MW01030590

THE GERMAN RIGHT IN THE WEIMAR REPUBLIC

THE GERMAN RIGHT IN THE WEIMAR REPUBLIC

Studies in the History of German
Conservatism, Nationalism, and Antisemitism

Edited by
Larry Eugene Jones

berghahn
NEW YORK · OXFORD
www.berghahnbooks.com

Published in 2014 by

Berghahn Books

www.berghahnbooks.com

© 2014, 2016 Larry Eugene Jones
First paperback edition published in 2016

Library of Congress Cataloging-in-Publication Data

The German right in the Weimar Republic : studies in the history of German
conservatism, nationalism, and antisemitism / edited by Larry Eugene Jones.
     pages cm
     Includes bibliographical references and index.
     ISBN 978-1-78238-352-9 (hardback) -- ISBN 978-1-78533-201-2 (paperback)
-- ISBN 978-1-78238-353-6 (ebook)
     1. Germany—Politics and government—1918–1933. 2. Conservatism—
Germany—History—20th century. 3. Nationalism—Germany—History—
20th century. 4. Antisemitism—Germany—History—20th century. I. Jones,
Larry Eugene, editor, author.
DD237.G448 2014
320.520943'09042—dc23

                                                                    2013041920

British Library Cataloguing in Publication Data

A catalogue record for this book is available from the British Library

ISBN: 978-1-78238-352-9 hardback
ISBN: 978-1-78533-201-2 paperback
ISBN: 978-1-78238-353-6 ebook

 Contents

Abbreviations

ADV	Alldeutscher Verband / Pan-German League
BMP	Bayerische Mittelpartei / Bavarian Middle Party
BVP	Bayerische Volkspartei / Bavarian People's Party
DDP	Deutsche Demokratische Partei / German Democratic Party
DKP	Deutsch-Konservative Partei / German Conservative Party
DNF	Deutschnationale Front / German National Front
DNVP	Deutschnationale Volkspartei / German National People's Party
DSTB	Deutschvölkischer Schutz- und Trutzbund / German-Racist Protection and Defense League
DvAG	Deutschvölkische Arbeitsgemeinschaft / German-Racist Coalition
DVFP	Deutschvölkische Freiheitspartei / German-Racist Freedom Party
DVP	Deutsche Volkspartei / German People's Party
KVP	Konservative Volkspartei / Conservative People's Party
NSDAP	Nationalsozialistische Deutsche Arbeiterpartei / National Socialist German Workers' Party
RjF	Reichsbund jüdischer Frontsoldaten / National Association of Jewish Front Soldiers
RKA	Reichskatholiken-Ausschuß der Deutschnationalen Volkspartei / Reich Catholic Committee of the German National People's Party
RLB	Reichs-Landbund / National Rural League

 Introduction

THE GERMAN RIGHT IN THE WEIMAR REPUBLIC
New Directions, New Insights, New Challenges
Larry Eugene Jones

The German Right in the Weimar Republic was a complex amalgam of political parties, economic-interest organizations, patriotic associations, paramilitary combat leagues, and young conservative salons of one sort or the other. What held these disparate organizations together, however, was not so much an ideology as a profound sense of bitterness over the lost war, a deep and abiding distrust of the democratic theory of government with its emphasis upon the principle of popular sovereignty, and a longing for the hierarchical and authoritarian values of the Second Empire. "To stand on the Right" did not mean membership in any particular political party but rather a disposition that expressed itself in a sense of contempt toward the symbols and institutions of Germany's new republican order. All of this represented a dramatic contrast from the last years of the Second Empire where many of those who "stood on the Right" staunchly defended the existing political order against those of their colleagues who sought to replace it with some form of national dictatorship capable of containing the forces of social and political change more effectively than the constitutional system devised by the Iron Chancellor Otto von Bismarck at the beginning of the 1870s. Although the schism within the German Right would become even more pronounced with Germany's defeat in World War I, the establishment of the Weimar Republic, and the imposition of the Versailles Peace Treaty, these differences would be papered over by the fact that virtually all of the factions on the German Right remained unalterably opposed to the changes that had taken place in the fabric of Germany's national life. It was precisely this "unity of the no," as Hans-Erdmann von Lindeiner-Wildau formulated it in an essay from 1929, that provided the largest of Germany's postwar conservative parties, the German National People's Party (Deutschnationale Volkspartei or DNVP), with its integrative potential in the first years of the Weimar Republic.[1] But with the economic and political stabilization of the Weimar Republic in the second half of the 1920s, the "unity of the no" began to lose much of its integrative appeal, with the result that the DNVP was no longer capable of mediating the differences that had existed on the German Right since before the outbreak of World War I and now began to fragment into its constituent social and economic interests. And with the onset of the Great Depression at the beginning of the 1930s, a badly fragmented German Right proved incapable of responding to the rise of National Socialism, a phenomenon that was spawned in no small measure by the disunity and organizational fragmentation of the German Right. From this perspective, the disunity of the Right was every bit as important as a prerequisite for the establishment of the Third Reich as the schism on the socialist Left or the fragmentation of the political middle.[2]

This is the new master narrative that currently governs the history of the German Right in the Weimar Republic. It supplants an older, more traditional narrative that established a direct line of continuity from the political configurations of the late Second Empire to the "alliance of elites" that negotiated the terms under which Nazi party leader Adolf Hitler assumed power in January 1933.[3] It has the advantage of nuance and differentiation, avoids the teleological determinism of the older narrative, and affirms the agency of the individual historical actor in the fateful series of events that culminated in Hitler's installation as chancellor.[4] Not only does this narrative underscore the extent to which the German Right in the Weimar Republic was riddled by all sorts of internal divisions that severely hampered its political effectiveness, but it also calls into question the "alliance between an old and a new Right" that a more recent cohort of historians from the late 1970s and 1980s has postulated as the ideological and organizational foundation upon which Hitler's assumption of power took place.[5] Its obvious appeal as an organizing motif notwithstanding, the distinction between an "old" and a "new" Right greatly oversimplifies the divisions that existed on the German Right in the Weimar Republic and fails to define these two terms with sufficient precision to make such an argument convincing. In point of fact, the "old Right"—epitomized by the Pan-German League (Alldeutscher Verband or ADV) and Alfred Hugenberg, the DNVP party chairman from 1928 to 1933—had by the end of the Weimar Republic been reduced to such a state of impotence that it could no longer negotiate with Hitler or anyone else from a position of strength.[6]

All of this underscores the need for a more nuanced and differentiated approach to the study of the German Right in the Weimar Republic. Here it is important to bear in mind not only that the German Right was a composite of economic interests that were often working at cross purposes with each other but also that the ideologies of the German Right were a hodgepodge of different theoretical positions ranging from the racist and antisemitic pronouncements of the Pan-Germans to the young conservative longing for the political and spiritual rebirth of the German nation with all kinds of variants and hybrids in between.[7] The social and economic infrastructure of the German Right was complex and varied, with heavy industry and big business, large landed agriculture and the small peasant proprietor, Christian labor and the white-collar unions, and the independent middle class in all of its various iterations struggling for survival in a rapidly contracting economy. To bring all of this under a single umbrella, particularly in light of the fact that not of all of those who comprised these groups identified themselves with a conservative political agenda, was a daunting task fraught with difficulties and frustration at every turn. Traditional German conservatism—and particularly Prusso-German conservatism with its defense of the inherited hierarchies of crown, state, rank, church, and the military—had lost much of its integrative potential by the beginning of the twentieth century and had already been forced on the defensive by an increasingly aggressive radical nationalism with distinctly populist and anti-elitist overtones. None of the ideologies on the German Right in the Weimar era, however, were capable of mediating the increasingly bitter conflict between the different factions on the German Right over how the social and economic burden of Germany's lost war was to be distributed throughout German society. As a result, neither the DNVP nor any other organization on the German Right succeeded in bridging the social, economic, regional, and confessional divisions that had become so deeply embedded in the fabric of Germany's national life, at least not until the meteoric rise of National Socialism at the end of the 1920s and early 1930s.[8]

The purpose of this collection is not so much to challenge the new master narrative on the history of the German Right in the Weimar Republic as to underpin it with examples of some of the most recent scholarly work on right-wing politics in the Weimar era. To be sure, this runs into the very teeth of the eclipse that has taken place in the political history of the Weimar Republic over the course of the last two or three decades. Nowhere is this eclipse more apparent than in North America and the United Kingdom, where the number of monographs on different aspects of Weimar's political history and the number of graduate students working on topics related to that history have declined dramatically after reaching a peak in the period from 1970 to 1990. The reasons for this are complex and varied. In part it reflects the sea change that has taken place in modern historical writing since the last decades of the previous century and represents a paradigmatic shift in the profession at large from the traditional fields of political, diplomatic, and intellectual history to the more popular sub-genres of social and cultural history. It also reflects a shift in the frontiers of German historical research from the Weimar period to the period after 1945, a shift that received much of its impetus from the sudden availability of sources on the German Democratic Republic after the fall of the Berlin wall and the unification of Germany in 1989–90. By the same token, research on the Third Reich seems to have been galvanized by access to archives in the former Soviet Union that had previously been inaccessible to Western scholars. Another factor contributing to the decline of new historical writing on the history of the Weimar Republic is the feeling that all of the major questions have been answered and that there is little in the way of original research and writing that remains to be done. Certainly the publication of magna opera by such giants in the profession as Hans Mommsen, Gerhard Schulz, and Heinrich August Winkler would only confirm that impression.[9] At the same time, fewer graduate students in modern German history in North America and the United Kingdom are being initiated into the techniques of archival research as opposed to less empirical and more theoretical methodologies appropriated from ancillary disciplines such as literary and film criticism, anthropology, and gender studies. With the decline in the levels of funding for graduate and postgraduate research students and scholars from North America in particular but from the United Kingdom as well are finding it increasingly difficult to spend long periods of time in Germany conducting the empirical research required for projects in Weimar political history. As a result, American scholars have all but abandoned the writing of the political history of the Weimar Republic to their German colleagues.

By no means does the dearth of recent English-language scholarship on the political history of the Weimar Republic mean that the study of Weimar politics—and particularly Weimar party politics—is at a dead end. To the contrary, the study of Weimar party politics remains quite vigorous in Germany, although even here this displays a peculiar configuration in that there has been relatively little recent literature of note on the Social Democrats and liberal parties. Although the two Catholic parties—the German Center Party (Deutsche Zentrumspartei) or the Bavarian People's Party (Bayerische Volkspartei or BVP)—continue to receive close scholarly attention, it is the German Right that has been the focal point of the most vigorous scholarly research on the politics of the late Second Empire and Weimar Republic in the last ten to fifteen years. Not only have there been four recent publications of outstanding merit on the DNVP as well as a superbly researched biography of DNVP party leader Otto Schmidt-Hannover,[10] but the agrarian milieu upon which the DNVP depended for a large part of its electoral support has come under particularly close scrutiny in a series of excellent monographs of the National Rural League (Reichs-Landbund or RLB), its regional affiliate in Brandenburg, the Christian-National Peasant and Farmers' Party (Christlich-Nationale Bauern- und Landvolkpartei), and the conservative parties in Württemberg in the Second Empire and Weimar Republic.[11] By the same token, there has been a spate of important new publications on the role that women played in the politics of the German Right, including a rare English-language contribution by Raffael Scheck on the place of women in the DNVP and the other organizations of the German Right.[12] All of this would suggest that while there has been a relative decline in the volume of literature on the Social Democrats and the liberal parties, interest in the politics of the German Right remains vibrant and productive.

Much of the recent literature on the history of the German Right is part of a more general inquiry into Germany's conservative-nationalist milieu. As problematic as the idea of a "conservative-nationalist milieu" might be, it has nevertheless served as an attractive strategy for bringing the plethora of political parties, economic interest groups, patriotic associations, and paramilitary organizations that constituted the German Right under a single umbrella.[13] One must bear in mind, however, that the integrity of this milieu was under continuous assault throughout the Weimar Republic and that, as Wolfram Pyta has shown in his detailed study of the Nazi breakthrough into the Protestant sector of Germany's rural population,[14] it began to show signs of serious erosion with the radicalization of its primary constituencies as a result of the general course of German economic development in the 1920s and early 1930s. The increasing radicalization of Germany's conservative-nationalist milieu could also be seen in the heightened activity of the Pan-German League before its steady eclipse in the second half of the 1920s[15] and in the rise of a paramilitary Right that sought to counter the social and economic cleavages that had become so deeply embedded in the fabric of Germany's national life with an aggressive and militantly anti-republican nationalism.[16] Historians have also begun to devote increasing attention to the specific features of Germany's Catholic-conservative milieu as something that was distinctive from its Protestant counterpart but with which it nevertheless shared much in common. The radicalization of Germany's Catholic aristocracy in the last years of the Weimar Republic played an important role in the collapse of the Weimar Republic and in Franz von Papen produced the one person who arguably bears more responsibility than anyone else for Hitler's installation as chancellor.[17]

A particular focal point of recent research on the history of the German Right has been the role of Germany's conservative elites and their efforts to salvage whatever they could of their status and influence in the face of the revolutionary turmoil that transformed German political life at the end of World War I. In this respect, it is important to draw attention to the fact that the German Right after 1918 was not the same as the German Right before World War I. Not only had the party political organization of the German Right undergone a profound transformation as a result of the war and revolution,[18] but the extra-parliamentary Right—the conglomerate of organizations that Geoff Eley discusses in his book *Reshaping the German Right*[19]—was no longer the same as it had been before the war. Of the various organizations that made up the extra-parliamentary Right before World War I, only the Pan-German League survived into the postwar period to play a significant role in Weimar political culture. What emerged in their stead were veterans' organizations, the so-called political combat leagues like the Civil Defense Leagues or *Einwohnerwehren* of the early Weimar Republic, the Young German Order (Jungdeutscher Orden), and the Stahlhelm.[20] But even here there had been a significant change in the leadership of the patriotic Right. Before the war the leadership of organizations like the Pan-German League, the German Naval League (Deutscher Flottenverein), and the League for the Eastern Marches (Deutscher Ostmarkenverein) had been recruited almost exclusively from disaffected elements of Germany's National Liberal constituency. But if one looks at the social pedigree of those who moved into leadership positions in organizations like the Pan-German League, the Stahlhelm, and the United Patriotic Associations of Germany (Vereinigte Vaterländische Verbände Deutschlands)—and this is particularly true of their leadership at the state and regional level—the titled nobility is much more prominently involved in the leadership and activities of the patriotic Right than it had been before the war. At the heart of this is a phenomenon that has not been fully accounted for in the political histories of the Weimar Republic, a phenomenon that, for the lack of anything better, might be called a "displaced elite." What this term suggests is that many of those from aristocratic backgrounds who had contemplated a career in the military or civil service only to find those career paths blocked by the events of 1918–19 now began to gravitate to leadership roles in those organizations that were most resolutely opposed to Germany's new republican system and the odium of defeat with which it was so intimately identified.

Much of the credit for pioneering the study of elites, or *Elitenforschung*, as a new subfield of historical research—and that of the aristocracy in particular—goes to Heinz Reif. In 2000–2001 Reif, himself the author of a authoritative study on the schism in Germany's titled aristocracy in the middle of the nineteenth century,[21] edited two volumes of conference papers on the nobility and bourgeoisie in nineteenth- and twentieth-century Germany that brought the study of elites back to the forefront of historical research. By far the most important work to emerge from Reif's stable of young historians is Stefan Malinowski's path-breaking study of the German nobility that appeared in 2003 under the title *Vom König zum Führer*. Based upon extensive primary research in sources that are not easily accessible and that in some cases had been closed for purposes of scholarly research, Malinowski's detailed and richly nuanced study of the German nobility from the last years of the Second Empire to the establishment of the Third Reich underscores the extent to which the combination of political displacement, economic decline, and social marginalization rendered the German aristocracy increasingly susceptible to National Socialism as a panacea for all the ills to which it found itself subjected.[22] Malinowski's work, in turn, has spawned a series of more specialized studies on the German aristocracy by Eckhart Conze, Bernd Kasten, and Rainer Pomp to take their place alongside an earlier study on Pomerania by the American scholar Shelley Baranowski.[23] By no means, however, has the study of elites been confined to the aristocracy. The political behavior of Germany's industrial and financial elites had long been the subject of scholarly attention, although the approach here has tended to be more biographical than institutional. Even then, none of the recent studies by Reinhard Neebe, Hans-Otto Eglau, Richard Overy, Boris Gehlen, and Werner Abelshauser have succeeded in displacing Henry Turner's *Big Business and the Rise of Hitler* as the preeminent monograph on the politics of Germany's industrial elite in the last years of the Weimar Republic. And the general thrust of this research has been to emphasize, as it did in the case of the titled nobility, the fragmentation of Germany's industrial leadership in the last years of the Weimar Republic and its inability to manipulate the course of political events as effectively as the initial forays into this field of research had assumed.[24] Nowhere is the political ineptitude of Germany's industrial elite in the face of National Socialism more convincingly exposed than in Peter Langer's exhaustive biography of arguably the most politically astute of the Ruhr industrial barons, the Gutehoffnungshütte's Paul Reusch.[25]

Topping this off is a series of new biographical studies on various individuals connected with the German Right, the most impressive of which is Wolfram Pyta's magisterial biography of World War I hero and Reich president Paul von Hindenburg. Based upon extensive research that includes access to materials in the possession of the Hindenburg family that had not previously been made available for purposes of scholarly research, Pyta argues that Hindenburg assiduously sought to base his claim to political leadership upon a charismatic appeal that overrode the partisan political divisions of Weimar political life only to make him in the last years of his presidency increasingly susceptible to the appeal of National Socialism.[26] Particularly noteworthy as complements to Pyta's biography of Hindenburg are two exemplary studies of Heinrich Brüning by William Patch and Herbert Hömig—the latter a two-volume biography that also covers his activities during World War II and the postwar period—as well as the more thematic monograph by Peer Oliver Volkmann that clearly places the principal executor of Hindenburg's experiment in presidential government on the moderate or governmental Right.[27] Germany's military leadership has also come in for its share of attention with new biographies of Wilhelm Groener, Werner von Blomberg, and the retired yet politically active World War I Field Marshal August von Mackensen,[28] while Kurt Schleicher, the most enigmatic of Germany's military leader and the last chancellor of the Weimar Republic, continues to fascinate a new cohort of historians with his behind-the-scenes struggle to decouple the exercise of executive authority from the vicissitudes of Weimar democracy. Recent research has focused on Schleicher's plans for a reform of the Weimar constitution and the question of whether or not he could have prevented Hitler's appointment as chancellor by having Hindenburg declare a state of national emergency.[29] On Schleicher, however, nothing has surpassed Thilo Vogelsang's *Reichswehr, Staat und NSDAP* since it was published in 1962,[30] while F. L. Carsten's *The Reichswehr and Politics* from 1966 still remains the best general overview of the military's political activities during the Weimar Republic.[31]

The last caveat notwithstanding, recent historical scholarship on the German Right in the Weimar Republic has demonstrated enormous vitality. The fact remains, however, that there is still important work that needs to be done, and the collection of essays assembled here indicates the different directions this might take. A thread that ties together all but one of the essays in this collection is the theme of antisemitism. There can be little doubt that antisemitism permeated the social, cultural, and political fabric of the German Right from the middle of the 1870s right through the end of the Weimar Republic. But antisemitism and the so-called Jewish question meant different things to different groups, and there was no unanimity on just how the different factions on the German Right should address this problem. For some it was the bread and butter of their politics; for others it was simply a matter of striking the right tone in their efforts to mobilize the masses; and for others it was an unwelcome distraction from the hard and often demoralizing challenges they faced in rescuing Germany from total collapse. Moreover, the intensity of antisemitic feeling and the rationale behind it differed not only from group to group but also from time to time depending upon the precise set of circumstances that were in play at any particular point in time. In other words, antisemitism had a temporal as well as a social variant that makes it all the more difficult to assess the precise role that antisemitism played in Weimar political culture and in the politics of the German Right. This endeavor is not well served by those who, in the footsteps of George L. Mosse's classic *Crisis of the German Ideology*,[32] posit a direct line of continuity from the antisemitism of the late Second Empire to the establishment of the Third Reich without appreciating all the intervening variables that lent German antisemitism—and particularly the antisemitism of the German Right—its peculiar contours and efficacy.[33] Antisemitism and racism may very well have been constants that in one way or another permeated virtually every aspect of Germany's right-wing political culture. But the specific forms in which they manifested themselves, their efficacy as instruments of mass mobilization, and the hostility they engendered among specific sectors of the German population were not. Not only was there no consensus as to precisely what constituted the "Jewish problem," but there was no agreement as to how that problem was to be solved.[34]

A question closely related to the place or racism and antisemitism in the morphology of the German Right is the relationship of the non-Nazi Right to National Socialism. The dramatic rise of National Socialism in the last years of the Weimar Republic stemmed in no small measure from the way in which it was able to occupy the spaces inhabited by more traditional forms of political sociability, in part by replicating and appropriating the rituals and forms of bourgeois associational life that in almost every case dated back to the prewar era.[35] What this produced was a Nazi-conservative symbiosis that was, as a number of recent regional studies have demonstrated,[36] particularly potent at the local or grassroots levels of German political life and that often belied the fragmentation of bourgeois and particularly right-wing politics at the national level. None of this has been adequately addressed in either the standard histories of the NSDAP[37] or by the spate of recent biographical literature on the leaders of the Nazi movement, including Ian Kershaw's magisterial biography of Adolf Hitler[38] and Ludolf Herbst's no less fascinating study of the origins of Hitler's charisma in the earliest days of the Weimar Republic.[39] All of this leaves a great deal to be done in the history of the NSDAP before 1933. Among other things, there is no systematic investigation of the NSDAP's relations with non-Nazi Right in the critical period from the 1929 crusade against the Young Plan to Franz von Papen's unfortunate appointment as chancellor in the early summer of 1932.[40] By the same token, there is no study of the way in which the increasingly potent Nazi-bourgeois symbiosis at the local or grassroots levels of German political life influenced or constrained the negotiating tactics of the leader of the DNVP, Stahlhelm, or other right-wing organizations in the last years of the Weimar Republic. The platitudes about the fusion of an old and a new German Right simply do not suffice. This is also one of the deficits in the existing body of historical literature on the German Right in the Weimar Republic that this collection of essays seeks to address.

In his essay on "Hindenburg and the German Right" Wolfram Pyta examines one of the great icons of the German Right, retired Field Marshall and Reich President Paul von Hindenburg. The only politician of his day who commanded the respect and admiration once accorded to Otto von Bismarck, Hindenburg towered over the rest of his contemporaries both literally and figuratively. But Hindenburg's relationship to the German Right was never as harmonious as either he or the leaders of the German Right had hoped. By the end of the 1930s Hindenburg was vilified by the leaders of the radical Right for his failure to fulfill the hopes they had attached to his election to the Reich presidency in 1925. But, as Pyta maintains, the reasons for Hindenburg's estrangement from the German Right go much deeper than disagreements over strategy and tactics. At the heart of this estrangement lay the fact that Hindenburg, unlike his contemporaries on the German Right, based his claim to authority upon a myth that he and his associates had assiduously cultivated since the first months of World War I and that he now deployed to full effect in the political struggles of the late 1920s and early 1930s. Drawing upon Max Weber's typology of political legitimation, Pyta demonstrates how Hindenburg both before and after his election as Reich president invested his claim to primacy over the German Right—and indeed over the German nation as a whole—with the force of a charismatic vision that not only sought to override the social and political cleavages that had become so deeply embedded in the fabric of Germany's national life but also enabled Hindenburg to present himself as the embodiment of the German nation itself in all its manifest diversity.[41] It was precisely Hindenburg's mythic stature and his self-conscious deployment of charisma as a way of legitimating his claim to political primacy that set him apart from his more traditional rivals on the German Right. But it was also Hindenburg's sense of himself as the personification of the German nation that, according to Pyta, left him vulnerable to the seductive appeal of Hitler's own charisma, so vulnerable, in fact, that he eventually overcame his deep-seated antipathy toward the Nazi party leader to appoint the man whom he had disparaged as "that Bohemian corporal" as chancellor in the last days of January 1933.[42]

Daniela Gasteiger's essay on Count Kuno von Westarp, arguably the most important conservative politician of the Weimar era, focuses on a politician who, like Hindenburg, identified himself with the best of the Prussian tradition but whose ties to that tradition became increasingly strained as he struggled to adapt himself and the force of German conservatism to the hard realities of Weimar political life.[43] Gasteiger points out through a careful analysis of Westarp's relationship to two of the most important lynchpins to his prewar political life—the outspoken racist politician Albrecht von Graefe and the bastion of Prussian conservatism, the Central Association of German Conservatives (Hauptverein der Deutschkonservativen)—that whatever hopes he may have had of keeping them within the orbit of the DNVP were doomed to failure. At the heart of this endeavor lay two issues, the so-called Jewish question and the DNVP's decision first in 1925 and then again in 1927 to enter the national government as part of an experiment in stabilization from the Right. In the first case, what separated Graefe and Westarp was not so much any disagreement over the threat the Jews allegedly posed to the health of the German nation as a difference of priorities. For Westarp regarded the Jewish question as only one of a host of different issues the DNVP had to address in the postwar period and refused to accord it the primacy that Graefe and his colleagues in the party's racist faction demanded as a condition of their willingness to stay in the party, with the result that in the final showdown between the racists and the party leadership Westarp sided with the latter. Similarly, Westarp's decision to support the DNVP's two experiments in government participation seemed an act of betrayal to the leaders of the Central Association of German Conservatives and produced a break in 1927–28 that was every bit as painful as that with Graefe and the racists. While Gasteiger's essay highlights the extent to which Westarp had moved away from the hard-line conservative politics of the late Wilhelmine and early Weimar eras, it also reveals just how hard it was to bring all the various factions of the German Right under a single umbrella.

The third chapter by Larry Eugene Jones offers an even more detailed examination of the DNVP's antisemitism. Here Jones argues that the DNVP's position on the Jewish question was "neither constant nor consistent" and that its "embrace of antisemitism" rose and ebbed with "the vicissitudes of the German economy and the stability of the Weimar Republic." Moreover, the expulsion of the racists around Graefe, Wilhelm Henning, and Reinhold Wulle at the DNVP's Görlitz party congress in October 1922 did not mean a complete rupture with the party's antisemitic elements. For, as the establishment of the DNVP's Racist National Committee (Völkischer Reichsausschuß der Deutschnationalen Volkspartei) in 1923–24 clearly indicated, the DNVP party leadership bent over backward to keep its racist wing within the party fold and to prevent its defection to the newly founded German-Racist Freedom Party (Deutschvölkische Freiheitspartei or DVFP) in the prelude to the May 1924 Reichstag elections. The campaign for the May 1924 elections represented the high-water point in the DNVP's use of antisemitism as an instrument of mass mobilization, and party leaders were indeed satisfied with the elections results and the establishment of the DNVP as the second largest party in the Reichstag. But as party leaders began to explore how it might be possible to leverage the DNVP's strength at the polls into a role in the national government, the party's antisemitism receded more and more into the background to the point where it played virtually no role whatsoever in the DNVP's campaign for the December 1924 Reichstag elections. During the so-called Westarp era from 1924 to 1928 the leaders of the DNVP's Racist National Committee festered as a result of their exclusion from the party's inner circles and formed the core of the anti-Westarp coalition that succeeded in dethroning Westarp as party chairman and in electing press and film magnate Alfred Hugenberg to the DNVP party chairmanship in October 1928. But although Hugenberg had been a founding member of the militantly antisemitic Pan-German League in the 1890s and enjoyed close ties with Pan-German chairman Heinrich Claß, the new DNVP party chairman refused to emulate the antisemitism of the rival NSDAP and eschewed antisemitism for anti-Marxism in his efforts to unite the German Right into a solid phalanx committed to the destruction of Germany's parliamentary institutions and the establishment of a more authoritarian system of government.

The next three essays all deal with the history of the Pan-German League, the most influential of Germany's prewar nationalist associations and the only to survive into the Weimar Republic. Rainer Hering's essay examines the appeal that Pan-Germanism exercised on Germany's academic elites and the role that they played in the dissemination of the Pan-German worldview. Hering argues that academics played a critical role in the "construction" of a Pan-German nation that rested upon the exclusion of women, Jews, and minorities from any sort of meaningful role in the life of the German *Volk*. What drove this project, Hering insists, was a fear of the modern age and the categorical rejection of democracy, socialism, and workers' and women's rights — in short, the emancipatory impulses that were in the process of transforming the larger world around them. It was precisely this fear that accounted for the disproportionately high percentage of academics in both the leadership and membership of the Pan-German League. Hering's argument connects quite well to Björn Hofmeister's exploration of the reasons responsible for the ADV's sudden rise and then its equally sudden eclipse as a viable force in Weimar politics. Following the defeat and revolution of 1918 the Pan-German League quickly positioned itself as the most uncompromising and resolute opponent of the changes that had just taken place in the structure of German political life and saw its membership swell to a peak of 38,000 in 1922 before falling to between 13,000 and 15,000 by the end of the decade. According to Hofmeister, the ADV's decline stemmed from a variety of factors, not the least of which that it never quite succeeded in adapting itself as an association of *Honoratioren* in the prewar period to the changes that took place in the structure of German political life after 1918. In particular, the Pan-Germans found themselves eclipsed by more militant and populist forms of political activism such as the civil defense leagues, or *Einwohnerwehren*, of the immediate postwar period, the Stahlhelm and other paramilitary combat leagues, and lastly by Hitler and the NSDAP. It is to this last relationship that Barry Jackisch turns in his essay on the question of continuity and change on the German Right in the Weimar Republic. Jackisch's essay focuses in particular on the relationship between the Pan-German League and the NSDAP from the time of ADV chairman Heinrich Claß's first contacts with Hitler in early 1920 to Hitler's installation as chancellor thirteen years later. Here Jackisch stresses that despite far-reaching ideological affinities between the ADV and NSDAP—a point that Hofmeister has also made in his contribution to this volume—the Pan-Germans had become increasingly estranged from the Nazi movement in the last years of the Weimar Republic and regarded Hitler's rise to prominence with a mixture of begrudging respect, bewilderment, and apprehension.

The Pan-German League was of all the major forces on the Weimar the most resolute and relentless in its antisemitism and pursuit of the Jewish question. But, as Brian Crimm and Ulrike Ehret illustrate in their respective chapters on the paramilitary Right and the Catholic Right, antisemitism on the non-Nazi Right was by no means confined to the Pan-Germans and their allies in the DNVP. Crimm's essay focuses on the two of Germany's most politically active and durable paramilitary organizations, the Stahlhelm and the Young German Order. Though ostensibly nonpolitical, or *überparteilich* as the Germans liked to put it, the Stahlhelm clearly stood on the Right and harbored a militantly antisemitic wing that gained more and more influence over the organization's affairs before it finally adopted an "Aryan paragraph" that excluded Jews from membership in March 1924. Artur Mahraun and the leaders of the Young German Order, on the other hand, were much more militantly antisemitic in the early years of the Weimar Republic but moderated their antisemitism in the second half of the 1920s in what was a strategic move to the middle. In both cases Crimm argues that the antisemitism of the paramilitary Right was "situational," that is to say that a particular organization's stance on the Jewish question was formed "in response to internal and external experiences" and that this frequently "reflected an organization's changing priorities resulting from demographics, fluctuating political fortunes, and bitter feuds with rival groups." As such, Crimm concludes, the "situational antisemitism" practiced by the Stahlhelm and Young German Order revealed "the ephemeral nature" of antisemitism on the German Right and was not as much of a constant as the standard histories of German antisemitism have tended to argue. Ehret's essay on the antisemitism of the Catholic Right, however, takes a somewhat different point of view. Ehret stresses religious antisemitism as a constant on the Catholic Right, although it was no longer exclusively rooted in religion but had acquired more modern accoutrements such as the concept of race along the way. The concept of the Catholic Right is itself elusive and refers to a relatively small percentage of Germany's Catholic population that identified itself with the political agenda of the German Right and that in some cases embraced a conspiratorial view of history that saw the Jew and the Free Mason as the archenemies of Germany's Christian national culture and the "ideas of 1789" as the corrosive poison that was slowly, but surely, destroying the social and spiritual fabric of the German nation.

The last two chapters by Edward Snyder and Joseph Bendersky focus on two individuals who were only peripherally involved in the politics of the German Right but who nevertheless enjoyed close ties to Germany's conservative establishment: Friedrich von Bodelschwingh and Carl Schmitt. Of the two, Bodelschwingh is by far the lesser known, while Schmitt has emerged as one of the most enigmatic and controversial figures in twentieth-century German history. As one of Germany's foremost Protestant theologians and director of the Bethel Institutions in Bielefeld, Bodelschwingh was unquestionably one of the most important representatives of social Protestantism in the Weimar Republic. But, as Snyder points out, Bodelschwingh is important not only because of his emphasis on work therapy as a corrective to the psychological and mental illnesses that afflicted the patients at Bethel but also because he and many of his closest associates at Bethel endorsed the practice of eugenics, including measures like sterilization, to "restore a fallen Germany to its place among the *Kulturnationen* of Europe." While Bodelschwingh was careful to keep his feelings about Jews to himself, his emphasis on the nation's racial health as a prerequisite for its recovery from the twin shock of defeat and revolution clearly suggested a bias that was not altogether different from that of main-line conservatives like Westarp or the leaders of the Stahlhelm. Carl Schmitt, on the other hand, is one of the most difficult individuals to classify or categorize. To be sure, Schmitt stood on the Right and, if his private diaries are any indication, shared the animus toward Jews that pervaded the right-wing political. But Schmitt assiduously avoided identification with any of the major organizations on the German Right, preferring for himself the role of the politically unaffiliated intellectual and legal expert. It was only in the last months of the Weimar Republic that Schmitt stepped into the political limelight, first as the head of the government's legal defense team in the trial over the legality of the deposition of the Prussian cabinet in July 1932 and then as one of a handful of legal specialists that Schleicher tapped for the task of drafting a new constitution for the German Reich. But, as Bendersky argues, Schmitt's most enduring contribution to Weimar political life was the destabilizing effect that his legal writing, his assaults on liberalism, and his hostility to Marxism had upon the intellectual legitimacy of the Weimar Republic and thus helped fuel the anti-republican discourse of the German Right.

As the essays in this volume clearly indicate, historical scholarship on the German Right in the Weimar Republic remains remarkably vigorous and productive. The essays presented here tend to confirm and perhaps modify in some detail or the other the general narrative that was outlined at the beginning of this essay for the history of the political Right in the Weimar Republic. In the light of recent research on right-wing politics in Weimar Germany it becomes increasingly clear that the German Right was anything but a homogeneous political force, but in reality was so riddled by internal divisions—some that were social, economic, and even ideological in nature, some that had more to do with strategy and tactics than anything else, some that were rooted in personal animosities and distrust—that it was incapable of articulating a coherent response to the paralysis of Germany's parliamentary institutions in the ever deepening economic crisis at home and abroad. It was precisely the fractious nature of right-wing politics in the last years of the Weimar Republic that left the more traditional elements of the German Right so vulnerable to penetration by the most radical group on the German Right, namely the NSDAP. In the final analysis, the dramatic rise of National Socialism stemmed in no small measure from a deep sense of public frustration with the rivalries among the various factions on the non-Nazi Right. Not only were the Nazis adept at exploiting the divisions between their rivals on the German Right, but Hitler and his party succeeded in articulating a vision of the nation that was so powerful in terms of its emotional appeal that it simply overrode the factionalism that had become so deeply embedded in the fabric of German right-wing politics. At the same time, the disunity of Hitler's rivals on the German Right meant that he was negotiating from a position of strength and they from a position of weakness in the critical deliberations that preceded the installation of the Hitler cabinet in the last fateful days of January 1933. This also accounted for the ease with which Hitler and his party were able to reverse the terms of the arrangement under which Hitler had assumed power and brush aside the conditions that his coalition partners had implicitly, if not explicity, attached to his appointment as chancellor.

Acknowledgments

The editor would like to thank Bridget Sendziak for her help in preparing, editing, correcting, and indexing the book.

Notes

1. Hans-Erdmann von Lindeiner-Wildau, "Konservatismus," in *Volk und Reich der Deutschen. Vorlesungen gehalten in der Deutschen Vereinigung für Staatswissenschaftliche Fortbildung*, ed. Bernhard Harms, 3 vols. (Berlin: R. Hobbing, 1929), 2:35–61, here 59.
2. For a fuller statement of this argument, see Larry Eugene Jones, "Nazis, Conservatives, and the Establishment of the Third Reich, 1932–34," *Tel Aviver Jahrbuch für deutsche Geschichte* 23 (1994): 41–64.
3. For the classic statement of this argument, see Fritz Fischer, *Bündnis der Eliten. Zur Kontinuität der Machtstrukturen in Deutschland 1875–1945* (Düsseldorf: Droste, 1979). A more recent iteration of this argument is to be found in Hans-Ulrich Wehler, *Deutsche Gesellschaftsgeschichte*, vol. 4: *Vom Beginn des Ersten Weltkriegs bis zur Gründung der beiden deutschen Staaten 1914–1989* (Munich: C. H. Beck, 2003), 580–93. For a telling critique of this argument, see Henry Ashby Turner, "'Alliance of Elites' as a Cause of Weimar's Collapse and Hitler's Triumph," in *Die deutsche Staatskrise 1930–1933*, ed. Heinrich August Winkler (Munich: R. Oldenbourg, 1992), 205–14.
4. For a fuller development of this argument, see Larry Eugene Jones, "Why Hitler Came to Power: In Defense of a New History of Politics," in *Geschichtswissenschaft vor 2000. Perspektiven der Historiographiegeschichte, Geschichtstheorie, Sozial- und Kulturgeschichte. Festschrif für Georg G. Iggers zum 65. Geburtstag*, ed. Konrad H. Jarausch, Jörn Rüsen and Hans Schleier (Hagen: Margit Rottmann Medienverlag, 1991), 256–76.
5. In particular, see Geoff Eley, "Conservative and Radical Nationalists in Germany: The Production of Fascist Potentials, 1912–1928," in *Fascists and Conservatives*, ed. Martin Blinkhorn (London: Unwin Hyman, 1990), 50–70. The argument is developed further in David Abraham, "Constituting Bourgeois Hegemony: The Bourgeois Crisis of Weimar Germany," *Journal of Modern History* 51 (1979): 417–37.
6. For example, see Larry Eugene Jones, "'The Greatest Stupidity of My Life': Alfred Hugenberg and the Formation of the Hitler Cabinet, January 1933," *Journal of Contemporary History* 27 (1992): 63–87. For a more sustained argument on the role of contingency in the formation of the Hitler cabinet, see Henry Ashby Turner, Jr., *Hitler's Thirty Days to Power: January 1933* (Reading, MA: Addison-Wesley, 1996), esp. 163–83.
7. Stefan Breuer has been particularly relentless in his dissection of the values and ideas of the German Right. Of his numerous publications, see in particular *Anatomie der konservativen Revolution* (Darmstadt: Wissenschaftliche Buchgesellschaft, 1993); *Grundpositionen der deutschen Rechten 1871–1945* (Tübingen: Edition Diskord, 1999); *Ordnungen der Ungleichheit. Die deutsche Rechte im Widerstreit ihrer Ideen 1871–1945* (Darmstadt: Wissenschaftliche Buchgesellschaft, 2001); and most recently *Die radikale Rechte in Deutschland 1871–1945. Eine politische Ideengeschichte* (Frankfurt: Reclam, 2010). Of particular value among the more specialized

contributions to this literature are Berthold Petzinna, *Erziehung zum deutschen Lebensstil. Ursprung und Entwicklung des jungkonservativen "Ring"-Kreises 1918–1933* (Berlin: Akademie Verlag, Berlin, 2000), and Claudia Kempner, *Das "Gewissen" 1919–1925. Kommunikation und Vernetzung der Jungkonservativen* (Munich: Oldenbourg, 2011). Of the recent English-language literature, see Roger Woods, *The Conservative Revolution in the Weimar Republic* (New York: St. Martins Press, 1996). See also the essays in Walter Schmitz and Clemens Volkenhals, eds., *Völkische Bewegung— Konservative Revolution—Nationalsozialismus. Aspekte einer politisierten Kulture* (Dresden: Thelem, 2005).

8. On the concept of the NSDAP as a "catch-all party of middle-class protest," see Thomas Childers, *The Nazi Voter: The Social Foundations of Fascism in Germany, 1919–1933* (Chapel Hill, NC, and London: University of North Carolina Press, 1983), 262–69.

9. For example, see Hans Mommsen, *Die verspielte Freiheit. Der Weg der Republik von Weimar in den Untergang 1918 bis 1933* (Berlin: Propylaen, 1989); Gerhard Schulz, *Zwischen Demokratie und Diktatur. Verfassungspolitik und Reichsreform in der Weimarer Republik*, 3 vols. (Berlin: de Gruyter, 1987–92); and Heinrich August Winkler, *Weimar 1918–1933. Die Geschichte der ersten deutschen Demokratie* (Munich: C. H. Beck, 1998).

10. In this respect, see Andreas Müller, *"Fällt der Bauer, stürzt der Staat." Deutschnationale Agrarpolitik 1928–1933* (Munich: Herbert Utz Verlag, 2003); Kirsten Heinsohn, *Konservative Parteien in Deutschland 1912 bis 1933. Demokratisierung und Partizipation in geschlechterhistorischer Perspektive* (Düsseldorf: Droste, 2010); Elina Kiiskinnen, *Die Deutschnationale Volkspartei in Bayern (Bayerische Mittelpartei) in der Regierungspolitik des Freistaats während der Weimarer Zeit* (Munich: C. H. Beck, 2005); Maik Ohnezeit, *Zwischen "schärfster Opposition" und dem "Willen zur Macht." Die Deutschnationale Volkspartei (DNVP) in der Weimarer Republik 1918–1928* (Düsseldorf: Droste, 2012); and Maximilian Terhalle, *Deutschnational in Weimar. Die politische Biographie des Reichstagsabgeordneten Otto Schmidt(-Hannover) 1888–1971* (Cologne, Weimar, and Vienna: Böhlau, 2009).

11. Stephanie Merkenich, *Grüne Front gegen Weimar. Reichs-Landbund und agrarischer Lobbyismus 1918–1933* (Düsseldorf: Droste, 1998); Rainer Pomp, *Bauern und Großgrundbesitzer auf ihrem Weg ins Dritte Reich. Der Brandenburgische Landbund 1919–1933* (Berlin: Akademie Verlag, 2011); Markus Müller, *Die Christlich-Nationale Bauern- und Landvolkpartei 1928–1933* (Düsseldorf: Droste, 2001); and Reinhold Weber, *Bürgerpartei und Bauernbund in Württemberg. Konservative Parteien im Kaiserreich und in Weimar (1895–1933)* (Düsseldorf: Droste, 2004).

12. Raffael Scheck, *Mothers of the Nation: Right-Wing Women in Weimar Germany* (Oxford and New York: Berg Publishers, 2004). In addition to the book by Heinsohn cited above (n.10), see also Andrea Süchting-Hänger, *Das "Gewissen der Nation." Nationales Engagement und politisches Handeln konservativer Frauenorganisationen 1900 bis 1937* (Düsseldorf: Droste, 2002), and Christiane Streubel, *Radikale Nationalistinnen. Agitation und*

Programmatick rechter Frauen in der Weimarer Republik (Frankfurt and New York: Campus Verlag, 2006). For a comprehensive survey of this literature, see Christiane Streubel, "Frauen der politischen Rechten in Kaiserreich und Republik. Ein Überblick und Forschungsbericht." *Historical Social Research/Historische Sozialforschung* 28 (2003): 103–66.

13. For the classic statement of the milieu thesis, M. Rainer Lepsius, "Parteiensystem und Sozialstruktur: zum Problem der Demokratisierung der deutschen Gesellschaft," in *Wirtschaft, Geschichte und Wirtschaftsgeschichte. Festschrift zum 65. Geburtstag von Friedrich Lütge,* ed. Wilhelm Abel, Knut Borchardt, Hermann Kellenbenz, and Wolfgang Zorn (Stuttgart: Fischer, 1966), 371–93. See also the reassessment and modification of Lepsius's thesis by Karl Rohe, "German Elections and Party Systems in Historical and Regional Perspective: An Introduction," in *Elections, Parties, and Political Traditions: Social Foundations of German Parties and Party Systems, 1867–1987,* ed. Karl Rohe (Oxford, 1990), 1–26. For two recent studies of Weimar political culture based upon the concept of milieu, see Siegfried Weichlein, *Sozialmilieus und politische Kultur in der Weimarer Republik. Lebenswelt, Vereinskultur und Politik in Hessen* (Göttingen, 1996). On the conservative milieu in particular, see Frank Bösch, *Das konservative Milieu. Vereinskultur und lokale Sammlungspolitik in ost- und westdeutschen Regionen (1900–1960)* (Göttingen, 2002), as well as the exemplary empirical studies by Helge Matthiesen, *Greifswald in Vorpommern. Konservative Milieu im Kaiserreich, in Demokratie und Diktatur 1900–1990* (Düsseldorf, 2000), esp. 75–301, and Mechthild Hempe, *Ländliche Gesellschaft in der Krise. Mecklenburg in der Weimarer Republik* (Cologne, Weimar, and Vienna: Böhlau, 2002).

14. Wolfram Pyta, *Dorfgemeinschaft und Parteipolitik 1918–1933. Die Verschränkung von Milieu und Parteien in den protestantischen Landgebieten Deutschlands in der Weimarer Republik* (Düsseldorf, 1996).

15. In this respect, see Rainer Hering, *Konstruierte Nation. Der Alldeutsche Verband 1890–1939* (Hamburg: Christians, 2003); Barry A. Jackisch, *The Pan-German League and Radical Nationalist Politics in Interwar Germany, 1918–39* (Farnham: Ashgate Press, 2012); and Björn Hofmeister, "Between Monarchy and Dictatorship: Radical Nationalism and Social Mobilization of the Pan-German League, 1914–1939" (PhD diss., Georgetown University, 2012); as well as the recent biography of ADV leader Heinrich Claß by Johannes Leicht, *Heinrich Claß 1868–1953. Die politische Biographie eines Alldeutschen* (Paderborn: Schöningh, 2012).

16. Although the Stahlhelm and the other organizations of the paramilitary Right have been discussed in the context of the milieu studies by Bosch and Matthiesen (see n.13), nothing has yet surpassed Volker R. Berghahn, *Der Stahlhelm—Bund der Frontsoldaten 1918–1935* (Düsseldorf: Droste, 1966). Two works of special note are Wieland Vogel, *Katholische Kirche und nationale Kampfverbände in der Weimarer Republik* (Mainz: Matthias-Grünewald, 1989), and Gerd Krüger, *"Treudeutsch allewege!" Gruppen, Vereine und Verbände der Rechten in Münster (1887–1929/30)* (Münster: Aschendorff,

1992). Also valuable for the insight they provided into the cohesion that the Stahlhelm and other paramilitary organizations provided at the local political level, see Peter Fritzsche, "Between Fragmentation and Fraternity: Civic Patriotism and the Stahlhelm in Bourgeois Neighborhoods during the Weimar Republic," *Tel Aviver Jahrbuch für deutsche Geschichte* 17 (1988): 123–44, as well as his longer, more detailed study, *Rehearsals for Fascism: Populism and Political Mobilization in Weimar Germany* (New York and Oxford: Oxford University Press, 1990).

17. On Papen, see the recent articles by Larry Eugene Jones, "Franz von Papen, the German Center Party, and the Failure of Catholic Conservatism in the Weimar Republic," *Central European History* 38 (2005): 191–217, and "Franz von Papen, Catholic Conservatives, and the Establishment of the Third Reich, 1933–1934," *The Journal of Modern History* 83 (2011): 272–318, as well as the problematic but nonetheless important biography by Joachim Petzold, *Franz von Papen. Ein deutsche Verhängnis* (Munich and Berlin: Buchverlag Union, 1995). On the Catholic aristocracy, see in particular Gerhard Kratzsch, *Engelbert Reichsfreiherr von Kerckerinck zu Borg. Westfälischer Adel zwischen Kaiserreich und Weimarer Republik* (Münster: Aschendorff, 2004), as well as the detailed essay by Horst Conrad, "Stand und Konfession. Der Verein der katholischen Edelleute. Teil 2: Die Jahre 1918–1949," *Westfälische Zeitschrift* 159 (2009): 91–154. See also two recent studies on the Benedictine Order as the spiritual vanguard of Catholic conservatism in the Weimar Republic by Brigitte Lob, *Albert Schmitt O.S.B. in Grüssau und Wimpfen. Sein kirchengeschichtliches Handeln in der Weimarer Republik und im Dritten Reich* (Cologne and Weimar: Böhlau, 2000), and Marcel Albert, *Die Beneditinerabtei Maria Laach und der Nationalsozialismus* (Paderborn: Schöningh, 2004).

18. Gerhard A. Ritter, "Kontinuität und Umformung des deutschen Parteiensystems 1918–1920," in *Entstehung und Wandel der modernen Gesellschaft. Festschrift für Hans Rosenberg zum 65. Geburtstag*, ed. Gerhard A. Ritter (Berlin, 1970), 342–84.

19. Geoff Eley, *Reshaping the German Right: Radical Nationalism and Political Change after Bismarck* (New Haven, CT, and London: Yale University Press, 1980). I would be remiss if I did not also acknowledge my debt to James Retallack for having greatly enriched and influenced my understanding of the Wilhemine Right. In particular, see James Retallack, *Notables of the Right: The Conservative Party and Political Mobilization in Germany, 1876–1918* (Boston: Unwin Hyman, 1988), and the collection of essays published in *The German Right, 1860–1920: Political Limits of the Authoritarian Imagination* (Toronto, Buffalo, and London: University of Toronto Press, 2006), esp. 3–31, 76–107, 273–324.

20. On the militarization of German politics in the immediate postwar period, see above all else the recent contributions that place this phenomenon in a broader comparative perspective by Robert Gerwarth, "The Central European Counter-Revolution: Paramilitary Violence in Germany, Austria and Hungary after the Great War," *Past and Present* 200 (2008): 175–209; and

Robert Gerwarth and John Horne, "Vectors of Violence: Paramilitarism in Europe after the Great War, 1917–1923," *Journal of Modern History* 83 (2011): 489–512; as well as the collection of essays published in Robert Gerwarth and John Horne, eds. *War in Peace: Paramilitary Violence in Europe after the Great War* (Oxford: Oxford University Press, 2012). For a recent study of this phenomenon in the German context, see Bernhard Sauer, "Freikorps und Antisemitismus in der Frühzeit der Weimarer Republik," *Zeitschrift für Geschichtswissenschaft* 56 (2008): 5–29.

21. Heinz Reif, ed., *Adel und Bürgertum in Deutschland I. Entwicklungslinien und Wendepunkte im 19. Jahrhundert* (Berlin: Akademie Verlag, 2000), and idem., *Adel und Bürgertum in Deutschland II. Entwicklungslinien und Wendepunkte im 20. Jahrhundert* (Berlin: Akademie Verlag, 2001).

22. Stephan Malinowski, *Vom König zum Führer. Sozialer Niedergang und politische Radikalisierung im deutschen Adel zwischen Kaiserreich und NS-State* (Berlin: Akademie Verlag, 2003). In a more similar vein, see Eckart Conze, "'Only a dictator can help us now': Aristocracy and the Radical Right in Germany," in *European Aristocracies and the Radical Right, 1918–1939*, ed. Karina Urbach (Oxford: Oxford University Press, 2007), 129–47. For an earlier exploration of this theme, see Wolfgang Zollitsch, "Adel und adlige Machteliten in der Endphase der Weimarer Republik. Standespolitik und agrarische Interessen," in *Die deutsche Staatskrise 1930–1933. Handlungsspielräume und Alternativen*, ed. Heinrich August Winkler (Munich:" R. Oldenbourg, 1992), 239–56.

23. In this respect, see Eckart Conze, *Von deutschem Adel. Die Grafen von Bernstorff im 20. Jahrhundert* (Stuttgart and Munich: Deutsche Verlags-Anstalt, 2000); Bernd Kasten, *Herren und Knechte. Gesellschaftlicher und politischer Wandel in Mecklenburg-Schwerin 1867–1945* (Bremen: Edition Temmen, 2011); and Pomp, *Bauern und Grossgundbesitz* (see n.11); and Shelly Baranowski, *The Sanctity of Rural Life: Nobility, Protestantism, and Nazism in Weimar Prussia* (New York and Oxford: Oxford University Press, 1995).

24. Henry Ashby Turner, Jr., *German Big Business and the Rise of Hitler* (New York and Oxford: Oxford University Press, 1985). Of the older literature, the most important is Bernd Weisbrod, *Schwerindustrie in der Weimarer Republik. Interessenpolitik zwischen Stabilisierung und Krise* (Wuppertal: Peter Hammer Verlag, 1978), and Reinhard Neebe, *Großindustrie, Staat und NSDAP 1930–1933. Paul Silverberg und der Reichsverband der Deutschen Industrie in der Krise der Weimarer Republik* (Göttingen: Vandenhoeck & Ruprecht, 1981). For a sample of the more recent biographical literature, see Hans Otto Eglau, *Fritz Thyssen. Hitlers Gönner und Geisel* (Berlin: Seidler, 2003); R. J. Overy, "'Primacy Always Belongs to Politics': Gustav Krupp and the Third Reich," in *War and Economy in the Third Reich* (Oxford: Oxford University Press, 1994), 119–43; Boris Gehlen, *Paul Silverberg. Ein Unternehmer (1876–1959)* (Stuttgart: Franz Steiner Verlag, 2007); and Werner Abelshauser, *Ruhrkohle und Politik. Ernst Brandi 1875–1937. Eine Biographie* (Essen: Klartext, 2009).

25. Peter Langer, *Macht und Verantwortung. Der Ruhrbaron Paul Reusch* (Essen: Klartext, 2012). See also Peter Langer, "Paul Reusch und die 'Machtergreifung'." *Mitteilungsblatt des Instituts für soziale Bewegungen. Forschungen und Forschungsberichte* 28 (2003): 157–202.
26. Wolfram Pyta, *Hindenburg. Herrschaft zwischen Hohenzollern und Hitler* (Munich: Siedler, 2007). On Hindenburg see also Jesko von Hoegen, *Der Held von Tannenberg. Genese und Funktion des Hindenburg-Mythos.* (Cologne: Böhlau, Weimar, and Vienna, 2007); and Anna von der Goltz, *Hindenburg: Power, Myth, and the Rise of Nazism* (Oxford and New York: Oxford University Press, 2009).
27. On Brüning, see William L. Patch, *Heinrich Brüning and the Dissolution of the Weimar Republic* (Cambridge: Cambridge University Press, 1998); and Herbert Hömig, *Brüning—Kanzler in der Krise der Republik. Eine Weimarer Biographie* (Paderborn: Schöningh, 2001); and idem., *Brüning—Politiker ohne Auftrag. Zwischen Weimarer und Bonner Republik* (Paderborn, Schöningh, 2005); as well as Peer Oliver Volkmann, *Heinrich Brüning (1885–1970). Nationalist ohne Heimat. Eine Teilbiographie* (Düsseldorf: Droste, 2007).
28. In this respect, see Wilhelm Hürter, *Wilhelm Groener. Reichswehrministerium am Ende der Weimarer Republik (1928–1932)* (Munich: R. Oldenbourg, 1993); Kristin A. Schäfer, *Werner von Blomberg. Hitlers erster Feldmarschall* (Paderborn: Schöningh, 2006); and Theo Schwarzmüller, *Zwischen Kaiser und "Führer." Generalfeldmarschall August von Mackensen. Eine politische Biographie* (Paderborn: Schöningh, 1996).
29. The most important contribution to this literature is Eberhard Kolb and Wolfram Pyta, "Die Staatsnotstandsplanung unter den Regierungen Papen und Schleicher," in *Die deutsche Staatskrise 1930–1933. Handlungsspielräume und Alternativen*, ed. Heinrich August Winkler, (Munich: R. Oldenbourg, 1992), 155–82; while the recent study by Irene Strenge, *Kurt von Schleicher. Politik im Reichswehrministerium am Ende der Weimarer Republik* (Berlin: Duncker & Humblot, 2006) is generally disappointing and fails to understand Schleicher's long-term strategic goals. See also Eberhard Kolb, *Was Hitler's Seizure of Power on January 30, 1933, Inevitable?* With a comment by Henry Ashby Turner, Jr. (Washington, DC: German Historical Institute, 1997).
30. Thilo Vogelsang, *Reichswehr, Staat und NSDAP. Beiträge zur Deutschen Geschichte 1930–1932* (Stuttgart: Deutsche Verlags-Anstalt, 1962).
31. F. L. Carsten, *The Reichswehr and Politics 1918 to 1933* (Oxford: Clarendon Press, 1966).
32. George L. Mosse, *The Crisis of the German Ideology: Intellectual Origins of the Third Reich* (New York: Grosset & Dunlap, 1964). A more recent example of this tendency is to be found in Peter Walkenhorst, *Nation—Volk—Rasse. Radikaler Nationalismus im Deutschen Kaiserreich 1890–1914* (Göttingen: Vandenhoeck & Ruprecht, 2007), esp. 333–42.
33. For an important corrective to this tendency, see Heinrich August Winkler, "Die deutsche Gesellschaft der Weimarer Republik und der Antisemitismus—Juden als Blitzableiter," in *Vorurteil und Völkermord.*

Entwicklungslinien des Antisemitismus, ed. Wolfgang Benz and Werner Bergmann (Freiburg, Basel, and Vienna: Herder, 1997), 341–62.

34. Of the recent literature, by far the best overview of racism and antisemitism is Stefan Breuer, *Die Völkischen in Deutschland. Kaiserreich und Weimarer Republik* (Darmstadt: Wissenschaftliche Buchgesellschaft, 2008). For three important specialized studies, see Hans Reif, "Antisemitismus in den Agrarverbänden Ostelbiens während der Weimarer Republik," in *Ostelbische Agrargesellschaft im Kaiserreich und in der Weimarer Republik. Agrarkrise—junkerliche Interessenpolitik—Modernisierungsstrategien*, ed. Heinz Reif (Berlin: Akademie Verlag, 1994), 378–411; Peter Wulf, "Antisemitismus in bürgerlichen und bäuerlichen Parteien und Verbände in Schleswig-Holstein (1918–1924)," *Jahrbuch für Antisemitismusforschung* 11 (2002): 52–75; and Stefan Malinowski, "Vom blauen zum reinen Blut. Antisemitischer Adelskritik und adliger Antisemitismus 1871–1944," *Jahrbuch für Antisemitismusforschung* 12 (2003): 147–69. An important recent contribution to this literature is Martin Ulmer, *Antisemitismus in Stuttgart 1871–1933. Studien zum öffentlichen Diskurs und Alltag* (Berlin: Metropol Verlag, 2011).

35. For the classic statements of this argument, see William Sheridan Allen, *The Nazi Seizure of Power: The Experience of a Single Town, 1922–1945* (New York: Franklin Watts, 1984); and Rudy Koshar, *Social Life, Local Politics, and Nazism: Marburg, 1880–1935* (Chapel Hill, NC: University of North Carolina Press, 1986); then restated more forcefully in Roger Chickering, "Political Mobilization and Associational Life: Some Thoughts on the National Socialist German Workers' Club (e.V.)," in *Elections, Mass Politics, and Social Change in Modern Germany: New Perspectives*, ed. Larry Eugene Jones and James Retallack (Cambridge: Cambridge University Press, 1992), 307–28.

36. For example, see Shelley Baranowski, "Convergence on the Right: Agrarian Elite Radicalism and Nazi Populism in Pomerania, 1928–33," in *Between Reform, Reaction, and Resistance: Studies in the History of German Conservatism from 1789 to 1945*, ed. Larry Eugene Jones and James Retallack (Providence, RI, and Oxford: Berg, 1993), 407–32; Bernd Kasten, "Deutschnationale Führungsschichten und der Aufstieg der NSDAP in Mecklenburg-Schwerin 1930–1933," *Mecklenburgische Jahrbücher* 115 (2000): 233–57; and Larry Eugene Jones, "Catholic Conservatives in the Weimar Republic: The Politics of the Rhenish-Westphalian Aristocracy, 1918–1933," *German History* 18 (2000): 60–85.

37. In this respect, see Dietrich Orlow, *The History of the Nazi Party: 1919–1933* (Pittsburgh, PA: University of Pittsburgh Press, 1969), and Wolfgang Horn, *Führerideologie und Parteiorganisation in der NSDAP* (Düsseldorf: Droste, 1972).

38. Ian Kershaw, *Hitler 1889–1936: Hubris* (New York and London: W. W. Norton, 1998).

39. Ludolf Herbst, *Hitlers Charisma. Die Erfindung eines deutschen Messias* (Frankfurt: S. Fischer, 2010).

40. A partial corrective to this deficit is to be found in Larry Eugene Jones, "Adolf Hitler and the 1932 Presidential Elections: A Study in Nazi Strategy and Tactics," in *Von Freiheit, Solidarität und Subsidiarität—Staat und Gesellschaft der Moderne in Theorie und Praxis. Festschrift für Karsten Ruppert zum 65. Geburtstag*, ed. Markus Raasch and Tobias Hirschmüller (Berlin: Duncker and Humblot, 2013), 549–73.

41. For an elaboration of this argument, see Wolfram Pyta, "Paul von Hindenburg als charismatischer Führer der deutschen Nation," in *Charismatische Führer der deutschen Nation*, ed. Frank Möller (Munich: R. Oldenbourg, 2004), 109–47.

42. In this respect, see Wolfram Pyta, "Geteiltes Charisma. Hindenburg, Hitler und die deutsche Gesellschaft im Jahre 1933," in *Das Jahr 1933. Die nationalsozialistische Machteroberung und die deutsche Gesellschaft*, ed. Andreas Wirsching (Göttingen: Wallstein Verlag, 2009), 47–69.

43. For a sample of the most recent research on Westarp, see Larry Eugene Jones and Wolfram Pyta, eds., *"Ich bin der letzte Preuße": Kuno Graf von Westarp und die deutsche Politik (1900–1945)* (Cologne, Weimar, and Vienna: Böhlau, 2006).

1

HINDENBURG AND THE GERMAN RIGHT

Wolfram Pyta

How does one situate Hindenburg in the German Right? The answer to this question offers important insights into the processes of political change that ran through the German Right in the first third of the twentieth century. For in the case of Hindenburg one can easily trace the deformation of Prussian-German conservatism in its classical form as it gravitated into the orbit of an increasingly powerful and emergent nationalism. Hindenburg's political views and the political position he represented render an impressive account of the changes that took place in the structure and form of the German Right: the retreat from traditional values and the turn toward ideas that belonged to the political arsenal of German nationalism. Hindenburg's political career thus offers important new perspectives on the transition from the "old" to the "new" Right, a transition that has already been the subject of extensive historical research.[1]

It is by no means a disservice to Hindenburg when one places him in the genealogy of the German Right. Hindenburg had always situated himself on the Right and left no doubt that his basic values and way of thinking belonged to the Right. To be sure, Hindenburg avoided statements to this effect during his tenure as Reich president for fear of compromising the spirit of bipartisan neutrality that was part and parcel of his office. But in private statements he made no secret of his political convictions. As he wrote to his eldest daughter on 16 February 1932: "First, let me state for the record that inwardly I stand on the Right."[2] And to his second adjutant Wedige von der Schulenburg he expressed himself with equal clarity: "You know that inwardly by all means I stand on the Right."[3] The self-description "on the Right," or *rechts*, however, offers only a vague sense of Hindenburg's political self-understanding because since the late nineteenth century the German Right had undergone a political metamorphosis during the course of which it had become more and more differentiated. To which variant of the German Right, therefore, is Hindenburg to be assigned?

Hindenburg's Conservatism and Its Limits

As a general rule, Hindenburg has been characterized as a prototypical German conservative without, however, systematically dissecting his political views and penetrating to their essential core. Hindenburg has thus been assigned the classical attributes of the conservative world-view: devotion to the monarchy and the monarchal form of government, commitment to the welfare of the state as a whole as the guiding principle of his political activity, respect for God, and an unwavering sense of duty.[4] One will also find testimonials from Hindenburg himself in which he expressed his sympathy for that party that regarded itself as the political trustee of Prussian-German conservatism. Until the end of 1918 this function was exercised by the German Conservative Party (Deutsch-Konservative Partei or DKP). Speaking to the DKP parliamentary leader Count Kuno von Westarp on 11 November 1916, Hindenburg characterized himself as "conservative even though he abstained from all forms of party politics. In the interest of the Fatherland," Westarp reported, "he believed that it was necessary that the Conservative Party not be pushed to the side by the course of future events but that it retain its influence."[5] After the German Conservative Party was absorbed into the newly founded German National People's Party (Deutschnationale Volkspartei or DNVP) at the end of 1918, Hindenburg transferred his political sympathies to the new party, which he saw as a continuation of the old conservative party and "to [whose supporters] I have counted myself fully and without qualification [*voll und ganz*]."[6] To be sure, Hindenburg declined Westarp's invitation to head the DNVP's ticket in East Prussia for the January 1919 elections to the constitutional national assembly because in his capacity as chief of the supreme military command he did not want to be seen as the exponent of any particular political party.[7] Still his ties to the new party went so far that he recommended to Westarp that he choose as his replacement his close personal friend and old military comrade cavalry general Friedrich von Bernhardi.[8]

Still, what do Hindenburg's expressions of support for the DKP and DNVP within his own circle of trusted confidantes actually mean? For although they certainly help describe Hindenburg's political habitat in fairly general terms, they do not provide an answer to the more specific and ultimately more important question of where Hindenburg is to be situated within the broad spectrum of political tendencies represented first by the German Conservatives and then by the German Nationalists. For both the German Conservative Party and to an even greater extent the German National People's Party brought together diverse political forces that pursued political goals with different nuances and emphases. Political conservatism embraced both archconservatives who regarded the expansion of state power with a certain reserve and viewed the monarchy as the fixed point of departure for their political activity and governmental conservatives for whom the state and not the monarchy served as their ultimate point of reference. At the same time, the last years of the Second Empire witnessed the emergence of new political formations on the German Right that had less and less in common with the classical conservatism of the nineteenth century and for which the concept of the nation tended to displace the traditional conservative dependence on the monarchy and state. Not only had the skepticism that classical conservatism originally manifested toward the basic ideas of nationalism all but disappeared among the exponents of the new Right, but they regarded the nation and a nationally homogeneous *Volk* as the axis around which their entire system of political beliefs revolved.[9]

Without a doubt Hindenburg's *Duz-Freund* Friedrich von Bernhardi belonged to this new species of politician who could no longer be described as "conservative" in the traditional sense of the word. If the term "conservative" is not to lose all of its conceptual specifcity, then it is important to draw a clear line of distinction between those conservatives who subscribed to a worldview that was rooted in monarchism and an authoritarian conception of the state and the representatives of a new Right for whom the monarchy and the state were subordinate to the nation. Bernhardi was every bit as critical of Wilhelm II as he was of the government the monarch had placed in office, for in his mind both were equally guilty of having lost contact with "the sense of the German nation."[10] The appeal to a nationally aroused *Volk* as a court of ultimate political legitimation bore indisputable testimony to the ways in which the boundaries of a traditional conservative perspective had been overstepped in the move toward the new Right.

From a preliminary survey of Hindenburg's political and intellectual horizon one can safely assume that Hindenburg and Bernhardi were political soul mates and that it is therefore no longer possible to look at Hindenburg as someone who subscribed to the classical conservatism of the old Right. In this respect we will be taking a closer look at Hindenburg's political position in an attempt to differentiate it even further from the more traditional forms of German conservatism. No one better serves our purpose in this respect than Elard von Oldenburg-Januschau, the prototype of the archconservative

East-Elbian conservatives. Oldenburg-Januschau enjoyed close personal and political contact to Hindenburg from 1914 to 1934,[11] and after Hindenburg's death he made no secret of the fact that Hindenburg
had deserted the conservative cause and that at heart he had never
belonged to the conservative camp.[12]

This is not to suggest, however, that Hindenburg's general demeanor
and lifestyle made him at first glance the perfect example of a conservative. Without a doubt Hindenburg possessed genuine conservative secondary virtues. He led an ordered family life and possessed a marked
sense of family. Also his appreciation of religion and church suggested
a strong affinity to basic conservative values. In his personal and political behavior Hindenburg was led by a genuine, not affected religiosity.[13] As a humble Christian he asked for God's help in prayer and felt
secure in the belief that God as the all-powerful master of human destiny stood at his side.[14] That God protected not only the individual but
the German Reich as well was also a view that was widely held in conservative circles. By the same token, God's protective majesty extended
also to the German nation. As Hindenburg wrote to his daughter in
January 1931: "God will not abandon our Fatherland—nor us as individuals."[15] And with this faith came the fact that Hindenburg searched
for God's counsel in the exercise of his office as Reich president. For the
deeply religious Hindenburg there could be no doubt that those who
were responsible for the welfare of the state "bring their concerns and
resolutions before God's throne in order to seek from Him the strength
and wisdom to bear the burden of their high office."[16] Similarly, Hindenburg's attitude to the church was that of a conservative who attended church regularly and regarded himself as a faithful member of
his Protestant church.[17]

Closely tied to Hindenburg's religiosity was his outspoken sense of
duty. Hindenburg embodied the conservative ideal of duty and responsibility. To subordinate one's own interests to the welfare of the whole
lay at the heart of Hindenburg's sense of who he was as a person and
as a servant of the German nation. Hindenburg would evoke this ethos
of duty whenever he would need to legitimize his intervention into the
political realm, beginning with his political activity in World War I.[18]
By the same token, Hindenburg justified his candidacy for the Reich
presidency in the spring of 1925 with words that were characteristic
for him and his need to find a synthesis between one's sense of duty
and one's faith in God. As he wrote to his daughter Irmengard after accepting the nomination of the *Reichsblock*: "Did it reluctantly, but out of
a sense of duty. May God see to it that everything from here on out is

good for the Fatherland!"[19] Nor can Hindenburg's willingness to stand again as a presidential candidate in 1932 be understood without reference to the preeminent place the concept of duty held in his catalog of political values.[20]

It would, however, be a serious mistake to reduce Hindenburg and his sense of mission to those values and attitudes that correspond to the fundamental ideas of a conservative worldview. Of even more significance are those ideas and values—but also the political actions resulting from them—that extended beyond the terrain of classical conservatism.

The Paradoxes of Hindenburg's Monarchism

First let us take a look at Hindenburg's attitude toward the monarch. It does not require a detailed explanation that Hindenburg, born in 1847 into the family of an army officer, supported the Prussian monarchy and the German Empire from the depths of his soul as the best conceivable system of government for the German people. Even then Hindenburg was not an ultramonarchist who clung to the monarchy with every heartbeat and who saw himself bound to his monarch by an insoluble relationship of faith and duty. Hindenburg was not a typical Prussian conservative who, as in the case of the DKP parliamentary leader Count Westarp, had closed his eyes to the personal deficits of Wilhelm II, but he remained dedicated to the monarchy as a form of government and therefore protected it against infringements upon the prerogatives of the monarch.[21] On the contrary, Hindenburg did not hesitate during the course of World War I to arrogate to himself rights, powers, and privileges to which, from the perspective of a traditional conservative viewpoint, only Wilhelm II could lay legitimate claim.

From the summer of 1917 on Hindenburg would claim for himself sovereign powers in the most important personnel decisions related to the governance of the Reich. This meant that it was no longer Wilhelm II but the chief of the German general staff who would determine the composition of the government. Hindenburg's intervention would be the decisive factor in the Kaiser's decision to break with his most important advisors: first in July 1917 from Reich Chancellor Theobald von Bethmann Hollweg, then in November 1917 from Vice Chancellor Karl Helfferich, and finally in June 1918 from the Secretary of State in the Foreign Office Richard von Kühlmann.[22] To be sure, these politicians were a thorn in the side of the conservatives in the Reich and Prussia because they stood for a program of moderate reform in both domestic and foreign policy.

But to pressure the Kaiser in this way and to force him into acquiescence, as Hindenburg did particularly in the case of Bethmann Hollweg's dismissal from office, was irreconcilable with the way in which conservatives traditionally understood their role in German political life. And absolutely irreconcilable with a conservative view of politics was the fact that Hindenburg failed to respect the extra-constitutional prerogatives of the Kaiser in forcing the dismissal of his personal chief of the privy council, Rudolf von Valentini, in January 1918.

Hindenburg's attacks against Bethmann Hollweg were on the one hand an expression of deep-seated differences of opinion between the field marshal and the Reich chancellor. The moderate conservative Bethmann Hollweg wanted to modernize Prussia and the Reich by ending the reactionary three-class franchise in Prussia and by elevating the position of the Reichstag, projects that in Hindenburg's mind would have turned the chancellor into the gravedigger of Prussia.[23] In this respect, however, Bethmann Hollweg proved to be a many-faceted defender of the rights and prerogatives of the monarch. For under the conditions of a people's war Bethmann Hollweg believed that the Kaiser could maintain his privileged position in the political system only by redefining himself as a *Volkskaiser* who, in this spirit, was committed to a systematic reform of the German political system from above.[24] But in doing so the Reich chancellor also infringed upon the legitimacy of Hindenburg's claim to power, a claim that was rooted in part in the fact that for some time Hindenburg had built up a position of his own that was independent of the authority of Wilhelm II and that legitimized itself through the plebiscitarian support of the German people. The bitter conflict between Hindenburg and Bethmann Hollweg was therefore part of a more fundamental conflict between the plebiscitarian legitimacy of Hindenburg's claim to power and that of the monarch as modified according to the precepts of a reformed *Volksstaat*. From this perspective Bethmann Hollweg can be seen as a far-sighted defender of monarchal authority, particularly in the realm of military command,[25] whereas the field marshal exercised a claim to power that was all-encompassing and that refused to recognize the legitimacy of any higher political authority.[26] In this respect Hindenburg's success in forcing Bethmann Hollweg's dismissal on 13 July 1917 by threatening to resign his military command represented a deep caesura in the history of the Prussian-German monarchy, a caesura that could have not been captured with greater pathos than in the words of the Kaiser himself: "It is high time for him to abdicate since for the first time that a Prussian monarch will be forced by his generals to do something that he didn't want to do."[27]

Through his infringement upon the prerogatives of monarchal power Hindenburg had placed himself outside the orbit of classical conservatism. This had presumably occurred with the dismissal of Wilhelm II's closest domestic advisor, the chief of his secret privy council Rudolf von Valentini. Valentini embodied the best virtues of the archconservative civil servant for whom the preservation of the rights of the crown took precedence over everything else and who had therefore expressed reservations regarding Bethmann Hollweg's plans for a reform of the Prussian-German monarchical system from above.[28] At the same time, Valentini was a picture-book conservative, and it speaks for itself that Hindenburg pursued this absolutely loyal servant of his king and emperor with such bitterness that he eventually brought him down on 16 January 1918. Hindenburg regarded the leader of the privy council as a "sinister [*unheilvolle*] person" who had allegedly advised the Kaiser "in one-sided tendency that came sharply from the left."[29] What were the standards that guided Hindenburg in accusing precisely this prototype of the archconservative of a tendency toward the left? What system of political coordinates was Hindenburg using when he went so far as to denounce Valentini to the Kaiser as the "enemy in the rear" who sabotaged the supreme high command in its military endeavors?[30]

At first glance one is inclined to place Hindenburg in the ranks of those military leaders who during World War I harbored plans for a disguised military dictatorship. Fleet Admiral Alfred von Tirpitz, Hindenburg's closest collaborator Erich Ludendorff, and several junior staff officers such as Colonel Max Bauer toyed with the idea of totally subordinating Germany's domestic political leadership to the power of the supreme high command. That this would disempower not only the Reichstag but also the Kaiser, the remaining dynastic princes, and the Bundesrat was perfectly clear to those who envisaged such a solution as the only way out of the political crisis that had descended upon Germany in the last years of the war. The concept of a military dictatorship brought together all of those ideas that had already found a home in the so-called new Right. Above all else, these ideas were characterized by a radical nationalism that sought to entrust the leadership of the state to those forces with the ruthless determination necessary to eliminate all internal adversaries that stood in the way of the establishment of an imperialist *Machtstaat* capable of imposing its will at home and abroad. The new Right thus delegitimized the monarchal principle and replaced it with the principle of political leadership. In the context of World War I, this meant making the supreme military command a sovereign power in its own right that, from the perspective of the new

Right, was alone capable of establishing aggressive nationalism as a doctrine of the state.[31]

Hindenburg's specific understanding of politics and power, however, did not go so far as to include the idea of a military dictatorship. In the first place, Hindenburg was not prepared to jettison the institutional order of the monarchy. To be sure, Hindenburg had not hesitated to press his political will upon the monarch particularly in questions of personnel, but he was not ready to abandon the monarchal principle and to replace it with a new concept of rule based upon the principle of leadership. Second, the concept "dictatorship" is inappropriate because it ignores the fact that Hindenburg's usurpation of monarchal prerogative rested upon the implicit consent of the German nation that he had gained more or less informally during the course of the war. As Hindenburg's old friend Bernhardi expressed it at the end of 1916: "You can accomplish whatever you want and dismiss whomever you want when everything falls apart. In you and you alone has the German nation placed its confidence."[32]

After his victory at Tannenberg at the end of August 1914 Hindenburg attracted the spontaneous adoration of the German people, and by the middle of the following year this had been transformed into a stable and lasting Hindenburg myth.[33] At first Hindenburg reacted with disbelief to the fact that he who had been completely unknown before the war had suddenly been elevated to "hero of the heart [*Helden der Herzen*]." Originally he had interpreted this turn of fortune according to classical conservative precepts: as a gift of God's providence. On 4 September 1914 he shared his feelings with the member of his family circle to whom he felt closest, his daughter Irmengard von Brockhusen: "I am honored and celebrated from all sides. . . . But that should not make me conceited [*übermütig*]. Without God I would have never had done it."[34] Yet four weeks later Hindenburg's self-confidence had grown to the point where he recognized that his great victory at Tannenburg was no "one-day success [*Eintagsfliege*]" and that his subsequent successes in Poland were directly attributable to his own talents: "Here things are quite good. It may sound arrogant, but it is so: Since my arrival there has been a great turn-around in this theater of the war."[35] It was not long before Hindenburg not only came to enjoy this situation but to take an active role in the cultivation of his myth, so much so in fact that in 1919 he curtly dismissed the criticism that ultraconservative circles had leveled against him as *lèse-majesté*: "The only existing idol of the nation, undeservedly my humble self, runs the risk of being torn from the pedestal once it becomes the target of criticism."[36]

If one attempts to categorize Hindenburg's style of leadership, one can best do it with the adjective "charismatic." What distinguished Hindenburg's style of leadership and claim to authority was an interactive relationship between the hero of Tannenburg and broad sectors of German society. In this respect Hindenburg performed a remarkable symbolic function in that he helped to highlight the longing for national unity that had become so deeply rooted in Germany's political culture. At the same time, Hindenburg was an exceedingly active agent of cultural meaning that pursued an active politics of symbolism and skillfully placed himself in the limelight in order to intentionally nurture his myth. In Hindenburg two particular faculties were brought together: the use of symbols as a mode of political representation and the staging of politics in symbolic terms.[37] And it was precisely the combination of the two that allowed Hindenburg to lay a claim to authority legitimized not by virtue of the office he held but rooted in a broad base of popular support that was directly related to his careful and conscious use of political symbols.

Hindenburg's claim to authority was not tied to any particular form of government; it could be effective under the terms of republican as well as under monarchist government. Through its constant evocation of the *Volk* as the subject upon whose acclamation his authority ultimately rested, Hindenburg's claim to leadership quickly exploded a typically conservative concept of political legitimation. Hindenburg's claim to authority, therefore, had little to do with conservative patterns of political legitimation but depended instead upon a constantly renewable popular consensus that extended to all sectors of German society and that bound the German people to his person and the project of national unity that had become synonymous with his person.

Nowhere was this more apparent than in his behavior on 9 November 1918. To be sure, Hindenburg was profoundly disturbed by the collapse of the Prussian monarchy and the German Empire and by the triumph of the revolution in Berlin.[38] Nevertheless Hindenburg moved quickly to adapt himself to the new order. After all, Hindenburg was the driving force behind the efforts to relocate the former monarch in the Netherlands, something that could only appear to the broader public as a flight on the part of the exiled Kaiser. Nothing damaged the prestige of the Hohenzollerns more than the fact that on the morning of 10 November the descendant of Friedrich the Great escaped to neutral Netherlands because he feared—and in this respect his fears were greatly strengthened by Hindenburg—falling into the hands of revolting soldiers. In other words, a Kaiser who preferred the drawing room to a hero's death at the front. Hindenburg was not only subjectively concerned about the personal security of Wilhelm II, but from his perspective the deposed Kaiser was a political liability for the army at the front, which had not yet been "infected" by the revolutionary turmoil and which Hindenburg wanted to preserve intact at all costs, including that of sending Wilhelm II as a potential troublemaker to the Netherlands.[39]

For Hindenburg the nation took precedence over the form of government, something that expressed itself in the fact that on 9 November 1918 Hindenburg placed himself at the service of the new revolutionary government in Berlin. Hindenburg did this precisely because he wanted to preserve the army intact as a power factor for the German Reich in the difficult armistice negotiations and peace negotiations that lay ahead. In this respect, Hindenburg's personal authority was so far beyond reproach that he could lead the front army back to Germany without signs of internal dissolution. The problem was that by now many conservatives expected from Hindenburg that he would use his position as commander-in-chief of the German army to dispose of the hated new government. What made these expectations particularly poignant for Hindenburg was the fact that his son-in-law Hans-Joachim von Brockhusen sympathized with such ideas and demanded that his father-in-law take appropriate action. Even then Brockhusen was aware that proposals to this effect might not meet with favor. As he explained to his father-in-law in a letter from 9 November: "I will do it even though I fear that I might anger you."[40] Brockhusen can be seen as a particularly authentic representative of a strong monarchal conservatism for whom the events of 9 November 1918 signaled the collapse of a world, all the more so because Hindenburg seemed to have joined forces with the revolutionaries and did not shy away from allying himself with the provisional government. When Brockhusen learned of this, it was as if his entire world had collapsed: "It suddenly flashed before my eyes as if I had been struck by lightning. So, I thought, this is what it must be like when one suffers a stroke."[41]

Hindenburg's son-on-law thus received a sharp rebuff as he tried to enlist the venerable field marshal for the ultraconservative course that he and many of his peers in the Prussian aristocracy hoped to pursue. Testily Hindenburg rejected all of this as ignorant and out of touch with reality for the simple reason that it failed to recognize that the central task to which he had devoted himself since the upheaval of 9 November 1918 was precisely to preserve the military and political substance of the German Reich without which the survival of the nation would be impossible. Hindenburg sought to save the German Reich through the difficult phase of the revolution and coming to terms with Germany's military defeat in the hope of better times in the future. Hindenburg's political pragmatism thus alienated him from those conservatives who could not accept the collapse of the monarchy and who now demanded that Hindenburg ally himself with the forces of the counterrevolution. Hindenburg clearly recognized just how deep the rift between himself and the Prussian conservatives had become as he wrote to his son-in-law on 13 March 1919: "It may very well be that I will be forced to separate myself from the Conservative Party to [whose supporters] I have counted myself fully and without qualification [*voll und ganz*]."[42]

Hindenburg's position on the monarchy did not change after his election to the Reich presidency gave rise to new expectations on the part of conservative monarchists that he would now take the lead in restoring the monarchy. Hindenburg sharply rejected advice to this effect because he feared that raising the question of restoration would only lead to new domestic and diplomatic turmoil. For not only would the restoration of the monarchy exacerbate the internal fragmentation of the German nation about which Hindenburg had already bitterly complained, but it would invite foreign powers to take countermeasures against the German Reich at precisely the moment that efforts to restore Germany to great power status through the revision of the Versailles Peace Treaty were beginning to show their first signs of real success.[43] Hindenburg therefore reacted negatively to Heinrich Brüning on the two occasions the Reich chancellor tried to warm him up to the idea of a restoration of the monarchy.[44] And in the fall of 1933 when a small group of royalists around retired general August von Cramon, one of Hindenburg's closest personal confidantes, tried to enlist the Reich president's support for another attempt at restoring the monarchy and implored him to recall the former Kaiser Wilhelm II to Germany from his exile in the Netherlands, Hindenburg rejected such an idea, though with words that revealed the inner dilemma in which he found himself: "Of course I recognize your fidelity to our Kaiser, king, and lord without reservation. But precisely because I share this sentiment, I must urgently warn against the step you plan to take. . . . The domestic crisis is not yet completely over, and foreign powers will have a hard time imagining me on the sidelines if it comes to a restoration of the monarchy. . . . To say this is unbelievably painful for me."[45]

Hindenburg belonged to the same cadre of politicians as Gustav Stresemann that was emotionally attached to the German Empire and who, if they had had their way, would like to have seen the restoration of the

monarchy. But a rational and realistic appraisal of the domestic and diplomatic situation in which Germany found itself made it clear that such
a project was politically irresponsible and placed at risk what was far
more important than the monarchical form of government, namely, the
integrity of the German Empire and the restoration of Germany's internal unity to the highest possible degree. Some of those who fell into this
category—Stresemann being the most prominent—found it possible to
support the Weimar Republic because they believed it capable of developing into a genuine *Volksstaat* in which all sectors of German society
were inwardly united. Hindenburg, on the other hand, did not belong to
the category of "Vernunftrepublikaner"[46] because he did not think that
the Weimar Republic was capable of fulfilling this task.

Hindenburg and the Quest for Germany's Inner Unity

By now we have identified the guiding principle that Hindenburg
inscribed on his political banner from 1914 on: the inner unity of the
German nation. Throughout his political career Hindenburg remained
committed to one goal that took precedence over all else, namely, that
of fusing the German nation into a united and homogeneous political will. In this respect Hindenburg stood, like many of his contemporaries, under the spell of the national awakening that had occurred
in almost all of the belligerents at the beginning of the war in August
1914. In a single moment it seemed as if all of the divisions that had
become so deeply entrenched in the fabric of German society were suddenly gone: the estrangement of the socialist labor movement, the bitter confessional strife between Protestants and Catholics, the conflict
over the allocation of resources between the agrarians and those who
sought to accelerate the pace of Germany's industrialization, the antagonism between the experiments in modernist culture that had captivated the large cities and the culturally conservative small towns and
villages. For a moment it seemed as if the profound fragmentation of
German society into a plethora of separate milieus had been overcome
as a patriotic wave spread throughout the country in August 1914.[47] To
be sure, not all sectors of German society were equally affected by this
phenomenon. But for those in the nationalist camp the August experience provided reassuring evidence that the German people could find
its way to that inner unity for which they had always longed.[48]

Hindenburg experienced the August days of 1914 in a very similar way. In Hanover and on a previous trip through Berlin he had had

sufficient opportunity to witness the storm of patriotic enthusiasm first hand. As he wrote to his son-in-law: "How glorious [*herrlich*] is the bearing of our people."[49] During the course of the war Hindenburg came to think of himself more and more as the trustee of the will to national unity that had made itself manifest in August 1914 and in doing so began to occupy a position that was more properly reserved for the Kaiser. "May we never lose the spirit of 1914!"[50] wrote Hindenburg in early March 1915 as he sought to help the German people orient itself with regard to the difficult struggles that lay ahead.

Though somewhat diffuse in their initial iterations, the "Ideas of 1914" came to form the spiritual basis of a new concept of the political order that gradually emerged during the course of the war, the concept of the *Volksgemeinschaft*.[51] To be sure, the term had enjoyed a certain cachet during the war,[52] but it was only after the defeat of 1918 that it developed into a widely accepted code for the longing for national unity to which the "Ideas of 1914" had given such eloquent expression. Not only did the concept of the *Volksgemeinschaft* underscore the fact that the German nation was to be regarded as a homogeneous community capable of expressing a single political will, but it also elevated the nation to the status of a court of legitimation for the exercise of political authority. And it was precisely this that accounted for the appeal of the idea of the *Volksgemeinschaft* deep within the ranks of the democratic camp both during and after the war. That the nation was no longer seen as a politically inconsequential community of those who defined themselves as German but was inseparably linked to the idea of the people as a political subject entitled to determine its own national destiny was a principle of political legitimation to which both the liberals and Social Democrats were attracted.[53]

The concept of the *Volksgemeinschaft* and its increasingly widespread acceptance during the course of World War I meant that the forces of the German Right could no longer ignore the demands of a politically aroused nation for a more meaningful role in shaping its own political destiny.[54] This, in turn, brought about a shift within the German Right from its fixation on a monarchal state whose legitimacy was not based upon a broad popular consensus to an acceptance of new forms of authority whose legitimation appeared indispensably tied to the consent of a nation capable of expressing itself as a united political will.

The conceptual vagueness of the idea of the *Volksgemeinschaft* as the translation of the "Ideas of 1914" into a new concept of the political order made it possible in the postwar period to use the terms *Volksgemeinschaft* and *Volksstaat* more or less as synonyms. The newly created

Weimar Republic conceived of itself as a *Volksstaat,* a system of government that for the first time in the history of the German people based
itself upon the principle of popular sovereignty. In this context the
Volksgemeinschaft had a two-fold meaning. On the one hand, it meant
that all sectors of the German nation were entitled to take part in the
political process and that representatives of the German working class
could rise to the highest offices in the state. This interpretation of the
Volksgemeinschaft explicitly criticized the German *Kaiserreich* in which
leadership positions were always reserved for socially privileged
groups. Social Democrats and liberals were thus attracted to a concept
of the *Volksgemeinschaft* that entailed political participation across social
barriers.[55] On the other hand, the concept of the *Volksgemeinschaft* implied that in the most fundamental questions of national policy those
who were now entitled to take part in the political process must subordinate the pursuit of their own particular interests to the welfare of the
nation as a whole. The notion of the *Volksgemeinschaft* thus presumed
that the various forces in German political life were committed to a set
of universally accepted fundamental principles that were no longer
subject to political dispute.

It should be no surprise, therefore, that at least until the end of the
1920s the concept of the *Volksgemeinschaft* was not limited exclusively
to the German Right but that it also received considerable support in
the political center and on the democratic Left. It was in this spirit that
the joint candidate of the Center, Social Democrats, and liberals for the
Reich presidency in 1925, the former Reich chancellor Wilhelm Marx,
conducted his campaign with the promise to lead "the German nation
and all the strata of which it is composed into a true *Volksgemeinschaft*
that transcends the cleavages of social and political division."[56] In prop-
agating the idea of the *Volksgemeinschaft,* however, Marx was simply
following in the footsteps of his predecessor, the Social Democrat Friedrich Ebert.[57] The concept of the *Volksgemeinschaft* thus enjoyed a broad
base of support within the ranks of the liberal and Social Democratic
parties because it offered a basis upon which the various sectors of
German society could be integrated into a viable and durable political
unity.[58] No German should avoid his or her responsibilities to the principle of national solidarity; no German could remain excluded from the
national community.

And it was precisely this point that distinguished the right-wing
variant of the idea of the *Volksgemeinschaft* from that of the political
middle and democratic Left. To be sure, the Right propagated the ideal
of national integration, but it combined this with the exclusion of those

whom it alleged to be the enemies of the nation. The German Right clung to the conviction that national unity could be achieved only when the internal enemy had been defeated and excluded. As presumed enemies of the nation the Right took aim not only at the Social Democrats and Communists but also at the Jews and those Catholics who supposedly took their cue from Rome. In so far as the political Right embraced the concept of the *Volksgemeinschaft*, this automatically implied the relentless pursuit of those forces that from its perspective stood in the way of internal unity.[59]

Without a doubt Hindenburg's understanding of *Volksgemeinschaft* exhibited a tendency toward exclusion similar to that of the new Right. For even in World War I Hindenburg believed that the internal enemy was already hard at work and characteristically included the archconservative chief of Wilhelm's privy council Rudolf von Valentini and the Reich chancellor Bethmann Hollweg among those who presumably sought to sabotage the victorious efforts of Germany's military leadership. In retrospect Hindenburg was a faithful student of Carl Schmitt, who defined the friend-foe antagonism as the salient criterion of the political realm.[60] Even after Hindenburg resigned as commander-in-chief of the German military, he retained the distinction between friend and foe as a prominent feature in his system of political coordinates. Although as a symbol of the longing for national unity Hindenburg exercised restraint in his public statements, the distinction between friend and foe would occasionally flare up. A particularly powerful use of the friend-foe antagonism could be seen in the "stab-in-the-back legend," in whose promulgation and spread Hindenburg had a major hand. On 18 November 1919 Hindenburg used the hearings of the Reichstag committee investigating the causes of Germany's military defeat as a forum for proclaiming *ex cathedra* that it was not the military but Germany's internal enemy that had to bear ultimate responsibility for the loss of the war.[61]

Even then Hindenburg could still feel comfortable with both sides of the idea of the *Volksgemeinschaft*, that is, not only with the tendency toward segregation and exclusion but also with the more inclusive implications of the concept. Even during the war Hindenburg had become the focal point of the longing that most Germans felt for a higher and more perfect form of national integration. It was therefore only natural that when he stood for public office for the first time in his life and became a candidate for the Reich presidency in the spring of 1925 that he would reprise the integrative aspect of the *Volksgemeinschaft* idea. His only programmatic statement in the campaign, the so-called "Easter

Appeal" of 11 April 1925, stood under the motto "reconcile rather than split [*versöhnen statt spalten*]" and was carefully crafted to place Hindenburg's will to integration at the heart of his candidacy: "I extend my hand to every German who thinks nationally, preserves the value of the German name at home and abroad, and who desires confessional and social peace."[62]

As Reich president Hindenburg—and here he was following in the tradition of his predecessor Ebert—spent the first five years of his presidency as a clarion for German national unity and did not hesitate to entrust high political office to politicians from the ranks of the Social Democrats, democratic liberalism, and political Catholicism. In doing so he had to endure massive criticism from an anxious and confused German Right that began to lose faith in Hindenburg because in the area of foreign policy he supported Stresemann's tempered and realistic policy of understanding with Germany's erstwhile enemies and in the area of domestic policy had failed to initiate a change in the political system. Through an accommodation with the Weimar Republic Hindenburg wanted to test whether or not it would be possible to proceed with the project of the *Volksgemeinschaft*. From 1925 to 1930 Hindenburg embraced an inclusive concept of the *Volksgemeinschaft* that stretched as far to the left as the Social Democrats and that sought to determine whether or not the basis for a fundamental consensus reaching from the Social Democrats to the German Nationalists existed.[63] During this phase of political experimentation Hindenburg therefore worked with cabinets in which ministers from the ranks of German Nationalists, the right-liberal German People's Party, the left-liberal German Democratic Party (Deutsche Demokratische Partei or DDP), the Catholic-conservative Bavarian People's Party (Bayerische Volkspartei or BVP), the Center, and the Social Democrats were all represented. After the 1928 Reichstag elections Hindenburg even went so far as to appoint as Reich chancellor the Social Democrat Hermann Müller, who in the course of time formed a government that stretched from the SPD to the DVP.

Measured by the standard of a politically homogeneous community of national will, the result of these experiments could only have had a sobering effect on the Reich president. In the spring of 1930 German society seemed as fragmented as it had been in 1925, something for which Hindenburg, with profound implications for the anti-pluralistic tendency of the *Volksgemeinschaft* concept, held the influence of the Reichstag directly responsible. To Hindenburg the Reichstag was a mirror of Germany's inner fragmentation in large part because the parties represented in it, at least from his perspective, were all committed to the pursuit of special interests. It was as a result of this insight, therefore, that in the spring of 1930 Hindenburg decided to move in a more authoritarian direction toward the construction of a political system in which the corrupting influence of the parties would be minimized at the same time that the influence of the Reich president on the legislative process—and particularly when it came to the appointment and formation of the cabinet—would increase.[64]

Hindenburg stood to benefit from the fact that the basic principle of the *Volksgemeinschaft* was not tied to a particular arrangement of political institutions and that it was therefore perfectly compatible with an interpretation that regarded the restriction of parliamentary prerogatives as a logical consequence of the idea of the *Volksgemeinschaft*. This indifference to the fate of Germany's political institutions extended well into the ranks of democratic liberalism, where an increasingly anti-parliamentary tone had made itself apparent,[65] as well as into those of political Catholicism, where ideas of community had begun to take on stronger and stronger anti-parliamentary contours.[66] In one decisive point, however, there was a fundamental distinction between the versions of the *Volksgemeinschaft* that existed in the liberal and Catholic camps and that embraced by Hindenburg. For the representatives of liberalism and political Catholicism the Social Democrats constituted an integral component of the *Volksgemeinschaft*, something that they had proven beyond any doubt by the strength and passion of their loyalty to the nation in World War I. In the 1932 presidential campaign Reich chancellor Heinrich Brüning therefore forged an alliance between political Catholicism, liberalism, and Social Democracy in order to demonstrate to Hindenburg that the democratic Left was also committed to the ideas of the *Volksgemeinschaft* and, in doing so, secured Hindenburg's reelection.[67]

Nevertheless Hindenburg proceeded to exclude the democratic Left from the realization of his *Volksgemeinschaft* project because he stood under the spell of the friend-foe way of thinking. For in the final analysis Hindenburg believed that the Social Democratic Party belonged to the inner enemies of national unity, so that the realization of a genuine *Volksgemeinschaft* necessarily required the exclusion of the Social Democrats. Hindenburg thus turned a deaf ear to Fritz Schäffer, chairman of the Catholic-conservative Bavarian People's Party, when on 17 February 1933 he made an impassioned plea on behalf of the national loyalty of the German Social Democrats. Schäffer's exchange with Hindenburg was indeed the only time after 30 January 1933 that a representative of those forces that had supported him in his campaign for reelection as

Reich president went to him personally and pleaded the case for the inclusive concept of the *Volksgemeinschaft*. For the candor with which they were spoken, Schäffer's words deserve to be cited at length: "We will reject the notion that million of Germans are not to be designated as national. The socialists served in the trenches [of World War I] and will serve in the trenches again. They also voted for the banner of Hindenburg. . . . I know many socialists who have earned acclaim for their service to Germany; I only need to remember the name Ebert."[68] But Hindenburg was unmoved by Schäffer's appeal because by now he had fully internalized the exclusive version of the *Volksgemeinschaft* and therefore regarded Social Democracy as an anti-national organization even though individual socialists were patriotic.

For Hindenburg the realization of the *Volksgemeinschaft* therefore meant standing shoulder to shoulder with the political Right. "What pains and angers me most," Hindenburg wrote to his daughter Irmengard in the summer of 1931, "is being misunderstood by a part of the Right."[69] Since the middle of 1931 he had sent unmistakable signals to the hopelessly divided German Right, which he hoped would submit to his political leadership and close ranks under his guidance at the expense of their own party political interests. As early as February 1932 Hindenburg had made it clear that after the presidential elections he would sever ties with Brüning as Reich chancellor in order to work for the creation of a new government in which all of the forces on the German Right, including the National Socialists, were represented. The only condition that Hindenburg attached to Nazi participation in such a government was that Hitler submit to his claim to leadership. In a letter to his daughter Hindenburg revealed unmistakably "that I stand inwardly on the Right. . . . If the Right proves itself willing to submit [*willfährig*], I shall welcome it with all my heart."[70] Equally clear were his statements in a personal exposé of his reasons for running for re-election that he sent to a number of his confidants on 25 February 1932. In what was a key document for understanding his own sense of mission Hindenburg wrote: "Please see from the following that the charge that I opposed a government of the Right is completely false. It was not I . . . but *solely the disunity of the Right* [emphasis Hindenburg's] and its inability to come together in the main points that constituted the obstacle for such a development. . . . Despite all the blows to the neck [*Nackenschläge*] I have taken, I will not abandon my efforts on behalf of a healthy move to the Right."[71]

On 30 January 1933 the constellation that Hindenburg had had in mind for the balance of his political life had been finally created. The various forces of the German Right were prepared under his guidance to participate in a "cabinet of national concentration." With this his wish to breathe new life into the "Ideas of 1914" had been fulfilled. Nowhere were his hopes expressed more clearly than in a radio address from 10 March 1932: "We can only reach our great goal when we come together in a genuine *Volksgemeinschaft*. . . . I recall the spirit of 1914 and the mood at the front, which asked about the man and not about his class or party."[72] On 30 January 1933 the venerable field marshal Paul von Hindenburg and the parvenu corporal Adolf Hitler sealed their pact with a symbolic handshake and went forward in realizing their version of the *Volksgemeinschaft*. Following the installation of the Hitler-Papen-Hugenberg cabinet Hindenburg recalled once again the sense of national awakening that had captivated him in August 1914: "Patriotic revival very gratifying; may God preserve our unity!"[73]

Notes

1. In this respect, see Geoff Eley, *Reshaping the German Right: Radical Nationalism and Political Change after Bismarck* (New Haven, CT: Yale University Press, 1980), and Larry Eugene Jones and James Retallack, "German Conservatism Reconsidered: Old Problems and New Directions," in *Between Reform, Reaction, and Resistance: Studies in the History of German Conservatism from 1789 to 1945*, ed. Larry Eugene Jones and James Retallack (Oxford: Berg, 1993), 1–30; as well as Axel Schildt, *Konservatismus in Deutschland. Von den Anfängen im 18. Jahrhundert bis zur Gegenwart* (Munich: C. H. Beck, 1998).
2. Hindenburg to Irmengard von Brockhusen, 16 February 1932, in private possession.
3. This word-for-word statement by Hindenburg to his adjutant Wedige von der Schulenburg is to be found in the entry of 24 October 1929 in the diary of Oswald von Hoeyningen-Huene, a collaborator in the Bureau of the Reich President, notebook 14, in the private possession of Dr. Uta Treu-Neubourg.
4. Walther Hubatsch, *Hindenburg und der Staat. Aus den Papieren des Generalfeldmarschalls und Reichspräsidenten von 1878 biw 1934* (Göttingen: Musterschmidt, 1966), esp. 145–48.
5. This statement from Hugenberg is based on the extremely reliable account in Kuno Graf von Westarp, *Konservative Politik im letzten Jahrzehnt des Kaiserreiches*, 2 vols. (Berlin: Deutsche Verlagsgesellschaft, 1934–35), 2:334. Westarp relied upon his own handwritten notes of the meeting that have been preserved in the family archives of the Freiherren Hiller von Gaertringen, Nachlaß Westarp, in Gärtringen (hereafter cited as NL Westarp, Gärtringen).

6. Hindenburg to his son-in-law Hans-Joachim von Brockhusen, 13 March 1919, in private possession.
7. Hindenburg to Westarp, 23 December 1918, reprinted in Hubatsch, *Hindenburg*, 56f.
8. Hindenburg to Westarp, 28 December 1918, NL Westarp, Gärtringen, Mappe "Briefwechsel mit Hindenburg."
9. Wolfram Pyta, "Das Zerplatzen der Hoffnung auf eine konservative Wende. Kuno Graf von Westarp und Hindenburg" in *"Ich bin der letzte Preuße". Der politische Lebensweg des konservativen Politikers Kuno Graf von Westarp (1864—1945)*, ed. Larry Eugene Jones and Wolfram Pyta (Cologne: Böhlau, 2006), 163–87, esp. 164–66.
10. Bernhardi to Hindenburg, 26 December 1916, in Friedrich von Bernhardi, *Denkwürdigkeiten aus meinem Leben nach gleichzeitigen Aufzeichnungen und im Lichte der Erinnerung* (Berlin: Mittler, 1927), 460–63, n.460. For Bernhardi's fixation on the nation, see 528–33.
11. Wolfram Pyta, *Hindenburg. Herrschaft zwischen Hohenzollern und Hitler* (Munich: Siedler, 2007), 564f.
12. See Oldenburg's lecture in the Hamburg National Club of 1919 (Hamburger Nationalklub von 1919), 18 January 1935, based on an entry into the diary of the future mayor of Hamburg Carl Vincent Krogmann for 19 January 1935, Forschungsstelle für Zeitgeschichte, Hamburg, 11/K5, Krogmann-Tagebücher 1934–35.
13. See Pyta, *Hindenburg*, 22, as well as the contribution by the military pastor Zierach, "Hindenburg als Mensch und Christ," in *Hindenburg. Was er uns Deutschen ist*, ed. Friedrich Wilhelm von Loebell (Berlin: Reimar Hobbing, 1927), 162–84.
14. Hindenburg's faith in God is reflected, for example, is his correspondence with his eldest daughter, Irmengard von Brockhusen, with whom he enjoyed a particularly close relationship. For example, see his letters from 24 January, 21 July, 14 October, 12 and 24 November, 1 and 10 December 1931, as well as from 17 March and 8 April 1932, all in private possession.
15. Hindenburg to Irmengard von Brockhusen, 24 January 1931, private possession.
16. Hindenburg to the Saxon Crown Prince Georg, 10 October 1928, in the Sächsisches Hauptstaatsarchiv, Dresden, Verein Haus Wettin.
17. See Pyta, *Hindenburg*, 22, as well as Dieter von der Schulenburg, *Welt um Hindenburg. Hundert Gespräche mit Berufenen* (Berlin: Buch- und Tiefdruck Gesellschaft, 1934), 107–14.
18. See the letter from Hindenburg to his confidant Hermann von Wartensleben, 22 May 1917, in Elisabeth Gräfin von Wartensleben, ed., *Hermann Graf von Wartensleben-Carow. Königl. Preuß. General d. Kavallerie.: Ein Lebensbild 1826–1921* (Berlin: E. S. Mittler & Sohn, 1923), 203.
19. Hindenburg to Irmengard von Brockhusen, 9 April 1925, private possession. See also Pyta, *Hindenburg*, 472, as well as Hubatsch, *Hindenburg*, 72.
20. See his letters to his daughter Irmengard, 28 February and 8 April 1932, private possession.

21. See Kuno Graf von Westarp, *Konservative Politik im Übergang vom Kaiserreich zur Weimarer Republik*, ed. Friedrich Freiherr Hiller von Gaertringen (Düsseldorf: Droste, 2001), 407–10.

22. For further information, see the detailed account in Pyta, *Hindenburg*, 267–83, 308, 315–23.

23. Pyta, *Hindenburg*, 277–79.

24. See Bethmann Hollweg's presentation to the Kaiser, 10 July 1917, reprinted in Bernhard Schwertfeger, *Kaiser und Kabinettschef. Nach eigenen Aufzeichnungen und dem Briefwechsel des Wirklichen Geheimen Rats Rudolf von Valentini* (Oldenburg: Stalling, 1931), 161–62.

25. Telegramm from Bethmann Hollweg to Hindenburg, 14 March 1917, in *Militär und Innenpolitik im Weltkrieg 1914–1918*, ed. Wilhelm Deist, 2 vols. (Düsseldorf: Droste, 1970), 2:672–73.

26. Letter from Hindenburg to Bethmann Hollweg, 17 March 1917, ibid., 677–80, as well as Hindenburg's Denkschrift from August 1917, reprinted in the *Hannoverscher Kurier*, 26 August 1919.

27. According to the extremely well-informed National Liberal Reichstag deputy Eugen Schiffer in the manuscript of his memoirs, "Ein Leben für den Liberalismus," Bundesarchiv Koblenz, Nachlaß Schiffer, 5/90.

28. Schwertfeger, *Kaiser*, 153.

29. Hindenburg to Wilhelm II, 16 January 1918, in Deist, ed., *Militär und Innenpolitik*, 2:1125.

30. Draft of a letter from Valentini to Hindenburg, January 1918, Bundesarchiv Koblenz, Nachlaß Valentini, 206/45.

31. Pyta, *Hindenburg*, 286–87. See also Stephan Malinowski, *Vom Königtum zur Führer. Sozialer Niedergang und politische Radikalisierung im deutschen Adel zwischen Kaiserreich und NS-Staat*, 2nd ed. (Berlin: Akademie-Verlag, 2003), 176–79; Hans-Ulrich Wehler, *Deutsche Gesellschaftsgeschichte*, vol. 4: *Vom Beginn des Ersten Weltkrieges bis zur Gründung der beiden deutsche Staaten 1914–1949* (Munich: C. H. Beck, 2003), 106–9; and Raffael Scheck, *Alfred von Tirpitz and German Right-Wing Politics, 1914–1930* (Atlantic Highlands, NJ: Humanities Press, 1998), 65–77.

32. Bernhardi to Hindenburg, 26 December 1916, in Bernhardi, *Denkwürdigkeiten*, 460.

33. Jesko von Hoegen, *Der Held von Tannenberg. Genese und Funktion des Hindenburg-Mythos* (Cologne: Böhlau, 2007).

34. Hindenburg to Irmengard von Brockhusen, 4 September 1914, private possession.

35. Hindenburg to Irmengard von Brockhusen, 6 October 1914, private possession.

36. Hindenburg to his longtime friend Count Wartensleben, 26 December 1919, cited in Wolfgang Ruge, *Hindenburg: Porträt eines Militaristen* (Cologne: Paul-Rugenstein, 1981), 191.

37. For further details, see Pyta, *Hindenburg*, 57–67. See also Hans-Georg Soeffner and Dirk Tänzler, "Figurative Politik. Prolegomena zu einer Kultursoziologie politischen Handelns," in *Figurative Politik*, ed. Hans-

Georg Soeffner and Dirk Tänzler (Opladen: Leske & Budrich, 2002), 17–33.

38. See the entry for 9 November 1918 in the diary of Hindenburg's son-in-law Christian von Pentz, excerpted in Hubatsch, *Hindenburg*, 36.

39. For a detailed analysis of Hindenburg's thinking on 9 November 1918, see Pyta, *Hindenburg*, 361–79.

40. Draft of a letter from Brockhusen to Hindenburg, 11 January 1919, private possession.

41. Hans-Joachim von Brockhusen-Justin, *Der Weltkrieg und ein schlichtes Menschenleben* (Greifswald: Bamberg, 1928), 280.

42. Hindenburg to Brockhusen, 13 March 1919, private possession.

43. Pyta, *Hindenburg*, 625–27.

44. Ibid., 650–53.

45. Hindenburg to Cramon, 25 October 1933, Bundesarchiv-Militärarchiv, Freiburg, Nachlaß Cramon, 25/1f.

46. On the concept of "Vernunftrepublikanismus," see Harm Klueting, "'Vernunftrepublikanismus' und ,Vertrauensdiktatur'. Friedrich Meinecke in der Weimarer Republik," *Historische Zeitschrift* 242 (1986): 69–98.

47. Reinhard Rürup, "Die Ideologisierung des Krieges: 'Die Ideen von 1914,'" in *Deutschland und der Erste Weltkrieg*, ed. Helmut Böhme and Fritz Kallenberg (Darmstadt: Technische Hochschule Darmstadt, 1987), 121–41.

48. Steffen Bruendel, *Volksgemeinschaft oder Volksstaat. Die "Ideen von 1914" und die Neuordnung Deutschlands im Ersten Weltkrieg* (Berlin: Akademie Verlag, 2003), esp. 67–71; and Sven Oliver Müller, *Die Nation als Waffe und Vorstellung. Nationalismus in Deutschland und Großbritannien im Ersten Weltkrieg* (Göttingen: Vandenhoeck & Ruprecht, 2002), 84–95.

49. Hindenburg to his son-in-law Brockhusen, 10 August 1914, private possession.

50. Hindenburg copied this phrase from 1 March 1915 in his own hand. This has been reproduced in facsimile in Hermann Schmökel, *Hindenburg. Ein Lebensbild* (Potsdam: Stiftungsverlag, 1915), 31. See also Pyta, *Hindenburg*, 113.

51. Bruendel, *Volksgemeinschaft*, 286f.

52. Bruendel, *Volksgemeinschaft*, 259. See also Gunther Mai, "'Verteidigungskrieg' und 'Volksgemeinschaft.' Staatliche Selbstbehauptung, nationale Solidarität und soziale Befreiung in Deutschland in der Zeit des Ersten Weltkrieges (1900–1925)," in *Der Erste Weltkrieg: Wirkung, Wahrnehmung, Analyse*, ed. Wolfgang Michalka (Munich: Piper, 1994), 583–602, here 590.

53. See Moritz Föllmer and Andrea Meissner, "Ideen als Weichensteller? Polyvalenz, Aneignung und Homogenitätsstreben im deutschen Nationalismus 1890–1933," in *Ideen als gesellschaftliche Gestaltungskraft im Europa der Neuzeit*, ed. Lutz Raphael and Heinz-Elmar Tenorth (Munich: R. Oldenbourg, 2006), 313–36.

54. Bruendel, *Volksgemeinschaft*, 132, 140f., 288f.

55. Jürgen C. Heß, *Theodor Heuß vor 1933* (Stuttgart: Klett, 1973), 75.

56. Election Appeal from the Rheinland Center Party, 24 March 1925, in *Volk, Kirche und Vaterland. Wahlaufrufe, Aufrufe, Satzungen und Statuten des Zentrums 1870–1933*, ed. Herbert Lepper (Düsseldorf: Droste, 1998), 453.

57. A wealth of examples can be found in the impressive study by Walter Mühlhausen, *Friedrich Ebert 1871–1925* (Bonn: Dietz, 2006), esp. 816ff.

58. Mai, "'Verteidigungskrieg' und 'Volksgemeinschaft,'" 591–93. See also Thomas Mergel, "Führer, Volksgemeinschaft und Maschine," in *Politische Kulturgeschichte der Zwischenkriegszeit 1918–1939*, ed. Wolfgang Hardtwig (Göttingen: Vandenhoeck & Ruprecht, 2005), 91–127, esp. 98f.

59. For further details, see Bruendel, *Volksgemeinschaft*, esp. 282–87.

60. See Pyta, *Hindenburg*, 259f. and 310.

61. Ibid., 407ff.

62. Reprinted in Hubatsch, *Hindenburg*, 187.

63. Pyta, *Hindenburg*, 489–93, 543

64. Ibid., 506, 510, 519, 544f.

65. Thomas Hertfelder, "'Meteor aus einer anderen Welt.' Die Weimarer Republik in der Diskussion des Hilfe–Kreises," in *Vernunftrepublikanismus in der Weimarer Republik*, ed. Andreas Wirsching and Jürgen Eder (Stuttgart: Steiner, 2008), 29–55.

66. Elke Seefried, "Verfassungspragmatismus und Gemeinschaftsideologie: 'Vernunftrepublikanismus' in der deutschen Zentrumspartei," in *Vernunftrepublikanismus*, ed. Wirsching and Eder, 57–86.

67. Pyta, *Hindenburg*, 658.

68. Schäffer's notes on his conversation with Hindenburg, 17 February 1933, in the unpublished Nachlaß of Josef Müller, Archiv für Christlich-Soziale Politik, Munich, V11.

69. Hindenburg to Irmengard von Brockhusen, 19 July 1931, private possession.

70. Hindenburg to Irmengard von Brockhusen, 16 February 1932, private poessession.

71. Persönliche Darlegung Hindenburgs, 25 February 1932, reprinted in Hubatsch, *Hindenburg*, 313f.

72. Ibid, 318.

73. Hindenburg to Irmengard von Brockhusen, 12 February 1933, private possession.

2

From Friends to Foes
Count Kuno von Westarp and the
Transformation of the German Right

Daniela Gasteiger

Through a long political career that lasted from the late Second Empire to the end of the Weimar Republic, the politician and publicist Count Kuno von Westarp (1864–1945) was eager to stress the continuities in his conservative view of the world.[1] Even years after the fall of the German monarchy Westarp's opponents still claimed to hear tones of Wilhelmine reaction in his speeches,[2] while his supporters looked upon him as the "embodiment [*Fortführer*] of the conservative tradition" and pinned their hopes for the creation of a united German Right on his leadership.[3] His writings were inspired by a strong desire to shape German conservatism in the light of his own principles, particularly through his weekly column on domestic politics in the *Kreuzzeitung*. In Westarp's eyes conservative politics were inextricably linked to a set of values embodied in what he called the "Prussian tradition," a term that above all else implied a strong monarchy supported by faithful civil servants united by their determination to curb the emancipatory ambitions of the plebian masses.

Born in Posen in West Prussia in 1864 Westarp entered the Reichstag in 1908 as a deputy for the German Conservative Party (Deutschkonservative Partei or DKP) after having served as a jurist in the Prussian administrative service. In 1913, on the eve of World War I, Westarp rose to the rank of the DKP's parliamentary leader. The loss of his political home with the collapse of the Prusso-German monarchy in the great caesura of 1918 did little to shake Westarp's political convictions. A determined adversary of Germany's new republican order, Westarp joined the newly founded German National People's Party (Deutschnationale Volkspartei or DNVP), which emerged at the end of 1918 as a *Sammelbewegung* of the German Right.[4] But despite his efforts to retain his political identity as a Conservative bound to the traditions of the

Second Empire, the alliances that he had forged before 1914 proved increasingly fragile and over time eventually fell apart.[5] Of these relationships two were particularly significant as barometers of Westarp's increasing estrangement from the residues of the prewar German Right. The first was his relationship with the *völkisch* politician Albrecht von Graefe-Goldebee (1868–1933),[6] who left the DNVP much to Westarp's dismay in the fall of 1922 to found the German-Racist Freedom Party (Deutschvölkische Freiheitspartei or DVFP). Equally telling was the collapse of Westarp's ties to the Central Association of German Conservatives (Hauptverein der Deutschkonservativen), the organization in which the prewar DKP had preserved itself after 1918 and the last fragment of Westarp's earlier political home to survive into Germany's postwar republican system.[7]

The following essay examines these two relationships as points of fracture in Westarp's network of political alliances against the background of the ideological and organizational conflicts that marked the German Right in the interwar period.[8] For example, how would the relationship between those conservatives and *völkisch* politicians who now found themselves together in the DNVP take shape over time? How would conservatives with their rejection of modern theories of sovereignty accommodate themselves to Germany's new republican order and to what extent would the DNVP afford them a permanent political home?[9] Was it legitimate for a monarchist like Westarp to become involved in the vicissitudes and compromises of republican politics instead of waging unconditional warfare against the system itself? The answer to these questions—and with them the fate of Westarp's conservatism—were hotly contested. At the heart of the problem lay a fundamental disagreement between Westarp and his old allies over how conservatism itself was to be defined and how conservative goals were to be pursued in the bitterly hated Weimar Republic. Much to the dismay of his former associates on the prewar German Right, Westarp tried to secure for himself and his party a role in the decision-making processes of the new German parliament. This did not mean, however, that Westarp became an adherent of the republican order or that he had abandoned his monarchist convictions.[10] For even after he accepted a key leadership role first as the chairman of the DNVP Reichstag delegation in 1925 and then as the party's national chairmanship in 1926,[11] Westarp never relented in his struggle against Social Democracy or in his unforgiving attitude toward Germany's adversaries in World War I.[12]

Westarp's relationships with Graefe-Goldebee and the Central Association of German Conservatives can be used as keys to understanding the way in which Westarp struggled to come to terms with the changes that had taken place in the structure of German political life after 1918. Not only did these conflicts end with various politicians on the German Right going their own separate ways, but more importantly they represented critical episodes in the political crisis of the postwar German Right and in the struggle over the heart and soul of the DNVP. Westarp's own search for a place on the German Right did not end with the DNVP. His refusal to pursue a policy of uncompromising opposition to Germany's new republican order met with strong resistance within his own party. In 1928 he lost the DNVP national party chairmanship to Alfred Hugenberg, who successfully rallied his supporters behind a policy of unconditional opposition.[13] When a year and a half later Westarp and his followers in the DNVP Reichstag delegation threw their support behind the newly formed cabinet of Heinrich Brüning, tensions within the DNVP escalated to the point where the group around Westarp left the DNVP to found the Conservative People's Party (Konservative Volkspartei or KVP), a party that received only a handful of votes in the 1930 Reichstag elections. Depressed by the failure of this project and the rise of the National Socialist movement, Westarp withdrew from active political life in 1932.

Westarp and the Völkisch-Conservative Symbiosis

Albrecht von Graefe, four years younger than Westarp, entered in the Reichstag in 1912 as a deputy for the German Conservative Party. In the same year he resigned from military service.[14] As in the case of Westarp, Graefe did not come from one of those Junker families that defined the popular profile of the party with which he had affiliated himself. In the eyes of their critics, however, both Westarp and Graefe were irremediably identified with this group. After the acquisition of his estate Goldebee and his subsequent entry into the Mecklenburg state parliament Graefe received the nickname "Talmijunker" because of the way he behaved as if he were a longtime and well-established landowner despite the fact that his family had received its patent of nobility only in the generation of his grandfather, a highly respected eye doctor.[15] Westarp, on the other hand, came from a family of Prussian civil servants and army officers and enjoyed the advantages of neither property nor personal fortune.[16] Westarp had to support himself and his family and was therefore in the jargon of the day classified as a member of the "Etagen-Adel," that is, as an aristocrat who lived in an urban apartment building rather than on a rural estate.[17] Rumors that Westarp owned over eighty manors or was the descendant of a Junker dynasty dogged him throughout the entire Weimar Republic.[18] Westarp's habitus as a retired Prussian civil servant and a conservative leader after 1918 combined with his functions as an agrarian lobbyist—though without landholdings of his own—made it difficult for his contemporaries to classify him as a typical *Berufspolitiker* whom the *Honoratioren* of the DKP would have treated dismissively as a party secretary.[19]

Westarp's and Graefe's political careers in the DKP were markedly different. As leader of the DKP Reichstag delegation from 1913 until the end of the war, Westarp firmly established himself alongside the party chairman Ernst von Heydebrand und der Lasa,[20] the "uncrowned king of Prussia," in the ranks of the party leadership. Since Heydebrand lived on his estate in Klein-Tschunkawe and remained generally aloof from the rhythms of everyday political life in Berlin, the work in the committees, assemblies, and informal discussions lay to a large extent in Westarp's hands. Graefe, on the other hand, was a member of the Pan-German faction in the DKP Reichstag delegation, where he earned for himself a reputation as one of the party's most outspoken critics of the weakness of the DKP Reichstag delegation vis-à-vis the government.[21]

On what did the friendly relations between two politicians as dissimilar as Westarp and Graefe rest? What above all else they shared in common was the perception of an "authority crisis" of the Second Empire, a crisis whose symptoms became even more pronounced from the perspective of the German Right after the turn of the century.[22] The emancipatory impulses at work within the working-class and women's movement threatened the foundations of what Stefan Breuer has defined as the conservative "Ordnungen der Ungleichheit" in the last years of the Second Empire.[23] After Bismarck's resignation in 1890, but no more so than during the First Moroccan Crisis of 1905–6, the Right criticized German foreign policy as weak and passive. The repeated scandals and affairs of the headstrong Wilhelm II left the defenders of the monarchy deeply embarrassed.[24] Relations between the government and the leaders of the DKP continued to deteriorate to the point where in 1909 conservative opposition to elements of the finance reform cost Bernhard von Bülow the chancellorship. From the very beginning German conservatives viewed his successor Theobald von Bethmann-Hollweg as weak and acquiescent in the face of the democratic forces that seemed to be threatening the very structure of German political life.[25] "There could be no doubt," wrote Westarp in his memoirs twenty-five years later, "that for reasons of state we took a strong stand against his weakness in the face of Social Democracy and the democratic tendencies of the day and against the thirst for power of the parties in the Reichstag."[26] Summing up the DKP's position and sense of itself in a single sentence, Westarp wrote: "Since Bethmann we were an outspoken opposition party without a majority."[27]

The shock of defeat in World War I, opposition to the revolution, and the rejection of the new republican order only strengthened the alliance between the two politicians. In the days after 9 November Westarp and Graefe were together far from Berlin in the vicinity of Graefe's estate Goldebee. Upon their return to Berlin they proceeded to join the DNVP. The German National People's Party had come together in the immediate aftermath of the revolution in an attempt to unite the various right-wing parties, patriotic groups, and individuals from the Second Empire into a single party.[28] Within the DNVP Graefe quickly found allies in the erstwhile National Liberal and Pan-German Alfred Hugenberg,[29] Gottfried Traub from the German Fatherland Party (Deutsche Vaterlandspartei),[30] and the *völkisch* women's leader Käthe Schirmacher,[31] in the so-called sharp wing of the party's delegation to the National Assembly."[32] Along with the publicist Reinhold Wulle and the former general staff officer Wilhelm Henning, Graefe emerged as one of the leading spokesmen for the party's völkisch wing.[33] In the National Assembly, where he represented his home state of Mecklenburg, Graefe was particularly outspoken in his attacks upon the DNVP's governmental conservatives who were intent upon laying the groundwork for some sort of role within the new republican system.[34] Westarp's decision to join the DNVP, on the other hand, was motivated first and foremost by his desire to use the party as the crystallization point for a conservative *Sammelbewegung* committed to saving what still remained of the conservative position in the Second Empire, namely, the monarchal concept, the unity of the Reich, the primacy of Prussia, and uncompromising opposition to the Social Democrats.[35] From the perspective of the more reform-minded conservatives Westarp clearly stood at that particular point in time on the extreme right wing of the party. Yet even though Westarp remained on good terms with the leaders of the party's *völkisch* faction, he did not want to compromise his independence and effectiveness as the leader of the DNVP's Conservative faction and rejected efforts to unite the two groups.

Efforts to discredit the Conservatives as enemies of reform and annexationists after 1918 had a profound effect on Westarp. His name had become so closely identified with the crusade for a German *Siegfrieden* that the DNVP party leadership refused to nominate him as a candidate for the January 1919 elections to the Weimar National Assembly. His exclusion from a role in parliament came as a severe blow and only added fuel to the strong oppositional sentiments that he brought into the Weimar Republic from the Second Empire. Revolutionary Berlin with its political turmoil and constant strikes evoked his unremitting hatred. In his memoirs Westarp portrayed the immediate postwar period as different phases of a civil war that extended over a half decade as a direct result of governmental failure. Westarp was convinced that the Weimar National Assembly and the constitution it promulgated in the summer of 1919 were the direct result of the revolution itself and that the way in which it violated the historically legitimated rights of the crown, the titled nobility, and the military amounted to a latent state of national emergency. Through his contacts to Wolfgang Kapp, a one-time member of the DKP who had played a prominent role in the founding of the German Fatherland Party, Westarp was initiated into the preparations for the Kapp Putsch and worked as part of a secret planning committee on the draft of a new constitution.[36] Westarp, however, was able to avoid being brought into direct connection with the ill-fated undertaking, all the more so since at the time of the putsch he was no longer part of the inner circle around Kapp.[37] Westarp's proximity to the Kapp Putsch marked the high point of his anti-republican activities in the early Weimar Republic. Its failure convinced him that the use of force was not an effective strategy for the defeat of democracy, and in 1920 he returned to the Reichstag and was able to regain his voice in parliament.

In the DNVP Reichstag delegation the relationship between Westarp and Graefe quickly assumed all the features of a "junior partnership."[38] In the summer of 1920 Westarp wrote to his friend Gottfried Traub: "Graefe and I are once again rather closely forged together."[39] At the core of this relationship lay a division of labor according to which Westarp used his membership in the party executive committee, his parliamentary experience, his far-reaching connections, his popularity as a public speaker, and his journalistic skills to gain influence within the party and promote it as the basis of a strong and united German Right, while Graefe, since April 1921 himself a member of the DNVP executive committee,[40] was the popular agitator who, in complete agreement with Westarp, waged the party's public crusade on a wide range of opposition themes, not the least of which were the vendetta against Matthias Erzberger, resistance to Allied demands for the surrender of alleged war criminals, and the restoration of the monarchy.[41] That this division of labor, however, was not compatible with the increasing consolidation of the DNVP became apparent in a dispute between the two politicians in January 1922. For when Westarp conveyed to Graefe the wish of the German National Youth League (Deutschnationaler Jugendbund) for "a fiery irredenta speech,"[42] Graefe bitterly replied: "I know that the party wants to use my sharp tongue [*Schnauze*] for agitation without allowing me to work on political tasks. In light of the current situation a fiery irredenta speech seems stupid. . . . As long as the *völkisch* principle has not been grasped in its innermost core but remains little more than a popular phrase, the very idea makes me shiver with disgust [*schüttelt mich so etwas wie Ekel*]."[43]

The disagreement between Westarp and Graefe was the outward sign of an emerging conflict within the DNVP over control of the party and the direction in which it should be headed. At the center of this conflict stood the question of antisemitism, the role it should assume in the party's agitation, and the place of the DNVP's *völkisch* wing in the party's internal affairs.[44] As the conflict drew to a climax in the late summer and early fall of 1922, the demands of the *völkisch* faction under the leadership of Graefe, Wulle, and Henning focused on two central themes: the expulsion of Jews from the party and the establishment of a German-Racist Working Group (Deutschvölkische Arbeitsgemeinschaft) that would operate independently of the party's national leadership with authorization to solicit contributions of its own.[45] This set the stage for an open conflict with the party's national leaders, who were not opposed to the use of antisemitism as a technique of political mobilization but sought to keep it within certain limits. Not only would the establishment of an organization for the DNVP's *völkisch* wing that operated outside of the existing party organization result in a dramatic increase in the party's antisemitic agitation but it would also have strengthened the position of those within the party who were fundamentally opposed to any move on the part of the DNVP in the direction of a role in the national government.[46] Antisemitism and hostility toward Germany's new republican order were linked to each other in a close symbiotic relationship in as much as the *völkisch* faction held the revolutionaries of 1918–19 responsible for introducing the "Jewish" ideas of Marxism and democracy into German political life.[47] For politicians like Graefe opposition to Germany's new democratic system went hand in hand with his desire to move antisemitism to the forefront of the DNVP's public profile, while for reform-minded conservatives like the Munich historian Otto Hoetzsch, who hoped that the DNVP could adapt to the demands of German democracy, antisemitism should assume a subordinate role in the party's agitation and public presence.[48]

On the question of antisemitism Westarp found himself caught between two stools. On the one hand, Westarp did not place the "Jewish question" at the center of all political, economic, and cultural questions. For him the root cause of German misery was Germany's domination by foreign powers, or what was commonly referred to as *Fremdherrschaft*, that it had experienced as a consequence of its defeat in World War I. The Allies had usurped Germany's power and freedom as a nation state and had subjected it to their will through the imposition of the Versailles Treaty. But after 1918 antisemitism would become an even more important component of Westarp's political thought. In this respect, it constituted an important part of a cultural code that spanned a wide range of social, political, and economic assumptions.[49] A particularly conspicuous example of this was the semantic linkage of "Jewish money" and the political influence it supposedly brought to capitalism and the emancipatory aspirations of the working class, in other words the linkage between the "gold" and the "red" internationals.[50] Westarp clearly recognized just how effective antisemitism could be as an instrument of political mobilization,[51] like many other conservatives he was careful to distance himself from the gutter antisemitism, or *Radau-Antisemitismus*, of the more radical elements on the German Right.

Profoundly influenced by the political-cultural antisemitism of Heinrich von Treitschke and his five-volume *Deutsche Geschichte* of the late 1880s and early 1890s,[52] Westarp saw the Jewish problem primarily as a nationality problem that along with a host of similar problems threatened the homogeneity of the Prussian-German nation state.[53] As a disciple of the nation state as it had evolved under Bismarck's tutelage, Westarp saw an authoritarian state as an essential precondition without which a people could not develop and flourish according to its own unique character.[54] But as Westarp himself expressed it, antisemitism as one of the exclusionary factors that defined the boundaries of the German nation state had changed over time from the religious antisemitism of the Tivoli Program from 1892 to a view of the Jewish question that was informed by the concept of race.[55] In fact, in an unpublished autobiography from the early 1940s Westarp defined himself as an adherent of the racial theories of Hans F. K. Günther, an important antisemitic publicist who played a major role in popularizing the concept of race in the Weimar Republic.[56]

From all of this Westarp deduced two concrete political demands. In the first place, he advocated limiting the immigration of Jews from

Eastern Europe, a demand that was widely discussed in the early years of the Weimar Republic. And secondly, he wanted to go on the attack wherever the "Jewish" component came together with Bolshevism and Social Democracy. "Namely, it must be made clear to the German worker," wrote Westarp in late November 1919 in words that illuminated the close relationship in his thought between antisemitism and hostility toward the republic, "that he risks placing himself under the influence of an alien people when he accepts the leadership of a Cohn and a Hirsch, a Haase and a Wurm and all the countless Jews in Social Democracy."[57] In Westarp's concept of the DNVP there was a clear place for a strong *völkisch* wing. Westarp was not alone in believing that antisemitic propaganda was a technique of taming and control—and not just in form and volume. But in contrast to many of those who belonged to his party's racist faction Westarp rejected efforts to deprive those Jews who lived in Germany of their civil or religious rights. And when it came to the question of expelling Jews from the DNVP, Westarp consistently sided with the party leadership around Oskar Hergt and Karl Helfferich.[58] Rather than attack such proposals on fundamental grounds, Westarp preferred to cite practical objections such as whether or not the requirement of an ancestry certificate, or *Stammbaumzeugnis*, attesting to the purity of one's racial pedigree was politically feasible or whether it would even be possible to arrive at a commonly accepted definition of a Jew. Even though Westarp went so far as to have such a certificate prepared for himself and his family so as to dispel rumors that he was related to Jews,[59] his antisemitic views were fraught with ambivalence. The high level of abstraction with which he often spoke of the "Jewish danger" and the role this played in the slogans and ideology of the DNVP stood in a curious relationship to his efforts to limit its dissemination and to exercise a measure of control over antisemitism in his own party.

In the first years of the Weimar Republic Graefe appeared to agree with Westarp that the exclusion of Jews from membership in the DNVP did not lie in the party's best interests provided that the Jews could be dissuaded from joining the party and gaining any significant influence within it.[60] But the agreement that had once existed between Westarp and himself on Jewish membership in the DNVP began to unravel as Graefe's own position on this question underwent considerable radicalization in the wake of the increasingly bitter conflict between the *völkisch* faction and the DNVP party leadership between 1920 and 1922. In November 1921 Karl Helfferich, one of the leading figures in the party until his death in a railroad accident in Switzerland in April 1924, succeeded in pushing through a resolution that effectively blocked the expulsion of Jews from the DNVP. In the meantime the DNVP party chairman Oskar Hergt refused to provide the *völkisch* faction with an independent power base that was not subject to the control of the party leadership. After the assassination of the German Foreign Minister Walther Rathenau in the summer of 1922, the conflict within the party became increasingly heated. The party leadership summarily expelled Wilhelm Henning from the DNVP Reichstag delegation because of a particularly inflammatory article he had written against the foreign minister only a few weeks before. Graefe and Reinhold Wulle declared their solidarity with Henning, resigned their seats in the DNVP Reichstag delegation, and against the explicit instructions of the DNVP party leadership founded a *völkisch* organization of their own outside the DNVP party organization. Because of his close ties to all of those involved in the conflict, Westarp was given the task of mediating between the various protagonists in the interest of party unity.[61]

Westarp's initial sympathies clearly lay with the *völkisch* wing. As he wrote to Gottfried Traub several weeks after Henning's expulsion from the Reichstag delegation: "Although I could never be in total agreement with Henning's manner . . . I have set for myself the goal of working with Graefe and Wulle for reunification despite the meager prospects of success this holds. It is also important to me to keep the *völkisch* tendency and men of character like Graefe and Wulle in the party and delegation and to strengthen their influence vis-à-vis the other tendencies [in the party]."[62] In his efforts as a mediator Westarp, however, had a larger goal in view, namely, to hold together the greater German Right and to prevent its fragmentation as a result of the conflict with the racists. Westarp's ambitions were focused above all else on keeping his old friend and comrade Graefe in the party. In the past—for example in an article for the *Eiserne Blätter* and then more recently in his speech on German foreign policy at the DNVP's national convention in October 1920—Graefe had spoken out against an intensification of the conflict in the party.[63] While this only seemed to confirm Westarp's hopes that a compromise might still be possible, Graefe however took an increasingly pessimistic point of view. After the 1920 DNVP party convention failed to produce a compromise on the *völkisch* question, Graefe thanked Westarp for his "loyal comradeship in arms" while complaining bitterly that the party leadership only wanted to "strangle" Wulle, himself, and the leaders of the party's *völkisch* faction and was never interested in a reconciliation.[64]

After his efforts at the negotiating table had failed, Westarp sought a compromise between the DNVP party leadership and the party's *völkisch* wing in his column "Innere Politik der Woche" for the *Neue Preußische (Kreuz-)Zeitung*. Here Westarp sought to clarify the different concepts and definitions that had surfaced in the conflict over antisemitism and the racist movement in the hopes of formulating a position designed specifically for the DNVP. Westarp began by distinguishing between "positive" and "negative" antisemitic efforts that differed by virtue of their methods of conflict.[65] Next he sought to connect these efforts to specific Prussian virtues.

> In so far as the struggle [of the völkisch movement] is directed against the domination of an alien Jewish race and has as its goal the purification of the German race, what they are seeking—and in only part of the völkisch movement is it a question of antisemitism—is one of those points in the DNVP party program that require its full attention. . . . But defense and struggle, hate and rage against the enemy of the German essence constitutes only a complement, a prerequisite for what forms the principal task of all völkisch endeavors, namely the constructive nature of German uniqueness and the German essence . . . , of all that the Prussian state once stamped upon the German essence—obedience and loyalty, discipline and order, honor and love of fatherland—once again finds validity (*Geltung*) in German lands.[66]

Westarp's efforts to contain antisemitism within the DNVP by definition met with little enthusiasm in the racist camp and prompted public polemics against the "Anti-Antisemitismus des Herrn Grafen Westarp."[67] The radicals rebuked Westarp for the abstractness of his antisemitic arguments and for his refusal to deprive Jews of their civil rights. In the final analysis Westarp failed to hold the different wings of the party together. Even threats that a swing to the left that might possibly result from the expulsion of the *völkisch* faction could also lead to the secession of the Conservatives from the DNVP had little effect.[68] Although Westarp clearly favored the *völkisch* wing, he was reluctant to become too closely associated with this group. He rejected suggestions that he should become a member of the racist working group with the argument that he remained the leader of the Conservatives and as such stood in a cartel relationship with the *völkisch* organization.[69]

In view of the irreconcilable differences within the party Westarp's position as an intermediary was no longer tenable. His support of the *völkisch* faction brought him into an open conflict with the DNVP party chairman Oskar Hergt. It was time for him to decide. At the DNVP Görlitz party congress in October 1922 Westarp repositioned himself by moving more closely to the party leadership and affirming his strong support for a declaration by the DNVP's national leaders that in any future cabinet negotiations they would not enter into a coalition with the Social Democrats, thus satisfying what was for Westarp an unshakable constant of his political career. Writing to Graefe, Westarp acknowledged that this would cost him the support of the racists but stressed that his statement of support for the position of the party leadership was necessary because the struggle against Social Democracy was for him and his Conservative friends decisive for their relationship to the party.[70] Graefe, who regarded Westarp's declaration of confidence in the DNVP leadership as a "retreat [*Abrücken*]" from his earlier position, responded: "I feel genuine pain over your most recent steps. . . . In my eyes that is a two-fold blow to the once beautiful dream of a conservative-*völkisch* alliance."[71]

At the DNVP Görlitz party congress Graefe, Wulle, and Henning were expelled from the DNVP. For Westarp this was a bitter blow that left him tired and in a state of nervous exhaustion.[72] From this point on the relationship between Westarp and Graefe was effectively shattered. In December 1922 the secessionists founded the DVFP and dissociated themselves as forcefully as possible from the DNVP.[73] The final break came three years later when Graefe attacked Westarp for allegedly having delivered the *Kreuz-Zeitung* into the hands of what he defined as a "large-scale capitalism infected by international Social Democracy [das internationale, sozialdemokratisch infizierte Großkapital]." After the long, sometimes passionate exchange that followed, Westarp wrote to Graefe: "Never in my long political life have I been more deeply hurt by the substance, form, and source of an attack than here. . . . Given the close relationship in which we once stood I would have expected that you would have listened to me before denouncing me in such a fashion."[74] On the same day Graefe wrote: "Out of respect for our earlier comradeship I have used a calm, objective tone. . . . But to my bitter disappointment I have to say after your behavior yesterday that my personal attitude toward you, always rooted in a deep respect even after we parted ways, must now undergo a regrettable revision."[75]

Westarp and the Dilemma of the Conservatives

For Westarp the secession of the *völkisch* faction in the fall of 1922 was a bitter political defeat. His erstwhile confederates from the DKP who had come together after 1918 in the Central Association of German Conservatives, on the other hand, viewed the secession with renewed optimism. As Max Brauer, the Central Association's corresponding secretary, wrote to its chairman: "We have often talked, highly re-spected Herr von Heydebrand, about the need for a large mass of *Völkischen* . . . as a reservoir out of which the Conservatives would once again fill its ranks."[76] The dreams of recapturing their lost power and greatness dominated the debates in the Central Association of German Conservatives in the newly founded Weimar Republic. This remnant was all that still existed of the DKP after 1918. Through the elimination of the three-class franchise in Prussia the Conservatives had lost more than their Prussian power bastion. There seemed in the short term first no way of surviving politically than to swim along in the melting pot, or *Sammelbecken*, of the DNVP. Most of the DKP's town and county or-ganizations had already gone over to the DNVP.[77]

In the negotiations that culminated in the founding of the DNVP, We-starp functioned as the spokesman for the German Conservatives. Even when it became clear that there was no longer any possibility of an inde-pendent Conservative party politics, Westarp refused to completely dis-solve the old organization. Conservatives harbored deep reservations against the "experiment" of a right-wing unity party whose founding proclamation did not include demands for the restoration of the mon-archy.[78] At the same time, he feared that the presence of Christian-Social politicians would lead the party to the left. In his correspondence with Heydebrand, Westarp reported how he had directly confronted the DNVP party executive committee with his doubts: "[I] said that as a matter of principle it must be decided . . . whether the party will become the new German Right and represent the Conservative position with-out which no orderly political system can exist." Otherwise the Conser-vatives must make certain that a new group to the right of the DNVP takes shape.[79] Given the uncertain prospects of the new party, Westarp struggled mightily against the resistance of the DNVP leadership cadre around Oskar Hergt to make certain that the Central Association of German Conservatives as an independent entity along with several im-portant state and provincial organizations were kept alive. Whatever remained of the prewar DKP, however, would have to abstain from all political activity.[80] It was also Westarp who devised the linguistic con-vention that would govern relations between the DNVP and Conserva-tives. In a declaration before the DNVP executive committee on 11 July 1919 Westarp made the important concession that "the followers of the old Conservative tendency . . . would seek their political futures in and with the German National People's Party and place their energies with-out reservation in the service of a shared patriotic mission."[81] Westarp subsequently joined the party executive committee.

Westarp's ties to the Central Association of German Conservatives remained an important component of his political self-conception. His willingness to pursue his objectives within the framework of the DNVP made him a hinge or link between the Conservatives and the German Nationalists. For more than a decade he filled this delicate role in that he served as a mediator, confidential reporter, and public speaker for both groups. In the DNVP executive committee Westarp softened sharply worded declarations from the Central Association against "the opportunism of the German Nationalist party leadership,"[82] assuaged suspicions of rivalry, and supported Conservative candidates for parliamentary election and offices in the DNVP leadership structure. In the Central Association, on the other hand, Westarp sought to create greater sympathy for the voting processes of parliamentary government and for the strategy and tactics of the DNVP party leadership. Yet the consensus that existed between Westarp and the German Conservatives in the early years of the Weimar Republic concealed differences that would later become critical. For whereas Westarp continued to practice what he had learned as a parliamentary deputy in the last years of the Second Empire, leading figures within the Central Association of German Conservatives remained implacably opposed to any sort of cooperation with the new democratic state.[83] Occasionally members of the Central Association's inner circle, like estate owners and former members of the Prussian Upper House (Herrenhaus) Dietlof von Arnim-Boitzenburg and Ernst von Seidlitz-Sandreczki, accepted offices in the DNVP for short periods of time but still remained aloof from the party and its national leadership.[84] The same could be said of Friedrich Everling, a leading monarchist who represented the DNVP in the Reichstag, men like Wilhelm von Müffling and Max Wildgrube from the Pan-German League (Alldeutscher Verband or ADV),[85] and Hermann Kreth, who served as president of the Berlin National Club (Berliner Nationalklub) from 1927 to 1930, all of whom were well integrated into the associational life of the militantly anti-republican German Right.[86]

The activities of the Central Association of German Conservatives as "a platform of the Prussian landed aristocracy with bourgeois newcomers"[87] picked up only slowly after 1918. As Heydebrand wrote to Westarp in late January 1919: "But for God's sake we must not retreat into a world of dreams or allow a sense of guilt to plunge us into pessimism. The main thing now is that in the midst of all the tumult and in the flood of events [*Fluth der strömenden und stürzenden Dinge*] we hold the party banner firm and upright [as a beacon] around which a future can take shape."[88] For his own part, Westarp tried to reassure his erstwhile Conservative colleagues that his goal was not to make difficulties for the DNVP but to lead "conservative elements" to it and hold it in reserve in the event of emergency.[89] Heydebrand, in turn, pinned his hopes for a better conservative future on the person of Westarp, whom he thought most capable of bringing a conservative party to life. In this respect, however, there were already profound differences of opinion between the two conservative leaders. With his decision to temporarily abandon the idea of an independent conservative politics Westarp had taken leave of one of the most important principles of conservative self-awareness and practice: the primacy of conservative independence at all costs.[90] During the war Westarp and Heydebrand had defended and practiced this code of behavior to the point of parliamentary isolation.[91] That Westarp no longer saw any chance of going it alone in the pursuit of a conservative agenda met with Heydebrand's bitter agreement.[92] As Heydebrand had written to Westarp on the occasion of his candidacy for the Weimar National Assembly in 1919:

> For the Conservative Party it is certainly a great advantage that you have decided to make this sacrifice. Whether from a purely personal point of view this is something we should celebrate seems doubtful, for . . . the composition of the new entity, composed as it is of predominantly Free Conservative and middle-class elements, [will] make it difficult to lend sufficient material support to the conservative concept that you have always represented to our great satisfaction.[93]

Heydebrand closed by alluding to the goals he and Westarp had shared in the prewar period, namely, their defense of the monarchical, authoritarian, and agrarian state against Social Democracy and their commitment to the idea of a *Volk* whose access to political participation was carefully graduated.

Concerns over the "dilution" of conservative principles and values found widespread resonance in the Central Association of German Conservatives. For many of its adherents "conservative politics," in its Prussian-Protestant form, meant preventing the DNVP's drift into the quagmire of the middle parties and exercising political pressure from the Right.[94] As late as 1924—over a year and half after the *völkisch* secession—the frustration that Conservatives felt over the course of the DNVP stood very much at the center at various meetings of the Central Association of the German Conservatives. Seidlitz-Sandreczki blamed the secession on the DNVP and recommended a rapprochement between the Conservatives and the *völkisch* organizations on the radical Right.[95] At the end of March 1924 the executive committee of the

Central Association released a statement that in the future the German Conservatives wanted to build a "bridge" between the German Nationalists and the *völkisch* camp. The Central Association had thus given a clear signal of where it stood in the spectrum of German party politics. This resolution also defined the political guidelines for the Central Association, principles that were deeply inscribed in Westarp's convictions like "political freedom" at home and abroad, the restoration of Prussian primacy, and the reinstitution of the Hohenzollern monarchy in the Reich and Prussia. Monarchy was hailed as the sole legitimate form of state most compatible with the German and Prussian sense of law. In light of Heydebrand's deteriorating health, Westarp was elected to the chairmanship of the Central Association with Seidlitz-Sandreczki as his deputy.[96]

Although newspapers like the *Zeit* greeted this resolution with the comment that the bridge between the racists and the German Nationalists was indeed in need of repair, the question remained as to whether or not Westarp, in light of his deteriorating relationship with Graefe, was the right person to build that bridge. As Westarp wrote to former member of the Prussian Upper House Leopold von Buch at the beginning of 1924, he remained deeply skeptical about the prospects of reconciliation between the DVFP and the DNVP. The demands of the Central Association for a joint slate of candidates between the DNVP and the German-Racist Freedom Party, Westarp explained, were doomed to failure by the attitude of Graefe and his supporters even if one were willing to go down that road. The DVFP was doomed to failure, Westarp concluded, if it chose to test its strength in the next national elections.[97]

The idea that the Conservative Party could be resurrected became increasingly attractive among certain circles in the Central Association. In the late summer of 1924 the moment for the founding of a new conservative party seemed to have arrived after the final vote on the Dawes Plan in the Reichstag. Despite the fact that the German Nationalist party leadership had branded the Dawes Plan a "Second Versailles," nearly half of the DNVP Reichstag delegation voted for the controversial bill and thus helped provide the government with the two-thirds majority it needed to suspend those provisions of the Weimar Constitution that pertained to the national railway system.[98] The day on which the vote took place—29 August 1924—went down as a day of disgrace in the collective memory of the German Nationalists. All of the talk about the powerful oppositional unity of the party, of a clear "no" against Stresemann's foreign policy proved illusory. Stresemann's enemies in the Central Association were speechless. On the day after the vote Westarp received a letter from Arnim-Boitzenburg announcing that he would be leaving the DNVP and that it was time to call the old Conservative Party back into life.[99]

On the evening of the vote Westarp had left Berlin in order to resume a cure that he had interrupted so that he could take part in the deliberations in the Reichstag.[100] But Westarp's absence did little to shield him from the excitement in the capital or from the sense of outrage among certain sectors of the party over the split in the DNVP's vote in the Reichstag. As Westarp's daughter Adelgunde reported to her sister in Gärtringen: "Today and yesterday [the Conservatives] have bombarded us with dispatches and special delivery letters insisting that Father should return to Berlin and reopen the Conservative shop [*Laden*]. That's not going to happen. First, Father's health. And second, Father wants to allow the excitement to die down a bit and gain a certain sense of distance from all that's going on."[101]

In October and November the Central Association met to discuss the events of 29 August. As usual the meetings began with a report by Westarp over the political situation. In the course of his remarks Westarp addressed two key problems: the possibility of a Conservative secession on the right wing of the DNVP and the sharp criticism of the DNVP party leadership and party chairman Oskar Hergt. Not only did Westarp urge the Conservatives to stay with the DNVP in order to continue infusing it with conservative ideas and values, but he carefully avoided a denunciation of those who had voted with the government parties. Instead Westarp described the dynamic that had accounted for the increase in the size and influence of the pro-government faction, namely the pressure of organized economic interests and an overture on the part of Foreign Minister Stresemann and the German People's Party (Deutsche Volkspartei or DVP) to support an extension of the existing governmental coalition to the right in the event that the German Nationalists supported the Dawes Plan.[102]

For reasons he was reluctant to disclose, Westarp's account of the split within the DNVP Reichstag delegation was remarkably restrained. His reserve stemmed in no small measure from the fact that although he had voted against the Dawes Plan, he was not adverse to using the DNVP's support of the Dawes Plan as a bargaining chip to secure a favorable position for the party in future cabinet negotiations. Two days before the decisive vote in the Reichstag Westarp and DNVP party chairman Hergt had worked out a strategy based upon the assumption that the DNVP's refusal to support those provisions in the Dawes Plan legislation that affected the status of the government-owned railway system and thus required a two-thirds majority for approval would lead to their rejection in the Reichstag. Stresemann would then have no alternative but to make the Nationalists an even better offer in order to secure their support in a second vote on the Dawes recommendations.[103] Not only was this strategy rendered null and void when the controversial railway laws found a two-thirds majority in the first round of voting, but the DNVP now found itself in a much weaker negotiating posture when the DNVP Reichstag delegation split down the middle in the fateful vote on 29 August.

As the DNVP and DVP resumed cabinet negotiations in the aftermath of the fateful vote on the Dawes Plan, Westarp was to be found once again among the ranks of the skeptics. His position on the DNVP's participation in the government always depended upon how influential the Nationalist ministers would be in the cabinet. After the vote on the Dawes Plan it no longer seemed likely that the DNVP would be able to secure the influence within the government to which it was entitled on the strength of its impressive victory in the May 1924 Reichstag elections. Instead, as Westarp wrote to Hergt: "On the road to power that I am willing to walk I see an intermediary phase of sharp opposition and national resistance as inescapable."[104] What this reveals is just how important it was to Westarp to keep the Conservatives in the DNVP and to reconcile them to reform-minded Hergt. But while Westarp could not prevent a devastating assault against Hergt's leadership of the DNVP at a meeting of the executive committee of the Central Association on 11 October 1924, he was able to dissuade the Conservatives from raising their own party banner in the upcoming Reichstag elections.[105]

Westarp's role in the Dawes Plan crisis and his rise to prominence in the DNVP confronted the Conservatives with the dilemma of dealing with his dual role as a Conservative and German Nationalist. In 1922 Heydebrand had warned Westarp that loyalty conflicts were inescapable and concluded with the observation that "your personal character is too fixed [festgelegt] for you in a Sammelpartei not to become involved in internal and external conflicts that tear it apart and damage the cause itself."[106] Heydebrand's fears about the strength of Westarp's resolve only reinforced the ambivalence the Conservatives had felt about his involvement in the DNVP. On 11 October 1924 the executive committee of the Central Association decided that Westarp's entry into the national cabinet was not desirable.[107] When Westarp subsequently accepted the chairmanship of the DNVP Reichstag delegation at the beginning of 1925 despite Conservative reservations about his increasingly prominent role in the party, Seidlitz's congratulatory note reflected all too well the ambivalence with which the Conservatives greeted this decision. "With a laughing and a crying eye," wrote Seidlitz, "I read yesterday of your election as chairman of the delegation and hurry to congratulate you even though my Conservative eye cries because you will have precious little time for our special mission in the Central Association and the *Kreuzzeitung*. I regard your election as a victory for the Conservative tendency in the party and hope that this will continue to be effective. I further hope that the coterie Hergt, Lindeiner [Hans-Erdmann von Lindeiner-Wildau] and Graef [Walther Graef-Anklam] will now finally be pushed to the wall [*nun endgültig an die Wand gequetscht ist*]."[108] For Westarp, on the other hand, the divided loyalties resulting from his rise to prominence within the DNVP party leadership had become increasingly unbearable, and in April 1925 he tendered his resignation as chairman of the Central Association and proposed Seidlitz as his successor.[109]

Conservative hopes that Westarp's rise to prominence would now tilt the DNVP more and more toward a policy of sharp opposition failed to materialize. The more deeply he became involved in parliamentary procedures and the DNVP's internal affairs, the greater the gap between Westarp and his old comrades in arms. Nowhere would this become more apparent than in the wake of the DNVP's decision to join the national government first in January 1925. The rules of political communication had changed for Westarp when his party abandoned the camp of the opposition. It was no longer possible for Westarp and the DNVP party leadership to criticize Stresemann's foreign policy as harshly as before, in particular in light of the government's impeding overtures to the French about the possibility of a security pact for Germany's western borders and the subsequent conclusion of the Locarno accord in the fall of 1925. This would put Westarp's talents not only as a broker between the DNVP and the government but also his ties to the Conservatives to the ultimate test.

Most Conservatives, but also significant sectors within the DNVP, were united in their opposition to Stresemann's initiative because of the territorial concessions that Germany would most likely have to make in order to secure Allied support for the proposed pact. For the Conservatives, Westarp had been too soft on Stresemann and his plans for a diplomatic accord with the Allies. Max Wildgrube, a member of the Central Association, even complained about Westarp's "un-Conservative" attitude.[110] At the end of May 1925 Westarp seized the opportunity to rally the Conservatives to the DNVP's support by outlining his strategic objectives in considerable detail. In particular Westarp went on to explain that after the debacle of 29 August 1924 it was no longer possible for the DNVP to pursue a credible hardline policy of uncompromising opposition to the proposed security pact and claimed that he sought to avoid a cabinet crisis for fear that this would cost the Nationalists influence over the future course of events. Though urging the Conservatives to show greater understanding for a Stresemann as one who seemed to be tilting to the right, Westarp insisted that this did not mean that he was in agreement with the government's foreign policy initiatives, which he hoped would fail before the renunciation of German claims to the contested province of Alsace-Lorraine ever came up for discussion.[111]

Only the DNVP's resignation from the national government in the fall of 1925 in protest to the conclusion of the Locarno accord prevented an open break between Westarp and the Conservatives.[112] Westarp's situation, however, was to become even more difficult when early the following year he accepted the party's national chairmanship in addition to the post he already held as chairman of the DNVP Reichstag delegation.[113] Writing to Westarp shortly after his election, the irascible Seidlitz exclaimed: "I find it impossible to congratulate you on your recent election, even though it may have been unanimous, because it means that you will be lost to us even more than before."[114] Seidlitz's fears were confirmed less than a year later when under Westarp's leadership the DNVP rejoined the national government in January 1927. Part of the price the DNVP had to pay for its entry into the national government was a statement that Westarp issued before the Reichstag in which he conceded that his party's entry into the government was predicated upon de facto acceptance of the existing political system. At the same time, Westarp tried to reassure his party's faithful that this did not mean that the DNVP was abandoning its commitment to the restoration of the monarchy as its long-term political goal.[115] Westarp's distinction between the DNVP's short-term and long-term goals, however, did little to assuage the suspicions and fury of his erstwhile colleagues in the Central Association of German Conservatives.

For the Conservatives this was tantamount to betrayal. As Seidlitz, Westarp's successor as chairman of the Central Association of German Conservatives, reported from Silesia: "I sit here at my desk for several hours every day trying to calm down those people who demand from me the separation of the Conservatives from the German Nationalists."[116] The fury that the Conservatives felt about the DNVP's drift into the morass of Weimar party politics reached its peak in October 1927 when the German Conservative Party—as some Conservatives preferred to call what still remained of their organization—adopted a resolution at its Frankfurt congress that reiterated its hostility toward the existing system of government in clear and unequivocal terms: "We reject the form of government born of treason, the breach of faith, and selfishness [*Verrat, Treubruch und Eigennutz*]."[117] The adoption of this resolution placed Westarp in an impossible situation. As the DNVP party leader he had underwritten the guidelines for his party's work in the governmental coalition that included, among other things, protection of the constitution. As a Conservative, on the other hand, he was directly tied to the official declaration of the Frankfurt congress. In a letter to Seidlitz, Westarp expressed dismay over the position of the Conservatives:

> This path [of participating in the government] is all the more narrow because it can only be taken if I loyally abide by the terms of the guidelines, which protect the constitution and its symbols against disparaging vilification [*herabsetzender Verunglimpfung*]. To me that does not seem to be all that great a sacrifice since the sharpness of one's tone alone does not accomplish anything. The Conservative resolution with its introductory words that ascribe the constitution to treason and the breach of faith . . . must, as I know from all my experience, work or be used as a thrust in this direction.[118]

Contemporary observers were quick to draw attention to Westarp's "two souls," one Conservative and therefore hostile to the constitution, the other German nationalist and committed to fulfilling the obligations the DNVP had incurred when it entered the government.[119] What all of this reveals is just how divergent conservative strategies for overcoming the crises of the Weimar Republic had become by the end of the 1920s. Uncompromising opposition and "positive cooperation," if only within clearly defined limits, formed the two poles between which the different nuances and meanings of political conservatism played out. The shift in Westarp's position from a course of fundamental opposition that did not preclude a forceful change of the political system to a more gradualist strategy that entailed participation in the existing political system was accompanied by reflections on political morality by which he tried to salvage his reputation as an upright conservative. As a publicist Westarp tried to explain the state-supporting traditions of German conservatism by emphasizing the distinctly Prussian concept of political obligation while at the same time legitimizing his course of political action by stressing the frustrating potential of uncompromising opposition:

> Here we have to be clear that affirmation of the state [*Bekenntnis zum Staat*] is not to be equated with the affirmation of the democratic form of the state but is a sacred duty to serve the German Reich in whatever form

it might exist with all of the strength and energy at our disposal. . . . Such a statement . . . will, I hope, help to overcome the tired resignation that comes from the notion that one cannot perform useful work on the reconstruction of the fatherland without the complete rejection of everything from the past, without the abandonment of the monarchal principle.[120]

The state to which Westarp swore his "sacred duty" to defend was not a neutral entity but an authoritarian monarchal state that had been shaped by history whose essential substance had not changed even though it had been usurped by enemy forces. Defending the authority of the state despite rejecting the form in which it currently existed was tantamount to walking on a tightrope and fraught with inner conflict. If the Conservatives returned to the comfort of uncompromising opposition by making demands that were impossible to meet, they ran the risk of losing all influence and capitulating to the status quo. The "revulsion and loathing for the existing system," cautioned Westarp at an internal party training session in preparation for the 1928 Reichstag elections, must not lead to "resignation and the refusal to take part in the elections."[121]

As Westarp failed to meet the demands of the Pan-Germans, the United Patriotic Associations of Germany (Vereinigte Vaterländische Verbände Deutschlands), and the Conservatives for favorable treatment in the nomination of candidates for the upcoming national elections,[122] the situation quickly escalated. Once again Seidlitz countered with the threat of a Conservative secession from the DNVP, though going one step further to release the Conservatives from their obligation to vote for the DNVP.[123] The Conservatives in the electoral districts of Potsdam II and Berlin intensified the conflict by endorsing a radical Völkisch-National Bloc (Völkisch-Nationaler Block), a move that was particularly insulting since Potsdam II was Westarp's own district.[124] Although this went even too far for Seidlitz, he could not keep Westarp from resigning from the Central Association and thus cutting the last ties to his old political home.[125]

The Völkisch-National Bloc, a fusion of right-wing parties and associates around Wulle and Graefe, quickly established itself as the long-awaited possibility of intensifying contacts between the *völkisch* movement and the old-line Conservatives in the Central Association. Several members of the Central Association went so far as to join the bloc and pressured the association's executive committee to make a final break with the DNVP and take up negotiations with Wulle and Graefe.[126] This idea, however, encountered strong opposition from Seidlitz, who despite his previous threats was still reluctant to sever ties to the DNVP.[127]

Arnim-Boitzenburg, on the other hand, was less apprehensive. In a letter to Graefe he welcomed the founding of the bloc since in his opinion nothing could be accomplished with the existing political parties.[128] Graefe responded that it was "painful" for him to witness the failure of the old Conservatives with whom he had his political start. "The pathetic development of the once so impressive Westarp serves as a chilling example of where one ends when one no longer musters the [necessary] will!"[129]

The poor showing of the Völkisch-National Bloc in the 1928 Reichstag elections caused the Conservatives to back away once again. In the DNVP, on the other hand, a promising ally began to move to the foreground in the person of Alfred Hugenberg. The powerful press and film magnate was a strong opponent of the Westarp faction in the DNVP Reichstag delegation and began to assert more and more influence over the party's internal affairs. In October 1928 Westarp lost the party chairmanship to Hugenberg. Seidlitz, who had kept up contact with Westarp after his resignation from the Central Association, consoled the deposed party chairman with the words: "My sincerest regrets over your removal from the party leadership. Perhaps, however, is this parting of the ways also the right thing to do. We must now place ourselves unconditionally behind Hugenberg."[130] Although Seidlitz stepped down from the Central Association's chairmanship, its course remained the same. With the new chairman Ewald von Kleist-Schmenzin the Conservatives stood behind the radical wing of the DNVP.[131]

In July 1930 the power struggle within the DNVP had been resolved in Hugenberg's favor. Westarp, who had come out in support of the presidential chancellorship of Heinrich Brüning, left the DNVP and cast his lot with the newly founded KVP.[132] His goal, as he wrote to his political friend von Maltzahn in 1932, had been to create a "national governmental bourgeois party between the National Socialists on the one side and the Center and Social Democrats on the other."[133] But for Westarp's erstwhile colleagues in the Central Association of German Conservatives the vast majority found it impossible to follow his example. It was impossible, wrote Arnim-Boitzenburg to a fellow conservative in July 1930, to imagine that the voters would now rally to a party that called itself "conservative" but that has nothing to do with Conservative politics. "I have had great [respect] for Westarp but must now say that his attitude in the last years, but particularly now, is difficult to understand."[134] Several months earlier Arnim-Boitzenburg had taken the time to outline his own vision of a rejuvenated conservative politics to Hugenberg: the Conservatives must come together with a part of the German Nationalists and the National Socialists to create a "genuine opposition against the system."[135]

Conclusion

Westarp's relations with the political racist Albrecht von Graefe-Goldebee and the Central Association of German Conservatives offer a rich insight into the intellectual and organizational processes of reorientation and redefinition that took place on the German Right during the Weimar Republic. The increasing distance between Westarp and his former comrades in arms in the period between the two world wars can be seen as a barometer of Westarp's conflict-prone efforts at strategic realignment and participation in the decision-making process of Germany's new republican order that his former allies were not willing to make. While the friendship between Graefe and Westarp in the Second Empire and early Weimar Republic rested upon a shared appreciation of the crises that besieged Germany, differences between the two become increasingly pronounced over the course of time. As Westarp rose to prominence in the DNVP, Graefe became increasingly radicalized by the struggles over the direction in which the party should be headed and eventually left it in order to organize the *völkisch* Right as a rival to the DNVP. As the DNVP's national chairman and as chairman of its delegation in the Reichstag, Westarp struggled to set a conservative political agenda that would influence the course of political development at the national level in the hope that political success would soften the uncompromising attitude of the hardliners on the extreme Right. But when success proved elusive and the DNVP suffered at the polls as a consequence, Westarp found himself at odds with the Central Association of German Conservatives and its commitment to a policy of radical opposition as a strategy for overcoming Germany's endemic crises.

Westarp's involvement in the new order provided those who had maintained their distance from Weimar democracy with delegitimating narratives that included accusations that he had been corrupted by the republican system and that he had lost all political credibility. In his own mind Westarp saw the contradiction between his monarchal ideals and his efforts to achieve a measure of influence within the Weimar political system as a "dilemma" that could not be solved. In the meantime, the old networks that Westarp had forged in the Second Empire proved unequal to the challenges of the Weimar Republic and collapsed under the weight of those challenges. Allies who, out of the shared experience of war, defeat, and revolution, had taken up the struggle against the Weimar Republic would become enemies by the end of the 1920s, divided by conflicting conceptions of what conservative politics meant and how it should be integrated into the everyday life of the republic itself. In the eyes of the radical Right Westarp's involvement with the Republic went too far. But from the perspective of more reform-minded conservatives, the continuities in his political thought and his emotional ties to the old imperial order kept him from making an unconditional commitment to the Republic.

Notes

I would like to take this opportunity to thank Larry Jones for his translation of my essay. This chapter presents the preliminary results of my ongoing research on Westarp.

1. On Westarp see the collection of essays published in *"Ich bin der letzte Preuße": Der politische Lebensweg des konservativen Politikers Kuno Graf von Westarp (1864–1945)*, ed. Larry Eugene Jones and Wolfram Pyta (Cologne, Weimar, and Vienna: Böhlau, 2006); as well as his published memoirs, Kuno von Westarp, *Konservative Politik im letzten Jahrzehnt des Kaiserreichs*, 2 vols. (Berlin: Deutsche Verlagsgesellschaft, 1935); and *Konservative Politik im Übergang vom Kaiserreich zur Weimarer Republik*, ed. Friedrich Freiherr Hiller von Gaertringen in collaboration with Karl J. Mayer and Reinhold Weber (Düsseldorf: Droste, 2001).
2. For example, see "Westarp mit dem Januskopf," *Vorwärts*, 20 August 1927, no. 393, in the Pressearchiv des Reichs-Landbundes, Bundesarchiv Berlin-Lichterfelde, Bestand R 8034 II (hereafter cited as BA Berlin, R 8034 II), 6152.
3. Anspach to Westarp, 12 October 1931, in the Familienarchiv der Freiherren Hiller von Gaertringen, in Gärtringen (hereafter cited as NL Westarp, Gärtringen), VN 3. On the DKP, see James Retallack, *Notables of the Right: The Conservative Party and Political Mobilization in Germany, 1876–1918* (Boston: Unwin Hyman, 1988); and *The German Right 1860–1920: Political Limits of the Authoritarian Imagination* (Toronto: The University of Toronto Press, 2006); as well as Volker Stalmann, "Vom Honoratioren- zum Berufspolitiker. Die konservativen Parteien (1867–1918)," in *Regierung, Parlament und Öffentlichkeit im Zeitalter Bismarcks. Politikstile im Wandel*, ed. Lothar Gall (Paderborn, Munich, Vienna, and Zurich: Schöningh, 2003), 91–125.
4. On the history of the DNVP, see the recent publication by Maik Ohnezeit, *Zwischen "schärfster Opposition" und dem "Willen zur Macht." Die Deutschnationale Volkspartei (DNVP) in der Weimarer Republik 1918–1928* (Düsseldorf: Droste, 2012); and Kirsten Heinsohn, *Konservative*

Parteien in Deutschland, 1912–1933. Demokratisierung und Partizipation in geschlechterhistorischer Perspektive (Düsseldorf: Droste, 2010). See also the recent work by Thomas Mergel, "Das Scheitern des deutschen Tory-Konservativismus. Die Umformung der DNVP zu einer rechtsradikalen Partei 1928–1932," *Historische Zeitschrift* (276) 2003: 323–68; and *Parlamentarische Kultur in der Weimarer Republik. Politische Kommunikation, symbolische Politik und Öffentlichkeit im Reichstag* (Düsseldorf: Droste, 2002). For the older literature consult Werner Liebe, *Die Deutschnationale Volkspartei 1918–1924* (Düsseldorf: Droste, 1956); and on the last years of the party Friedrich Hiller von Gaertringen, "Die Deutschnationale Volkspartei," in *Das Ende der Parteien 1933. Darstellungen und Dokumente*, ed. Erich Matthias and Rudolf Morsey (Düsseldorf: Droste, 1984), 543–652.

5. On the relationship between the concept of identity and biography, see Thomas Etzemüller, *Biographien. Lesen–erforschen–erzählen* (Frankfurt: Campus Verlag, 2012), 49. See also Andreas Gestrich, "Einleitung: Sozialhistorische Biographieforschung," in *Biographie–sozialgeschichtlich. 7 Beiträge*, ed. Andreas Gerlich, Peter Knoch and Helga Merkel (Göttingen: Vandenhoeck and Ruprecht, 1988), 5–28.

6. On antisemitism and the *völkisch* movement, see Stefan Breuer, *Die Völkischen in Deutschland. Kaiserreich und Weimarer Republik* (Darmstadt: Wiss. Buchgesellschaft, 2008), esp. 183–93, as well as his earlier work, *Ordnungen der Ungleichheit. Die deutsche Rechte im Widerstreit ihrer Ideen 1871–1945* (Darmstadt: Wissenschaftliche Buchgesellschaft, 2001). On the role of the racists in the DNVP, see Jan Striesow, *Die Deutschnationale Volkspartei und die Völkisch-Radikalen 1928–1922*, 2 vols. (Frankfurt a.M.: Haag + Herchen, 1981).

7. On the Central Association see Jens Flemming, "Konservatismus als 'nationalrevolutionäre Bewegung.' Konservative Kritik an der Deutschnationalen Volkspartei 1918–1933," in *Deutscher Konservatismus im 19. und 20. Jahrhundert. Festschrift für Fritz Fischer zum 75. Geburtstag und zum 50. Doktorjubiläum*, ed. Dirk Stegmann et al. (Bonn: Verlag Neue Gesellschaft, 1953), 295–331; Striesow, DNVP, 315–34.

8. In this context Heinsohn speaks of "gedachte Ordnungen." See Heinsohn, *Konservative Parteien*, 251.

9. Axel Schildt, *Konservatismus in Deutschland von den Anfängen im 18. Jahrhundert bis zur Gegenwart* (Munich: Beck, 1998), 119.

10. Ibid., 156. See also Andreas Wirsching, "Koalition, Opposition, Interessenpolitik. Probleme des Weimarer Parteienparlamentarismus," in *Parlamentarismus in Europa. Deutschland, England und Frankreich im Vergleich*, ed. Marie-Luise Recker (Munich: Oldenbourg, 2004), 41–64. On the contours of this position within the DNVP, see Friedrich Hiller von Gaertringen, "Das konservative Preußen und die Weimarer Republik," in *Preußen. Nostalgischer Rückblick oder Chance zu historischer Aufarbeitung*, ed. Francesca Schinzinger and Immo Zapp (Ostfildern: Scripta Mercaturae Verlag, 1984), 52–69. On the process of political integration through parliamentary collaboration, see Mergel, *Parlamentarische Kultur in der Weimarer Republic*, 323–31.

11. For this phase of Westarp's political career, see Larry Eugene Jones, "Kuno Graf von Westarp und die Krise des deutschen Konservatismus in der Weimarer Republik," in *Ich bin der letzte Preuße*," ed. Jones and Pyta, 109–46.

12. Ibid.

13. Mergel, "Scheitern," 345–67.

14. *Handbuch der verfassungsgebenden deutschen Nationalversammlung, Weimar 1919. Biographische Notizen und Bilder*, ed. Bureau des Reichstags (Berlin: Carl Heymanns Verlag, 1919), 169.

15. Westarp, *Übergang*, 70, n.7.

16. "Personalia," n.d. [ca. 1916], Geheimes Staatsarchiv Preußischer Kulturbesitz (GStPrK), HA I, Rep. 184, Personalakten Nr. 3040.

17. Stephan Malinowski, "Kuno Graf von Westarp—ein missing link im preußischen Adel. Anmerkungen zur Einordnung eines typischen Grafen," in *Ich bin der letzte Preuße*", ed. Jones and Pyta, 9–32, 14.

18. Westarp, *Übergang*, S. 126.

19. Stalmann, "Honoratiorenpolitiker," 116–21.

20. James Retallack, "Zwei Vertreter des preußischen Konservatismus im Spiegel ihres Briefwechsels: Die Heydebrand-Westarp-Korrespondenz," in *Ich bin der letzte Preuße*", ed. Jones and Pyta, 33–60, esp. 34–39.

21. On Graefe's position in the DKP, see Westarp, *Konservative Politik im Kaiserreich*, 2:309–11.

22. Bruno Thoß, "Nationale Rechte, militärische Führung und Diktaturfrage in Deutschland 1913–1923," *Militärgeschichtliche Mitteilungen* 38/2 (1987): 27–76, here 32.

23. Breuer, *Ordnungen*, 11–19. On the threat posted by the women's movement, see Heinsohn, *Konservative Parteien*, 10f.

24. For further details, see Martin Kohlrausch, *Der Monarch im Skandal. Die Logik der Massenmedien und die Transformation der wilhelminischen Monarchie* (Berlin: Akademie Verlag, 2005).

25. Retallack, *German Right*, 398.

26. Westarp, *Konservative Politik im Kaiserreich*, 1:379.

27. Westarp to Beyendorff, 13 March 1920, NL Westarp, Gärtringen, VN 30.

28. On the founding of the DNVP, see Lewis Hertzman, *DNVP. Right-Wing Opposition in the Weimar Republic, 1918–1924* (Lincoln: University of Nebraska Press, 1963), 8–30, as well as the more recent and superbly documented study by Ohnezeit, *DNVP in der Weimarer Republik*, 30–46.

29. Heidrun Holzbach, *Das "System Hugenberg." Die Organisation bürgerlicher Sammlungspolitik vor dem Aufstieg der NSDAP* (Stuttgart: Deutsche Verlags-Anstalt, 1981), 70–89.

30. On Traub, see Willi Henrichs, *Gottfried Traub (1869–1956). Liberaler Theologe und extremer Nationalprotestant* (Waltrop: Spenner, 2001).

31. Heinsohn, "Das konservative Dilemma und die Frauen," 101.

32. Westarp, *Konservative Politik im Übergang*, 92.

33. Breuer, *Die Völkischen in Deutschland*, 184–85.

34. Striesow, *DNVP und die Völkisch-Radikalen*, 82, 135.

35. Declaration by Westarp at the meeting of the DNVP central executive committee (Hauptvorstand), 9 April 1920, in Westarp's unpublished

Nachlaß, Bundesarchiv Berlin-Lichterfelde, Bestand N 2329 (hereafter cited as BA Berlin, NL Westarp), 25.

36. Westarp, *Konservative Politik im Übergang*, 200.
37. Ibid., 212.
38. Stefan Breuer, *Die radikale Rechte in Deutschland 1871–1945. Eine politische Ideengeschichte* (Stuttgart: Reclam, 2010), 248.
39. Westarp to Traub, 3 July 1920, NL Westarp, Gärtringen, VN 115. See also Westarp, *Konservative Politik im Übergang*, 511.
40. Striesow, *DNVP und die Völkisch-Radikalen*, 77–82.
41. Westarp, *Konservative Politik im Übergang*, 361, 534. See also Boris Barth, *Dolchstoßlegenden und politische Desintegration. Das Trauma der deutschen Niederlage im Ersten Weltkrieg 1914–1933* (Düsseldorf: Droste, 2003), 308.
42. Westarp to Graefe, 6 January 1922, NL Westarp, Gärtringen, VN 25.
43. Graefe to Westarp, 8 January 1922, NL Westarp, Gärtringen, VN 25.
44. In this respect, see the contribution in this volume (chapter 3) by Larry Eugene Jones.
45. Striesow, *DNVP und die Völkisch-Radikalen*, 311–12.
46. In this respect, see Breuer, *Völkischen in Deutschland*, 184.
47. This has been persuasively argued by Martin H. Geyer, *Verkehrte Welt. Revolution, Inflation und Moderne: München 1914–1924* (Göttingen: Vandenhoeck & Ruprecht, 1998), 278–88.
48. Striesow, *DNVP und die Völkisch-Radikalen*, 118–19.
49. In this respect, see "Antisemitismus als kultureller Code," in Shulamit Volkov, *Antisemitismus als kultureller Code. Zehn Essays* (München: Beck, 2000), 13–36.
50. Helmut Berding, *Moderner Antisemitismus in Deutschland* (Frankfurt: Suhrkampf, 1988), 93.
51. Westarp, *Konservative Politik im Übergang*, 149.
52. On Treitschke, see Ulrich Wyrwa, "Genese und Entfaltung antisemitischer Motive in Heinrich von Treitschkes 'Deutscher Geschichte im 19. Jahrhundert,'" in *Antisemitische Geschichtsbilder*, ed. Werner Bergmann and Ulrich Sieg (Essen: Klartext, 2009), 83–101, here 97–99.
53. For example, see Westarp, "Innere Politik der Woche," *Neue Preußische (Kreuz-)Zeitung* (hereafter cited as *NPKZ*), 11 November 1919.
54. Westarp, "Was ist konservativ?" in *Deutsches Adelsblatt* 34 (1927): 754–56.
55. Westarp, *Konservative Politik im Übergang*, 144–46.
56. Ibid, 144.
57. Ibid.
58. Striesow, *DNVP und die Völkisch-Radikalen*, 314.
59. Westarp, *Konservative Politik in Übergang*, 141–42.
60. Graefe, "Partei und Judenfrage," 5 February 1920, NL Westarp, Gärtringen, VN 29.
61. Pfannkuche to Westarp, 14 August 1922, NL Westarp, Gärtringen, VN 86.
62. Westarp to Traub, 10 August 1922, NL Westarp, Gärtringen, VN 86.
63. Striesow, *DNVP und die Völkisch-Radikalen*, 253, 271–73.
64. Graefe to Westarp, 17 September 1922, NL Westarp, Gärtringen, VN 88.
65. Westarp, "Innere Politik der Woche," *NPKZ*, 20 August 1922.

66. Westarp, "Innere Politik der Woche," *NPKZ*, 24 January 1922.
67. "Der Anti-Antisemitismus des Herrn Grafen Westarp," *Der Deutsche Volksrat. Eine politische Wochenschrift*, 13 January 1920.
68. Brauer-Berichte, 3 October 1922, NL Westarp, Gärtringen, VN II/83.
69. Brauer-Berichte, 19 September 1922, NL Westarp, Gärtringen, VN II/83.
70. Westarp to Graefe, 2 November 1922, NL Westarp, Gärtringen, VN 88.
71. Graefe to Westarp, 4 November 1922, NL Westarp, Gärtringen, VN 88.
72. Brauer-Berichte, 18 October 1922, NL Westarp, Gärtringen, VN II/83.
73. The secondary literature on the *völkisch* secession from the DNVP is already extensive. For the most recent accounts of this, see Breuer, *Völkische in Deutschland*, 183–93; and Ohnezeit, *DNVP in der Weimarer Republik*, 120–38; as well as the contribution by Jones, chapter 3, in this volume.
74. Westarp to Graefe, 1 August 1925, NL Westarp, Gärtringen, VN 52.
75. Graefe to Westarp, 1 August 1925, NL Westarp, Gärtringen, VN 52.
76. Brauer-Berichte, 21 November 1922, NL Westarp, Gärtringen, II/83.
77. Flemming, *Konservative Kritik*, 300.
78. Klitzing to Westarp, 27 February 1919, BA Berlin, NL Westarp, 37. For the text of the founding proclamation, see Liebe, *Deutschnationale Volkspartei*, 9–11.
79. Westarp to Heydebrand, 13 Feb 1919, NL Westarp, Gärtringen, II/78.
80. Circular from the Central Association of German Conservatives to the chairmen of the DKP state and provincial organizations, n.d., NL Westarp, Gärtringen, II/1. See also Hertzman, *DNVP*, 38.
81. Westarp, *Konservative Politik im Übergang*, 47.
82. Müffling to Westarp, 8 March 1924, NL Westarp, Gärtringen, VN 49.
83. Pyta, *Dorfgemeinschaft*, 297.
84. On Arnim, see the biography Sieghart von Arnim, *Dietlof Graf von Arnim-Boitzenburg. Ein preußischer Landedelmann und seine Welt im Umbruch von Staat und Kirche* (Limburg an der Lahn: Starke, 1998).
85. Flemming, "Konservative Kritik," 304.
86. Westarp, *Konservative Politik im Übergang*, 584.
87. Flemming, "Konservative Kritik," 301.
88. Heydebrand to Westarp, 23 January 1919, NL Westarp, Gärtringen, II/78.
89. Westarp an Stolberg-Wenigerode, 22 June 1923 [?], NL Westarp, Gärtringen, VN 38.
90. Retallack, *Notables on the Right*, 220.
91. "Die Isolierung der konservativen Reichstagsfraktion bis Anfang November 1917," text with Westarp's handwritten alterations from November 1917, BA Berlin, NL Westarp, 73. See also Westarp, *Konservative Politik im Kaiserreich*, 2:10–14, 162.
92. Heydebrand to Westarp, 16 February 1919, NL Westarp, Gärtringen, II/79.
93. Heydebrand to Westarp, 4 January 1919, NL Westarp, Gärtringen, II/78.
94. Sontag to Westarp, 30 July 1920, in the unpublished Nachlaß of Franz Sontag, Bundesarchiv Koblenz, Bestand N 1064, 14. See also Müffling to Westarp, 8 March 1924, NL Westarp, Gärtringen, VN 49.
95. Brauer-Berichte, 12 February 1923, NL Westarp, Gärtringen, VN II/84.

96. "Die deutschkonservative Brücke," *Germania*, 25 March 1923, and "Die Konservativen," *Die Zeit*, 27 March 24, both in BA Berlin, R 8034 II, 6152. See also Striesow, *DNVP und die Völkisch-Radikalen*, 323–34.

97. Westarp to Buch, 19 January 1924, NL Westarp, Gärtringen, VN 49. See also Westarp, *Konservative Politik im Übergang*, 574.

98. Much of the following has been taken from Michael Stürmer, *Koalition und Opposition in der Weimarer Republik 1924–1918* (Düsseldorf: Droste, 1967), 38–78; and Robert Grathwol, *Stresemann and the DNVP: Reconciliation or Revenge in German Foreign Policy 1924–1928* (Lawrence: Regents Press of Kansas, 1980), 8–20.

99. Flemming, "Konservative Kritik," 310.

100. Bureau Westarp to Wiegand, 1 September 1924, NL Westarp, Gärtringen, VN 50.

101. Adelgunde von Westarp to Gertraude Hiller von Gaertringen, n.d. [September 1924], Familienarchiv der Freiherren Hiller von Gaertringen, Gärtringen, in an uncataloged collection of family correspondence organized by year.

102. Westarp's remarks at the meeting of the expanded executive committee of the Central Association of German Conservatives, 6 November 1924, in the unpublished Nachlaß of Count Dietlof von Arnim-Boitzenburg, Brandenburgisches Landeshauptarchiv Potsdam, Repertorium 37 (hererafter cited as BLHA Potsdam, Rep. 37, NL Arnim-Boitzenburg), 4426. For the overall political context, see Stürmer, *Koalition und Opposition*, 61–71.

103. Ibid.

104. Westarp to Hergt, 18 September 1924, NL Westarp, Gärtringen, II/11.

105. Meeting of the executive committee of the Central Association of German Conservatives, 11 October 1924, BLHA Potsdam, Rep. 37, NL Arnim-Boitzenburg, 4426.

106. Heydebrand to Westarp, 6 August 1922, NL Westarp, Gärtringen, II/83.

107. Meeting of the executive committee of the Central Association of German Conservatives, 11 October 1924, BLHA Potsdam, Rep. 37, NL Arnim-Boitzenburg, 4426.

108. Seidlitz to Westarp, 5 February 1925, NL Westarp, Gärtringen, II/13.

109. Meeting of the executive committee of the Central Association of German Conservatives, 1 April 1925, BLHA Potsdam, Rep. 37, NL Arnim-Boitzenburg, 4426.

110. In this respect, see Wildgrube's remarks at the meeting of the executive committee of the Central Association of German Conservatives, 25 May 1925, BLHA Potsdam, Rep. 37, NL Arnim-Boitzenburg, 4429.

111. Westarp's report at the meeting of the executive committee of the Central Association of German Conservatives, 25 May 1925, BLHA Potsdam, Rep. 37, NL Arnim-Boitzenburg, 4429.

112. On the Locarno crisis and the DNVP's resignation from the national government, see Barry R. Jackisch, "Kuno Graf von Westarp und die Auseinandersetzung über Locarno: Konservative Außenpolitik und die deutschnationale Parteikrise 1925," in *"Ich bin der letzte Preuße"*, ed. Jones

and Pyta, 147–62; as well as the two party histories by Manfred Dörr, "Die Deutschnationale Volkspartei 1925 bis 1928" (PhD diss., Universität Marburg, 1964), 167–80; and Ohnezeit, *DNVP in der Weimarer Republik*, 319–39.

113. On Westarp's election as DNVP party chairman, see Ohnezeit, *DNVP in der Weimarer Republik*, 343–44.
114. Seidlitz to Westarp, 18 March 1926, NL Westarp, Gärtringen, VN 79.
115. Walther Graef-Anklam, "Der Werdegang der Deutschnationalen Volkspartei 1918–1928," in *Der nationale Wille. Werden und Wirken der Deutschnationalen Volkspartei 1918–1928*, ed. Max Weiß (Essen, 1928), 50.
116. Seidlitz to Westarp, 22 May 1927, NL Westarp, Gärtringen, VN 40.
117. "Verrat und Würdelosigkeit," *Berliner Tageblatt*, 11 October 1927, BA Berlin, R 8034 II, 6152.
118. Westarp to Seidlitz, 20 October 1927, NL Westarp, Gärtringen, VN 40.
119. "Westarps zwei Seelen," *Vorwärts*, [16?] October 1927, BA Berlin, R 8034 II, 6152.
120. Westarp, "Innere Politik der Woche," *NPKZ*, 5 February 1927.
121. Speech by Westarp on 28 March 1928 at a DNVP training conference, 26–31 March 1928, BA Berlin, R 8005, 58/73–96.
122. In this connection, see Seidlitz to Westarp, 28 February 1928 and 14 March 1928, NL Westarp, Gärtringen, VN 40.
123. Seidlitz to Westarp, 12 April 1928, NL Westarp, Gärtringen, VN 40.
124. Ibid.
125. Westarp to Seidlitz, 13 April 1928, NL Westarp, Gärtringen, VN 40.
126. Ernst to Arnim-Boitzenburg, 9 June 1928, BLHA Potsdam, Rep. 37, NL Arnim-Boitzenburg, 4429.
127. Arnim-Boitzenburg to Graefe, 5 January 1928, BLHA Potsdam, Rep. 37, NL Arnim-Boitzenburg, 4429.
128. Ibid.
129. Graefe to Arnim, 30 December 1927, BLHA Potsdam, Rep. 37, NL Arnim-Boitzenburg, 4429.
130. Seidlitz to Westarp, 10 November 1928, NL Westarp, Gärtringen, VN 100.
131. On Kleist, see Bodo Scheurig, *Ewald von Kleist-Schmenzin: Ein Konservativer gegen Hitler* (Oldenburg: Stalling, 1968).
132. For further details, see Larry Eugene Jones, "German Conservatism at the Crossroads: Count Kuno von Westarp and the Struggle for Control of the DNVP, 1928–30," *Contemporary European History* 18 (2009): 147–77. On the founding of the KVP, see Erasmus Jonas, *Die Volkskonservativen 1928–1933. Entwicklung, Struktur, Standort und staatspolitische Zielsetzung* (Düsseldorf: Droste, 1965), 79–86.
133. Westarp to Maltzahn, 16 June 1932, NL Westarp, Gärtringen, VN 131.
134. Arnim-Boitzenburg to Schönemarck, 25 July 1930, BLHA Potsdam, Rep. 37, NL Arnim-Boitzenburg, 4429.
135. Arnim-Boitzenburg to Hugenberg, 16 April 1930, BLHA Potsdam, Rep. 37, NL Arnim-Boitzenburg, 4429.

3

Conservative Antisemitism in the Weimar Republic

A Case Study of the German National People's Party

Larry Eugene Jones

The extent to which antisemitism constituted an essential component of German political culture both before and after World War I remains a question of considerable historical interest. This is particularly true of recent investigations on the history of the German Right. The purpose of this essay will be to examine the history of antisemitism in the Weimar Republic through the lens of the German National People's Party (Deutschnationale Volkspartei or DNVP), a party that was founded in November 1918 as the point around which a badly fragmented prewar German Right could crystallize. Although antisemitism had figured prominently in the politics, ideology, and self-definition of the German Right before World War I, the new party demonstrated considerable ambivalence on the so-called Jewish question, a fact that has not been fully appreciated in the existing body of secondary literature on the DNVP.[1] For, as the following essay will argue, the DNVP's position on the Jewish question was neither constant nor consistent. Just as there was no consensus on the Jewish question between the various factions that had come together in the fall and early winter of 1918 to found the DNVP, so did the party's embrace of antisemitism rise and ebb with the vicissitudes of the German economy and the stability of the Weimar Republic. By the same token, conservative antisemitism itself consisted of all sorts of different strands that can only be disentangled from each other with great difficulty and subtlety. All of this suggests that a more nuanced and differentiated interpretation of the party's position on the Jewish question that one finds in the existing body of secondary literature on the DNVP and German Right is long overdue.

The DNVP and the Jewish Question, 1918–23

Of the four groups that came together in November 1918 to found the German National People's Party,[2] two, the German Conservative Party (Deutsch-Konservative Partei or DKP) and the German Social Party (Deutschsoziale Partei), were explicitly and militantly antisemitic, the third, the Christian Socials (Christlichsoziale Partei), had antisemitic antecedents they had tried to mute in the latter years of the Second Empire, and the fourth, the Free Conservatives (Reichs- und freikon-servative Partei), had attached no particular significance to the Jewish question in the period before 1918.[3] Moreover, the leaders of the new party—most notably the newly elected DNVP national chairman Oskar Hergt—were recruited in large part from the ministerial bureaucracy and sought to distance themselves from the political organizations of prewar German conservatism. From their perspective, the German National People's Party was a totally new party unencumbered by the mistakes of the past, and in the campaign for the January 1919 elections to the Weimar National Assembly and Prussian constitutional convention the founders of the new party did their best to avoid the antisemitic diatribes that had characterized the political agitation of the DKP and other prewar conservative political parties. But whatever their intentions might have been, the efforts of the DNVP's national leadership to steer clear of antisemitism in their initial foray into the arena of electoral politics were undercut by the fact that at the state and regional levels of the party's national organization antisemitic themes and imagery came to play a more and more important role in the latter stages of the campaign. This was true not only of the East Prussian districts where antisemitism had played a significant role in conservative politics before 1914 but also in Bavaria and Württemberg where new political organizations with only loose ties to the national DNVP had sprung up. Given the decentralized structure of the DNVP party organization, the party's national leadership had little control over the conduct of the campaign at the state, regional, and local levels of the party organization and felt increasingly uncomfortable with much of what was taking place during the latter stages of the campaign.[4]

The first years of the Weimar Republic were characterized by a veritable explosion of antisemitism that was related to four specific factors. Germany's defeat in World War I and the emergence of the "Stab-in-the-Back Legend," the omnipresent threat of Bolshevism and social revolution, the runaway inflation of the early 1920s and, last but certainly not least, the large-scale influx of east European Jews combined to excite the antisemitic imagination of the German people and to transform what in the Second Empire had been a widespread, yet essentially benign, undercurrent of German political culture into open hostility to all Jews at home and abroad.[5] During this period the DNVP both fed and fed off of the tide of rising antisemitism.[6] Even relative moderates like Friedrich Edler von Braun who campaigned in Bavaria on a joint ticket shared by the DNVP and German People's Party (Deutsche Volkspartei or DVP) felt compelled to address the Jewish question. While acknowledging the great service that individual Jews had rendered Germany in the areas of scholarship, literature, and art and carefully dissociating himself from the agitation of radical antisemites, Braun continued:

> The Jewish question is one of the most deeply touching problems of the current scene, and one cannot ignore it in formulating guidelines for policy. The Jews are a people without a home and destroy every national body in which they gain a decisive influence, for they are international and cosmopolitan in their disposition and historical development and must therefore necessarily disrupt the processes of national development. Proof of this can be seen in their close connection with Social Democracy, whose teachings come from Marx and Lassalle and is therefore born from the Jewish spirit. So also were the majority of the leaders of the revolution in Russia and Germany Jews. Here I do not need to remind you of their names but only point to the fact that far more than a half of the ministers in the revolutionary government consisted of Jews. . . . It is against this overgrowth of the Jewish influence [*Überwuchern des jüdischen Einflusses*] in politics, against its domination of capital and the press, that we must turn and protect ourselves if we are not to fail in our obligations to our own people. We must protect the German oak from the being choked by these usurous weeds [*Wucherpflanze*] if one day we do not want to appear decayed and rotten to the core.[7]

What this revealed was an almost schizophrenic contradiction in the party's self-image that was temporarily obscured by the turmoil of 1918–19 but that would become increasingly apparent with the passage of time. In this respect, the DNVP found itself the target of a concerted campaign by Heinrich Claß and the leaders of the Pan-German League (Alldeutscher Verband or ADV), one of the most influential vehicles of prewar antisemitism, to transform the party into an instrument of the racist Right.[8] At the same time, the leaders of the DNVP found antisemitism to be a particularly useful tool in recruiting the support of the German farmer. Antisemitism had been a prominent feature of prewar rural political culture not just in the conservative strongholds east of the Elbe[9] but also in regions with historically liberal profiles like Württemberg and Schleswig-Holstein.[10] It is therefore not surprising that the National Rural League (Reichs-Landbund or RLB), which had been founded in January 1921 as the principal agent for the representation of conservative agricultural economic interests, exhibited a high degree of antisemitism in its programmatic statements and the speeches of its leading figures.[11] In a separate development, the leaders of the prewar DKP—and here the key figure was Count Kuno von Westarp, the DKP's last parliamentary leader—began to reassert themselves as a force within the DNVP. Not only did Westarp play an important role in drafting the program the DNVP promulgated in April 1920, but he and a number of other erstwhile DKP politicians succeeded in their bid for election to the Reichstag in the May 1920 national elections.[12] The net effect of these developments was to tip the balance within the DNVP in favor of those elements who pressed for a more aggressive course of action with respect to the Jewish question.

In the campaign for the June 1920 Reichstag elections the leaders of the DNVP's racist wing launched a concerted effort to move antisemitism to the center of the party's electoral agitation. A telling barometer of the rising antisemitism within the party was the secession of a group of party moderates around Siegfried von Kardorff, a former Free Conservative and an outspoken opponent of antisemitism in any form who left the party in April 1920 to protest the ascendancy of the Westarp faction and the way in which the campaign was being conducted.[13] This was followed by the curious case of Anna von Gierke, a member of the DNVP delegation to the Weimar National Assembly and a conservative feminist renowned for her work in the field of social and child welfare. The fact that Gierke's mother was Jewish made her a conspicuous target for the agitation of the party's racist wing, which celebrated a major triumph in blocking her nomination to a secure candidacy in the upcoming national elections. As a result both Gierke and her father Otto, a highly respected law professor at the University of Berlin, resigned from the party in a move that clearly represented another setback for the leaders of the DNVP's moderate wing and prompted a renewed debate on the role of antisemitism in the party's future political development.[14] Although the DNVP managed to increase its share of the popular vote by more than two-thirds in the 1920 Reichstag elections, the party's antisemites were still disappointed by the outcome of the election and argued that the party would have done better had it pursued a more aggressively antisemitic campaign.[15]

Over the course of the next two years, the leaders of the DNVP's antisemitic wing intensified their efforts to gain control of the party. Here the key figure was Albrecht von Graefe-Goldebee, a Silesian noble who had belonged to the DKP before World War I. But in their efforts to steer the DNVP in a more antisemitic direction,[16] Graefe and his associates soon found themselves on a collision course with the party's national leadership, the so-called four-H group of Hergt, Helfferich, Otto Hoetzsch, and Alfred Hugenberg who were widely perceived as the party's leadership cadre. Of the four, only Hugenberg, who had been active in the Pan-German League since before the war, was at all sympathetic to the agitation of the antisemites, but even he was cautious about reducing the myriad problems that Germany faced in the immediate postwar period to the Jewish question and felt little inclination to make the Jewish question the end-all and be-all of the DNVP's political existence. The other three were adamantly opposed to the agitation of the party's antisemites, partly out of conviction and partly out of the fear that it would make it impossible for the DNVP to gain access to the corridors of power should the appropriate opportunity present itself. In November 1921 the DNVP leadership dealt the leaders of the party's racist wing a sharp setback when it rejected three motions that would have had the effect of barring Jews from party membership and then proceeded to adopt a resolution introduced by Helfferich that blocked a change in the party statutes on the Jewish question. According to the terms of this resolution, the party's district organizations were barred from amending their statutes to exclude Jews from membership in the party, although precisely how this would pertain to the two or three district organizations that had already adopted a so-called Jewish paragraph remained unclear.[17] Infuriated by this turn of events, the leaders of the DNVP's racist faction began to organize themselves and their followers into a special alliance at both the national and district levels of the DNVP organization but ran into strong opposition from Hergt, Helfferich, and Hugenberg, while Westarp, who privately agreed with Graefe on the nature of the Jewish threat, remained cool to the idea of a separate racist organization within the party.[18]

The crisis drew to a head in the early summer of 1922 when Wilhelm Henning, one of the leaders of the DNVP's racist faction and a member of the DNVP Reichstag delegation, broke ranks with the party leadership with a particularly scurrilous attack against Germany's Jewish foreign minister, Walther Rathenau, for having allegedly betrayed Germany in negotiating the Rapallo Treaty with Soviet Russia.[19] When Rathenau was assassinated by right-wing extremists in late June, the agitation of the party's racist wing suddenly became a source of political embarrassment for the DNVP's national leadership, with the result that Helfferich, who in this and other matters exercised far more influence over the DNVP's political course than the party's duly elected national chairman Hergt, began to press for a resolution of the crisis. With the quadrumvirate of Hergt, Helfferich, Hoetzsch, and Hugenberg leading the charge, the DNVP Reichstag delegation formally expelled Henning from the delegation, though not from the party, by more than a two-thirds majority in both the delegation and the party executive committee on 19 July 1922.[20] The final showdown, however, came at the DNVP's Görlitz national party congress later that October. The issue at stake was whether or not the DNVP's racist faction would be allowed to maintain its own organization as an independent agency within the party apparatus for the purpose of uniting the various elements within the party that were committed to transforming the DNVP into an instrument of the racist cause. As the conflict drew to a resolution, Westarp tried to mediate between the racists and the party's national leadership in a desperate attempt to prevent secession by the leaders of the DNVP's racist faction. In doing this, Westarp stated a position on the Jewish question that in many respects is a classic statement of conservative antisemitism when he wrote for the *Neue Preußische (Kreuz-) Zeitung* in August 1922:

> As a large political party it is impossible for us to adopt a position that treats Jewry as the sole cause of the damage [that Germany has suffered] and that regards it as the singular object not just of the racial struggle as such but of all political combat. Here it is safe to say that the various political tendencies that make this mistake are doomed to a short and unsuccessful existence. The clearer one is about the limits that must be placed on antisemitism, however, the more determined one must also be that the German National People's Party, for the sake of the issue and its effectiveness as a party, must lead the struggle not just against the destructive Jewish spirit but against the political, economic, and social dominance of Jewry within the entirety of its political and racial labors and not as a single issue.[21]

In the final analysis, however, Westarp and the DNVP party leadership were unable to devise a formula on the racist question that was acceptable to the leaders of the party's racist wing.[22] At Görlitz Graefe-Goldebee, Henning, and the other leaders of the DNVP's racist wing were expelled from the party after they refused to dissolve the German-Racist Coalition (Deutschvölkische Arbeitsgemeinschaft or DvAG) they had founded in Berlin-Charlottenburg at the end of the previous month.[23] The secession of the racists, who two months later founded a new political party of their own in the German-Racist Freedom Party (Deutschvölkische Freiheitspartei or DVFP), came as a bitter setback for Westarp but represented a major victory for Hergt, Helfferich, and those in the DNVP party leadership who perceived of the DNVP as a party of loyal opposition modeled more or less after the British Tories. At the same time, however, the Nationalists were concerned about the threat that the founding of the DVFP posed to their own party's electoral prospects, and in February 1923 they moved to minimize the risk of defections to their racist rival by founding the Racist National Committee (Völkischer Reichsausschuß der Deutschnationalen Volkspartei) within the DNVP national organization. The two-fold purpose of this committee was to provide what remained of the DNVP's racist faction a voice at the highest levels of the party's national leadership and to cement the racist principle as firmly as possible in the party's program and political profile.[24] More importantly, the creation of the Racist National Committee provided the Pan-German League a platform within the DNVP's national organization from which it could directly influence the policies and decision-making process of the party's national leadership. Claß and the leaders of the ADV had sharply criticized Graefe and his associates for their decision to leave the DNVP and remained true to their original strategy of pursuing their objectives within the framework of the DNVP.[25]

The High Water Mark, 1924

At no point in the history of the DNVP was the influence of the party's racist faction more apparent than in the campaign for the May 1924 Reichstag elections. The DNVP's racist rivals had scored significant gains in recent state elections in Mecklenburg and Thuringia, and the leaders of the DNVP were determined to meet the racist challenge head on by actively wooing the support of those racist groups that had been left politically homeless by the demise of the Nazi Party (Nationalsozialistische Deutsche Arbeiterpartei or NSDAP) following Hitler's abortive Beer Hall Putsch in November 1923.[26] Even Hergt, who had previously taken great pains to dissociate himself from the racist rhetoric of the radical Right, acquiesced in the decision to move racism and antisemitism to the forefront of the Nationalist campaign.[27] The DNVP racists celebrated their first triumph in April 1924 when the DNVP party congress in Hamburg approved a resolution that barred full Jews and those who were married to Jews membership in the party.[28] In the meantime, Walther Graef-Anklam and the leaders of the DNVP's National Racist Committee had already begun work on a set of guidelines, or *Leitsätze*, on the *völkisch* principle and its place in the party's public profile.[29] Although the original draft was too radical for Hergt and his associates and underwent further revision at the hands of the party's national leaders,[30] it nevertheless served as the basis for the position the DNVP took on racism and antisemitism for the duration of the campaign. This position was rooted in a biological racism that stressed not just the unique properties of the German national character but also the need to preserve the purity of the Nordic-German blood that flowed through the veins of the German nation as the foremost responsibility of the state. Through a program of racial hygiene those of alien racial stock were to be segregated from the nation as a whole and rendered morally harmless. This, in turn, would be accompanied by the introduction of a new educational curriculum with the five-fold objective of strengthening the Christian foundations of Germany's national culture, developing a greater understanding of the history of the German race and its place in the history of the world, fostering a greater appreciation of the German language and its impact upon the cultures of other races, promoting a German sense of beauty in the fine arts, and instructing the German nation in the sciences of biology and racial hygiene.[31]

On 21 February 1924 the DNVP tried to steal the racists' political thunder by introducing a resolution in the Prussian Landtag that would have required all Jews who had entered Prussia since 1 August 1914 to register with the police by 15 April 1924 in preparation for leaving the state by 1 July. Those Jews who did not comply with this ordinance would be subject to confinement in refugee camps prior to their expulsion from Prussian territory.[32] While this was an obvious ploy to capitalize upon the resentment that many Germans felt over the large-scale influx of East European Jews into Germany after the end of World War I, Nationalist propagandists were anxious to meet the racist Right on the latter's own terms and stressed their party's commitment to the *völkisch* principle at every conceivable opportunity.[33] Speaking at a party rally in Stettin, estate owner Hans Schlange-Schöningen lapsed into demagogy that was scarcely discernible from that of the racist Right. "Jewry," Schlange-Schöningen exclaimed, "not only brought us the war and delivered us into slavery but it keeps us in this deplorable situation because it serves its oldest purposes. . . . In the final analysis it was not France, not England, not even America but the international Jewish stock market that was the true victor in the war."[34] Even relative moderates like Hans-Erdmann von Lindeiner-Wildau, a member of the DNVP delegation to the Prussian Landtag who was campaigning for a seat in the Reichstag, cloaked his critique of the modern democratic state and his defense of the conservative conception of the state in the language of the racist antisemite.[35] Yet for all of the passion with which they embraced the racist cause and exposed the clandestine machinations of international and German Jewry, the Nationalists drew a crucial distinction between their brand of antisemitism and that of the racists to their right. The Nationalists were particularly critical, for example, of the hostile attitude the leaders of the racist parties manifested toward religion, the monarchy, and the capitalist economic system. At the same time, there was a plebeian quality to racist agitation against the Jews and their place in German economic life that the leaders of the Nationalist party found difficult to accept.[36]

Nowhere did the racial Right pose a more serious threat to the DNVP's electoral prospects than in the south German state of Bavaria, where the situation was complicated by the fact that state elections were scheduled to take place less than a month earlier than the national elections set for the first week of May. The Bavarian Middle Party (Bayerische Mittelpartei or BMP), as the DNVP's Bavarian chapter was generally known, was still recoiling from the racist crisis at the end of 1922 and the defection of several prominent racists, most notably Rudolf Xylander and Rudolf Buttmann, to the rival German Racist Freedom Party.[37] But the abortive Hitler-Ludendorff putsch at the end of 1923 sent a shock wave through the ranks of Bavaria's conservative establishment and prompted the leaders of the Bavarian Rural League (Bayerischer Landbund) to propose an alliance of all right-wing forces for the upcoming state elections.[38] Ideally this alliance would include the racists, but should they refuse to cooperate, the fallback position would be an alliance of all other right-wing groups including the BMP, the DVP, the National Liberal State Party of Bavaria (Nationalliberale Landespartei Bayerns), and several lesser-known monarchist and conservative organizations. Although the racists declined to participate, the proposed alliance known as the United National Right (Vereinigte Nationale Rechte) received strong support from Hans Hilpert and the BMP party leadership, who announced its formation with a series of broadsides directed against the more radical racists for having sabotaged the cause of right-wing unity.[39] But in the final analysis this did little to inoculate the DNVP's Bavarian electorate, and in the Bavarian Landtag elections of 6 April 1924 the BMP suffered unexpectedly heavy losses that set off a virtual panic within the DNVP's national party organization.[40] To shore up their party's position in Bavaria, the DNVP's national leaders intervened in the nomination of candidates for the upcoming Reichstag elections on behalf of retired admiral and naval secretary Alfred von Tirpitz in the hope that a man of his stature and national pedigree could unite the splintered forces of the Bavarian Right and help the DNVP win back the votes it had lost to the radical racists.[41]

Although racism and antisemitism were eventually overshadowed as in the May 1924 Reichstag elections by the furor over Germany's decision to accept the recommendations of the Dawes commission as the basis of a provisional reparations settlement,[42] party leaders continued to stress their party's commitment to the *völkisch* principle at every conceivable opportunity. Even the DNVP's Reich Catholic Committee (Reichskatholikenausschuß der Deutschnationalen Volkspartei or RKA) that had been founded in the fall of 1920 in an attempt to attract Catholic conservatives to the DNVP banner lent its voice to the rising crescendo of racist and antisemitic rhetoric that the party unleashed in the spring of 1924.[43] Although it is impossible to determine the precise effect that the DNVP's embrace of racism and antisemitism had upon the outcome of the election, the DNVP went on to score a smashing victory in the May 1924 elections with 19.5 percent of the popular vote and ninety-six seats in the Reichstag, a victory to which the party's racist faction reacted with jubilation and for which it took immediate credit.[44] In the months that followed, however, the leaders of the DNVP's racist wing found themselves increasingly marginalized as the party's national leadership tried to leverage promises of support for ratification of the Dawes Plan into a place in the cabinet. The leaders of the DNVP's Racist National Committee remained adamantly opposed to the tactics of their party's national leadership and voted unanimously against ratification of the Dawes Plan when it came before the Reichstag in late August 1924.[45] Moreover, in the campaign for the new national elections that followed the collapse of the DNVP's efforts to join the government, the racist issue was pushed to the sidelines and in no way whatsoever played the central role that it had played in the campaign earlier that spring. Here one can only assume that the exigencies of coalition politics and the fact that the leaders of the DNVP were angling for a place in a new national government required making the DNVP more palatable to potential coalition partners by disentangling it as discretely as possible from the racist Right.

Antisemitism in Retreat and Resurgence, 1924–28

Notwithstanding the role that racism and antisemitism played in the DNVP's stunning victory at the polls in May 1924, the leaders of the party's racist faction found themselves increasingly marginalized in the party's internal affairs and electoral politics in the period between 1924 and 1928. This was the period of Westarp's ascendancy as the dominant figure in the DNVP party leadership. Though by no means free from the antisemitic prejudices of those who made up the leadership of the party's racist faction, Westarp did not believe that all of Germany's problems could be reduced to the Jewish question and automatically subordinated it to issues of greater political priority.[46] With the DNVP's entry into the national government in January 1925 the leaders of the party's racist faction found themselves relegated to the sidelines from where they waged a determined and unrelenting struggle against the compromises that Westarp and the DNVP party leadership had been obliged to make in the interest of coalition solidarity.[47] In the summer of 1925 the DNVP's Racist National Committee took a strong and uncompromising stand against the Locarno Accords that Germany had negotiated with Great Britain, France, and Italy and played a major role in mobilizing opposition to the proposed security pact at the grassroots level of the DNVP's national organization and in eventually forcing the DNVP's withdrawal from the national government in October 1925 after efforts to block the treaty's ratification had failed.[48] But victories like this did little to endear the leaders of the DNVP's racist faction to Westarp and party moderates who were committed to pursuing a conservative political agenda on the basis of the existing political system and who hoped to return to the national government at the earliest possible opportunity.

If anyone kept the DNVP's racist fires burning during the period of Weimar's relative political and economic stabilization, it was the group of women activists affiliated with the DNVP's National Women's Committee (Reichsfrauenausschuß der Deutschnationalen Volkspartei) that had been founded in December 1918 as the first step toward the mobilization of the women's vote for the upcoming elections to the Weimar National Assembly.[49] The women's committee played an important role in drafting the new party program the DNVP promulgated in April 1920 and succeeded in projecting an essentially conservative image of women and their role in Germany's national life by highlighting the virtues of domesticity, religion, and patriotic sacrifice. Above all, it was the task and responsibility of women to protect the cherished values of Germany's national culture—family, faith, nation, racial hygiene—against the forces of decay that had been unleashed by the November Revolution and that had become synonymous with the hated Weimar system.[50] In the campaign for the 1920 Reichstag elections, however, the women's committee was careful to distance itself from

Anna von Gierke and, with the notable exception of committee chair-
woman Margarete Behm, lined up behind the DNVP racists and their
efforts to cast the DNVP as the vanguard of racial purity.[51] Following
the founding of the DNVP's Racist National Committee in the spring
of 1923, women activists like Annagrete Lehmann, Käthe Schirmacher,
and Paula Müller-Otfried were welcomed into the leadership of the
new committee, where they played an important role in keeping racism and antisemitism on the party's agenda despite the reluctance of
the DNVP's national leadership to jeopardize its strategic situation
by publicly identifying itself too closely with the racist cause.[52] At the
heart of their commitment to racism was the conviction that as the
biological vessels of the German nation, women bore a particular responsibility for protecting the purity of German blood against pollu-
tion through contact with inferior races such as the Jews.[53] As a result,
the DNVP's women activists generally opposed the efforts of Westarp
and the DNVP's national leadership to reach some sort of an accommodation with the existing political system, in part because they were
opposed to compromises of any sort and in part because this necessarily required sacrificing the party's racist objectives for the sake of
short-term political gains.[54]

Powerless to prevent the DNVP from joining the national government for a second time in January 1927, the leaders of the party's racist wing retreated to the sidelines where they joined forces with the
Pan-German League in its efforts to take over control of the DNVP.[55]
The party's racists felt vindicated by the heavy losses the DNVP sustained in the May 1928 Reichstag elections as its share of the popular
vote declined from 21.5 to 14.2 percent and the size of its Reichstag
delegation by thirty deputies.[56] The Nationalist campaign had been
dominated by the struggle against special-interest parties, a struggle
in which social and economic issues took precedence over those of
race and antisemitism. In the aftermath of the defeat the leaders of the
DNVP's racist wing spearheaded the efforts to bring about a change in
the party leadership and the DNVP's political course. In this respect,
the DNVP's racists threw their full support behind the candidacy of
press and film magnate Alfred Hugenberg for the DNVP party chairmanship and played a major role in forcing Westarp's resignation as
DNVP party chairman at a meeting of the DNVP party representation
on 8–9 July 1928.[57] In the struggle for control of the party that followed
Baron Axel von Freytagh-Loringhoven as chairman of the DNVP's
Racist National Committee openly embraced the idea of a smaller but
ideologically purer DNVP and demanded that those who still placed

the pursuit of special economic interests ahead of the national welfare should be driven from the party.[58] Though by a margin so small it was never made public, Hugenberg's subsequent election as DNVP party chairman at a meeting of the DNVP party representation on 20 October represented a sensational victory for the party's racist wing and its allies in the Pan-German League.[59] Over the course of the next two years Hugenberg would succeed in transforming the DNVP from a sociologically and ideologically heterogeneous conservative *Sammelpartei* into a strong bloc fused together by what Hugenberg called "the iron hammer of *Weltanschauung*," as first the party moderates and then the more traditional conservatives around Westarp left the party.[60]

Antisemitism and Its Limits under Hugenberg

Although the leaders of the DNVP's racist wing had actively supported Hugenberg's bid for the party chairmanship and rejoiced in his election,[61] the fruits of their victory were ambiguous. For Hugenberg, despite his impeccable right-wing pedigree, was not an ideological racist but a radical nationalist whose entourage included both hardline racists like Axel von Freytagh-Loringhoven, Paul Bang, and ADV chairman Heinrich Claß and someone like Reinhold Quaatz, a man of mixed racial ancestry whose cousin, Ludwig Holländer, was director of the Central Association of German Citizens of the Jewish Faith (Centralverein deutscher Staatsbürger jüdischen Glaubens).[62] Moreover, in his programmatic statements and in particular in his directions for the overall design for the DNVP's Kassel party congress in November 1929 Hugenberg featured anti-Marxism as the axis around which he sought to unify the German national camp.[63] For Hugenberg—and this was a consistent thread of his political worldview from the end of World War I through his eventual withdrawal from active political life in 1933— it was Marxism that constituted the most serious single threat to the unity of the German people and Germany's return to great power status. Defending Germany against the threat of Marxism was for Hugenberg the highest priority of all political activity. To be sure, for the racial antisemite Marxism was generally synonymous with the Jew and but one more manifestation of the international Jewish conspiracy to conquer the world. In the linguistic code of the antisemite Marxism contained a not-all-too-carefully concealed and widely accepted reference to the Jew and his ubiquitous influence. But for Hugenberg, who was by no means oblivious to this code, it was Marxism and not the

Jew that constituted the greatest and most immediate danger to the German nation. For someone who clearly tolerated antisemites among his closest advisors, Hugenberg's speeches and private correspondence were remarkable for their lack of explicit references to the Jewish question. Only rarely, as in a speech in Detmold on 4 January 1932, did Hugenberg invoke the language of German racism—and then only in an obligatory, if not innocuous, embrace of "racist belief and racist strength [*völkischer Glauben und völkische Kraft*]" as the basis of national unity without referring specifically to the threat that Jews presumably posed to the health and unity of the German nation.[64]

What this meant in practical terms was that Hugenberg's ascendancy to the DNVP party leadership did not signal a return to the rabid antisemitism of the party's early years. In fact, anti-Marxism remained the central leitmotif around which Hugenberg organized the DNVP's campaign in the September 1930 Reichstag elections[65] and continued to be at the very heart of the party's sense of mission through the last years of its existence. What is perhaps most striking about the public statements of Hugenberg and other DNVP leaders in the last years of the Weimar Republic was the absence of almost any reference to the Jewish question. Not even after relations between the DNVP and NSDAP had begun to deteriorate in the first half of 1932 did Hugenberg and his associates in the DNVP party leadership make a serious attempt to differentiate the position of their party from that of the Nazis on the issues of racism and antisemitism. To be sure, the Nationalists waged a bitter struggle against the Nazis in the campaign for the July 1932 Reichstag elections as they tried to recover the ground their party had lost to the NSDAP in the April 1932 state elections in Prussia, Bavaria, and Württemberg.[66] But this revolved almost entirely around the social and economic issues like private property and the defense of capitalism where the Nationalists sought to differentiate their position from the socialism of the Nazi party and made no mention of the differences that presumably set them apart from the Nazis on the so-called Jewish question.[67] The most important programmatic statement the DNVP issued during the course of the campaign—the *Freiheitsprogramm der Deutschnationalen Volkspartei* by Quaatz and Bang—assiduously avoided any reference to the Jewish question or the need for action to deal with the threat that international Jewry presumably posed to Germany's vital interests at home and abroad.[68] Similarly, in the development and articulation of the Nationalist campaign strategy at a special meeting of the party's national leadership on 25 July 1932 two of the party's most renowned racists, Axel von Freytagh-Loringhoven and Paul Bang, spoke not on questions of racial hygiene or the international Jewish conspiracy but on foreign and social policy respectively.[69]

From this one can draw three possible conclusions, none of which is in any way exclusive of the other two. In the first place, the Nationalists may not have had much faith in the efficacy of racism and antisemitism as instruments of political mobilization and therefore subordinated them to issues that they thought would be more effective in attracting the support of prospective voters. Second, by granting racists like Freytagh-Loringhoven and Bang a prominent role in the articulation of Nationalist objectives in the campaign for the July 1932 elections the leaders of the DNVP may have been trying to send a coded signal to their party's racist wing that the issues of racial hygiene and the need to address the Jewish threat were still very much in the minds of the party leaders despite the fact that there was no explicit mention of these issues in the way in which the campaign was being organized. And third, this might also suggest that there was actually very little to separate the Nationalists from the Nazis when it came to the matter of racism and antisemitism and that the DNVP therefore stood little to gain by trying to elaborate on these differences.[70] Whatever the reasons might have been, issues of race and antisemitism did not play a significant or conspicuous role in the Nationalist campaign for the Reichstag elections of 31 July 1932. All of this, however, would begin to change following the dissolution of the Reichstag in September 1932 and in the campaign for the Reichstag elections of 6 November.

Still reeling from the heavy losses their party had suffered in the state elections earlier that April, the leaders of the DNVP were devastated by the outcome of the July 1932 Reichstag elections. For although the Nationalists had anticipated a sharp swing to the Right, they were unprepared for the fact that it was the National Socialists and not their own party that had been the principal beneficiary of this swing. With over thirteen million votes and 230 seats in the newly elected Reichstag, the NSDAP had clearly established itself as the largest party in the Reichstag, while the DNVP, on the other hand, saw its share of the popular vote slip from 7.0 to 5.9 percent and lost four of its forty-one seats in the Reichstag.[71] Moreover, the DNVP had come under heavy attack from the Nazis for its lack of a strong and consistent position on the Jewish question and in particular for having extended its protective mantle over Theodor Duesterberg, the Stahlhelm leader whom the DNVP had supported in the 1932 presidential elections only to have the Nazis reveal during the course of the campaign that unbeknownst to the candidate his paternal grandfather had been Jewish.[72] Forced on to the defensive by the ferocity and persistence of the Nazi attacks, the DNVP had no choice but to define its position on Jews and their place in German public life more precisely and moved quickly to reprise their racist credentials by publishing articles on Paul de Lagarde, Houston Stewart Chamberlain, and the forefathers of modern racist thought in *Unsere Partei* and other party organs.[73] At the same time, Nationalist pundits took issue with the Darwinian and materialist assumptions that lay at the heart of the Nazi concept of race and asked how was this compatible with the spiritual values that Hitler had proudly extolled as the essence of Germandom.[74] But, as in the case of elections earlier that summer, issues related to race and the Jewish question were clearly subordinate to those of a social and economic nature. It was precisely in the areas of social and economic policy that Hugenberg and the leaders of the DNVP tried to put the greatest distance between themselves and the socialist schemes of the NSDAP. Once again it was the fear of socialism, whether in its Marxist or Nazi iterations, that dominated the DNVP's campaign in the fall of 1932.[75]

All of this, however, was framed in the discursive context of German racism. At no point in the campaign for the November 1932 elections or at any other point in the last years of the Weimar Republic did the Nationalists go head-to-head with the Nazis on the questions of race and antisemitism or question the validity of race as a political or analytical category. It was as if there was an implicit agreement between the two right-wing parties on the existence of a "Jewish problem" and that it was only a difference of approach and emphasis that separated the two parties when it came to solving this problem. Here it is important to note that the issues of antisemitism and how one might go about solving the "Jewish problem" were never addressed in the negotiations that preceded Hitler's installation as chancellor on 30 January 1933. Not only was there an implicit consensus that something called the Jewish problem did exist, but the various parties that were involved in the negotiations were careful to avoid addressing the specifics of the issue for fear that this would only complicate the already tedious and difficult negotiations that eventually culminated in the formation of the Hitler cabinet.[76] The fact that Hugenberg was already trying to find a suitable position for Quaatz in the private sector would suggest that he had accepted some sort of exclusionary policy with respect to German Jewry as the price of doing business with the Nazis.[77] Nor did racism or antisemitism figure prominently in the campaign for the Reichstag elections on 5 March 1933. Here Hugenberg campaigned with Vice Chancellor Franz von Papen and the Stahlhelm's Franz Seldte under the umbrella of the Combat Front Black-White-Red (Kampffront Schwarz-Weiß-Rot) as allies of the National Socialists in a common crusade to establish the foundations of a new and more authoritarian form of government.[78] Whereas there was much talk in the campaign pronouncements of Hugenberg and his allies about the Christian-national concept of the state,[79] the implications this held for Germany's half million or so Jews were never spelled out.

All of this would, of course, become abundantly clear as the Nazis began to push aside their conservative allies in the spring of 1933 and take the initial steps toward the creation of a racial state, that is, a state in which the categories of race determined one's political status and in which those of inferior racial stock would be driven from positions of influence, academic appointments, and gainful employment first in the public and then ultimately in private sector as well. Not only were Jews subjected to a veritable reign of terror that the Nazi Storm Troopers unleashed against enemies of the regime in the aftermath of the March elections, but the Law for the Restoration of the Civil Service from 7 April 1933 dealt a severe blow to the economic livelihood of German Jewry. Under these circumstances many German Jews—and particularly those who regarded themselves as *Nationaljuden* and identified themselves with the basic values of Germany's national culture—began to petition the DNVP for membership and assistance in the hope that this might afford them a measure of protection against the malevolence of the Nazi regime.[80] For a while the DNVP party leadership equivocated as to how it should respond to this sudden wave of interest on the party of politically conservative Jews who privately sympathized with the social and economic goals of the DNVP but who had been kept from taking part in its affairs by the racist sentiments of many of its leading members. After a period of initial equivocation the DNVP showed its true colors when on 27 March 1933 Hans Nagel from the DNVP headquarters in Berlin responded to a query from the party's Berlin district organization: "The DNVP statues include the passage that Jews are not allowed to join the party. The statutes do not contain a precise definition of who is a Jew. In the committees responsible for accepting new members the opinion has, however, gained ground that persons who are born Jewish and then convert to Christianity must not be accepted into the party."[81] Or, as a similar response to a party member whose name had been removed from the party roster because of his Jewish ancestry read: "According to party statutes Jews cannot be accepted into the German National Front (Deutschnationale Front or DNF). It is not religion but ethnic origin that is decisive in the characterization of 'Jewish.' If you have been accepted into our party and are a member of the Jewish race, it is only because we were not aware of that fact. Therefore, we cannot consider the expulsion from your local group as unjustified."[82] By then, of course, the DNVP itself had become a target of Nazi violence and was in no position to protect its own officials, let alone Jews who were looking for sanctuary from the Nazis.[83]

Conclusion

Assessing the place of antisemitism in the DNVP and of the DNVP's antisemitism in the broader spectrum of conservative antisemitism in the Weimar Republic requires a fine sense of nuance and an ability to distinguish between the various strands of racism and antisemitism that came together in Weimar's largest and most influential conservative party. After all, not all antisemitisms were the same either in how they defined the Jew, the significance they attached to the Jewish question, or the way in which they thought the Jewish question should be solved. The antisemitism of the DNVP was a hodgepodge of different threads of antisemitic thought and practice. Some of it was rooted in inherited religious prejudice, both Lutheran and Catholic. Some of it was of a more recent provenance and had to do with the perception that since their emancipation in the previous century the Jews had come to exert an influence over German social, economic, and cultural life that was incommensurate with their meager numbers. Some of it stemmed from the way in which the Stoeckerite tradition at the end of the nineteenth century had identified Jewishness with the worst excesses of an unbridled capitalism. Some of it was certainly related to the increasingly palpable fear of Bolshevism and social revolution that gripped bourgeois Europe in the wake of World War I. And some of it was rooted in an aggressive and virulent form of racism and in a racial theory of history that saw the Jews as the heart and soul of a vast and multifaceted conspiracy aimed at the subjugation, if not the destruction, of the German nation and the last remaining reservoirs of unpolluted Aryan racial stock that still existed there. All of this had come together in one degree or another to define the DNVP's profile on antisemitism and the Jewish question.

Under these circumstances it would be unrealistic to expect a single, consistent, and homogeneous position on the Jewish question from the DNVP. As one might expect, there were sharp divisions both within the DNVP's national leadership and between the party's national leadership and the leaders of its local and regional organizations on the position the DNVP should adopt with respect to the Jews and their place in German social and political life and on the role that racism and antisemitism should play in the party's public profile. As a general rule, racist and antisemitic sentiment was far stronger and far more persistent at the local and regional levels of the DNVP party organization than the party's national leadership was willing to recognize or admit. Although the party provided a political home for hardline racial antisemites who sought to transform the DNVP into an instrument of their own political agenda and who were constantly pushing the party's national leadership to adopt a more stridently racist and antisemitic tone in its campaign propaganda, the DNVP's national leadership—at least until Hugenberg's election as DNVP party chairman—sought to mute or tone down the racist rhetoric of the party's right wing so as not to alienate prospective coalition partners and jeopardize its chances of becoming part of the national government. And Hugenberg, despite the massive support he received from the leaders of the DNVP's racist wing in his bid for the party chairmanship, remained skeptical about the utility of antisemitism as a technique of mass mobilization and placed his faith instead in anti-Marxism as the key to uniting a badly fragmented German nation behind his party's political banner. But the lack of significance Hugenberg attached to the "Jewish question" cut both ways. For not only did he disdain appeals to race hatred as a way of mobilizing his party's electorate, but it blinded him to the fanaticism of Nazi antisemitism to the point where in January 1933 he agreed to form a government with a man whom he described as "the greatest demagogue in the history of the world"[84] without so much as raising a single question about what Hitler and his followers planned to do with the Jews.

Notes

1. All students of the antisemitic discourse in the Weimar Republic remain deeply indebted to the path-breaking essay by George L. Mosse, "Die deutsche Rechte und die Juden, in *Entscheidungsjahr 1932. Zur Judenfrage in der Endphase der Weimarer Republik*, 2nd ed., ed. Werner E. Mosse (Tübingen: J. C. B. Mohr, 1966), 184–246, esp. 226–35. Also useful, particularly for the early years of the Weimar Republic, is the detailed study by Jan Striesow, *Die Deutschnationale Volkspartei und die Völkisch-Radikalen 1918–1922*, 2 vols. (Frankfurt: Haag und Herschen, 1981). See also the incisive but by no means exhaustive discussion of the DNVP's antisemitism in the early years of the Weimar Republik in the recently published book by Maik Ohnezeit, *Zwischen "schärfster Opposition" und dem "Willen zur Macht."*

Die Deutschnationale Volkspartei (DNVP) in der Weimarer Republik 1918–1928 (Düsseldorf: Droste, 2012), 120–58. On the role of the Jewish question in the DNVP after the formation of the Hitler cabinet, see Hermann Beck, *The Fateful Alliance: German Conservatives and Nazis in 1933. The* Machtergreifung *in a New Light* (New York and Oxford: Berghahn Books, 2009), 174–218, esp. 176–82, 188–94. For a particularly obtuse, historically insensitive, and methodologically flawed study of the DNVP's antisemitism, see Hans Dieter Bernd, "Die Beseitigung der Weimarer Republik auf 'legalem' Weg: Die Funktion des Antisemitismus in der Agitation der Führungsschicht der DNVP" (PhD diss., Fernuniversität Hagen, 2004).

2. By far the most detailed account of the founding of the DNVP is to be found in the recent publication by Ohnezeit, *DNVP in der Weimarer Republik*, 25–46. See also see Striesow, *DNVP und die Völkisch-Radikalen*, 9–43, as well as the earlier studies by Lewis Hertzman, "The Founding of the German National People's Party, November 1918–January 1919," *Journal of Modern History* 30 (1958): 24–36, and Werner Liebe, *Die Deutschnationale Volkspartei 1918–1924* (Düsseldorf: Droste, 1956), 7–15.

3. On prewar political antisemitism, see the recent studies by Peter Walkenhorst, *Nation—Volk–Rasse. Radikaler Nationalismus im Deutschen Kaiserreich 1890–1914* (Göttingen: Vandenhoeck & Ruprecht, 2006); and Stefan Breuer, *Die Völkischen in Deutschland. Kaiserreich und Weimarer Republik* (Darmstadt: Wissenschaftliche Buchgesellschaft, 2008), 68–83; as well as the short essay by Werner Bergmann, "Völkischer Antisemitismus im Kaiserreich," in *Handbuch zur "Völkischen Bewegung" 1871–1918*, ed. Uwe Puschner, Walter Schmitz, and Justus H. Ulbricht (Munich: Saur, 1996), 449–63. Still valuable is the classic study by Richard S. Levy, *The Downfall of the Anti-Semitic Parties in Imperial Germany* (New Haven, CT, and London: Yale University Press, 1975), esp. 225–53. On the antisemitism of the DKP, see James Retallack, "Anti-Semitism, Conservative Propaganda, and Regional Politics in Late Nineteenth Century Germany," *German Studies Review* 11 (1988): 377–403, reprinted in a revised and much expanded version in James Retallack, *The German Right, 1860–1920: Political Limits of the Authoritarian Imagination* (Toronto: University of Toronto Press, 2006), 273–324.

4. Striesow, *DNVP und die Völkisch-Radikalen*, 44–63.

5. In this respect, see Werner Jochmann, "Die Ausbreitung des Antisemitismus," in *Deutsches Judentum in Krieg und Revolution 1916–1923. Ein Sammelband*, ed.Werner E. Mosse (Tübingen: J. C. B. Mohr, 1971), 409–510. For a more recent survey of antisemitism in the Weimar Republic, see Heinrich August Winkler, "Die deutsche Gesellschaft der Weimarer Republik und der Antisemitismus—Juden als Blitzableiter," in *Vorurteil und Völkermord. Entwicklungslinien des Antisemitismus*, ed. Wolfgang Benz and Werner Bergmann (Freiburg, Basel, and Vienna: Herder, 1997), 341–62.

6. On the anti-Semitic discourse in the DNVP, see the discussions of the Jewish question at the evening workshops, or *Arbeitsabende*, of the State-Political Coordinating Committee of the German National People's Party (Staatspolitische Arbeitsgemeinschaft der Deutschnationalen Volkspartei),

6 and 27 June 1919, in the unpublished records of the Deutschnationale Volkspartei, Bundesarchiv Berlin-Lichterfelde, Bestand R 8005 (hereafter cited as BA Berlin, R 8005), 327. See also the discussion of the Jewish question in Kuno Graf von Westarp, *Konservative Politik im Übergang vom Kaiserreich zur Weimarer Republik*, ed. Friedrich Freiherr Hiller von Gaertringen in collaboration with Karl J. Mayer and Reinhold Weber (Düsseldorf: Droste, 2001), 139–48. For the most recent contribution to the literature on antisemitism and the DNVP in the early Weimar Republic, see Ohnezeit, *DNVP in der Weimarer Republik*, 120–58.

7. [Friedrich Edler von Braun], *Wahlrede des Kandidaten der Bayerischen Mittelpartei (DeutschNationale Volkspartei in Bayern und der Deutschen Volkspartei (Nationalliberale Partei) Staatsrat von Braun* (Augsburg, n.d. [1918–19]), 6.

8. In this respect, see the minutes of the meeting of the ADV managing committee, 16–17 February 1919, in the unpublished records of the Alldeutscher Verband, Bundesarchiv Berlin-Lichterfelde, Bestand R 8048 (hereafter cited as BA Berlin, R 8048), 123/13–14. See also Freytagh-Loringhoven, "Der Alldeutsche Verband und die Parteien," *Alldeutsche Blätter* 30, no. 28 (16 October 1920): 226–27. For a sample of the ADV's antisemitism, see Georg Fritz, "Die Überwindung der jüdischen Fremdherrschaft," in *Deutschvölkisches Jahrbuch 1920*, ed. Georg Fritz (Weimar, 1920), 63–74. The most comprehensive history of the ADV is Rainer Hering, *Konstruierte Nation. Der Alldeutsche Verband 1890 bis 1939* (Hamburg: Christians, 2003). On the ADV's views of the various German parties, see 396–488. On the ADV's activities in the Weimar Republic, see 138–53. For a more detailed discussion of Pan-German politics in the Weimar Republic, see Barry A Jackisch, *The Pan-German League and Radical Nationalist Politics in Interwar Germany, 1918–39* (Farnham: Ashgate, 2012), here 87–131; as well as the recent dissertation by Björn Hofmeister, "Between Monarchy and Dictatorship: Radical Nationalism and Social Mobilization of the Pan-German League, 1914–1939" (PhD diss., Georgetown University, 2012), esp. 185–244. See also the recent biography of the ADV leader by Johannes Leicht, *Heinrich Claß 1868–1953. Die politische Biographie eines Alldeutschen* (Paderborn: Schöningh, 2012), esp. 269–77.

9. For example, see Dewitz to Kriegsheim, 22 November 1923, in the unpublished records of the Reichs-Landbund, Bundesarchiv Berlin-Lichterfelde, Bestand R 8034 I, 66/9–11. For further information on the anti-Semitic prejudices of the German and more specifically East Elbian aristocracy, see Georg H. Kleine, "Adelsgenossenschaft und Nationalsozialismus," *Vierteljahrshefte für Zeitgeschichte* 26 (1978): 100–43, esp. 109–10; and more recently Stefan Malinowski, "Vom blauen zum reinen Blut. Antisemitische Adelskritik und adliger Antisemitismus 1871–1944," *Jahrbuch für Antisemitismusforschung* 12 (2003): 147–69.

10. On the strength of antisemitism among Württemberg conservatives, see Hans Peter Müller, "Antisemitismus im Königreich Württemberg zwischen 1871 und 1914," *Jahrbuch des Historischen Vereins für Württembergisch Franken*

86 (2002): 547–83. On the situation in Schleswig-Holstein, see Peter Wulf, "Antisemitismus in bürgerlichen und bäuerlichen Parteien und Verbände in Schleswig-Holstein (1918–1924)," *Jahrbuch für Antisemitismusforschung* 11 (2002): 52–75.

11. For further details, see Hans Reif, "Antisemitismus in den Agrarverbänden Ostelbiens während der Weimarer Republik," in *Ostelbische Agrargesellschaft im Kaiserreich und in der Weimarer Republik. Agrarkrise — junkerliche Interessenpolitik — Modernisierungsstrategien*, ed. Heinz Reif (Berlin: Akademie Verlag, 1994), 378–411.

12. This has been well documented in Westarp, *Konservative Politik*, ed. Hiller von Gaertringen, 83–88, 110–12. For an overview of Westarp's political career in the Weimar Republic, see Larry Eugene Jones, "Kuno Graf von Westarp und die Krise des deutschen Konservativismus in der Weimarer Republik," in *"Ich bin der letzte Preuße": Kuno Graf von Westarp und die deutsche Politik (1900–1945)*, ed. Larry Eugene Jones and Wolfram Pyta (Cologne, Weimar, and Vienna: Böhlau, 2006), 109–46, here 112–15.

13. For further details, see Streisow, *DNVP und die Völkisch-Radikalen*, 208–12.

14. In this connection, see the letters from Otto and Anna von Gierke to the DNVP party leadership, 12 May 1920, reprinted in Otto von Gierke, *Einige Wünsche an die Deutschnationale Volkspartei*, Als Manuskript gedruckt 20. Oktober 1920 (Berlin: Scherl, n.d. [1920]), 22–29. See also Westarp, *Konservative Politik*, ed. Hiller von Gaertringen, 143. For a critical assessment of the DNVP's position on the so-called Jewish question, see Friedrich von Oppeln-Bronikowski, *Antisemitismus? Eine unparteiische Prüfung des Problems* (Charlottenburg: Deutsche Verlagsgesellschaft für Politik und Geschichte, 1920).

15. For example, see Freytagh-Loringhoven to Westarp, 20 July 1920, in the Familienarchiv der Freiherrn Hiller von Gaertringen, in Gärtringen (hereafter cited as NL Westarp, Gärtringen), VN 25.

16. For Graefe's position, see his letter to Westarp, 8 January 1922, NL Westarp, Gärtringen, VN 25. In a similar vein, see Henning, "Gedanken zur grundsätzlichen Haltung unserer Partei," 30 June 1921, in the unpublished Nachlaß of Reinhard Mumm, Bundesarchiv Berlin-Lichterfelde (hereafter cited as BA Berlin, NL Mumm), 277/267–70. For an overview of the racists in the DNVP, see Breuer, *Völkischen in Deutschland*, 183–93.

17. Report from Brauer to Heydebrand, 1 December 1921, NL Westarp, Gärtringen, II/82, Brauer-Berichte, 43

18. Report from Brauer to Heydebrand, 16 January 1922, NL Westarp, Gärtringen, II/82, Brauer-Berichte, 55.

19. Henning, "Das wahre Gesicht des Rapallo-Vertrags," *Konservative Monatsschrift* 79, no. 6 (June 1922): 521–26. For the most detailed treatment of the crisis that ensued, see Striesow, *DNVP und die Völkisch-Radikalen*, 341–420.

20. Report by Brauer to Heydebrand, 20 July 1922, NL Westarp, Gärtringen, II/83, Brauer-Berichte, 149–50. For a fuller explanation of the DNVP's position, see the internal circular "Zur Abwehr" to the party's district

and precinct organizations as well as to the party's state and national parliamentarians, 29 July 1922, BA Berlin, NL Mumm, 277/281–87. For Henning's account of these developments, see "Darstellung des Abgeordneten Henning über die Ereignisse, die zu seinem Ausschluß aus der Fraktion geführt haben," n.d. [September–October 1922], NL Westarp, Gärtringen, VN 88. On Helfferich's role in the 1922 racist crisis, see John G. Williamson, *Karl Helfferich, 1872–1924: Economist, Financier, Politician* (Princeton, NJ: Princeton University Press, 1971), 368–71.

21. Statement by Westarp, 22 August 1922, cited in Walther Graef-Anklam, "Der Werdegang der Deutschnationalen Volkspartei 1918–1928," in *Der nationale Wille. Werden und Wirken der Deutschnationalen Volkspartei 1918–1928*, ed. Max Weiß (Essen: Wilhelm Andermann Verlag, 1928), 14–53, here 42.

22. In this respect, see Westarp's undated report of the two meetings of a special nine-member committee appointed by the DNVP party representation on 31 August 1922 to negotiate a compromise on the racist question in Munich, 3 and 9 November [1922], BA Berlin, NL Mumm, 277/271–73.

23. Report from Brauer to Heydebrand, 18 October 1922, NL Westarp, Gärtringen, II/83, Brauer-Berichte, 199–203. See also Radike's report on a meeting of the DNVP district organization in Berlin-Charlottenburg, 14 August 1922, BA Berlin, NL Mumm, 277/276–78. For further details on the racist secession, see Ohnezeit, *DNVP in der Weimarer Republik*, 134–58.

24. On the founding of this organization, see the minutes of the meeting of the DNVP National Racist Committee, 22 April 1923, BA Berlin, R 8005, 361/230–31, also in BA Berlin, R 8048, 223/5–6. For a statement of the committee's goals, see Graef-Anklam, "Die völkischen Zielen der Deutschnationalen Volkspartei," n.d. [April 1923], BA Berlin, R 8048, 223/219. For further information on the committee and its subsequent history, see Jackisch, *Pan-German League*, 89–100.

25. In this respect, see Freytagh-Loringhoven to Claß, 6 August 1923, BA Berlin, R 8048, 209/177.

26. For further details, see Brauer to Heydebrand, 23 February 1924, NL Westarp, Gärtringen, II/84, Brauer-Berichte, 374–77. On the role of the DNVP's Racist National Committee in the preparations for the party's campaign in the May 1924 Reichstag elections, see Westarp to Wedell, 19 March 1924, NL Westarp, Gärtringen, VN 49.

27. See Hergt's statement in the minutes of the DNVP's Racist National Committee, 17 February 1924, BA Berlin, R 8048/223/41, as well as Brauer's observations in his report to Heydebrand, 19 February 1924, NL Westarp, Gärtringen, II/84, Brauer-Berichte, 369–73.

28. See Brauer's report of Graef's announcement before the DNVP's Racist National Committee, 17 February 1924, in Brauer to Heydebrand, 19 February 1924, NL Westarp, Gärtringen, II/84, Brauer-Berichte, 369–73.

29. For the original draft of the DNVP's Racist National Committee, see "Leitsätze der völkischen Welt- und Staatsauffassung," n.d., appended to the meeting announcement from Graef, 2 February 1924, BA Berlin, R 8048,

223/32–37. For further details, see the minutes of the DNVP's National Racist Committee, 17 February 1924, BA Berlin, R 8048, 223/41–45.

30. For a critical perspective on the role that Hergt and the DNVP party leadership played in toning down the party's statement on racism and antisemitism, see Brauer to Heydebrand, 16 March 1924, NL Westarp, Gärtringen, II/84, Brauer-Berichte, 377–80. See also the detailed critique of the "Leitsätze" in Pfannkuche to the DNVP Racist National Committee, 12 February 1924, BA Berlin, R 8048, 223/36–40.

31. "Die völkischen Ziele der Deutschnationalen Volkspartei," n.d. [April 1924], DNVP-Werbeblatt, no. 217, in the unpublished Nachlaß of Luitpold von Weilnböck, Bundesarchiv Koblenz (hereafter cited as BA Koblenz, NL Weilnböck), 5b.

32. Georg Negenborn, *Die jüdische Gefahr*, Deutschnationale Flugschrift, no. 153 (Berlin: Deutschnationale Schriftenvertriebsstelle, 1924), 2–3.

33. For example, see [Deutschnationale Volkspartei], *Der völkisch-nationale Gedanke im Kampfe mit der Republik (Vier Jahre deutschnatl. Reichstagsarbeit)*, Deutschnationale Flugschrift: no. 147 (Berlin: Deutschnationale Schriftenvertriebsstelle, 1924).

34. Hans Schlange-Schöningen, *Wir Völkischen! Rede in Stettin 1924*, Deutschnationale Flugschrift, no. 142 (Berlin: Deutschnationale Schriftenvertriebsstelle, n.d. [1924]), 9–10.

35. Hans-Erdmann von Lindeiner-Wildau, *Aufgaben völkischer Politik. Vortrag vor dem Amt für staatspolitische Bildung der Studenschaft der Universität Berlin am 27. Februar 1924*, Deutschnationale Flugschrift, no. 148 (Berlin: Deutschnationale Schriftenvertriebsstelle, 1924), 10–14.

36. In this respect, see Schwarzer, "Das Ziel der Wahl," *Der Tag*, 9 March 1924, no. 60; as well as Walther von Graef-Anklam, *Völkische Mittel- oder deutschnationale Rechtspartei?*, Deutschnationale Flugschrift, no. 150 (Berlin: Deutschnationale Schriftenvertriebsstelle, 1924); and [Deutschnationale Volkspartei], *Die Deutschvölkische Freiheitspartei*, Deutschnationales Rüstzeug, no. 1 (Berlin: Deutschnationale Schriftenvertriebsstelle, 1924).

37. Minutes of the expanded BMP executive committee, 20 December 1922, BA R 8005, 26/46–49. For further details on the impact of the racist crisis on the BMP, see Striesow, *DNVP und die Völkisch-Radikalen*, 472–76.

38. In this respect, see Hilpert to Weilnböck, 12 January 1924, as well as the minutes of the BLB executive committee, 29 November 1923, both in BA Koblenz, NL Weilnböck, 5b.

39. Bayerische Mittelpartei, "Positive deutschvölkische Arbeit," n.d., appended to Otto to Westarp, 26 April 1924, NL Westarp, Gärtringen, VN 49.

40. For a detailed analysis of the BMP's losses in the 1924 Bavarian state elections, see Elina Kiiskinen, *Die Deutschnationale Volkspartei in Bayern (Bayerische Mittelpartei) in der Regierungspolitik des Freistaats während der Weimarer Zeit* (Munich: C. H. Beck, 2005), 244–48. On relations between the BMP and BLB in the first years of the Weimar Republic, see Manfred Kittel, "Zwischen völkischem Fundamentalismus und gouvernementaler Taktik. DNVP-Vorsitzender Hans Hilpert und die bayerischen

Deutschnationalen," *Zeitschrift für bayerische Landesgeschichte* 59 (1996): 849–901, here 974–77.

41. Hergt to the members of the DNVP executive committee, 8 April 1924, NL Westarp, Gärtringen, VN 44. For further information on the Tirpitz candidacy, see Raffael Scheck, *Alfred von Tirpitz and German Right-Wing Politics, 1914–1930* (Atlantic Highlands, NJ: Humanities Press, 1998), 144–50.

42. On the general contours of the DNVP's campaign in the May 1924 Reichstag elections, see Dirk Lau, *Wahlkämpfe der Weimarer Republik. Propaganda und Programme der politischen Parteien bei den Wahlen zum Deutschen Reichstag von 1924 bis 1930* (Marburg: Tectum Verlag, 2008), 265–70.

43. For further information on the antisemitism of the DNVP's Catholic wing, see the essay in this volume, chapter 8, by Ulrike Ehret. On the history of the RKA, see Larry Eugene Jones, "Catholics on the Right: The Reich Catholic Committee of the German National People's Party, 1920–33," *Historisches Jahrbuch* 126 (2006): 221–67, here 223–30.

44. For the reaction of the racists to the DNVP's gains in the May 1924 elections and their plans to intensify the party's racist agitation in the post-election period, see the circular from Gräf-Thüringen to the members of the DNVP's National Racist Committee and its regional affiliates throughout the country, 23 May 1924, BA Berlin, R 8048, 223/57.

45. In this respect, see the long letter from Freytagh-Loringhoven to Goldacker, 12 September 1924, in the unpublished Nachlaß of Otto Schmidt-Hannover, Bundesarchiv Koblenz, 34. For further indication of right-wing frustration with the direction in which the DNVP seemed to be headed, see the correspondence between Kriping and the Pan-German leadership, 19–29 October 1924, BA Berlin, R 8048, 210/94–95, 107, as well as Vietinghoff-Scheel to Gebsattel, 20 October 1924, BA Berlin, R 8048, 210/97, and Claß to Mündler, 1 November 1924, BA Berlin, R 8048, 210/110.

46. For a fuller explication of Westarp's views on the Jewish question, see Stefan Malinowski, "Kuno Graf von Westarp—ein *missing link* im preußischen Adel. Anmerkungen zur Einordnung eines untypischen Grafen," in *"Ich bin der letzte Preuße"*, ed. Jones and Pyta, 9–32, esp. 17–20; and Karl J. Mayer, "Kuno Graf von Westarp als Kritiker des Nationalsozialismus," ibid., 190–216, esp. 200–203; as well as the essay in this volume, chapter 2, by Daniela Gasteiger.

47. See in particular the minutes of the DNVP's Racist National Committee, 5 July 1925, BA Berlin, R 8005, 361/193–94, also in BA Berlin, R 8048, 223/74–76. On the inner-party controversy surrounding the DNVP's participation in the first Luther cabinet, see Manfred Dörr, "Die Deutschnationale Volkspartei 1925 bis 1928" (PhD diss., Universität Marburg, 1964), 93–110; and Ohnezeit, *DNVP in der Weimarer Republik*, 285–90.

48. In this respect, see the resolution adopted by the executive committee of the DNVP's Racist National Committee, 22 October 1925, NL Westarp, Gärtringen, VN 55, also in BA Berlin, R 8048, 223/96. On the DNVP's fight against the Locarno accords and its resignation from the national

government in October 1925, see Dörr, "Deutschnationale Volkspartei," 134–211.

49. On the founding and history of the DNVP's National Women's Committee, see Annagrete Lehmann, "Ziel und Entwicklung der deutschnationalen Frauenarbeit," in *Der nationale Wille*, ed. Weiß, 319–36. For further details, see Andrea Süchting-Hänger, *"Gewissen der Nation." Nationales Engagement und politisches Handeln konservativer Frauenorganisationen 1900 bis 1937* (Düsseldorf: Droste, 2002), 127–43; and Raffael Scheck, "German Conservatism and Female Political Activism in the Early Weimar Republic," *German History* 15 (1997): 34–55; as well as the recent study by Christiane Streubel, *Radikale Nationalistinnen. Agitation und Programmatik rechter Frauen in der Weimarer Republik* (Frankfurt and New York: Campus Verlag, 2006), 107–16.

50. On the DNVP's appeal to women voters in the 1920 elections, see Julia Sneeringer, *Winning Women's Votes: Propaganda and Politics in Weimar Germany* (Chapel Hill, NC, and London: University of North Carolina Press, 2002), 42–51. For further details, see Süchting-Hänger, *"Gewissen der Nation"*, 143–49.

51. See the discussion of the Gierke affair in Süchting-Hänger, *"Gewissen der Nation"*, 208–10.

52. On cooperation between the DNVP's National Women's Committee and Racist National Committee, see the word of acknowledgement by Freytagh-Loringhoven at the meeting of the DNVP's Racist National Committee, 7 July 1928, BA Berlin, 8005, 392/5.

53. For example, see Tiling, "Leitsätze zur völkischen Frage," n.d., BA Berlin, NL Mumm, 356/1.

54. In this respect, see Süchting-Hänger, *"Gewissen der Nation"*, 270–74. In a similar vein, see Raffael Scheck, *Mothers of the Nation: Right-Wing Women in Weimar Germany* (Oxford and New York: Berg Publishers, 2004), 85–106.

55. On the Pan-German plans to gain control of the DNVP, see Claß's remarks at the meeting of the ADV managing committee as well as the document "Richtlinien zur dezentralen Beeinflussung der DNVP," 26–27 November 1927, BA Berlin, R 8048, 152/19–25. See also Jackisch, *Pan-German League*, 146–53, and Hofmeister, "Between Monarchy and Dictatorship," 269–89.

56. For the racists' reaction to the 1928 election results, see the protocol of the meeting of the DNVP's Racist National Committee, 7 July 1928, BA Berlin, R 8005, 392/5–7. On the Nationalist losses in the 1928 Reichstag elections, see the analysis in Dörr, "Deutschnationale Volkspartei," 387–90.

57. For Westarp's account of the developments on 8–9 July 1928, see his memorandum to the chairmen of the DNVP state and provincial organizations, 12 July 1928, NL Westarp, II/30.

58. Freytagh-Loringhoven, "Nicht große, sondern starke Rechte," *Der Tag*, 25 July 1928, no. 177.

59. On Hugenberg's election to the DNVP party chairmanship, see John A. Leopold, "The Election of Alfred Hugenberg as Chairman of the German National People's Party," *Canadian Journal of History* 7 (1972): 149–71; as well

as the relevant chapters of Dörr, "Deutschnationale Volkspartei," 410–65. Heidrun Holzbach, *Das "System Hugenberg". Die Organisation bürgerlicher Sammlungspolitik vor dem Aufstieg der NSDAP* (Stuttgart: Deutsche Verlags-Anstalt, 1981), 192–253; Ohnezeit, *DNVP in der Weimarer Republik*, 425–28; and Hofmeister, "Between Monarchy and Dictatorship," 290–98.

60. In this respect, see Thomas Mergel, "Das Scheitern des deutschen Tory-Konservatismus. Die Umformung der DNVP zu einer rechtsradikalen Partei 1928–1932," *Historische Zeitschrift* 276 (2003): 323–68. For further details, see Larry Eugene Jones, "German Conservatism at the Crossroads: Count Kuno von Westarp and the Struggle for Control of the DNVP, 1928–30," *Contemporary European History* 18 (2009): 147–77.

61. In this respect, see the programmatic article by Claß, "Alldeutsche Ziele für Deutschlands Rettung," *Deutschlands Erneuerung. Monatsschrift für das deutsche Volk* 12, no. 10 (October 1928): 575–80.

62. On the question of Quaatz's ancestry, see the introduction by Hermann Weiß and Paul Hoser, ed., *Die Deutschnationalen und die Zerstörung der Weimarer Republik. Aus dem Tagebuch von Reinhold Quaatz 1928–1933* (Munich: Oldenbourg, 1989), 19–20. On Hugenberg's views on the Jewish question, see John A. Leopold, *Alfred Hugenberg: The Radical Nationalist Campaign against the Weimar Republic* (New Haven, CT, and London: Yale University Press 1977), 22.

63. For a clear statement of the anti-Marxist line the DNVP adopted at the Kassel congress, see Alfred Hugenberg, *Klare Front zum Freiheitskampf. Rede auf dem 9. Reichsparteitag der Deutschnationalen Volkspartei am 22. November 1929*, Deutschnationale Flugschrift, no. 339 (Berlin: Deutschnationale Schriftenvertriebsstelle, 1929). In a similar vein, see Otto Schmidt-Hannover, *Frontgeneration und Jugend im Freiheitskampf gegen den Marxismus. Rede, gehalten auf dem 9. Reichs-Partei-Tage der D.N.V.P. in Kassel am 23. November 1929* (Berlin: Brunnen-Verlag, 1929); and Karl Veidt, *Der Kulturkampf unserer Zeit: Christentum und Marxismus. Rede, gehalten auf dem 9. Reichsparteitag der Deutschnationalen Volkspartei in Kassel am 22. November 1929*, Deutschnationale Flugschrift, no. 338 (Berlin: Deutschnationale Schriftenvertriebsstelle, 1929).

64. "Kein dritter Tributplan! Rede Hugenbergs in Detmold," *Unsere Partei* 10, no. 2 (15 January 1932): 10–11.

65. For example, see the report of Hugenberg's speeches before the DNVP party representation and party executive committee, 25 July 1930, in *Unsere Partei* 8, no. 15 (1 August 1930): 461–63; and in the Berlin Sportpalast, 14 August 1930, *Unsere Partei* 8, no. 16 (15 August 1930): 197–201.

66. In this respect, see the report of Hugenberg's speech at the DNVP Reich leadership conference in Berlin, 25–26 June 1932, in *Unsere Partei* 10, no. 13 (1 July 1932): 167–70. For the most far-reaching Nationalist attack against the NSDAP in the campaign for the July 1932 Reichstag elections, see Ewald von Kleist-Schmenzin, *Der Nationalsozialismus—eine Gefahr*, Als Manuskript gedruckt (Berlin: Deutsche Verlagsgesellschaft, 1932).

67. For example, see Irmgard Wrede, *Deutschnationale und Nationalsozialisten. Die Unterschiede auf wirtschafts- und sozialpolitischem Gebiete. Vortrag gehalten am 12. Juni 1932 auf der Tagung des erweiterten Reichsfrauenausschusses der D.N.V.P.*, Deutschnationale Flugschrift, no. 365 (Berlin: Deutschnationale Schriftenvertriebsstelle, 1932); and Anton Scheibe, *DNVP und NSDAP. Was uns einigt und was uns trennt*, Deutschnationale Flugschrift, no. 367 (Berlin: Deutschnationale Schriftenvertriebsstelle, 1932).

68. R. G. Quaatz and Paul Bang, eds., *Das deutschnationale Freiheits-Program*, mit einem Vorwort von Alfred Hugenberg (Berlin: Deutschnationale Schriftenvertriebsstelle, 1932).

69. In this respect, see Axel von Freytagh-Loringhoven, *Nationale Außenpolitik. Rede gehalten auf der Reichsführertagung der DNVP. zu Berlin, am 25. Juni 1932*, Deutschnationale Flugschrift, no. 369 (Berlin: Deutschnationale Schriftenvertriebsstelle, 1932); and Paul Bang, *Sozialpolitik*, Deutschnationale Flugschrift, no. 364 (Berlin: Deutschnationale Schriftenvertriebsstelle, 1932). For a record of the conference, see *Unsere Partei* 10, no. 13 (1 July 1932): 167–73.

70. There is nothing in the historical record that sheds light on how the Nationalists constructed their campaign for the July 1932 Reichstag elections or why they chose to avoid the racist issue in their articulation of the DNVP's campaign objectives. This is not to say that the DNVP's district and local organizations or their auxiliaries in the regional agrarian organizations did not resort to anti-Semitic rhetoric and imagery in their efforts to mobilize the conservative electorate, but this does not seem to have been consistent with the general outlines of the campaign orchestrated by the DNVP party leadership. The recent article by Manfred Kittel, "'Steigbügelhalter' Hitlers oder 'stille Republikaner'? Die Deutschnationalen in neuer politikgeschichtlicher und kulturalistischer Perspektive," in *Geschichte der Politik. Alte und neue Wege*, ed. Hans-Christof Kraus and Thomas Nicklas, Historische Zeitschrift, Beiheft 44 (Munich: Oldenbourg, 2007), 201–35, rightly stresses the persistent strength of *völkisch* and antisemitic sentiment at the local and regional levels of the DNVP party organization, as does the study of the DNVP's Württemberg affiliate by Hans Peter Müller, "Die Bürgerpartei/Deutschnationale Volkspartei (DNVP) in Württemberg 1918–1933. Konservative Politik und die Zerstörung der Weimarer Republik," *Zeitschrift für Württembergische Landesgeschichte* 61 (2002): 374–433, esp. 378–79, 391–96.

71. Alfred Milatz, "Das Ende der Parteiein im Spiegel der Wahlen 1930 bis 1933," in *Das Ende der Parteien 1933*, ed. Erich Matthias and Rudolf Morsey (Düsseldorf: Droste, 1960), 743–93, here 772.

72. For example, see Heinz Franke, *Die Partei der "Köpfe"*, Kampfschrift Heft 22, Broschürenreihe der Reichspropaganda-Leitung der NSDAP (Munich: Franz Eher Verlag, 1932), 11–12. For an indication of Nationalist sensitivity on this issue, see Schmidt-Hannover to Hugenberg, 5 September 1932, in the unpublished Nachlaß of Alfred Hugenberg, Bundesarchiv Koblenz, 38/274–76, and the memorandum of a conversation between Hugenberg

and other DNVP party leaders, 8 September 1932, in the unpublished Nachlaß of Reinhold Quaatz, Bundersarchiv Koblenz, 17.

73. In this vein, see Porembsky, "Der völkische Gedanke in der DNVP," *Unsere Partei* 10, no 17 (1 September 1932): 259–60. For further details, see Mosse, "Die deutsche Rechte und die Juden," 228.

74. In this respect, see the brochure by the Berlin cathedral pastor and DNVP Reichstag deputy Bruno Döhring, *Die Fehlleitung der nationalen Bewegung durch Adolf Hitler. Aus seiner Weltanschauung erklärt* (Berlin: Buchdruckerei Gutenberg, n.d. [1932]), 3–5.

75. For the thrust and tone of the Nationalist campaign, see the report of Hugenberg's speech at a DNVP rally in the Berlin Sportpalast, 3 November 1932, in *Der Tag*, 5 November 1932, no. 206.

76. For a detailed reconstruction of the negotiations that led to the formation of the Hitler cabinet from the perspective of Hugenberg and the DNVP party leadership, see Larry Eugene Jones, "'The Greatest Stupidity of My Life': Alfred Hugenberg and the Formation of the Hitler Cabinet, January 1933," *Journal of Contemporary History* 27 (1992): 63–87.

77. In this respect, see the entry in Quaatz's diary, 30 January and 1 February 1933, in *Die Deutschnationalen und die Zerstörung der Weimarer Republik*, ed. Weiß and Hoser, 229–31.

78. For further details, see Klaus Peter Hoepke, "Die Kampffront Schwarz-Weiß-Rot. Zum Scheitern des national-konservativen 'Zähmungs'-Konzepts an den Nationalsozialisten im Frühjahr 1933," *Fridericiana. Zeitschrift der Universität Karlsruhe* 36 (1984): 34–52.

79. Papen, "Die Sammlung der christlich-konservativen Kräfte," *Die Kampffront. Pressedienst der Kampffront Schwarz-Weiß-Rot* 1, no. 7 (1 March 1933): 1–2.

80. Hermann Beck, "Between the Dictates of Conscience and Political Expediency: Hitler's Conservative Alliance Partner and Antisemitism during the Nazi Seizure of Power," *Journal of Contemporary History* 41 (2006): 611–40.

81. Nagel to DNVP, Landesverband Berlin, 27 March 1933, BA Berlin R 8005, 48/125, cited in Beck, "Between the Dictates," 639. For an elaboration of the DNVP's position on the Jewish question, see Nagel to the DNVP, Landesverband Pommern, 23 March 1933, BA Berlin, R 8005, 48/138–39.

82. Nagel to Fuch, 14 May 1933, BA Berlin, R 8005, 48/25, cited in Beck, "Between the Dictates," 639.

83. On the DNVP's fate in the first six months of the Third Reich, see Hermann Beck, "Konflikte zwischen Deutschnationalen und Nationalsozialisten während der Machtergreifung," *Historische Zeitschrift* 292 (2011): 645–80.

84. Gerhard Ritter, *Carl Goerdeler und die deutsche Widerstandsbewegung* (Stuttgart: Deutsche Verlags-Anstalt, 1954), 60.

4

ACADEMICS AND RADICAL NATIONALISM
The Pan-German League in Hamburg and the German Reich
Rainer Hering

What do Georg von Below, Ernst Haeckel, Karl Lamprecht, Franz von Lenbach, Alfred Lichtwark, Baron Hans von Liebig, Dietrich Schäfer, Reinhold Seeberg and Max Weber all have in common? They were all academics and belonged, if only briefly, to the extreme nationalistic Pan-German League (Alldeutscher Verband or ADV) at some point in its existence from 1891 to 1939. To be sure, many of them have never been recognized or thought of as Pan-Germans. Still, by virtue of the prominent social status they held and the role they played as professors, teachers, physicians, jurists, lawyers, journalists, and writers in the dissemination of ideas and culture, they exercised enormous influence in the public arena and contributed in no small measure to the spread of Pan-German ideas in broad sectors of the German population.

Since its founding in 1890–91 the Pan-German League demanded the far-reaching expansion of the German Empire in central Europe as well as the establishment of an overseas colonial empire. At the same time, the ADV called for the suppression of foreign and racially alien influences on Germany's national life. "Germany for the Germans [Deutschland den Deutschen]!" was the slogan that lay at the heart of the Bamberg Declaration from 1919 in which the Pan-German League proclaimed its radical antisemitic program for the postwar period.[1] Not only did the Pan-Germans play a major role—at least intellectually—in setting Germany's path to World War I, but central elements of its ideology were subsequently taken over and translated into practice by the National Socialists. There were far reaching and profound points of contact between the Pan-Germans and the National Socialists—ideological, personal, and financial. One might even go so far as to argue that the Pan-German League provided the "intellectual spark" that first prepared Germany's political landscape for the reception of racist thought. In this respect, its effects can hardly be overemphasized.

In point of fact, no other organization played a more important role in making racist thought acceptable, or *salonfähig*, or in implanting it in the ranks of Germany's academic elites than the ADV. From here, Pan-German ideas spread throughout the broader population. A closer investigation of its organization and its ideology will thus offer new insights into the nature of extreme nationalism and its acceptance in the German bourgeoisie between the German Empire and the Third Reich.

In the following essay the role of academics in the Pan-German League will be examined with respect to three general questions. First, what made the ADV so attractive for German academics? Second, what opportunities did they have to shape the political culture and society of the German Empire and Weimar Republic? And, third, exactly how were they able to accomplish this as individual historical agents? These three questions will be answered in part through a careful investigation of the ADV's second largest local organization or *Ortsgruppe*, namely that in the Hanseatic city of Hamburg. Not only are the source materials for an investigation of Pan-German activities in Hamburg extremely rich and varied, but the city's increasing importance in the political and economic life of the German Empire and its role in international trade underscore both the desirability and value of such an undertaking. Moreover, the study of the Pan-Germans in Hamburg offers a particularly striking example of the way in which conservative academics responded to what they perceived as the threat of modernity. With the collapse of the Second Empire the Hanseatic city began a profound and dramatic transformation in the areas of technical and economic modernization. The city's profile changed rapidly as its population reached a million in the first years of the Weimar Republic. At the same time, the introduction of a democratic franchise transformed the fabric of Hamburg political life by ending the domination of the bourgeois *Honoratioren* who had controlled city affairs since the end of the middle ages and by greatly increasing the opportunities of women and those with lower incomes to participate directly in the political life of the city.[2]

Notwithstanding the prominent role that commerce and international trade enjoyed in Hamburg's profile as a city, academics too were becoming increasingly important as a part of the urban landscape as education received more and more attention. In addition to a comprehensive, differentiated, and recently reformed public school system, Hamburg offered a rich array of educational opportunities for the city's adult population. The University of Hamburg was founded in 1919, and in 1926 it was given the task of preparing and certifying those who sought to teach in the city's school system. As a result, teachers in the public schools were also required to complete a university education.[3] All of this greatly enhanced the role and influence of academics in the cultural and political life of Weimar Hamburg.

The Pan-German League in the German Empire and Weimar Republic

"Remember that you are a German [Gedenke, daß Du ein Deutscher bist]!" —this had been the mantra of the Pan-German League from the very beginning of its existence. From its founding in 1890–91 as the Universal German League (Allgemeiner Deutscher Verband) until its dissolution in 1939, the Pan-German League was one of the most influential political lobbies in the German Empire and remained so throughout the Weimar Republic. Even though its membership never exceeded 50,000, the social and professional prominence of those whom it had recruited from the ranks of Germany's educated and propertied elites—professors, secondary school teachers, jurists, and physicians—greatly magnified the ADV's influence throughout German society. Nowhere was this more apparent than in politics. Moreover, the fact that a number of other organizations had affiliated themselves with the ADV as corporate members gave it another 150,000 followers who presumably shared some, if not all, of its political and ideological objectives. As a result, the Pan-German League assumed a central role in the public discourse of the various organizations on Germany's extreme Right from 1890 well into the twentieth century that enabled it to exercise a persistent, though imperceptible, influence upon the bureaucracy and state policy.[4]

The Pan-German League constituted an essential organizational and ideological component of the *völkisch* movement from the last decades of the Second Empire to the Third Reich.[5] At the same time, it formed an important connection between the nationalism of the Second Empire, the *völkisch* movement, and National Socialism. It contributed decisively to the dissemination and social respectability of antisemitic, racist, and *völkisch*-nationalist ideas and left a profound imprint upon the conglomeration of ideas that lay at the core of the National Socialist ideology. The Pan-German League was the most influential and effective representative of the so-called old nationalism of right-wing *Honoratioren* that continued to influence Germany's educated bourgeoisie for nearly fifty years despite the two great caesura of Germany's national history in 1918–19 and 1933. At the same time, the ADV was receptive to the "new" and more radical nationalism of the postwar period and contributed in no small measure to its spread during the Weimar Republic. The Pan-Germans thus served as a link or mediator between the two forms of German nationalism, the "old" and the "new."[6]

Around the Pan-German League there developed a thick network of institutional and personal connections. The ADV was thus a prototype for the close bond that developed between nationalism, anti-feminism, antisemitism, anti-parliamentarism, and anti-Slavism to become the defining characteristic of the radical Right in the Weimar Republic. These attitudes were all rooted in the rejection of the emancipatory impulses and consequences of the modern age and were part of a fundamental crisis that brought into question the identity of German educated bourgeois males. The goal of Pan-German discourse was the stabilization—or, more accurately, restabilization—of the social and economic supremacy of the educated bourgeoisie and of male primacy in the family and society. This would take place through a return to premodern and autocratic forms of domination.

The concept of the nation lies at the heart of a nation's political culture as well as the internal structure of its state. The Pan-German construct of the German state thus helped shape the way in which the ADV conceived of itself and its mission in the Wilhelmine and Weimar periods. Of relevance here is not just the way in which the ADV defined the external boundaries of the imagined Pan-German Reich, with its correlates of a unified economic region under German hegemony and a greatly expanded German colonial empire, but also how the status of those who lived inside this area was to be determined, that is to say, who would be allowed to participate and who would be excluded as a *Reichsfeind* or allowed to remain but only in a subordinate status with limited rights. Excluded from any sort of meaningful role in the administration and leadership of this Reich would be first of all women, Jews, and members of other races as well as the Communists, Social Democrats, Democrats, Catholics, and those national and regional minorities such as the Poles, Alsatians, Danes, and Guelfs who refused to submit to the Pan-Germans' national centralism but insisted on preserving their own national identity. At the same time, the Pan-German concept of the state would determine who would exercise influence within the Reich. This would be reserved first and foremost to those representatives of Germany's educated and propertied bourgeoisie that formed the social basis of the Pan-German movement. Income levels, property, education, and social influence were the criteria that the Pan-Germans adopted in defiant opposition to the concepts of equality and equal rights celebrated by the democratic ethos of nineteenth and early twentieth centuries.

After 1919 the Pan-German concept of the state with its racial and antisemitic elements underwent further radicalization. The concept "national" was replaced by *"völkisch."* The goal was now the establishment of a racial dictatorship through either the restoration of the monarchy or the installation of a leader who enjoyed the blessing of the Pan-Germans. To the outside world this would be justified as a concrete step toward the "rebirth" of the German nation after the defeat of 1918. Together with the "Stab-in-the-Back Legend," this ideology sought to compensate for the bitter defeat that Germany had suffered despite the valiant sacrifices of its people and to concentrate the nation's energies on the struggle for a revision of Versailles and the destruction of Germany's fledgling republican system. To accomplish these ends all means were justified. The Pan-Germans further insisted that the appropriate racial composition of the German population and the cultivation of a racial consciousness among the Germans were essential prerequisites for Germany's inner renewal.[7]

During the Weimar Republic the German National People's Party (Deutschnationale Volkspartei or DNVP) was profoundly influenced and ideologically saturated by Pan-German ideas until Alfred Hugenberg (1865–1951), one of the ADV's founding fathers, assumed the DNVP party chairmanship in 1928 and began to translate the ADV's radical demands into political practice.[8] Still, the Pan-Germans refrained from identifying themselves too closely with any particular party constellation for fear that this would weaken national unity. Nevertheless, there followed a period of close cooperation with the parties of the German Right in an attempt to gain a measure of influence over the legislative process. In this respect, however, the behavior of the Pan-Germans only reflected the all too familiar topos of conservative *Überparteilichkeit*, under the mantle of which conservative organizations had sought to pursue their own highly partisan interests. The ideology of *Überparteilichkeit* was particularly popular among academics, who used it to justify their own claim to leadership. But in the final analysis this ideology constituted a heavy burden on Weimar democracy and the Weimar party state.[9]

The Pan-Germans regarded the Second German Empire of 1871 as an incomplete national state that failed in its efforts to unite the entire German nation. As ethnic nationalists, they defined the nation as an "ethnic nation" or *Volksnation*, whereby over time the concept of the "cultural nation" or *Kulturnation"* played a much less significant role. *"Volk"* was a central category of Pan-German thought, which was defined through the German language, culture, tradition, history, and since the second decade of the twentieth century by race. It was the aim of the Pan-German League to establish a *völkisch* German national state in order to complete the task that had only been partially completed with the founding of the Second German Empire. Lastly, the Pan-Germans sought to establish a central European empire that would be complemented by overseas colonies. This would require mobilizing the German minorities living abroad as well as building up the strength of the German military. After 1919, however, as the ADV concentrated its energies on the struggle against democracy and for the revision of Versailles, these and other aspects of the Pan-German program retreated into the background.[10]

The close connection between gender, citizenship, and nation played a particularly important role in the Pan-German concept of the nation. In the Pan-German nation women would play a subordinate role in German public life and would be limited in their own area of activity to the private sphere of the family. The increasing politicization and democratization of women, particularly in the Weimar Republic, made a complete return to the way things had been beforehand all but impossible. Women would therefore be granted limited space in the public arena that over time would be reduced little by little. Although women had become increasingly involved in the ADV itself, only in exceptional cases were they able to achieve positions of influence.[11]

The Pan-German concept of the nation was constructed so that the elements of this construction and the manner in which they were combined with each other were largely invisible. Alongside the "soft" or *weiche* elements such as the common history, the collective memory, the shared recollections and myths, the single language, and narratives that imparted a sense of identity and that played a decisive function in Pan-German thought throughout the Wilhelmine Empire, there emerged since the eve of the World War I and above all in the Weimar Republic a "harder" fundamentalism that took precedence over everything else, namely, the notion that "blood" or "race" constituted the essence of the Pan-German nation.[12] After the military defeat of 1918 this factor became the sole determining factor for the Pan-German concept of the nation and its rebirth after the humiliation of Versailles. This represented a dramatic radicalization of ADV's profile, a process that had already begun with the assumption of the ADV chairmanship by Heinrich Claß in 1908, that had manifested itself in the prewar period after the 1912 Reichstag elections, and that culminated in the adoption of the Bamberg Declaration in 1919.[13]

Pan-German nationalism was inseparable from antisemitism. Arguing from a historical frame of reference, the Pan-Germans depicted Jews as the source of everything that threatened the German way of life, as the embodiment of all the negative features and tendencies of German society. In the Pan-German view of the world, it was the very essence of "the Jew," resting as it did in the role that "the Jew" played in international commerce throughout the world since the beginning of the modern era, who was responsible for all of the negative social and political developments with which those of German blood now found themselves confronted. Pan-German antisemitism was thus rooted in a profoundly conspiratorial view of history that saw "the Jew" as the all-powerful agent of social, economic, and political change who, from his secure position behind the scenes, was pulling the strings to which the rest of the world danced. For the Pan-German League "the Jew" personified the very counteridentity of what it meant to be German. The ADV thus provided a simplified explanation of what was happening in the world as well as a measure of security and constancy in both the individual and collective identity formation during a period a rapid social change and uncertainty. For the Pan-Germans it was never a question of returning to premodern social models from the time before the Enlightenment and Jewish emancipation but rather one of looking everywhere for "the hidden Jew" in the increasingly more complicated and rapidly changing social, economic, and life models of the modern era. In order to render complex social transformations palpable and explicable for the ordinary person, it is necessary to identify a concrete person or group as being responsible for that which is to be rejected. For this reason the Pan-Germans projected the negative attributes of a vague and incomprehensibly abstract notion of the modern on the Jews as the group responsible for these changes and declared them guilty. Thus, for the Pan-Germans "the Jew"—the homeless and rootless international and cosmopolitan Ahasver—embodied all of that which in the modern age was subverting inherited traditions and values and thus became the counteridentity to what the Pan-Germans hailed as the essence of one's personal and national identity. From this perspective, the Jews were not simply a rival minority entity with which the nation was in conflict but a counterentity for which there was no space whatsoever because of the very threat they posed to the ADV's own conception of the German *Volk*. The true cause of the decline and fall of the German nation was, in Pan-German parlance, "the corruption [*Zersetzung*] of Jewish blood and Jewish spirit." To counter the destructive force of Jewish blood and Jewish spirit, the rigid worldview of the Pan-Germans offered the fiction of social harmony and homogeneity, something that presupposed not only ethnic unity but the dissolution of all social and political contradictions.

Academics in the Pan-German League

Academics were prominently represented in the Pan-German League. An analysis of the social composition of the ADV membership shows that the majority of its members stemmed from the urban bourgeois middle class for which education and property were typical signs of social privilege. In 1901 approximately half of its members were either academics or belonged to the liberal professions, a quarter businessmen, 15 percent industrialists and artisans, and 2 percent farmers.

Scarcely 2 percent of those who belonged to the ADV were of noble pedigree, while less than a percent of the ADV members came from the working class. More than a third of those who sat on the ADV managing committee possessed the doctorate. Of those who served as chairmen of the ADV's local chapters, 20 percent were either the owners or managers of industrial enterprises, a further 20 percent were businessmen or administrative employees, and more than half teachers, civil servants, doctors, and lawyers. Most had received academic training; many belong to the ranks of Germany's intellectual *Honoratioren*. More than anything else, they conceived of themselves as custodians of Germany's national culture. By virtue of their status and their role in the education of Germany's professional elites, they played a critical role in the dissemination of the *völkisch*-racist *Weltanschauung*. Through their activities the Pan-German League was able to spread its ideology throughout broad sectors of the German population.[14]

Table 4.1. Vocational Statistics of the ADV Membership for 1901

academic careers	5.899 (29.80 percent)
liberal professions (artists, teachers, civil servants)	4.022 (22.32 percent)
farmers	444 (2.24 percent)
businessmen	5.288 (26.71 percent)
industrialists and artisans	2.859 (14.44 percent)
Total Membership	19.796 (100 percent)

Source: Der Alldeutsche Verband im Jahre 1901 (Berlin, 1902), 20f. The categories used above were taken from this source. Of the ADV's 22,300 members 19,796 are included in these statistics. The percentages were calculated on the basis of these statistics.

At the turn of the century approximately a third of the ADV's local leaders were fifty-five years of age or older, while 60 percent had been born after 1850. For both groups the founding of the Second Empire was the formative experience in the development of their political worldview. If the first cohort may have been somewhat disappointed by the subsequent course of political developments, the younger cadre of ADV leaders, to which Heinrich Claß belonged, was more engaged in pursuit of the Pan-German cause. Even though most were too young to have taken an active part in the founding of the Second Empire, this event continued to play a central role in their memory and political self-awareness.

The geographical center of gravity for the Pan-German movement lay in the coastal cities of northwest Germany and in the predominantly National Liberal and Protestant part of central Germany that stretched from the Grand Duchy of Hesse through Thuringia and Prussian Saxony to the Kingdom of Saxony itself. In the Ruhr industrial basin there was also an intensive Pan-German presence in the cities of Düsseldorf, Duisburg, Bochum, and Essen. Particularly in the new large metropolitan centers one could find comparatively high numbers of civil servants and members of the educated bourgeoisie. In predominantly Catholic cities, on the other hand, the Pan-German League found little support. In Münster, for example, the local ADV chapter had no more than thirty-one members, and its activities were almost completely ignored by the local press. All together, the Pan-Germans found their strongest support in the Protestant-National Liberal milieu in central and northern Germany, while they never succeeded in developing a strong foothold in southern Germany, where the prevailing liberal-democratic climate, the specific confessional structure, and their latent hostility toward Catholics effectively thwarted their efforts.[15]

By virtue of office and authority the Pan-Germans possessed excellent resources for the dissemination of their ideals, if for no other reasons than the fact that in Germany, university professors enjoyed a particularly high reputation and social status.[16] The specific significance of the Pan-Germans lay in their function as influential and effective agents for the circulation of their ideas and values, which led to an ideological saturation of key nationalist positions.[17] Over the course of time the influence of academics in the ADV, particularly at the local level, became more and more apparent. Nowhere was this more so than in Hamburg. For academics the Pan-German League remained as attractive as ever, as the following statistics clearly reveal.[18]

An examination of the three surviving membership lists for the ADV's Hamburg chapter from 1897, 1901, and 1914 shows—something that is hardly surprising for a city like Hamburg—that at the outset merchants were most strongly represented. But the percentage of ADV members who belonged to the merchant class declined steadily from 69.7 percent in 1987 to 54.9 percent in 1901 and finally to 46.1 percent in 1914. In contrast, the percentage of those who described themselves as academics, including engineers but excluding civil servants and employees, increased at a steady rate from 15.9 percent in 1897 to 17.4 and 25.3 percent in 1901 and 1914 respectively. Among the academics, physicians and pharmacists constituted the largest numerical group, but over time their numbers steadily declined in relationship to other sectors of the academic community. For if in 1897, 48.3 of all those in the Hamburg ADV who could be defined as academics were physicians and pharmacists, by 1901 this had declined to 44.1 percent and to 31.5 percent by 1914 during a period of time when the overall membership of the Hamburg ADV continued to climb. In contrast, the number of jurists—judges and lawyers—and teachers increased dramatically. The percentage of jurists among the academics who belonged to the Hamburg ADV grew from 18.9 percent in 1897 to 22.8 percent in 1901 and 23.5 percent in 1914. By the same token, the percentage of teachers as a sector of the academic community that belonged to the Hamburg ADV remained more or less stagnant from 1897 to 1901 before shooting up from 15.2 in 1901 to 23.5 percent in 1914.

Table 4.2. Vocational Groups in the Hamburg ADV

	1897	1901	1914
merchants	884	458	295
artisans / independent middle class	53	50	47
manufacturers	30	35	33
technicians and engineers	23	19	30
physicians and pharmacists	97	64	51
judges	14	8	12
lawyers	24	25	26
teachers and university professors	33	22	38
pastors		10	7
civil servants	22	14	34
employees	16	19	6
retirees	17	7	2
others	41	24	7
unknown professional status	4	82	54
Total Membership Numbers	1,268	834	640

In Hamburg the Pan-German League developed more and more into an organization that was dominated by academics, while the percentage of the local membership that belonged to the merchant class continued to make up scarcely half of the members. Still, if one compares the social composition of the Hamburg chapter of the Pan-German League with that of the national organization, it becomes immediately clear that in Hamburg merchants were much more prominently represented than in the rest of the Reich. While they represented 26.71 percent of the membership in the ADV's national organization, in the Hanseatic cities they represented 63.87 percent, in Hamburg as high as 69.16 percent.[19] Physicians formed the second strongest professional group in the Hamburg ADV, followed by jurists and teachers.[20] All in all, this analysis only confirms the impression of an organization that was anchored in the educated and propertied bourgeoisie. Even then, however, one has to be careful not to extrapolate from the social structure of the Hamburg ADV that all of those who belonged to this milieu subscribed to the Pan-German ideology, particularly in view of the fact that left-liberalism was particularly well represented among Hamburg's teachers. There were other political cultures than Pan-Germanism in the Hamburg bourgeoisie.[21]

The Pan-Germans in Hamburg operated both directly and indirectly. The focal point of their direct activity in Hamburg lay in the direction of the annual Bismarck celebration as well as in evening lectures, or *Vortragsabende*, on selected political or historical topics that attracted as many as three thousand listeners and reached broad sectors of the Hamburg bourgeoisie through extensive press coverage. Even more important than the ADV's direct influence on the public arena through special events and publications was the indirect dissemination of the Pan-German ideology for the simple reason that it could not always be traced back to the ADV itself, namely, the activity of those who belonged to the ADV in leadership roles in the state and city, for example in the Hamburg city government, political parties, and other organizations. Many Pan-Germans were extremely influential in the formation of public opinion and had the ability to shape the behavior of individual persons quite effectively.[22]

A small number of Pan-Germans were also active as teachers in higher education. In Hamburg this meant that before the founding of the university in 1919 they had been active either in the reorganized Universal Lecture Course (Allgemeines Vorlesungswesen) that had been adopted as recently as 1895 or in the Hamburg Colonial Institute (Hamburgisches Kolonialinstitut). The ADV's Albrecht Krause

(1838–1902), well known as a specialist on Kant, held a lectureship at the former of these two institutions, while the long-time chairman of the Hamburg ADV Paul Winter, as well as Justus Strandes, another prominent Pan-German, gave lectures at the Colonial Institute. Professor Justus Hashagen (1877–1961), who held the chair for medieval and modern history at the University of Hamburg University beginning in 1925, was also a long-time member of the ADV. Similarly, the university lecturer for the history of war and military science at the University of Hamburg from 1933 to 1937 Alfred Schüz (1892–1957) had belonged to the Pan-German League from 1919 to 1925. Of international renown was the meteorologist and director of the German Marine Observatory (Deutsche Seewarte) in Hamburg Erwin Knipping (1844–1922), who was elected to the committee of the ADV's local chapter in 1895. No less famous was the port physician and founder of the famous institute for ship and tropical sicknesses that bore his name, Professor Bernhard Nocht (1857–1945), who had been a member of the Hamburg ADV since 1897.

Pan-German Antisemitism in the Academy: The Geographer Siegfried Passarge

Of the numerous academics that were affiliated with the Pan-German League in Hamburg, almost no one was more influential or prominent than the geographer Siegfried Passarge (1867–1958). Passarge served as a professor in Hamburg beginning in 1909 and was a member of the ADV's Hamburg chapter from at least 1914 on. In his life and academic career Passarge combined scholarly teaching and publication with radical Pan-German views, and he was the most vehement antisemite on the faculty at the newly founded University of Hamburg. Although the university was a creation of the fledgling Weimar Republic, the political views of the university faculty were predominantly conservative. In so far as party membership for the time in question can be established, the German People's Party (Deutsche Volkspartei or DVP) and DNVP led the way with 9.6 percent of all professors and university lecturers belonging to the DVP, 6.3 percent to the DNVP, 4.8 percent to the pro-republican German Democratic Party (Deutsche Demokratische Partei or DDP) or its successor the German State Party (Deutsche Staatspartei), and 2.2 percent to the Social Democratic Party (Sozialdemokratische Partei Deutschlands). Only two Social Democrats ever held the rank of full professor.[23] Antisemitic resentment was widespread throughout the university. As early as the summer of 1919 university students had attacked Jewish lecturers with leaflets and boycotts, and the complaints of the renowned Jewish psychologist Wilhelm Stern (1871–1938) about the boycotts were handled dismissively by the university administration. Passarge's own behavior was downplayed by university officials, who never censured him for his views or dissociated themselves from antisemitism as such.[24]

Who was Siegfried Passarge? Otto Karl Siegfried Passarge was born in Königsberg in 1866, the son of a district judge whose wife was the daughter of a local merchant. Having grown up in Königsberg and Interberg, Passarge went on to study medicine, geography, and geology in Berlin, Jena, and Freiburg im Breisgau. In 1890 he was awarded the doctorate in geology, and in 1892 he passed the state medical exam. As a physician and scholarly collaborator, Passarge took part in 1893–94 in the expedition to north Cameroons that led to the establishment of German control over the Cameroon hinterland. Subsequent research trips in the following years led him to South America, Algeria, and Egypt. In 1903 he completed his habilitation for geography in Berlin and two years later was appointed full professor in Breslau. From 1908 to 1919 Passarge was a professor on the staff of the Hamburg Colonial Institute and then at the University of Hamburg, where he served as director of the Geographical Institute until his retirement in 1935. In 1925 he was elected to the German Academy of Naturalists Leopoldina (Deutsche Akademie der Naturforscher Leopoldina). In 1958 he died in Bremen.[25] In terms of quantity alone, Passarge was an extraordinarily productive scholar. Between 1891 and 1955 he authored well over 350 publications, while his private papers contain a number of unpublished manuscripts. Many of his publications, however, lack a scholarly apparatus with references to the sources of his information.[26]

Siegfried Passarge was actively involved in the politics of the German Right. In addition to his activity in the Pan-German League, Passarge campaigned for a seat in the Hamburg Senate in 1927 as a politically unaffiliated candidate on the DNVP ticket. In 1933 he joined the NSDAP and succeeded in being accepted into the party despite a ban on new members through the personal intervention of Martin Bormann (1900–45). In July 1933 Passarge spoke at the university on "Nationale Revolution, Hochschulen und Judentum," described Hitler as God's gift to the German people, and stressed that the survival of Germany depended upon a solution to the Jewish problem. Not only was Passarge politically radical, but his statements resonated throughout the public.[27]

Nothing attracted more attention or provoked greater controversy than Passarge's lecture in the summer of 1927 on the theme

"Rassenkunde des deutschen Volkes und der Juden." Here one finds Passarge's well-known thesis: "If the grandfather is a Social Democrat, the father is a Communist party secretary and the son a convict," a statement that set off a great debate over academic freedom. Passarge had frequently criticized the "Jewish-Marxist atmosphere" at the University of Hamburg and had made remarks to this effect even during the Second Empire. For Passarge, Germany's defeat in World War I and the collapse of the Hohenzollern monarchy were the great traumas of his life. In his almost pathological search for the cause of these calamities Passarge focused upon the Jews as a universal scapegoat.[28] His antisemitism became even more vehement during the Weimar Republic as he began to formulate specific solutions to the Jewish question.[29] This was particularly apparent in 1928 when Passarge edited the translation of the antisemitic *Buch vom Kahal*.[30] In the following year Passarge published a more ambitious book with the title *Das Judentum als landschaftskundlich-ethnologisches Problem* with the J. F. Lehmann publishing house in Munich.[31] Ten years earlier Passarge had established landscape science, or *Landschaftskunde*, as an academic discipline, but this had never gained academic respectability and had been universally rejected with the exceptions of the geography faculty in Königsberg and Hamburg.

The uniqueness of Passarge's work lay in how it stressed the ways in which landscape and culture interacted with each other.[32] Publications in which Passarge supported a ban on the import of foodstuffs as a way of addressing the famine of surplus populations were cited more and more frequently in the contemporary press. By the same token, Passarge rejected vaccinations and measures to combat epidemics so as not to interfere with the process of natural selection and was equally adamant in his condemnation of social welfare programs that would soften the struggle for existence. Throughout all of this, Passarge used his academic status and authority as a university professor to win support for the practical applications of his personal ideology. Since he regarded pacifism as a "degenerative sign of domestication," Passarge deliberately sought confrontation and provoked conflict with his opponents in which he invariably exceeded his own competence. Until the end of his life racist, antisemitic, and social Darwinist views remained decisive. That, however, did not prevent the Faculty of Mathematics and Natural Sciences at the University of Hamburg from awarding him an honorary doctorate in 1957. In the official testimonial that was read in his honor, Passarge's studies in the field of cultural geography—and by implication all of the ideologically racist and personal assumptions that informed his work—were explicitly cited.[33]

Passarge's 1928 edition of the *Buch von Kahal* for Leipzig's openly antisemitic Hammer Publishing House under the direction of the notorious Jew-hater Theodor Fritsch (1852–1933)[34] published the minutes of the Jewish self-administration organization, or Kahal,[35] of Minsk from 1789 to 1828 that the Jewish convert to Russian Orthodoxy and occasional spy for Russia's political policy Jacob Brafmann had edited a Russian-language version in 1869 that had already been exposed as a forgery.[36] What Passarge wanted to prove with this publication was that the Kahal and the orthodox Jews who stood behind it wanted to support Jewish merchants to ruin the competition from Christians.[37] In December 1927 news of this publication led to Passarge's censure by two DDP deputies in the Hamburg Senate, Dr. Max Eichholz (1881–1943) and Curt Albert Platen (1872–1941).[38] In their statement to the Senate the two Democrats stressed that

> the contents [of the book] left no doubt that by its publication Professor Dr. Passarge could only have been led by the wish to incite antisemitic feeling. The way in which the editor brought ancient and outmoded conditions in Russia together with current conditions both outside Russia and in Germany shows that he places little stock in scholarly objectivity. The "research" and teaching methods of Professor Dr. Passarge may be appropriate to disgrace the University of Hamburg in the eyes of all those who do not understand how a man with such opinions can serve as a respectable professor of geography.

The Senate, however, emphasized the principle of academic freedom, and the university authorities refused to introduce disciplinary proceedings against Passarge for his extreme views.[39]

Siegfried Passarge used his authority as a scholar to lend his antisemitic views legitimacy and emphasis. He claimed to investigate Jewry as a scientific and ethnological problem and insisted that his opinions were objective and based on the results of scholarly research.[40] In point of fact, however, he rarely paid attention to the current state of research and chose not to engage those few who actually mentioned his works. This was particularly true in the case of "Das Buch vom Kahal."[41]

Hamburg's most prominent Jewish citizen, the Chief Rabbi Joseph Carlebach (1883–1942), subjected Passarge's book to a devastating critique in which he confirmed in painstaking detail the same scholarly shortcomings and errors that the two DDP deputies Eichholz and Platen had complained about before the Hamburg Senate. In a sixteen-page brochure from February 1928 Carlebach attacked Passarge's scholarship with particular reference to the motives that stood behind his scholarly posture.[42]

Not only did Carlebach point out serious errors in the translation of the text, but he proved that the protocol as a whole constituted a forgery even though individual parts of it may have been based on original communal documents. Carlebach's final verdict was that Passarge's edition of the Kahal was not a product of academic integrity but of the author's own antisemitic prejudices and intentions.

The Pan-German Appeal for Academics

What attracted academics to the Pan-German League? Why were men who had been trained in the highest standards of scholarship, work methods, and argumentation and who were fully capable of rational thought as well as comprehensive and nuanced modes of analysis attracted to an organization whose very ideology stood diametrically opposed to these skills and dispositions?

The mental attitude of the Pan-Germans was rooted in the rejection of the emancipatory elements and consequences of the modern age and was above all else an expression of a fundamental identity crisis of Germany's male bourgeois educated elites. In the wake of industrialization and modernization in all of their multifold forms and manifestations the position of Germany's educated elites, the so-called *Bildungsbürgertum*, became increasingly insecure. Life itself seemed more and more opaque, complicated, and impersonal. As international developments began to play an increasingly important role in shaping the contours of German life, traditional values lost much of their meaning as time and time again leadership positions that had once rested on education and culture were brought into question and pushed to the periphery by the performance principle. In place of education based upon the classical humanist model of the nineteenth century, technical and practical intelligence became more and more important. Within the framework of the process of professionalization, specialization and expertise in a single subject became more important than what Hans-Ulrich Wehler called the "traditional ideal of the educated generalist [*überlieferte Generalisten-Ideal der Gebildeten*]." Since the 1880s an ideological differentiation that saw nationalism, social Darwinism, antisemitism, imperialism, monism, and a faith in the natural sciences move to the foreground undermined the self-image and self-confidence of the Germany's educated bourgeoisie. Economic opportunities in the world of scholarship—for example, the means to finance a high lifestyle by scholarly publications—completely collapsed. In the aftermath of World War I many academics suffered the loss of their fortunes through the government's inability to repay its war debt and the runaway inflation of the early 1920s. As a result, not only had the social status but also the economic circumstances in which academics lived deteriorated, something that the decline in purchasing power by two-thirds of what it had been in the prewar period clearly reflected. On the other hand, the economically more successful elements of the German bourgeoisie, the so-called *Wirtschaftsbürgertum*, gained in importance and emerged as a social competitor of the academic bourgeoisie. This, in turn, only intensified the search of the academic bourgeoisie for a new source of meaning and value that would stabilize its importance and self-image, whereby a purely materialistic point of view was roundly rejected. What academics sought was something that would compensate for what they perceived as the deformations of the modern age in the process of social leveling, the absorption of the individual in an anonymous mass, and the loss of easily comprehensible connections and structures as well as the general disdain for bourgeois norms of behavior.[43]

The Pan-German League afforded Germany's bourgeois academic elites an opportunity to protest the changes that were taking place in the world around them without any responsibility for actually changing them and in this way reinvested their own lives with value and purpose. The Pan-German League offered clear, simple, and catchy explanations that held specific individuals or groups responsible for the profound and virtually inexplicable changes that were associated with the passage to the modern age. Above all, Jews and international conspiracies of whatever kind were blamed for these changes. At the same time, the Pan-German League with its various proposals for the reorganization of German society sought the (re)stabilization of the increasingly problematic social and political primacy of Germany's *Bildungsbürgertum* as well as the reaffirmation of male supremacy in the family and society. This would take place through a return to premodern and autocratic forms of domination. In particular the Pan-Germans sought to exclude women, workers, Catholics, and Jews as well as national and regional minorities from social influence and participation in the political process.

Particularly attractive were the ADV's goals in the area of foreign policy. In the age of imperialism the creation of a strong and territorially large German Empire with colonies throughout the world was a goal that in Pan-German eyes was well worth the effort. The special attention the ADV devoted to the ethnic Germans who lived abroad or in the borderlands as a quasi-territorial symbol of the threat that existed on the fringes of the empire clearly played a role here as well. By the same token, a traditional authoritarian society along the lines propagated by the Pan-Germans—complemented in the political realm by a strong monarchy or even a dictatorship—offered those who felt threatened by the modern age a measure of inner security and strengthened the identity of many anxious individuals.

In this respect, the Pan-German league appeared at least to those academics that thought of themselves as "national" a possible alternative to the existing social and political situation. By seeking to (re) stabilize the social and political supremacy of the *Bildungsbürgertum* and to reaffirm the principle of male primacy in the family and society through the return to premodern and autocratic forms of domination, the Pan-German League offered a clear and constant fictional identity that suggested an end to the confusion and lack of transparency of the existing social and economic situation. Along with a measure of sociability and the opportunity to exchange ideas with men of similar background and political orientation, the League provided academics with positions of leadership and responsibility that were of great significance for one's own identity for the simple reason that they helped compensate for the declining political and social influence of the class from which they came. It is precisely here that the appeal of the Pan-German League for academics is to be found. At the same time, one cannot underestimate the importance of sociability as an aspect of the ADV's appeal, for this gave criticism of the culture and the times in which one lived a certain coziness or familiarity that reinforced the League's sense of political mission.

By virtue of their prestige and their role in the dissemination of political and social ideas, Pan-German academics were enormously influential in the Wilhelmine Empire and Weimar Republic. Not only did they help spread the Pan-German ideology above all else within the ranks of the German bourgeoisie, but they contributed in no small measure to the social respectability of nationalist, antisemitic, racist, and eventually National Socialist ideas. Even though they remained out of the public eye after the end of the World War II, they continued to occupy positions of influence and status until pushed to the periphery of German academic and intellectual life by the broad acceptance of democracy and fundamental changes in the structure of German society.

Notes

1. This slogan first originated in the 1870s. See Helmut Böhme, *Deutschlands Weg zur Großmacht. Studien zum Verhältnis von Wirtschaft und Staat während der Reichsgründungszeit 1848–1881* (Cologne and Berlin: Kiepenheuer & Witsch, 1966), 400.
2. In this respect, see Werner Jochmann, ed., *Vom Kaiserreich bis zur Gegenwart*, Hamburg—Geschichte der Stadt und ihrer Bewohner 2, (Hamburg: Hoffmann und Campe, 1986); and *Hamburg. Die Stadt im 20. Jahrhundert*, ed. Ortwin Pelc and Carsten Prange (Hamburg: Convent Verlag, 2002).
3. See the brief overview in Rainer Hering, "Bildung in Hamburg," in *Hamburg. Die Stadt im 20. Jahrhundert*, ed. Pelc und Prange, 64–67.
4. The development of the Pan-German League and the differences between its leadership and local organizations can only be discussed here in broad outlines. For further details, see the various publications of Rainer Hering, most importantly *Konstruierte Nation. Der Alldeutsche Verband 1890–1939* (Hamburg: Christians, 2003); as well as his essays, "'Es ist verkehrt, Ungleichen Gleichheit zu geben.' Der Alldeutsche Verband und das Frauenwahlrecht," *Ariadne* 43 (2003): 22–29; "Radikaler Nationalismus zwischen Kaiserreich und 'Drittem Reich' am Beispiel der Alldeutschen Blätter," in *Das konservative Intellektuellenmilieu in Deutschland, seine Presse und seine Netzwerke (1890–1960)*, ed. Michel Grunewald and Uwe Puschner in collaboration with Hans Manfred Bock (Bern: Peter Lang, 2003), 427–43; "Juden im Alldeutschen Verband?" in *Aus den Quellen. Beiträge zur deutsch-jüdischen Geschichte. Festschrift für Ina Lorenz zum 65. Geburtstag*, ed. von Andreas Brämer, Stefanie Schüler-Springorum, and Michael Studemund-Halévy, Studien zur jüdischen Geschichte 10 (Munich and Hamburg: Dölling und Galitz, 2005), 291–300; "Eliten des Hasses. Der Alldeutsche Verband in Hamburg 1892 bis 1939," in *Hamburger Arbeitskreis für Regionalgeschichte Mitteilungen* 43 (2005): 44–69; "'. . . eine sehr sympathische Stellung.' Der Kyffhäuser-Verband der Vereine Deutscher Studenten und der Alldeutsche Verband," in *125 Jahre Vereine Deutscher Studenten. 1881–2006*, Bd.1 *Ein historischer Rückblick*, ed. Marc Zirlewagen (Bad Frankenhausen: Akademischer Verein Kyffhäuser, 2006), 25–43; "*Dem besten Steuermann Deutschlands*". *Der Politiker Otto von Bismarck und seine Deutung im radikalen Nationalismus zwischen Kaiserreich und "Drittem Reich"*, (Friedrichsruh: Otto-von-Bismarck Stiftung, 2006); and "Alldeutsche Hansa? Zur Sozialstruktur des Alldeutschen Verbandes Lübeck," in: *Aus der Mitte des Landes. Klaus-Joachim Lorenzen-Schmidt zum 65. Geburtstag*. ed. Detlev Kraack and Martin Rheinheimer (Neumünster-Hamburg: Wachholtz, 2013), 451–62. On the ADV in Wilhelmian Germany, see the studies by Johannes Leicht, *Heinrich Claß 1868–1953: Die politische Biographie eines Alldeutschen* (Paderborn: Ferdinand Schöningh, 2012); Peter Walkenhorst, *Nation—Volk—Rasse. Radikaler Nationalismus im Deutschen Kaiserreich 1890–1914* (Göttingen, 2007); Michael Peters, *Der Alldeutsche Verband am Vorabend*

des Ersten Weltkrieges (1908–1914). Ein Beitrag zur Geschichte des völkischen Nationalismus im spätwilhelminischen Deutschland (Frankfurt and New York: Peter Lang, 1996); Roger Chickering, *We Men Who Feel Most German: A Cultural Study of the Pan-German-League 1886–1914* (Boston: Allen and Unwin, 1984). On the ADV in the Weimar Republic, see Barry A. Jackisch, *The Pan-German League and Radical Nationalist Politics in Interwar Germany, 1918–39* (Farnham: Ashgate, 2012); Edgar Hartwig, "Alldeutscher Verband (ADV), 1891–1939," in *Lexikon zur Parteiengeschichte*, ed. Dieter Fricke et al., 4 vols. (Cologne: Paul-Rugenstein, 1983–86), 1:13–47; and the unpublished doctoral dissertations by Edgar Hartwig, "Zur Politik und Entwicklung des Alldeutschen Verbandes von seiner Gründung bis zum Beginn des 1. Weltkrieges, 1891–1914" (Phil. diss., Friedrich Schiller Universität Jena, 1966); Brewster Chamberlin, "The Enemy on the Right: The Alldeutscher Verband in the Weimar Republic 1918–1926" (PhD diss., University of Maryland, 1972); and Willi Krebs, "Der Alldeutsche Verband in den Jahren 1918–1939—ein politisches Instrument des deutschen Imperialismus" (Phil. diss., Berlin [DDR], 1970); as well as the older study by Alfred Kruck, *Geschichte des Alldeutschen Verbandes 1890–1939* (Wiesbaden: Franz Steiner, 1954).

5. This terminology refers to a movement, or *Sammelbewegung*, that first surfaced in the last decades of the Second Empire and that brought together diverse individuals and organizations with differing ideas and goals that fought among themselves and occasionally united only to fall away from each other once again. What united them was that they all reacted to the process of modernization by falling back upon traditional, though radicalized concepts and models of explanation. The *völkisch* movement offered alternative models of the modern; it was a probative anti-movement characterized by antisemitism, anti-Slavism, anti-Romanism, anti-urbanism, and anti-internationalism. What the movement sought was a reaffirmation of what it presumed to be the essential attributes of the Germans and their culture that had been shaken by century-long processes of foreign infiltration and appropriation. For further information, see *Handbuch zur "Völkischen Bewegung" 1871–1918*, ed. Uwe Puschner, Walter Schmitz, and Justus H. Ulbricht (Munich: K. G. Saur, 1996), XIII–XVIII, the citations from XIV and XVIII.

6. For this and the following with documentation, see Hering, *Konstruierte Nation*.

7. Hering, "Wiedergeburt," 1079–84.

8. Hering, *Konstruierte Nation*, 413–26, 472–89.

9. Ibid., 396–412. See also Hering, "'Parteien vergehen, aber das deutsche Volk muß weiterleben': Die Ideologie der Überparteilichkeit als wichtiges Element der politischen Kultur im Kaiserreich und in der Weimarer Republik," in *Völkische Bewegung–Konservative Revolution–Nationalsozialismus. Aspekte einer politisierten Kultur*, ed. Walter Schmitz and Clemens Vollnhals (Dresden: Thelem, 2005), 33–43.

10. Hans-Peter Ullmann, *Interessenverbände in Deutschland* (Frankfurt: Suhrkamp, 1988), 105–8.

11. Hering, *Konstruierte Nation*, 380–96. See also Ute Planert, *Antifeminismus im Kaiserreich. Diskurs, soziale Formation und politische Mentalität* (Göttingen: Vandenhoeck & Ruprecht, 1998).

12. Friedrich Wilhelm Graf, "'Die Nation—von Gott erfunden?' Kritische Randnotizen zum Theologiebedarf der historischen Nationalismusforschung," in *"Gott mit uns". Nation, Religion und Gewalt im 19. und frühen 20. Jahrhundert*, ed. Gerd Krumeich and Hartmut Lehmann (Göttingen: Vandenhoeck & Ruprecht, 2000), 285–317, here 307.

13. For this and the following, see Hering, *Konstruierte Nation*, esp. 187–219. Racial concepts were already present in the thinking of Claß's predecessor Ernst Hasse. For example, see Hasse, "Die Zukunft des deutschen Volkstums," *Deutsche Politik* (Munich: J. F. Lemann, 1907), vol. 1, no. 4, 46–68. There was, however, no consensus in the ADV's local organizations for Hasse's goal of excluding Jews from membership in the ADV or for the inclusion of antisemitism in the Pan-German program.

14. For further information, see Uwe Puschner, *Die völkische Bewegung im wilhelminischen Kaiserreich. Sprache-Rasse-Religion* (Darmstadt: Wissenschaftliche Buchgesellschaft, 2001), 275f.; and Volker Ullrich, *Die nervöse Großmacht. Aufstieg und Untergang des deutschen Kaiserreichs 1871–1918* (Frankfurt: S. Fischer, 1997), 346, 380. On the opportunities afforded prominent members of the ADV to influence public discourse, see Kruck, *Geschichte des Alldeutschen Verbandes*, 18. See also John A. Moses, "Pan-Germanism and the German professors 1914–1918," *The Australian Journal of Politics and History* 15 (1969): 45–60; Fritz Klein, "Die deutschen Historiker im ersten Weltkrieg," in *Die bürgerliche deutsche Geschichtsschreibung von der Reichseinigung von oben bis zur Befreiung Deutschlands vom Faschismus*, ed. Joachim Streisand (Berlin [DDR]: Akademie Verlag, 1965), 227–48; and Wanda Kampmann, *Deutsche und Juden. Die Geschichte der Juden in Deutschland vom Mittelalter bis zum Beginn des Ersten Weltkrieges* (Frankfurt: Fischer-Taschenbuch, 1979), 321. Senior elementary and secondary school teachers identified themselves in particular with the Wilhelmine state and were therefore prominently represented in the membership of the various nationalist pressure organizations.

15. Chickering, *Men*, 102–21. For an exemplary analysis of the structure of the ADV's local organization, see 306–30. See also Christina Broberg von Seggern, "The Alldeutscher Verband and the German Nationalstaat" (PhD diss., University of Minnesota, 1974), 32–36; and Mildred S. Wertheimer, *The Pan German League 1890–1914* (New York: Octagon Books, 1971), 65–69.

16. For example, see Konrad H. Jarausch, *Students, Society and Politics in Imperial Germany: The Rise of Academic Illiberalism* (Princeton, NJ: Princeton University Press, 1982).

17. Gangolf Hübinger, "Ideenzirkulation und Buchmarkt," *Internationales Archiv für Sozialgeschichte der deutschen Literatur* 27 (2002): 116–24.

18. Hering, *Konstruierte Nation*, 280f.

19. For the 1897 membership figures, see *Der Alldeutsche Verband im Jahre 1901* (Berlin, 1902), 20f.
20. Analysis of membership statistics for 1897, 1901, and 1914.
21. Contemporary insights are to be found in Gustav Schiefler, *Eine Hamburgische Kulturgeschichte 1890–1920. Beobachtungen eines Zeitgenossen*, ed. Gerhard Ahrens, Hans Wilhelm Eckardt, and Renate Hauschild-Thiessen (Hamburg: Hamburger Vereine für Hamburgische Geschichte, 1985).
22. For the following with detailed examples, see Hering, *Konstruierte Nation*, 287–312.
23. This conclusion is based on the teaching faculty in the summer semester of 1933. For further information, see Rainer Hering: "Der 'unpolitische' Professor? Parteimitgliedschaften Hamburger Hochschullehrer in der Weimarer Republik und im 'Dritten Reich,'" in *Hochschulalltag im "Dritten Reich." Die Hamburger Universität 1933–1945*, ed. Eckart Krause, Ludwig Huber, and Holger Fischer (Berlin and Hamburg: Dietrich Reimer, 1991), 85–111. For the broader context, see Barbara Vogel, "Anpassung und Widerstand. Das Verhältnis Hamburger Hochschullehrer zum Staat 1919 bis 1945," in idem., 3–83.
24. Vogel, "Anpassung," 25f. See also Martin Tschechne, *William Stern* (Hamburg: Ellert and Richter, 2010).
25. Siegfried Passarge, "Das Geographische Seminar des Kolonial-Instituts und der Hansischen Universität 1908–1935," *Mitteilungen der Geographischen Gesellschaft in Hamburg* 46 (1939): 1–104. See also Passarge's autobiography, *Aus achtzig Jahren. Eine Selbstbiographie* (Ms., n.d. [1949?]), as well as the secondary studies by Herbert Louis, "Siegfried Passarge 29.11.1866–26.7.1958," in *Bayerische Akademie der Wissenschaften Jahrbuch 1959* (Munich: Verlag der Bayerischen Akademie der Wissenschaften, 1959), 180–83; and Holger Fischer and Gerhard Sandner, "Die Geschichte des Geographischen Seminars der Hamburger Universität im 'Dritten Reich,'" in *Hochschulalltag im "Dritten Reich"*, ed. Krause et al, 1197–222; as well as the unpublished manuscript by Marin Meyer, "Siegfried Passarge, Rassismus und die Geographie" (Ms., Hamburg, 1997), 2f.
26. "Schriftenverzeichnis und Nachlaß von Siegfried Passarge," compiled by Gerhard Sandner and Mechtild Rössler (Ms., Hamburg, 3rd rev. ed., 1998). See also Meyer, "Siegfried Passarge, Rassismus und die Geographie," 7f.
27. Hering, *Konstruierte Nation*, esp. 179, 295, 298, and 312.
28. Meyer, "Siegfried Passarge, Rassismus und die Geographie," 21.
29. Passarge's antisemitism leaves out none of the more well-known formulations and establishes a connection between Jewry and Bolshevism. Even then, however, it would be a mistake to see him as a racial antisemite like the National Socialists, since he denied the existence of separate races altogether. In this respect, see Hans Fischer, *Völkerkunde im Nationalsozialismus. Aspekte der Anpassung. Affinität und Behauptung einer wissenschaftlichen Disziplin* (Berlin and Hamburg: Dietrich Reimer, 1990), 53f.

30. Jacob Brafmann, *Das Buch vom Kahal. Auf Grund einer neuen Verdeutschung des russischen Originals,* ed. Siegfried Passarge, 2 vols. (Leipzig: Hammer-Verlag, 1928), vol. 1: *Materialien zur Erforschung der jüdischen Sitten,* with a foreword and introduction by Siegfried Passarge, v–viii; vol. 2: *Das Buch von der Verwaltung der jüdischen Gemeinde,* foreword, v–viii, and the chapter by Passarge, "Das jüdische Problem," 241–382. See also Karl Tschuppik, "Professor Passarges Wissenschaft. Der Geographieprofessor der Hamburger Universität gibt ein verschollenes Werk der Pogrom-Literatur heraus. Sein 'Buch vom Kahal', das Machwerk eines zaristischen Spitzels," in *Der Montag Morgen* (Berlin), 25 July 1927, and *Deutsches Adelsblatt* 46, no. 6 (21 February 1928).

31. In addition to medical literature the J. F. Lehmann Publishing House published a steady stream of nationalistic, racist, and antisemitic pamphlets and books. Julius Friedrich Lehmann (1864–1935) was an influential member of the Pan-German League and joined the NSDAP in 1920. See Gary D. Stark, "Der Verleger als Kulturunternehmer: Der J. F. Lehmanns Verlag und Rassenkunde in der Weimarer Republik," *Archiv für Geschichte des Buchwesens* 16 (1976): 291–318; as well as his broader study of the neoconservative press, *Entrepreneurs of Ideology: Neoconservative Publishers in Germany 1890–1933* (Chapel Hill: University of North Carolina Press, 1981), esp. 19–22 and 111–24. See also Hans-Günter Richardi, *Hitler und seine Hintermänner. Neue Fakten zur Frühgeschichte der NSDAP* (Munich: Süddeutscher Verlag, 1991), 230–32; and Hellmuth Auerbach, "Vom Trommler zum Führer. Hitler und das nationale Münchner Bürgertum," in *Irrlicht im leuchtenden München? Der Nationalsozialismus in der "Hauptstadt der Bewegung",* ed. Björn Mensing and Friedrich Prinz (Regensburg: Friedrich Pustet, 1991), 67–91, esp. 69. On the medical profession and its affinity for National Socialism, see Klaus-Dieter Thomann, "Auf dem Weg in den Faschismus. Medizin in Deutschland von der Jahrhundertwende bis 1933," in *Medizin, Faschismus und Widerstand. Drei Beiträge,* ed. Barbara Bromberger, Hans Mausbach, and Klaus-Dieter Thomann (Cologne: Pahl-Rugenstein, 1985), 15–185; Klaus-Dieter Thomann, "'Dienst am Deutschtum'—der medizinische Verlag J. F. Lehmanns und der Nationalsozialismus," in *Medizin im "Dritten Reich",* ed. Johanna Bleker and Norbert Jachertz, 2nd expanded ed. (Cologne: Pahl-Rugenstein, 1992), 54–69; Justus H. Ulbricht, "Völkische Publizistik in München. Verleger, Verlage und Zeitschriften im Vorfeld des Nationalsozialismus," in *München — "Hauptstadt der Bewegung." Bayerns Metropole und der Nationalsozialismus* (Munich: Klinkhardt und Biermann, 1993), 131–36; Justus H. Ulbricht, "Das völkische Verlagswesen im deutschen Kaiserreich," in *Handbuch zur "Völkischen Bewegung",* ed. Puschner, Schmitz, and Ulbricht, 277–301; and Sigrid Stöckel, ed., *Die "rechte Nation" und ihr Verleger. Politik und Popularisierung im J.F. Lehmanns Verlag 1890–1979* (Heidelberg: Lehmanns, 2002).

32. Siegfried Passarge, *Das Judentum als landschaftskundlich-ethnologisches Problem* (Munich: J. F. Lehmann, 1929). The book was advertised also in the *Alldeutschen Blättern* 39 (1929): 163. In this respect, see Karl Hoheisel,

"Siegfried Passarges 'Das Judentum als landschaftskundlich-ethnologisches Problem': Paradigma einer zeitgemäßen Religionsgeographie?" in *Religion und Siedlungsraum*, ed. Manfred Büttner et al. (Berlin: Dietrich Reimer, 1986), 55–81, esp. 60–65.

33. Staatsarchiv Hamburg (hereafter cited as StA Hamburg), 361–5 II Hochschulwesen II, U s 4; ebd., 361–6 Hochschulwesen–Dozenten- und Personalakten, I 310 and IV 765; ebd., 135–1 I-IV Staatliche Pressestelle I-IV, 5383. In this respect, see Fischer and Sandner, "Geschichte des Geographischen Seminars," esp. 1206–14; Hoheisel, "Siegfried Passarges 'Das Judentum als landschaftskundlich-ethnologisches Problem,'" 59–61; and Hering, *Konstruierte Nation*, 179, 295, 298, and 312. The effect of antisemitic slogans on Jewish students is the subject of the study by Gertrud Wenzel, *Granny. Greta Warburg und die Ihren. Hamburger Schicksale berichtet von Gertrud Wenzel-Burchard* (Hamburg: Christians, 1970), 72–75.

34. A scholarly history of this publishing house is long overdue. On Fritsch and the Reichshammerbund, see Uwe Lohalm, *Völkischer Radikalismus. Die Geschichte des Deutschvölkischen Schutz- und Trutz-Bundes 1919–1923* (Hamburg: Leibniz-Verlag, 1970), 56–66; Katja Hintze, "'Antisemiten-Katechismus' und 'Handbuch der Judenfrage': Antisemitische Vorurteile und Stereotypen bei Theodor Fritsch" (Unpubl. Master's thesis, Hanover 1997).

35. The Kahal (in Hebrew Kehila) refers to an organizational structure for the Jewish communities in Poland. Minsk became part of Poland in the sixteenth century and was assigned to Russia in the second partition of Poland at the end of the eighteenth century. The Kahal originated toward the end of the sixteenth century and shaped the lives of Polish Jews. In addition to its administrative authority, including raising taxes, the Kahal also exercised legal jurisdiction over the members of the community in order to make certain that their religious and cultural life was disturbed as little as possible. The Kahal consisted of three to five elders who would rotate its chairmanship every month. The members of the Kahal came mostly from the well-to-do merchantry and landowners. In 1822 the Kahal was abolished in the Russian Kingdom of Poland and replaced by a supervisory board from the synagogue, or *Synagogenaufsicht*. For further information, see Agnieszka Rudnicka, "Kahal," in *Neues Lexikon des Judentums*, ed. Julius H. Schoeps (Gütersloh: Gütersloher Verlags-Haus, 2000), 441f.

36. Herman Rosenthal, "Kahal," in Jewish Encyclopedia.com (www.jewishencyclopedia.com, consulted on 3 November 2003).

37. Meyer, "Siegfried Passarge, Rassismus und die Geographie," 5; and Hoheisel, "Siegfried Passarges 'Das Judentum als landschaftskundlich-ethnologisches Problem,'" 58.

38. The Jewish lawyer Eichholz was hated by the National Socialists because of his activity as an attorney in political trials and in 1943 was murdered in the Auschwitz concentration camp. See *M.d.L. Das Ende der Parlamente 1933 und die Abgeordneten der Landtage und Bürgerschaften der Weimarer Republik in der Zeit des Nationalsozialismus. Politische Verfolgung, Emigration und*

Ausbürgerung 1933–1945. Ein biographischer Index, ed. Martin Schumacher (Düsseldorf: Droste, 1995), 244. Platen was chairman of the Hamburg state organization of the German State Party and belonged to the Hamburg Senate from 1910 to 1933. See StA Hamburg, 731–1 Handschriftensammlung, 601, Verzeichnis der Bürgerschaftsmitglieder.

39. StA Hamburg 361–6 Hochschulwesen—Dozenten- und Personalakten, I 310, vol. 14, Abschrift der Anfrage Nr.74 vom 12 Dec 1927. In an official statement on behalf of university authorities senior government official Albrecht von Wrochem (1880–1944) emphasized that the university had "no grounds but also no opportunity to do anything with respect to the publication of the book. . . . The book," continued Wrochem, "did not contain attacks against German Jewry. . . . The book had received a tendentious mark only because it had appeared in the Hammer Publishing House." In the Senate's response of 22 March 1928, it read: "The Senate cannot condemn the research methods of Professor Passarge even after taking his most recent publications into consideration, since in its opinion it is not within its purview to judge scholarly publications without exposing itself to criticism for having unjustifiably violated the principle of academic freedom" (idem.). In his memoirs Passarge wrote the following about the incident: "When I edited with an extensive introduction the very interesting book of folklore that had appeared in Russian under the title 'Brafman, das Buch von Kahal,' a motion was introduced in the Senate to remove me from my office. A committee to investigate the matter was appointed, but the issue went away. Nothing compromising could be found." See Passarge, *Aus achtzig Jahren,* 453f. In point of fact, the imminent dissolution of the Senate was the reason that nothing came of the DDP inquiry from 12 December 1927. See StA HH, 361–6 Hochschulwesen—Dozenten- und Personalakten, I 310, Band 13. For further details, see Fischer and Sandner, "Die Geschichte des Geographischen Seminars der Hamburger Universität im 'Dritten Reich,'" 1202.

40. Passarge, *Kahal,* 1:v–vii, and liif.

41. In this respect, see Hoheisel, "Siegfried Passarges 'Das Judentum als landschaftskundlich-ethnologisches Problem,'" 58f. and 67; and Meyer, "Siegfried Passarge, Rassismus und die Geographie," 9 and 19.

42. *Öffentliche Dank- und Huldigungsadresse eines Odisten an den Sonnenmenschen Dr. Siegfried Passarge, o. ö. Professor der Geographie an der Universität Hamburg, Herausgeber des Buches vom Kahal. Überreicht von Dr. phil. nat. Joseph Carlebach, Oberrabiner des Bes Din Altona und der Kahale von Schleswig-Holstein* (Berlin: Philo-Verlag und Buchhandlung, 1928). Bet Din is the rabbinical term for the Jewish court. See Lutz Doering und Theodore Kwasman, "Bet Din," in *Neues Lexikon,* 125. For this and the following see Rainer Hering "Joseph Carlebach und die Hamburger Universität," in " *. . . die da lehren, werden leuchten wie des Himmels Glanz. . . ." (Daniel 12,3). Die Sechste Joseph Carlebach-Konferenz. Joseph Carlebach und seine Zeit. Würdigung und Wirkung,* ed. Miriam Gillis-Carlebach and Barbara Vogel (Hamburg: Dölling und Galitz, 2005), 116–40.

43. In this respect, see among others Gerd Krüger: *"Treudeutsch allewege!"
Gruppen, Vereine und Verbände der Rechten in Münster (1887–1929/30)*
(Münster: Aschendorff, 1992), 45f.; Hans-Ulrich Wehler, Deutsche
Gesellschaftsgeschichte, vol. 3: *Von der "Deutschen Doppelrevolution" bis zum
Beginn des Ersten Weltkrieges 1849–1914* (Munich: C. H. Beck, 1995), esp.
730–50, the citation on 735; Angelika Linke, *Sprachkultur und Bürgertum.
Zur Mentalitätsgeschichte des 19. Jahrhunderts* (Stuttgart and Weimar: J. B.
Metzler, 1996), esp. 19–31; Ullrich, *Großmacht*, 285–290; Volker Berghahn,
*Das Kaiserreich 1871–1914. Industriegesellschaft, bürgerliche Kultur und
autoritärer Staat* (Stuttgart: Klett-Cotta, 2003), esp. 174–79, 218–20; and
Andreas Schulz, *Lebenswelt und Kultur des Bürgertums im 19. und 20.
Jahrhundert* (Munich: Oldenbourg, 2005), esp. 25–40, 76–97.

5

REALMS OF LEADERSHIP AND RESIDUES OF SOCIAL MOBILIZATION

The Pan-German League, 1918–33

Björn Hofmeister

As the ideological and propagandistic vanguard of the radical Right in Imperial Germany, the Pan-German League (Alldeutscher Verband or ADV) aspired to influence right-wing politics in Weimar Germany. The Pan-Germans had consistently challenged the government by mobilizing public opinion in support of an aggressive foreign policy, cultural and ethnic homogenization, and the political containment of liberalism, pacifism, Social Democracy, and political Catholicism. The historiography on the Pan-German League has produced a number of important studies on Pan-German ideology and politics during its formative years in Imperial Germany and World War I.[1] Debates about the League's attempts to create a conservative-nationalist *Sammlungsbewegung* and its radical programs of authoritarian reform, racism, antisemitism, and territorial expansionism into the colonial periphery as well as on the European continent have traditionally dominated the way in which the Pan-German movement and its place in modern German history has been understood. Demands for ethnic resettlement in Europe, efforts to prevent democratic reform by means of a civilian-military dictatorship, and the use of antisemitism as a strategy for mass mobilization at the end of the war revealed far-reaching ideological proximities to the National Socialist movement of the postwar period. From a perspective that emphasized ideological cohesion and continuities between the "old" and the "new" Right after the war in the mobilization of popular support, this body of literature highlighted the way in which Pan-Germanism had helped to radicalize nationalist and *völkisch* associations at the turn of the century and then, in the wake of World War I and the November Revolution, assisted in the rise of National Socialism.

For all its inherent appeal, this narrative has severe methodological shortcomings. Among other things, it neglects the limitations that the Pan-German League encountered in competition with new mass political movements, most conspicuously the various paramilitary groups and the National Socialist German Workers' Party (Nationalsozialistische Deutsche Arbeiterpartei or NSDAP) that surfaced during the Weimar Republic. These phenomena signaled a comprehensive realignment of the German Right after 1918 with new competition over leadership and the emergence of new techniques of mass mobilization. This essay revisits the argument that there was a continuous path of political mobilization from Germany's "old" political elites to the "new" mass movements of the radical Right of the Weimar Republic with particular emphasis on the role and development of the Pan-German League. The following essay shows not only how ideological proximity and organizational cooperation facilitated strategic and fateful alliances with the "new" movements of the radical Right, but it also reveals how an "old" radical nationalist movement struggled to reconcile its exclusive claim to power with the need to energize mass mobilization after World War I.[2] The Pan-Germans retained the belief that they themselves still constituted a political and intellectual vanguard, that they, as *Bildungsbürger*, were entitled to educate the populace about the dangers of revolution and disunity through the "weapons of the mind [*geistigen Waffen*]."[3] But, as this essay argues, the Pan-German sense of mission was contested in Weimar Germany and eventually proved outdated in the face of right-wing mass politics, paramilitary street violence, the rise of charismatic leadership conceptions in political movements, and increasingly powerful expectations of a strong, popular *Führer*.

The historiography of the Pan-German League in the Weimar Republic has generally overlooked this conflicted nature of the ADV's role and place in Weimar political culture. Instead the ADV has been depicted as the most important and successful pressure group on Weimar's radical Right in terms of influencing public opinion, crafting networks among right-wing organizations, and shaping *völkisch* debates about territorial expansion, cultural homogeneity, and civil-military dictatorship.[4] This view has ignored the problems the Pan-Germans faced in reconciling the challenges of mass mobilization with their goal of creating a government based upon the principles of elite leadership in the hands of of educated experts. Situating the Pan-German League in the broader context of Weimar's radical Right makes it necessary to recognize the limitations of the Pan-German *Weltanschauung*, the social boundaries of the Pan-German milieu, and the cultural constraints of Pan-German mobilization. This essay thus traces the Pan-German League's transformation from a vanguard of the radical Right in Imperial Germany to an increasingly antiquated association of right-wing *Honoratioren* after World War I.

Revolution as Trauma

Between World War I and the dissolution of the Pan-German League in 1939, Germany experienced a fundamental restructuring of the radical Right as a result of war, revolution, and the rise of mass society. World War I represented a particularly critical watershed in the history of the Pan-German movement. Germany's military defeat and the collapse of the Second Empire traumatized the ADV's leadership, contributed to a deep sense of political and social dislocation, and challenged the foundations of the Pan-German ideology. In their utopian vision of a politically and culturally homogenized society—though one based on class divisions—the Pan-Germans had always placed the interests of the *Volk* at the center of politics. But the concept of elite governance had failed during the war in as much as the *Burgfrieden* that had been proclaimed in 1914 could not mediate the political and social conflict of the war itself. As the *Burgfrieden* eroded and another *Sammlungsbewegung* collapsed with the failure of the German Fatherland Party (Deutsche Vaterlandspartei) in 1918, the Pan-Germans became increasingly concerned about the success of its efforts to mobilize support for the war effort with the promise of compensation for the masses with world-power status for Germany, reparations to rebuild the German economy, and new land for German settlers. The collapse of the old monarchical order and the loss of the war underscored in particular the failure of the Pan-German League's use of radical antisemitism as a strategy for mobilizing mass support and effectively dashed their hopes for a civilian-military dictatorship.

In the immediate aftermath of the November Revolution and the armistice national headquarters of the Pan-German League issued a statement that revealed the ideological dislocation and frustration that the ADV felt over the failure of efforts to sustain the *Burgfrieden* throughout the war: "What surprised us—in comparison to the certainty of the downfall, which is almost certain under these circumstances—or what certainly hit us most, maybe even broke us, is 'how' the collapse happened, 'how' it expanded in all directions. . . . Given the events of the last weeks, together with millions of German *Volksgenossen* the

Pan-German League stands at the grave of its proudest hopes."[5] For the Pan-Germans the revolutionary upheaval that followed the end of the war represented a crisis of the state that found its most revealing expression in widespread social unrest and the breakdown of military order. In his memoirs ADV chairman Heinrich Claß described in vivid language his astonishment at the plundering of the Supplies Office, the Imperial Tin Factory, and the War Clothing Office in Kastel/Mainz by an "undisciplined mass." These events left a lasting impression on Claß. It was, he wrote, "terrible to see those streaming back from the communications zone in their trucks who had robbed their own store magazines and graciously distributed gifts to the starving and begging masses."[6] As the purported custodians of authority, the Pan-Germans instructed their members to promote social routine and political obedience by cooperating with the workers' councils in order to prevent further fragmentations of the *Volksgemeinschaft*, which had clearly split into "two different ideologies"—on the one hand those who demanded peace and democracy and on the other those who supported military victory by all means and authoritarian governance: "Where there exists a Pan-German local chapter, there is a mediating center for the maintenance of public order."[7]

The image of the "restless Pan-German" who had tried to sabotage every attempt at a negotiated peace in the last years of the war, however, left the Pan-Germans politically isolated in the immediate postwar period. To escape revolutionary unrest in Berlin, the League considered relocating its headquarters to Eisenach in Thuringia and briefly considered renaming itself the *Bismarckbund*. In the end both ideas were rejected, and in February 1919, after months of ideological dislocation and political inactivity, the ADV leadership rallied around Claß to organize the League's first postwar national convention in Bamberg. Here the Pan-German leadership unleashed a powerful attack on the Weimar Republic with demands for reform that were framed in language with clear antisemitic undertones. These demands, however, remained on paper as the ADV leadership pursued discussions with nationalist leaders such as Paul von Hindenburg and representatives of the Wettin and Wittelsbach dynasties in the hope that this might lead to counterrevolution or a restoration of the monarchal system. But these hopes failed to materialize as the royal houses proved unwilling to undertake action.[8] The same frustration dogged hopes the Pan-Germans had pinned on the Hohenzollern Crown Prince's eldest son, Prince Friedrich Wilhelm of Prussia, who joined the ADV after the publication of the Bamberg Declaration.[9] The death of the Crown Prince in 1925 removed the one man upon whom the Pan-Germans had pinned their hopes of a dictatorial regime. Similar disappointments resulted from the Pan-Germans' contacts to the leaders of the free corps, which by the spring of 1919 had 250,000 to 400,000 men under their command.[10] Pan-Germans such as Julius F. Lehmann in Munich and Otto Helmut Hopfen in Starnberg used their contacts to former commissioned officers in a futile effort to mobilize their troops as counterrevolutionary forces, while Gertzlaff von Hertzberg-Lottin and Leopold von Vietinghoff-Scheel traveled to the Baltics to contact units like the *Eiserne Division* in Mittau.[11]

All these efforts to craft a counterrevolutionary force to overthrow the Weimar Republic failed in part because of competition over the question of leadership—a phenomenon that had already plagued the Fatherland Party in its efforts to create a unified *Sammlungsbewegung* in the last years of World War I. The failure of the Kapp Putsch in March 1920—which had been organized by the founder of the Fatherland Party, Wolfgang Kapp, and in which a number of prominent Pan-Germans like Paul Bang, Major Otto Füsslein, Baron Axel von Freytagh-Loringhoven, and Alfred Jacobsen had been involved[12]—set the stage for an intensified leadership conflict among the leading movements of the postwar German Right. Claß himself was shocked to learn of the Kapp Putsch, and its failure convinced him that in order to succeed a dictatorship would have to be made palatable to the masses. The idea of a dictatorship, he concluded, should be introduced to the public in "homeopathic doses" in order to get those with "weak nerves" used to it.[13] Between 1920 and 1921 the Pan-Germans were therefore reticent about using the term "dictatorship" in public. At a crucial meeting of the ADV managing committee on 2 September 1921, however, Claß demanded that the League commit itself to a clear position on the question of dictatorship.[14] When a majority of the managing committee opposed him, Claß responded by opening a campaign on behalf of the idea in the pages of the *Deutsche Zeitung*. At the next meeting of the managing committee in late November, Claß won a majority for the proposition that dictatorship should henceforth define the League's position, albeit with an emphasis on educating the masses through a massive campaign of antisemitic propaganda.[15] In the meantime, negotiations with the free corps leader Georg Escherich in July 1920, the man who led the infamous Organization Consul after its founding in May 1920, had broken down. Claß and Escherich clashed over spheres of influence. Escherich wanted to establish the Bavarian Order Bloc (Bayerischer Ordnungsblock), an alliance of some forty right-wing associations and parties that served as a holding company for a right-wing putsch, while

Claß sought to create a similar organization in northern Germany that would be administered by the League's headquarters.

Rivalry over leadership in putschist activities invariably involved the head of the Reichswehr, Hans von Seeckt. Seeckt had been in contact with Claß since February 1923. But Seeckt pursued his own plans, as did Hitler, who in 1920 had used Claß to secure the funds he needed for the acquisition of the *Völkischer Beobachter* (formerly the *Münchener Beobachter*) but who was now planning his own putsch.[16] The abortive Hitler Putsch in November 1923 cut across the plans of the Pan-Germans, many of whom recoiled from the violent potential of nationalist ideology. With the eclipse of radical nationalism in the aftermath of the Munich putsch the Pan-German League reached the limits of its appeal and by the end of the decade was left with a membership that, in size as well as in social background, looked very much like that of the prewar years.

Strongholds and Outposts:
Pan-German Regional and Political Constituencies

While the Pan-Germans struggled to adapt to the political realities of Weimar democracy, membership in the League expanded well beyond its prewar dimensions. It increased from 14,000 at the beginning of the war to an all-time peak of 39,000 in 1922, before decreasing steadily to 15,500 in 1929 and to between 10,000 and 13,500 in 1933–36.[17] These fluctuations reflected a structural problem that had plagued the League ever since its founding in 1891. The departure of thousands of passive members—referred to as *Karteileichen* who would join for a short time without contributing anything more than their membership dues—had been a persistent irritant for the ADV leadership. But after the war inflation and the postwar reconstruction of the ADV's local chapters, many of which had collapsed during the war, left the ADV's national headquarters with only limited resources for recruiting new membership. Special collections among the League's wealthy supporters—particularly in the coal and steel industry in the Ruhr, the Blohm & Voss shipyards in Hamburg, and smaller Saxon entrepreneurs—helped balance the League's budget but did not permit major investments in the League's infrastructure.[18] The situation was compounded by the fact that the League suffered a turnover affecting a majority of its membership every seven to eight years, a factor that contributed to the increasing inactivity of many of the ADV's local chapters. As

Vietinghoff-Scheel noted in a report to the ADV managing committee in November 1921, fewer than 10 percent of the League's chapters were actively engaged in Pan-German activities.[19] In a similar vein August Gebhard, who chaired the ADV chapter in Friedberg and was a member of the League's managing committee, noted in 1927 that since the outbreak of the war the Pan-German League had been little more than a fashionable vehicle for nationalist activists to vent their fury without, however, ever intending to stay after the war.[20] This was a problem that both camouflaged and underscored the League's weakness in competing with other right-wing organizations and that made even short-term financial planning difficult.

The Pan-German League tried to find its way out of this dilemma by turning to antisemitism as the key to mobilizing popular support. In this respect, the ADV sponsored organizations like the German Racist Protection and Defense League (Deutschvölkischer Schutz- und Trutzbund or DSTB) in 1919, which soon became one of the largest movements on the German Right with between 160,000 and 180,000 members recruited primarily from the urban middle classes.[21] The founding of the DSTB was a strategic decision by the Pan-Germans to mobilize a mass following without opening their own rank-and-file to mass membership. The ADV's unwillingness to broaden its own membership base, however, had major implications for its relationship to the DSTB. The leaders of the Pan-German League chose to remain in the background in the Protection League, with the result that DSTB chairman Alfred Roth regarded himself as independent of Pan-German headquarters. Although the DSTB advisory council included a number of prominent Pan-Germans such as Georg von Stössel, Gustav Pezoldt, Erich Jung, Gebhard, Bang, and Lehmann, their presence remained largely cosmetic. As a result, the Protection League was plagued by endemic leadership quarrels from the very beginning as the Pan-Germans were pushed more and more from the center to the periphery of the organization. It was only after the dissolution of the Protection League in the wake of Walter Rathenau's murder in the summer of 1922 and the subsequent adoption of the Law for the Protection of the Republic that the Pan-Germans, most notably Konstantin von Gebsattel and Hertzberg from the ADV managing committee, assumed control of the DSTB, if only to oversee its liquidation at the same time that the Pan-German League was faced with the prospect of dissolution itself.[22]

The Protection League mobilized radical nationalists and socialized future political leaders, most of whom moved not to the Pan-German League but found their way to rival organizations like the NSDAP.

The Protection League was never a movement with charismatic national leaders and, rather than provide the ADV with a source of new members, served as a recruiting ground for the rival NSDAP. While the DSTB succeeded in mobilizing new members throughout Germany with strongholds in Munich, Berlin, Hamburg, Stettin, Hanover, and Dresden, the ADV remained tied to its traditional regional strongholds in the predominantly Protestant areas of central Germany such as Berlin, Saxony, Thuringia, Hesse, Brunswick, provincial Hanover, Anhalt, Saxony, and Westphalia, as well as in the Hanseatic cities of Bremen and Hamburg. In trying to expand its membership base, the ADV had to contend with strong liberal traditions in the southwest and well-organized agrarian interests in Prussia's north. The eastern provinces remained contested territories once the League expanded into Posen, Eastern Brandenburg, Pomerania, and Eastern and Western Prussia during the war. After the war the mobilization of new members was made even more difficult not only by the territorial losses to Poland but also by the fact that agrarian pressure groups dominated the areas east of the Elbe. The regional affiliates of the National Rural League (Reichs-Landbund or RLB) were particularly effective in mobilizing agrarian interests in Pomerania and Brandenburg. At the same time, the ADV headquarters neglected rural constituencies in Mecklenburg and Schleswig Holstein in large part because its chronic lack of finances made it impossible to provide speakers. In Bavaria, which remained a fertile base of recruitment for nationalist and paramilitary organizations, the Pan-Germans' room for maneuver was severely restricted by the rise of the NSDAP. At the same time, the League's infrastructure in the Rhine-Main basin was all but destroyed by the Allied occupation, and it was not until shortly before Allied troops left that it was reestablished in June 1929. But here the search for a chairman and members was hampered by the fact that former Pan-Germans had been threatened with imprisonment for the better part of a decade by Allied occupation forces. Paul Alt, who became district leader in 1929, complained bitterly that those who had once belonged to the ADV had either joined other organizations and parties, had become inactive politically, or had died.[23] Even Claß's own nephew, Eduard Lucius, refused to accept the chairmanship of the new chapter in Mainz because he feared imprisonment by the French.[24]

Structural problems continued to affect the League's ability to mobilize new supporters. The high turnover rate in the ADV membership led to severe financial problems, a fact that reflected the low morale of the ADV's rank-and-file and the reluctance of the League's members to pay membership dues. The fate of the Pan-Germans' movement in Austria, where the ADV had been founded in April 1919, was similarly doomed by financial difficulties. Between 1919 and 1924 the Austrian Pan-German League mobilized an impressive membership that peaked at 20,000 organized in 200 local chapters before decreasing to 10,000 in 1927.[25] As in Germany, however, the ADV's success in Austria was a function of the political turbulence of the era between the peace treaties of 1919 and the crisis of 1923. Still, expansion into Austria remained the Pan-German League's most significant accomplishment in its efforts to promote German unification with Austria and expand the organization's appeal south of its strongholds in Central Germany. In the final analysis, however, the leadership struggle within the Austrian Right rendered the League insignificant and prompted Claß to consider its dissolution. In 1927 the Pan-German organ in Austria, the *Deutschöster-reichische Tageszeitung*, was sold to save financial resources for the ADV headquarters in Berlin and to stabilize the *Alldeutsche Blätter*.

In the meantime, the problem of mobilization and participation remained a dilemma. In late 1926 Vietinghoff-Scheel complained that on paper the League had thirty-six districts, of which perhaps only six were active.[26] With the onset of the great depression the League found itself at the limits of its financial capacities as decreasing membership and the ineffectiveness of repeated fundraising efforts exacted such a heavy toll on the ADV infrastructure that Claß considered dissolving the League if its operations were not placed on a stable footing. These problems were only exacerbated by the centralization of power in the League and the Pan-Germans' failure to attract the support of younger people.

Realms of Cultural and Social Leadership: Political Sociability, Youth, and Women

After Hitler reestablished the NSDAP in February 1925, the National Socialists set out to expand their influence beyond their initial strongholds in Bavaria into bourgeois associational life in other parts of Germany. In this respect they sought not only to take over leadership roles in the associational milieu of the German *Bürgertum* but also to exploit mass demonstrations like the various paramilitary *Heerschauen* that had been introduced on the eve of the war with tens of thousands of participants.[27] The Pan-Germans, on the other hand, preferred more intimate surroundings. Itinerant speakers like Bang, Karl Grube, and Otto von Feldmann would attract between a dozen and a hundred people at chapter meetings throughout the country. Pan-German gatherings with a thousand or more attendees, which took place in Frankfurt Oder, Chemnitz, Bamberg, and Dresden between 1920 and 1922, became increasingly rare after 1923, as did the *Sonnenwendfeiern*, like the one in Teuteburg in 1921, which attracted 4,000 people.[28] The Pan-Germans were thus neither willing nor able to tap into the militant sociability that brought mass following to Germany's sport societies, paramilitary associations, and veterans' associations.[29]

A case in point was the annual Bismarck celebrations. Before the war the Pan-Germans had been actively involved in organizing the choreography of the celebrations at a time when the Iron Chancellor was in the process of establishing himself as an alternative power center of the "national opposition" to Wilhelm II following his resignation from office in 1890. From the turn of the century onward the League regarded itself as the principal heir to Bismarck's political legacy. After 1918 Bismarck would become an alternative symbol of political power, though now in opposition to Weimar.[30] Bismarck celebrations remained an important venue for the Pan-Germans as they sought to advance their claim to the leadership of the nationalist milieu in the struggle for an end to the Weimar Republic. The Pan-Germans, however, enjoyed no monopoly over the Bismarck-symbol as the annual Bismarck celebrations in Hamburg turned into a rallying point for nationalist associations that stood well outside the ADV's immediate orbit. While the League's Hamburg chapter still made annual pilgrimages to Bismarck's estate in Friedrichsruh, the Pan-Germans were now only one of the groups that took part in the demonstrations of the German Right before the Bismarck statute in Hamburg and found themselves amid thousands of participants from the DNVP, the German National Bismarck Youth (Bismarckjugend der Deutschnationalen Volkspartei), gymnastics clubs, student fraternities, veterans' societies, and scouting associations.[31] After 1929, when bloody clashes with Communists led to a decrease in the number of participants, the Pan-Germans began to hold smaller-scale celebrations with fewer than a hundred members at the mausoleum in Friedrichsruh. This represented a retreat into more intimate confines as the Pan-Germans, along with the DNVP and other local nationalist associations such as the Evangelical League (Evangelischer Bund), celebrated their devotion to the man whom they regarded as the symbol around which the entire German Right should coalesce.[32]

By this time there was no other *locus classicus* of the Pan-German League. After 1916 the League's small headquarters was centrally located in Berlin-Tiergarten, but Claß resided with the League's staff in the building's unfashionable *Hinterhof*. Claß was able to integrate himself rather quickly into Berlin's political life, cultivating a habitus that, according to several of his closest friends, was comparable to that of other political leaders. Berlin also served as a safe haven for the League national conventions as the occupation of the Rhineland and the territorial losses in the east limited the League's choices for venue cities. At the same time, the inflation forced the ADV leadership to keep its expenses as low as possible. The League was most successful in smaller cities. One of the most vital centers of Pan-German activity was Dresden. Here the League continued to exercise power over the city's nationalist festivities and to organize the city's annual Bismarck celebrations for the 143 associations that were affiliated with the United Patriotic Associations of Germany (Vereinigte Vaterländische Verbände Deutschlands).[33] The Pan-Germans' Bismarck celebrations in Dresden thus retained their appeal to the nationalist *Bürgertum* of the city as well as in other larger towns in Saxony. Still, as the developments in Hamburg revealed, the Pan-Germans had deep reservations about mass parades and demonstrations. Claß made no secret of his contempt for mass rallies, while Vietinghoff-Scheel dismissed them as empty populist spectacles and complained about the poor quality of speakers, especially from the Stahlhelm.[34] The Pan-Germans thus found themselves losing influence in the nationalist realm as the DNVP and NSDAP assumed the lead in organizing mass events in Hamburg and other German cities. Still, the Pan-Germans continued to organize mass demonstrations and paramilitary marches such as the "German Day" in Plauen, which in 1924 attracted as many as 25,000 participants.[35] But the increasingly military character of these "German Days" presaged the campaigns of the National Socialists, who usurped control over the organization of these events and moved the venue from cities in central Germany like Weimar (1920) and Detmold (1921) to their Bavarian strongholds in Coburg (1922) and Nuremberg (1923).

After 1928 the National Socialist invasion of the bourgeois associational culture became massive. The Pan-Germans retreated into semipublic spheres of sociability and politics only to find that these had become all but irrelevant in the era of mass politics. By the end of the Weimar Republic the League had become a niche of retreat and ideological fulfillment, if not an idyll of bourgeois authenticity, for the ADV's rank-and-file membership. Competition with the mass organizations of the German Right over authority and leadership was for the Pan-Germans an uneven contest. Unlike the Stahlhelm and other veterans' organizations, the ADV presented itself as a bastion of bourgeois sociability, which remained aloof from the mass appeal of National Socialism. For their own part, the Pan-Germans hoped to bridge the gap between bourgeois *Honoratiorenpolitik* and mass politics by negotiating compromises with mass organizations. The referendum against the Young Plan in 1929 and the ADV's participation at the mass rally in Bad Harzburg on 11 October 1931 were prime examples of this tactic and offered the ADV a brief respite from its decline in significance. However, competition over audiences and support during the campaign against the Young Plan, and in particular the tactics of the NSDAP, exposed the deeper structural problems involved in uniting such disparate movements. The Harzburg rally made this dilemma all too apparent to thousands of SA and Stahlhelm activists as well as to the hundred or more journalists from all over the world when at the last moment Hitler refused to join representatives from the other organizations on the podium as one of the event's keynote speakers. It was only after Alfred Hugenberg, a founding member of the ADV and one of Claß's closest political associates, persuaded the Nazi party leader of the damage his absence would do to the entire Right if he abused the political credibility he had gained between the elections of September 1930 and his audience with Hindenburg the day before the Harzburg rally that Hitler agreed to speak.[36] The campaign against the Young Plan and the Harzburg rally, which contemporaries judged as a threat to the political stability of the Republic, thus represented a significant departure from the League's preference for smaller venues and quieter surroundings in which they could pursue what they referred to as *"sachliche Politik."*[37] The League's own leadership conferences, which usually took place four times a year, were governed by a different choreography. With some five hundred members in attendance, these meetings emphasized sociability, official meetings, and cultural programs, including the recitation of patriotic poems, the performance of classical music and dance, and trips to local sites of interest.

Traditional forms of bourgeois associational life such as these were not well suited to the new demands of radical nationalism. Nowhere was this more apparent than in the Pan-Germans' failure to organize a youth movement of their own between 1919 and 1923. Although it was founded by individual chapters, the Pan-German Youth (Alldeutsche Jugend) was coordinated by the League's headquarters in Berlin, while the ADV's headquarters in Innsbruck oversaw youth chapters in Austria. Youth homes, or *Jugendheime*, and advisory boards to help members find jobs were designed to create a more coherent Pan-German membership. These efforts, however, were handicapped by a lack of personnel and resources. In the end, only a few hundred members ever joined the Pan-German Youth. Both the central importance of the Berlin chapter in the venture and the failure to recruit younger family members of Pan-Germans suggested that the Pan-German Youth was a sideshow in which the ADV invested little of its resources or prestige. Faced with the inflation, the Pan-Germans decided to hand the members of the Pan-German Youth over to the DNVP's organization, the Bismarck Youth, which had come into existence in 1922.[38] The failure of the Pan-German Youth reflected fundamental problems in the League, which could not commit itself to mobilizing youth. The Pan-Germans had no intention of passing the torch to a new generation despite talk among themselves about their own advancing age. By 1925 the Pan-Germans were well aware that they had lost the fight for Germany's youth and had lost interest in resurrecting the Pan-German Youth.[39]

All of this underscored not only the Pan-German League's difficulty in accommodating the interests of its younger members but also its indifference to the claims of the "front generation" of war veterans or the still younger cohorts of the "war-youth generation" born between 1900 and 1910 and the "postwar generation" born after 1910. Whereas younger activists were organized in the DNVP's Bismarck Youth or the Hindenburg Youth League (Hindenburg Jugendbund) of the right-liberal German People's Party (Deutsche Volkspartei or DVP), the cultural legacy of the "front generation" was administered on the Right primarily by the Stahlhelm and other veterans' associations as well as by the SA.[40] In the meantime, the National Socialists began to lose all interest in the Pan-German League, the erstwhile pioneer of radical nationalism. The antagonism between Claß and Hitler dated from their first meeting in 1920. Afterward Hitler idolized other more militant vanguard movements, most notably the Italian Fascist movement of Benito Mussolini. And while the Protection League had succeeded in bringing Pan-Germans and National Socialists together into a single association, its function was little more than to transfer antisemitism as a mobilizing strategy from the Pan-German League to other movements on the radical Right, including the NSDAP, many of whose future leaders had been socialized there.

The problem of mobilizing young people spoke to another challenge. The Pan-German League, which had established special women's groups in several chapters before the war, failed to make use of the broad participatory impulse that channeled female members into conservative parties and associations after the war. The exact number of female members in the Pan-German League cannot be determined. In 1927, however, the League included 1,300 family members, who were mostly the wives and daughters of male members, out of a total of 17,000 members.[41] Although the membership figure for the ADV as a whole declined significantly after 1919, the number of family members remained relatively stable. In August 1919, for example, the League counted 1,135 such members out of a total membership of 33,469.[42] Women thus accounted for between 3 and 14 percent of the League's membership with percentages that varied throughout Germany. Occasional attendance by wives "as guests" of members of the managing committee or executive council between 1929 and 1932 offered little compensation. Women were to become more visible in leading positions in the early 1930s, but they joined at an accelerated rate only after 1933, when they were also appointed to important posts, including chairwomen.[43] Hertha Schemmel took matters in her own hands in Berlin and organized events in the capital. Franziska von Porembsky from Rudolstadt was irreplaceable in the Thuringian district, as was Irmgard Wrede, who struggled to overcome the League's insignificance in Silesia.[44] In early 1931 Wrede, Schemmel, and Porembsky temporarily joined headquarters in Berlin as staff members but without defined portfolios. They offered advice and helped in revising the League's manuscripts for publication. They also supported Claß's busy political life, which demanded a great deal of travel, office work, meetings, and absence from home. All of this made Claß's wife and daughter substantial, though largely invisible, members of the ADV staff. The Pan-German League thus remained a bastion of patriarchy, which offered only niches for female activism. This, in turn, limited the ADV's appeal to female constituencies, which had been mobilized by the DNVP in various women's committees or by the Protection League with various national supervisors of women's activities, and made the Pan-German League an aging men's association that retreated into its well-established rituals of centralized power devoted to cultivating residues of sociability and political expression in small, confined circles.[45]

Pan-German *Honoratioren* and the Nazi Challenge

In an effort to strengthen the League's public influence by giving Claß enhanced leadership powers, the Pan-Germans instituted new forms of centralization. These significantly changed the League's outlook and politics after the war. Power within the ADV's leading institutions coalesced around the chairman and his handpicked advisors. By the time that Eduard Liebert from the ADV managing committee labeled Claß the *"Führer"* of the Pan-German League in April 1918,[46] Claß had already established himself as its undisputed leader, thus bringing to a conclusion a process of recruitment that had begun as early 1908. The Pan-German League thus became increasingly subject to the internal manipulation of Claß and his loyal servants, such as Count Ernst zu Reventlow, who served as a new member in the executive committee and editor of the *Alldeutsche Blätter* until 1910—at which time he was succeeded by Claß's nephew Eduard Lucius—and Vietinghoff-Scheel, who became the ADV's executive chairman, or *Hauptgeschäftsführer*, in 1913.[47] Claß's consolidation of power met with occasional resistance, but for the most part this only reinforced his position. To thwart his opponents, Claß offered to resign on several occasions when the managing committee refused to honor his request for a position to assist him at the ADV headquarters. At the height of internal discussions over Claß's war aims program at the beginning of World War I, however, the managing committee gave Claß full authority to speak on behalf of the League. Supported by an inner circle that included Gebsattel, Vietinghoff-Scheel, Karl Lohmann, Jacobsen, Hertzberg, and Bang, Claß instituted direct and centralized leadership based on the so-called leadership principle or *Führerprinzip*.[48] During the war personnel shortages at all levels of the ADV's organization made centralized leadership even more important. By the beginning of the Weimar Republic, Claß employed a devoted staff at the headquarters with Otto von Roeder as secretary and Emil Junghans as clerk, Vietinghoff-Scheel, Gebsattel, and Hertzberg as deputy chairmen, and Alexander von Brockdorff as the headquarters' executive. Claß also appointed a number of loyalists as chairmen of important local chapters in an effort to streamline the channels of power and to ensure agreement. A significant number of these men subsequently moved into the managing committee or the head council, a move that created a centralized power structure that revolved around Claß and that was channeled to the local chapters through the various executive bodies of the League. Erich Stolte from Berlin, Jacobsen from Hamburg, Gebsattel from Bamberg, Liebert from Munich, Pezoldt from Plauen, *Justizrat* Schlüter from Essen, Dr. Oertel from Chemnitz, Georg Beutel from Dresden, Gebhard from Friedberg, the Walbaum brothers Hermann and Friedrich Karl from Tübingen and Göttingen respectively, Ludwig Viereck from Brunswick, and Hugo Grell from Potsdam were the most prominent members of these bodies.[49]

While these personal alliances solidified Claß's position as the undisputed leader of the ADV, they also narrowed both the scope of ideological input and the recruitment of new personnel. After the war the death of leading Pan-Germans changed the League's infrastructure not only at the local and district levels, but also in the ADV's executive, with the result that Claß was able to appoint even more loyal followers to key positions within the League's leadership structure. Although the editors of the *Alldeutsche Blätter* estimated that in 1918, 2,000 new members had been recruited to serve in the war,[50] after the war almost every chapter experienced a membership loss that resulted in a perceptible "decay" of the ADV organization. The high rate of turnover, especially at the centers of decision making between 1914 and the early 1920s, was unparalleled in the League's history. Yet as the political hardships accumulated, leading members like Gebsattel, Hopfen, and even Claß himself began to show serious signs of physical and psychological strain since the outbreak of the war. This, however, did not keep the ADV managing committee from renewing Claß's authority to act in the name of the Pan-German League first in 1921 and then again in 1924.[51] His centralized power was reinforced by the prominence of men in leadership positions who were his own age or older. Most of those who attended the meetings of the executive committee between 1920 and 1934, for example, were born in the 1860s and 1870s. What Detlev Peukert once called the "Wilhelmine Generation" born between the late 1850s and 1870 thus dominated the Pan-German League. But it was especially the cohort of Claß (1868–1953) that constituted the League's core leadership.[52] The prominence of these radical nationalist "1868ers," who represented a generation too young to have shaped the new Imperial Germany of 1871 and too old to have fought in World War I as the apex of Germany's imperial aspirations as a world power, bred a sense of political determination and ideological cohesion. But it also blocked the aspirations of younger activists to turn the League into an association that could appeal to the "front generation." Younger generations of Pan-German activists followed older members only slowly and in small numbers. Members of the so-called *Reichsgründergeneration* born between 1870 and 1880, such as Bang (1879–1945) and Hertzberg (1880–1945), as well as younger activists such as Arthur Müller (1883–1957) and Otto Heine (1893–1956) from the managing committee, became influential in the League during the 1920s but were all loyal supporters of Claß and failed to inspire the ADV chairman to address the limits of Pan-German mobilization.

The problems the ADV experienced in asserting itself as a dynamic, new force on the German Right were compounded by the distractions of Claß's private and public life. Claß himself was only too aware of his weak health, particularly after he emerged from two trials in the mid-1920s both physically and politically weakened. By the beginning of 1924 Pan-German plans for a national dictatorship had been frustrated not only by the failure of the Hitler Putsch but also by public allegations that Claß had conspired against Seeckt and that he had in fact planned Seeckt's assassination after the Chief of the Reichswehr refused to support right-wing uprisings in the occupied Ruhr. For the Pan-Germans, these allegations came as a surprise and only compounded the stress that had surrounded Hitler's trial for treason. The Hitler trial from 26 February to 1 April 1924 revealed the feuds between the Pan-Germans and the Nazis, their struggle for leadership of the national movement, their disrespect for each other's political style, and their ignorance of each other's core constituencies. Claß was surprised that Hitler excused his own putsch by asserting that Claß had planned a similar scenario in the hope of installing Seeckt, the General State Commissar Gustav Ritter von Kahr, or even Hitler himself as dictator.[53] The fragility of the Pan-German claim to leadership of the national movement was particularly manifest in Claß's own physical and psychological frailty, especially after the police searched his home on 15 May 1926 in connection with rumors that the League had negotiated with Reich President Hindenburg and the exiled Emperor Wilhelm II in Doorn over the appointment of Hugenberg as a dictator.[54] The subsequent trial, which took place before the Supreme Court in Leipzig, lasted thirteen months from May 1926 to June 1927. Having been tried for putsch plans that had been discussed early in 1926 by paramilitary organizations like the Wiking League (Bund Wiking), Olympia, Ludendorffs's Tannenburg League (Tannenbergbund), the Stahlhelm, and Artur Mahraun's Young German Order (Jungdeutscher Orden),[55] the Supreme Court found no evidence that planning to use Article 48 as a vehicle to dictatorship could be considered high treason. Only after Claß had survived three such trials between 1924 and 1927 was he able to reassert his claim to the leadership of the national movement. In the meantime, the Pan-German League had been completely unsettled by the allegations of Weimar's legal executive and the media glare the trials had attracted.

Claß's successes in the courtroom exacted a heavy price. Especially after his wife, Mathilde, died in the summer of 1927 after suffering from nerve and cervical vertebra paralysis since 1924, Claß himself suffered from bouts of poor health and repeatedly remained absent from headquarters for weeks and months. Only in early 1928 did Claß once again become active in these efforts to organize a *Sammlungsbewegung* of the Right.[56] In the meantime, however, parallel centers of action had developed elsewhere. Nowhere was this more true than in the case of the DNVP. At the end of 1922 Freytagh-Loringhoven and several other Pan-Germans like Vietinghoff-Scheel and Walther Graef organized the party's racist wing into the DNVP's Racist National Committee (Völkischer Reichsausschuß der Deutschnationalen Volkspartei), a position from which they championed the party's racist outlook and fought against the compromises of the party's national leadership with the existing political system. Like Hitler, Claß now too rejected putschism as a means for overthrowing the Weimar Republic and grasped the necessity of adhering to a policy of legality as the only conceivable way to gain power.[57] Infiltrating and purging the DNVP seemed like the most effective course of action for such a strategy just as the DNVP seemed to be in the process of adapting itself to the demands of the new parliamentary system under the leadership of Count Kuno von Westarp.[58] Between 1925 and 1927, however, Claß was unable to persuade Alfred Hugenberg to challenge Westarp for the chairmanship of the party. As a result, the Pan-Germans in the DNVP Reichstag delegation and in local chapters throughout the country tried instead to mobilize a majority for Hugenberg at meeting of the DNVP's party representation (Parteivertretung) in Berlin on 20 October 1928. Hugenberg's election was followed by a purge of DNVP district organizations by Pan-German activists, particularly in traditional Pan-German strongholds like Bremen, Hamburg, Potsdam, Berlin, South Hanover, and Saxony.[59]

Despite the purge of party moderates and the ideological radicalization that followed Hugenberg's election as party chairman, the DNVP did not become a simple extension of the Pan-German League. Given Claß's physical frailty, the League more often served as little more than a propaganda instrument for Hugenberg. Under Hugenberg the DNVP remained irreconcilably opposed to the experiments in government participation that Westarp had pursued in 1925 and 1927–28. As representatives of the Christian labor unions and agrarian pressure groups such the National Rural League abandoned the party between 1928 and 1930, Hugenberg tried to streamline the DNVP according to the *Führerprinzip*.[60] The DNVP thus turned more and more into a radical splinter party, whose share of the vote dropped from 14.2 percent in May 1928 to 7.0 percent in September 1930 with a corresponding loss in its party membership. The elections of 1930 revealed the volatility of Germany's bourgeois electorate, intensified the fragmentation of Germany's more established non-socialist parties, and initiated a dramatic political realignment of forces to the right of the Social Democrats and Center. Every third person that had voted for the DNVP 1928 voted for the NSDAP two years later.[61] Particularly alarming was the NSDAP's success in the Pan-German strongholds of Protestant northern and central Germany. The independent middle classes and large numbers of civil servants as well as the self-employed now voted for the NSDAP. Farmers and estate-owning Junkers also turned increasingly to Hitler, reducing the DNVP's success in its traditional strongholds east of the Elbe.[62] Yet despite the loss of moderate members, the new "bloc" rhetoric did not produce ideological unity among what was left of the party's rank-and-file. The *Sammlung* of former conservative, National Liberal, and antisemitic constituencies failed to produce a coherent nationalist and conservative milieu. Neither the DNVP nor the Pan-German League could rely on the support of its own core constituencies. The DNVP was a fragile *Milieupartei*, the Pan-German League a fragile *Milieuverband*.

The 1930 Reichstag elections constituted a dramatic turning point in the history of the Pan-German League and DNVP. It represented a shift within the German Right in favor of the National Socialists, who had previously functioned as a junior partner to the DNVP. In the aftermath of the elections Claß realized that the DNVP and the Pan-German League were now both dependent on Hitler's NSDAP.[63] The 1929 campaign against the Young Plan and the rally at Bad Harzburg in October 1931 both confirmed the extent to which the DNVP and Pan-German League had lost out in their efforts to organize a right-wing *Sammlungsbewegung* amid the growing electoral successes of the NSDAP. Sensing that the disputes within the DNVP were damaging Hugenberg and that "one was wrong to assume that Hugenberg was a unifying figure to the DNVP's Reichstag delegation," Claß kept open the possibility of an alliance with Hitler as an alternative to the ADV's partnership with the DNVP. After discussions within the ADV managing committee in 1930, Claß reconsidered and endorsed the League's support for DNVP candidates and secured the placement of several Pan-German members on the DNVP ticket.[64] Between 1931 and 1933, however, Hitler's intransigence and his unwillingness to cooperate fully with other elements of the Right had produced a virtual breakdown in relations between the Pan-Germans and the NSDAP.

The Pan-Germans were increasingly helpless in the leadership quarrels that divided Germany's anti-republican Right. Claß concluded that the events at Bad Harzburg had demonstrated that the national opposition was in shambles.[65] The ADV's loss of relevance within the national movement gave rise to cautious opposition to Claß's leadership of the organization. At a meeting of the ADV managing committee in December 1931 the district leader of north Bavaria, Christoph Pickel, demanded the creation of a "leadership council" to mobilize a Pan-German *Volksbewegung*.[66] Pickel argued that now was the time for the Pan-German League to become the leader of the "national opposition." Fritz Schillmann, who chaired the ADV's Berlin district organization, reminded Pickel that the League remained an "aristocratic" movement.[67] Instead of appealing to the masses, the League had to remain a small organization with Claß as the "monarch," while the mobilization of the masses was delegated to the DNVP. In the debate that followed, Vietinghoff-Scheel agreed with Schillmann that the ADV's message would never reach large parts of German society, especially since members were no longer engaged in the politics of the local chapters while the ADV's headquarters in Berlin kept investing its dwindling resources in senseless political campaigns.[68] In fact, the local chapter lectures rarely drew more than a few hundred people, and the League lost an additional 2,400 members between September 1930 and December 1931, thanks in part to the necessary increase in the annual fees.[69]

The Reichstag elections of 31 July 1932 brought even more disastrous results. The DNVP's share of the vote fell from 7.0 percent in 1930 to 5.9 percent, while the NSDAP gained an astounding 37.3 percent.[70] The NSDAP's success underlined the inability of the DNVP to compete with the NSDAP. The DNVP seemed condemned to the role of a bystander. After the Reichstag was dissolved again on 12 September 1932, the split between Hitler and Hugenberg deepened as Hitler seemed willing to talk to almost any political party. The NSDAP's strategy for the election campaign was to attack every political opponent, including the DNVP. The game left everyone confused, including Claß. Hitler's negotiations with the Center Party infuriated him, and he argued for a public break with the NSDAP. Speaking before the ADV managing committee in early September 1932 Claß reminded his colleagues that he had supported the NSDAP before Hitler betrayed the League during his 1924 trial and that he had subsequently supported the NSDAP's participation in the crusade against the Young Plan. But Hitler had frustrated all efforts to form a unified radical Right, seeking instead to exact maximum political capital by appearing to cooperate in order to "skim the cream off the top."[71] Claß was willing to risk a complete break with the NSDAP and would rather see the Pan-German League lose half its members than place it at the mercy of the NSDAP. However, Claß also realized that the DNVP could not seize the power on its own and, insofar as it needed the mass support of the NSDAP, was reluctant to call for the break. In the last four months before Hitler's appointment as chancellor on 30 January 1933 the Pan-German League continued to lose whatever influence it still had over Hugenberg, whose authoritarian leadership style had already begun to alienate long-serving Pan-Germans in the DNVP.[72]

Under these circumstances Claß began to develop his own plans for a dictatorship and drafted a Pan-German "emergency program" as an alternative to the rival positions of the DNVP and the NSDAP. Claß's "emergency program" called for the establishment of a presidential dictatorship, the promulgation of a state of emergency, a prohibition of the German Communist Party (Kommunistische Partei Deutschlands or KPD) and labor strikes, censorship of the media, and the creation of an expert advisory council, or *Großrat*, to the Reich President.[73] But Claß's physical frailty and the centralization of power within the League proved fatal when at the end of 1932 the "emergency program" could only be published in parts starting in December. As one of the program's principal authors, Claß was suffering from influenza, and it was not until 31 December 1932 that the first part of his political program could be published.[74] Another bout of gastric flu forced him to leave for a cure in Schwarzeneck in Thuringia, where he remained until the middle of February 1933. As a result, he was not in Berlin when Hitler was installed as chancellor on 30 January 1933.[75]

The Pan-Germans greeted Hitler's installation as chancellor with great ambivalence. For although the Pan-Germans endorsed the fundamentals of Nazi antisemitism and hailed the racial laws of April 1933 as the first step toward the creation of a racial state in which the rights of political participation were determined by the purity of one's blood and not by some abstract concept of citizenship,[76] Claß himself expressed a sense of "shame" about the pressure that had been brought to bear on Hugenberg and privately lamented that the coalition with Hitler had been a mistake.[77] At the same time, Claß publicly accepted the mantle of a "pioneer [*Wegbereiter*] of the national opposition" but carefully avoided the label of "Hitler's stirrup-holder [*Steigbügelhalter*]."[78] The Pan-German League would manage to hang on for the next six years before it was finally proscribed in 1939 on the pretext that with the annexation of Austria and the Sudetenland all of its goals had been achieved. Throughout this period the ADV found itself pushed more and more to the margins of Germany's national life with little more to do than to bemoan Nazi populism, street violence, and the complete disregard for the conservative principle of autarky in managing the

German economy as Hitler and his associates moved toward a future war.[79] Both Claß and Hugenberg lived to witness the defeat and division of Germany, the dissolution of Prussia, and the loss of former German territories after the Word War II. At Hugenberg's funeral in 1951 and Claß's two years later their close friend and associate Otto Meesmann lamented that "we stand on the ruins of Bismarck's Empire."[80]

Conclusion

The dissolution of the Pan-German League in 1939 concluded a long descent into political insignificance. By then the Pan-Germans had long ceased to be a factor in German political life. The very fact that the ADV had played no role whatsoever in the deliberations that led to the formation of the Hitler cabinet in January 1933 only underscored the extent to which the Pan-Germans had been relegated to the margins of Weimar politics. All of this, however, was fraught with bitter irony. For the Pan-Germans were indeed "pioneers" of the national revolution, a vanguard of the national opposition, and the Nazis owed much of their success to the way in which the Pan-Germans had prepared and fertilized the soil in which Nazism took root and flourished. Not only were there profound and far-reaching ideological proximities between the Pan-Germans and National Socialism, but both the ADV and the NSDAP sought to mobilize the masses through a lethal combination of ethnic racism, territorial expansionism, anti-liberalism, anti-socialism, and anti-democracy, all of which was tied together in the emotionally packed concept of the *Volksgemeinschaft*. Although the Pan-Germans despised the principle of popular sovereignty and propagated instead a class-based concept of political representation under the leadership of educated experts and a monarchy that was reduced to little more than symbolic value, it was not so much their ideas that separated them from the Nazis as the means and methods by which they and their Nazi rivals sought to realize these ideas.

For the Pan-Germans the period from 1914 to 1939 was an era of both success and failure, ideological power and a loss of significance, illusions and delusions. The Pan-German League remained tied to conceptions and ideology from the Imperial era, and until 1923 it continued to exercise significant symbolic power in the political culture of the Weimar Republic. But the principal beneficiaries of the new paramilitary political culture that took shape as a consequence of the trauma of defeat and revolution were not the Pan-Germans but radical nationalist movements that spoke to broader constituencies and practiced new and ultimately more effective forms of political mobilization. The rise of Hitler and National Socialism was facilitated by a well-established discourse of radical nationalism that the Pan-Germans had helped shape since the turn of the century. But the NSDAP's successful infiltration of Germany's conservative milieu after the 1928 Reichstag elections and Hitler's charismatic appeal to the masses was in large part a response to the shortcomings of the radical Right of the late imperial era. The Pan-Germans could not meet the challenge of National Socialism; their resources were too limited and their mindset too narrow to move beyond the confines of the *Honoratiorenpolitik* of Wilhelmine Germany. The Pan-Germans offered neither innovative nor effective means of mass mobilization and were left to languish in the shadow of public politics. Although the ADV remained surprisingly immune to infiltration by the National Socialists, the Pan-Germans—and the party through which it sought to advance its agenda, the German National People's Party—suffered immensely from the erosion and fragmentation of the predominantly Protestant liberal and nationalist bourgeois milieu out of which the League had originally emerged. The cumulative effect of war, inflation, and the great depression had created fissures in the ranks of this milieu that were so deep and so pervasive that there was little the Pan-Germans could do to overcome them.[81]

MacGregor Knox has noted that there was a fundamental tension between the ADV's claim to speak for all of the German people and the limited appeal of its efforts at popular mobilization. The dilemma facing the Pan-Germans, Knox concluded, was that they "remained conservatives by provenance and milieu" while their assumptions and "convictions increasingly made them revolutionaries."[82] What made them revolutionaries was not just their rejection of the political systems of Wilhelmine and Weimar Germany and their unrelenting opposition to any sort of compromise with it but, more importantly, their efforts to stimulate a rebirth of the German nation based upon the concept of the *Volksgemeinschaft*, a concept that theoretically embraced all Germans regardless of their social class, confession, gender, age, or the region of German from which they came. But the Pan-Germans never succeeded in overcoming the cleavages of class, confession, gender, age, or even region in their own efforts to mobilize the public behind its political agenda. For all its rhetoric about a national solidarity that transcended these fissures, the ADV remained hopelessly trapped in its own milieu and failed to articulate a vision of national unity that was capable of mobilizing the support of those who did not belong to the

Bildungsbürgertum milieu out of which the ADV had mostly emerged at the end of the nineteenth century. This was particularly true of the failure of the ADV's efforts to secure a breakthrough into the ranks of those who had served during World War and who in the postwar period gravitated toward paramilitary combat leagues like the Stahlhelm and SA. By the same token, the Pan-German goal of creating an exclusive organization of political specialists and educated experts as a sort of advisory council to the national government only accentuated a sectarianism that made it all the more difficult for the ADV to reach out from its own narrow base into new social constituencies. While a strong *esprit de corps* saved the ADV from dissolution after 1918, its principal problem remained that it was incapable of mobilizing a durable core constituency of more than about 10,000 to 15,000 members, of whom probably no more than 10 percent could be labeled devoted activists.[83]

The rise of the NSDAP was due in no small measure to the Pan-Germans' ignorance of the masses and the inadequacy of their elitist conceptions of leadership as a response to the crisis in which Germany found itself after 1918. The ADV's hopes of establishing itself as the power center of a new spiritual aristocracy (*Geistesaristokratie*) only helped legitimate the claims that Hitler and the NSDAP made on behalf of a charismatic *Führer* who, endowed with the power with the force of a religious vision, would succeed in transcending the divisions that had become so deeply entrenched in German political life. Although the Pan-Germans shared Hitler's belief in the primacy of the state, his distrust of democratic parliamentary government, and his racism at the driving force of modern society, they remained hostage to the milieu that had given birth to their movement and failed to articulate a political vision that featured the masses as the agent of political change and legitimacy. By the same token, the Pan-Germans failed to develop alternate centers of national unity to help legitimate their claim to political leadership. After 1918 neither Hindenburg nor Hitler was willing to cooperate with the Pan-Germans in the pursuit of their political ideals, nor did Hugenberg fulfill Claß's expectations as a potential dictatorial successor to Bismarck. This, in turn, left the Pan-Germans with no alternative but to acquiesce in Hitler's installation as chancellor and to embrace him as the *Führer* who at last would translate their dreams into reality. In the final analysis, it was not the Pan-Germans but Hitler and the National Socialists who proved to be the real beneficiaries of their agitation. Although other right-wing movements espoused Pan-German demands as their own and used antisemitism as a strategy for mobilizing the masses, there had been a fundamental realignment of the radical Right in the period after 1918 that had left its leadership hopelessly fragmented and that, in turn, paved the way for the Nazi seizure of power in 1933. At the end the Pan-Germans found themselves excluded from the corridors of power and condemned to increasing isolation and impotence in the Third Reich.

Notes

1. The secondary literature on the history of the Pan-German League in the Second Empire is quite extensive. For the most important studies, see Roger Chickering, *We Men Who Feel Most German: A Cultural Study of the Pan-German League, 1884–1914* (Boston: Allen & Unwin, 1984); and Michael Peters, *Der Alldeutsche Verband am Vorabend des Ersten Weltkrieges (1908–1914). Ein Beitrag zur Geschichte des völkischen Nationalismus im spätwilhelminischen Deutschland* (Frankfurt: Peter Lang, 1992); as well as Alfred Kruck, *Geschichte des Alldeutschen Verbandes 1890–1939* (Wiesbaden: Steiner, 1954); and Rainer Hering, *Konstruierte Nation. Der Alldeutsche Verband 1890–1939* (Hamburg: Christians, 2003). For the broader context, see Dirk Stegmann, *Die Erben Bismarcks. Parteien und Verbände in der Spätphase des Wilhelminischen Deutschlands. Sammlungspolitik 1897–1918* (Cologne and Berlin: Kiepenheuer & Wietsch, 1970); Geoff Eley, *Reshaping the German Right: Radical Nationalism and Political Change after Bismarck*, 2nd ed. (Ann Arbor: University of Michigan Press, 1990); Peter Walkenhorst, *Nation-Volk-Rasse. Radikaler Nationalismus im Deutschen Kaiserreich 1890–1914* (Göttingen: Vandenhoeck & Ruprecht, 2007); and Axel Griessmer, *Massenverbände und Massenparteien im wilhelminischen Reich. Zum Wandel der Wahlkultur 1903–1912* (Düsseldorf: Droste, 2000); as well as the historiographical essay by Wolfgang Mock, "'Manipulation von oben' oder 'Selbstorganisation an der Basis'? Einige neuere Aufsätze der englischen Historiographie zur Geschichte des deutschen Kaiserreichs," *Historische Zeitschrift* 232 (1981): 358–75.
2. On the ideological dynamics of the German Right, see the three works by Stefan Breuer, *Grundpositionen der deutschen Rechten, 1871–1945* (Tübingen: Edition Diskord, 1999), 31–50, 103–32; *Ordnungen der Ungleichheit. Die deutsche Rechte im Widerstreit ihrer Ideen 1871–1945* (Darmstadt: Wissenschaftliche Buchgesellschaft, 2001); and *Die radikale Rechte in Deutschland 1871–1945* (Stuttgart: Reclam, 2010). For further information, see Axel Schildt, *Konservatismus in Deutschland vom 18. Jahrhundert bis in die Gegenwart*, (Munich: Beck, 1998), 102–81; Uwe Puschner, Walter Schmitz, and Justus H. Ulbricht, "Vorwort," in *Handbuch zur "Völkischen Bewegung" 1871–1918*, ed. Puschner, Schmitz, and Ulbricht (Munich: Saur, 1998), ix–xxiii; Lee McGowan, *The Radical Right in Germany: 1870 to the Present* (Harlow: Longman, 2002); and James Retallack, "Introduction," in *The*

German Right, 1860–1920: Political Limits of the Authoritarian Imagination (Toronto: University of Toronto Press, 2006), 3–31.

3. *Alldeutsche Blätter*, 23 January 1919.

4. On the history of the ADV in the Weimar Republic, see Willi Krebs, "Der Alldeutsche Verband in den Jahren 1918–1939. Ein politisches Instrument des deutschen Imperialismus" (PhD diss., Humboldt Universität zu Berlin, 1970); Brewster S. Chamberlain, "The Enemy on the Right: The Alldeutsche Verband in the Weimar Republic, 1918–1926" (PhD diss., University of Maryland, 1972); and Barry Andrew Jackisch, *The Pan-German League and Radical Nationalist Politics in Interwar Germany* (Farnham: Ashgate, 2012). For recent studies on leading Pan-German activists, see Stefan Frech, *Wegbereiter Hitlers? Theodor Reismann-Grone. Ein völkischer Nationalist 1863–1949* (Paderborn: Schöningh, 2009); and Johannes Leicht, *Heinrich Claß 1868–1953. Die politische Biographie eines Alldeutschen* (Paderborn: Schöningh, 2012).

5. "Aufruf des Alldeutschen Verbandes an seine Mitglieder," 15 November 1918, in the unpublished records of the Alldeutscher Verband, Bundesarchiv Berlin-Lichterfelde, Bestand R 8048 (hereafter cited as BA Berlin, R 8048), 601/46.

6. Heinrich Claß, "Wider den Strom," vol. 2, in the unpublished Nachlaß of Heinrich Claß, Bundesarchiv Berlin-Lichterfelde, Bestand N 2368, 3, ch. 3.12. A scholarly edition of Claß's memoirs by Björn Hofmeister is currently in preparation under the title *Politische Erinnerungen des Vorsitzenden des Alldeutschen Verbandes 1915–1933/36*. The memoirs are hereafter cited as Claß, *Erinnerungen*, by chapter and subchapter.

7. See *Alldeutsche Blätter*, 19 April 1919 and 16 November 1918.

8. Claß, *Erinnerungen*, ch. 5.13. See also Hopfen to Claß, 15 November 1919, BA Berlin, R 8048, 392/49–57, and 20 November 1919, BA Berlin, R 8048, 392/700–8.

9. See Claß, *Erinnerungen*, ch. 5.3, as well as Claß's remarks at the meeting of the ADV managing committee, 26 November 1921, BA Berlin, R 8048, 133/10.

10. See Hagen Schulze, *Freikorps und Republik 1918–1920* (Boppard: H. Boldt, 1969), 36–37; James Diehl, *Paramilitary Politics in Weimar Germany* (Bloomington: Indiana University Press, 1977); Richard Bessel, *Germany after the First World War* (Oxford: Oxford University Press, 1993), 258; and Boris Barth, *Dolchstoßlegenden und politische Desintegration. Das Trauma der deutschen Niederlage 1914–1933* (Düsseldorf: Droste, 2003), 237.

11. See Krebs, "Der Alldeutsche Verband," 54–60. See also J. F. Lehmann, *Verleger J.F. Lehmann. Ein Leben im Kampf für Deutschland. Lebensbild und Briefe*, ed. Melanie Lehmann (Munich: J. F. Lehmann, 1935), 46–58; as well as *Alldeutsche Blätter*, 6 December 1930.

12. See Claß, *Erinnerungen*, ch. 5.5. See also Hopfen to Claß, 14 March 1920, BA Berlin, R 8048, 392/102; and Claß's remarks at the meeting of the ADV managing committee, 19 June 1920, BA Berlin, R 8048, 128/7–9; as well as Chamberlain, "Enemy on the Right," 142–43, and Krebs, "Der Alldeutsche Verband," 63–64.

13. See Claß's remarks at the meeting of the ADV managing committee, 2 September 1921, BA Berlin, R 8048, 132/9–11.
14. Meeting of the ADV managing committee, 2 September 1921, BA Berlin, R 8048, 132/13–19.
15. Meeting of the ADV managing committee, 26–27 November 1921, BA Berlin, R 8048, 133/6–10, 24–27, 34.
16. See Claß, *Erinnerungen*, addendum. In this same context, see Joachim Petzold, "Claß und Hitler. Über die Förderung der frühen Nazibewegung durch den Alldeutschen Verband und dessen Einfluß auf die nazistische Ideologie," *Jahrbuch für Geschichte* 21 (1980): 247–88.
17. For further details, see Björn Hofmeister, "Between Monarchy and Dictatorship: Radical Nationalism and Social Mobilization of the Pan-German League, 1914–1939" (PhD diss., Georgetown University, 2012), statistical appendix, fig. 1.
18. On the ADV's finances, see Breusing [to Beutel], 30 October 1919, in the records of the Alldeutscher Verband, Ortsgruppe Dresden und Oberelbgau, Stadtarchiv Dresden, Bestand 13.1 (hereafter cited as StA Dresden 13.1, 2/59); Breusing at the meeting of the ADV managing committee, 14–15 February 1920, BA Berlin, R 8048, 127/27; and Roeder to Hartmeyer, 5 June 1925, BA Berlin, R 8048, 211/177. See also Krebs, "Der Alldeutsche Verband," 17, as well as Johannes Bähr, Ralf Banken, and Thomas Flemming, *Die MAN. Eine deutsche Geschichte* (Munich: Beck, 2008), 250; Heidrun Holzbach, *Das "System Hugenberg." Die Organisation bürgerlicher Sammlungspolitik vor dem Aufstieg der NSDAP* (Stuttgart: DVA, 1982), 142; and Henry A. Turner, "Emil Kirdorf and the Nazi Party," *Central European History* 1 (1968): 324–44.
19. Vietinghoff-Scheel's remarks at the meeting of the ADV managing committee, 26 November 1921, BA Berlin, R 8048, 133/20; and at the meeting of the ADV managing committee, 12–13 February 1927, BA Berlin, R 8048, 149/78.
20. Gebhard at the meeting of the ADV managing committee, 12–13 February 1927, BA Berlin, R 8048, 149/60.
21. On the DSTP, see Uwe Lohalm, *Völkischer Radikalismus. Die Geschichte des Deutschvölkischen Schutz- und Trutzbundes 1919–1923* (Hamburg: Leibnitz, 1970), 89–90, 361. See also Werner Jochmann, *Gesellschaftskrise und Judenfeindschaft in Deutschland 1871–1945* (Hamburg: Leibnitz, 1988), 99–170.
22. Circular from Hertzberg, 3 May 1923, BA Berlin, R 8048, 256/46–48.
23. In this respect, see Alt to Ernst, 24 January 1930, in the unpublished records of the Hessisches Polizeipräsidium, Hessisches Staatsarchiv Darmstadt, Bestand G12 B (hereafter cited as HStA Darmstadt, G 12 B), 32/3. For further details, see Alt to the ADV headquarters, 28 May 1930, and Alt to Ernst, 13 August 1930, both in HStA Darmstadt, G12 B, 32/3; as well as Alt to Ernst, 10 September 1929, HStA Darmstadt, G12 B, 31/1, n.p.; and Alt's report from, 7 March 1930, HStA Darmstadt, G12 B, 32/4, n.p.
24. See Ernst to the ADV headquarters, 9 August 1930, HStA Darmstadt, G12 B, 31/5, n.p.

25. See Hofmeister, "Between Monarchy and Dictatorship," statistical appendix, fig. 11.
26. Remarks by Vietinghoff-Scheel at the meeting of the ADV managing committee, 4–5 December 1926, BA Berlin, R 8048, 148/45.
27. On the forms of bourgeois associational life in small-town Germany, see William Sheridan Allen, *The Nazi Seizure of Power. The Experience of a Single German Town, 1922–1945*, 2nd ed. (New York: Watts, 1984); Rudi Koshar, *Social Life, Local Politics, and Nazism, 1880–1935* (Chapel Hill, NC, and London: University of North Carolina Press, 1986); and Frank Bösch, *Das konservative Milieu. Vereinskultur und lokale Sammlungspolitik* (Göttingen: Wallstein, 2002), 15; as well as the thoughtful essay by Roger Chickering, "Political Mobilization and Associational Life: Some Thoughts on the National Socialists German Workers' Club (e.V.)," in *Elections, Mass Politics, and Social Change in Modern Germany: New Perspectives*, ed. Larry Eugene Jones and James Retallack (Cambridge: Cambridge University Press, 1992), 307–30.
28. *Alldeutsche Blätter*, 17 January 1920, 18 January 1921, 17 December 1921, 11 March 1922, 6 May 1922, and 23 July 1921.
29. On the militarization of political life in the immediate postwar period, see Robert Gerwarth and John Horne, "Vectors of Violence: Paramilitarism in Europe after the Great War, 1917–1923," *Journal of Modern History* 83 (2011): 489–512; Martin Conway and Robert Gerwarth, "Revolution and Counter-Revolution," in *Political Violence in Twentieth-Century Europe*, ed. Donald Bloxham and Robert Gerwarth (Cambridge: Cambridge University Press, 2011), 140–75; and Robert Gerwarth and John Horne, eds., *Paramilitary Violence after the Great War* (Oxford: Oxford University Press, 2012). See also Frank Bösch, "Militante Geselligkeit. Formierungsformen der bürgerlichen Vereinswelt zwischen Revolution und Nationalsozialismus," in *Politische Kulturgeschichte der Zwischenkriegszeit 1918–1939*, ed. Wolfgang Hardtwig (Göttingen: Vandenhoeck & Ruprecht, 2005), 151–82. On the Stahlhelm, see, Volker Berghahn, *Der Stahlhelm. Bund der Frontsoldaten 1918–1935* (Düsseldorf: Droste, 1966); and Alois Klotzbücher, "Der politische Weg des Stahlhelm—Bund der Frontsoldaten in der Weimarer Republik" (PhD diss., 1965); as well as the thoughtful essay by Peter Fritzsche, "Between Fragmentation and Fraternity: Civic Patriotism and the 'Stahlhelm' in Bourgeois Neighbourhoods during the Weimar Republic," *Tel Aviver Jahrbuch für Deutsche Geschichte* 17 (1988): 123–44.
30. On the Bismarck myth and its role in German political culture, see Robert Gerwarth, *The Bismarck Myth: Weimar Germany and the Legacy of the Iron Chancellor* (Oxford: Oxford University Press, 2005); and Richard F. Fraenkel, *Bismarck's Shadow: The Cult of Leadership and the Transformation of the German Right, 1898–1945* (Oxford and New York: Berg, 2005).
31. See *Hamburger Echo*, 1 April 1926, *Hamburger Nachrichten*, 1 April 1926, *Hamburger Fremdenblatt*, 1 April 1927, *Hamburger Volkszeitung*, 27 March 1929.
32. *Hamburger Nachrichten*, 2 April 1928, 4 April 1932, and 3 April 1933.

33. See the report of the Hamburg police, 7 June 1926, in the records of the Hamburg political police, Staatsarchiv Hamburg, Bestand 331–3, ES 10977, 827–29; and the report of the Reichskommissar für die Überwachung der öffentlichen Ordnung to Planck, 28 January 1926, in the unpublished records of the Reich Chancery, Bundesarchiv Berlin-Lichterfelde, Bestand R 43/I (hereafter cited as BA Berlin, R 43/1), 770/78–80.

34. Vietinghoff-Scheel to "Fritz," 1 February 1928, BA Berlin, R 8048, 214/30.

35. See the report of 1 December 1924 in the records of the Reichskommissar für die Überwachung der öffentlichen Ordnung, Bundesarchiv Berlin-Lichterfelde, Bestand R 1507, 25/32.

36. See Claß, *Erinnerungen*, addendum. See also reports of the Harzburg rally in *Vorwärts*, 11–13 October 1931; and *Unsere Partei* 9, no. 20 (17 October 1931): 246–47.

37. In this respect, see Bang's report to the ADV managing committee, 6–7 December 1930, BA Berlin, R 8048, 164/37–45; and Claß's remarks at the meeting of the ADV managing committee, 9 September 1932, BA Berlin, R 8048, 171/10.

38. On the Bismarck Youth, see Wolfgang Krabbe, "Die Bismarckjugend der Deutschnationalen Volkspartei," *German Studies Review* 17 (1994): 9–32.

39. See the minutes of the meeting of the ADV managing committee, 31 January–1 February 1925, BA Berlin, R 8048, 141/33–36.

40. See Benjamin Ziemann, "Die Erinnerung an den Ersten Weltkrieg in den Milieukulturen der Weimarer Republik," in *Kriegserlebnis und Legendenbildung*, ed. Thomas Schneider (Osnabrück: Universitätsverlag Rasch, 1999), 249–70; Richard Bessel, "The 'Front Generation' and the Politics of Weimar Germany," in *Generations in Conflict: Youth Revolt and Generation Formation in Germany, 1770–1968*, ed. Mark Roseman (Cambridge: Cambridge University Press, 1995), 121–36; and Anke Hoffstadt, "Der 'Stahlhelm. Bund der Frontsoldaten' und der Nationalsozialismus," in *Nationalsozialismus und Erster Weltkrieg*, ed. Gerd Krumeich (Essen: Klartext, 2010), 191–206.

41. Vietinghoff-Scheel at the meeting of the ADV managing committee, 12–13 February 1927, BA Berlin, R 8048, 149/78.

42. "Mitgliederliste Alldeutscher Verband," August 1919, BA Berlin, R 8048, 125/14.

43. For example, see *Alldeutsche Blätter*, 3 October 1936 and 5 March 1938.

44. On the involvement of women in the activities of the radical Right, see in particular Christiane Streubel, *Radikale Nationalistinnen. Agitation und Programmatik rechter Frauen in der Weimarer Republik* (Frankfurt: Campus, 2006). Particularly useful for the DNVP and its prewar predecessors are Raffael Scheck, *Mothers of the Nation: Right-Wing Women in Weimar Germany* (Oxford: Berg, 2004); Andrea Süchting-Hänger, *Das "Gewissen der Nation." Nationales Engagement und politisches Handeln konservativer Frauenorganisationen 1900–1937* (Düsseldorf: Droste, 2002); and Kirsten Heinsohn, *Konservative Parteien in Deutschland 1912 bis 1933. Demokratie und Partizipation in geschlechterhistorischer Perspektive* (Düsseldorf: Droste, 2010).

45. In this respect, see Claß, *Erinnerungen*, 5.4, 8.2, and 8.8.

46. Quoted in *Alldeutsche Blätter*, 20 April 1918. See also Leicht, *Heinrich Claß*, 205–20 and 248–58.

47. For further details, see Hofmeister, "Between Monarchy and Dictatorship," 309.

48. *Alldeutsche Blätter*, 12 December 1925.

49. Hofmeister, "Between Monarchy and Dictatorship," 311–12.

50. See Alldeutscher Verband, "Voranschlag für 1918," BA Berlin, R 8048, 116/5–8.

51. See the minutes of the meeting of the ADV managing committee, 5–6 February 1921, BA Berlin, R 8048, 130/4–5; and 16–17 February 1924, BA Berlin, R 8048, 137/62.

52. On the generational component of Weimar political culture, see Detlev J. K. Peukert, *Die Weimarer Republik. Krisenjahre der klassischen Moderne* (Frankfurt: Fischer, 1987), 25–31.

53. For further details, see Claß, *Erinnerungen*, addendum.

54. Reichskommissar für die Überwachung der öffentlichen Ordnung, 17 November 1925, BA Berlin, R 43/I, 770/75–77; as well as the reports in *Vorwärts*, 18 February 1926; *Berliner Lokal-Anzeiger*, 9 January 1926; and *Deutsches Tageblatt*, 1 January 1926.

55. See also *Deutsche Zeitung*, 5 November 1927.

56. Roeder to Roon, 27 February 1928, BA Berlin, R 8048, 214/12–13; and Hertzberg-Lottin to Claß, 27 February 1930, in the unpublished Nachlaß of Gertzlaff von Hertzberg, Bundesarchiv Berlin-Lichterfelde, Bestand N 2353, 1/148.

57. Claß, *Erinnerungen*, addendum.

58. For example, see "Richtlinien zur dezentralen Beeinflussung der DNVP" at the meeting of the ADV managing committee, 26–27 November 1927, BA Berlin, R 8048, 152/23–24.

59. On the ADV and its role in Hugenberg's election, see Claß, *Erinnerungen*, ch. 8.1. For further information, see Holzbach, *Das "System Hugenberg"*, 241; Kruck, *Geschichte des Alldeutschen Verbandes*, 168–69; and Jackisch, *Pan-German League*, 133–58. For further information, see John A. Leopold, "The Election of Alfred Hugenberg as Chairman of the German National People's Party," *Canadian Journal of History* 7 (1972): 149–71; as well as the detailed account of these events in Hans Hilpert, "Meinungen und Kämpfe. Meine politischen Erinnerungen," in Hilpert's unpublished Nachlaß, Bayerisches Hauptstaatsarchiv Munich, Abteilung V, 10/3628–3749.

60. On Hugenberg and the fragmentation of the DNVP's left wing, see John A. Leopold, *Alfred Hugenberg: The Radical National Campaign against the Weimar Republic* (New Haven, CT: Yale University Press, 1977), 55–83; and Attila A. Chanady, "The Disintegration of the German National People's Party 1924–1930," *Journal of Modern History* 39 (1967): 65–91; as well as two more recent contributions by Thomas Mergel, "Das Scheitern des deutschen Tory-Konservatismus. Die Umformung der DNVP zu einer rechtsradikalen Partei 1928–1932," *Historische Zeitschrift* 275 (2002):

323–68; and Manfred Kittel, "'Steigbügelhalter' Hitlers oder 'stille Republikaner'? Die Deutschnationalen in neuerer politikgeschichtlicher und kulturalistischer Perspektive," in *Geschichte der Politik. Alte und neue Wege*, ed. Hans-Kristof Kraus and Thomas Nicklas (Munich: Oldenbourg, 2007), 201–35.

61. Jürgen Falter, *Hitlers Wähler* (Munich: Beck, 1991), 111.

62. Ibid., 67–117, 146–290. See Thomas Childers, *The Nazi Voter The Social Foundation of Fascism in Germany, 1919–1933* (Chapel Hill, NC, and London: University of North Carolina Press, 1983), 119–91. See also Shelley Baranowski, *The Sanctity of Rural Life: Nobility, Protestantism, and Nazism in Weimar Prussia* (New York and Oxford: Oxford University Press, 1995), 146–50; and Jeremy Noakes, *The Nazi Party in Lower Saxony, 1921– 1933* (Oxford: Oxford University Press, 1971), 108–55.

63. See Claß, *Erinnerungen*, addendum.

64. Claß to the executive committees of the ADV local organizations, 24 July 1930, StA Dresden, 13.1, 12/258–59.

65. Claß at the meeting of the ADV managing committee, 5–6 December 1931, BA Berlin, R 8048, 168/54–56.

66. See the discussion of Pickel's memorandum at the meeting of the ADV managing committee, 5–6 December 1931, BA Berlin, R 8048, 168/26–27.

67. Schillmann to Claß, 2 November 1931, BA Berlin, R 8048, 168/31–32.

68. Vietinghoff-Scheel to Müller, 5 November 1931, BA Berlin, R 8048, 168/37.

69. See the remarks of Schillmann and Vietinghoff-Scheel at the meeting of the ADV managing committee, 5–6 December 1931, BA Berlin, R 8048, 168/75, 71–72.

70. Childers, *Nazi Voter*, 192–261.

71. Claß's report at the meeting of the ADV managing committee, 9 September 1932, BA Berlin, R 8048, 171/6–10.

72. In this respect, see the entries for 22–23 February and 5 and 15 March 1933 in *Die Deutschnationalen und die Zerstörung der Weimarer Republik. Aus dem Tagebuch von Reinhold Quaatz 1928–1933*, ed. Hermann Weiss and Paul Hoser (Munich: Oldenbourg, 1989), 235–37, 242.

73. "Entwurf Sofortprogramm," n.d. [December 1932], BA Berlin, R 8048, 172/64–91.

74. See *Alldeutsche Blätter*, 31 December 1932.

75. See Claß, *Erinnerungen*, ch. 8.7.

76. In this respect, see Vietinghoff-Scheel, "Die Hauptaufgaben deutscher Bevölkerungs- und Raumpolitik," in *Reden und Vorträge vom Alldeutschen Verbandstage in Chemnitz, 3. September 1933* (Berlin: Neudeutsche Verlags- und Treuhandanstalt, 1933), 20–33; as well as the more elaborate statement of Pan-German racial philosophy from the summer of 1933 in Leopold von Vietinghoff-Scheel, *Vom Wesen und Aufbau des völkischen Staates* (Berlin: Vermögensverwaltung des Alldeutschen Verbandes, 1933).

77. Entry in Quaatz's diary, 7 March 1933, in *Die Deutschnationalen und die Zerstörung der Weimarer Republik*, ed. Weiß and Hoser, 238–39.

78. *Deutsche Zeitung*, 9 February 1933.

79. In this regard, see the reports in the *Alldeutsche Blätter*, 20 April 1934 and 5 November 1937, as well as the ADV Lagebericht, 30 October 1935, in the unpublished Nachlaß of August Gebhard, Stadtarchiv Friedberg, Box 7, Folder 3.
80. See Meesmann, "Lebensbuch über Alfred Hugenberg" [n.d.], BA Koblenz, NL Hugenberg, 172/262–67; and Meesmann, "Ansprache Otto Meesmann am Grabe Heinrich Claß in Mainz am 1. Juni 1953," in the Restnachlaß of Heinrich Claß in the private possession of Friedel Dürrschmidt–Wolfrathshausen.
81. On this process, see Larry Eugene Jones, "The 'Dying Middle': Weimar Germany and the Fragmentation of Bourgeois Politics," *Central European History* 5 (1972): 23–54; Konrad Jarausch, "Die Krise des deutschen Bildungsbürgertums im ersten Drittel des 20. Jahrhunderts," in *Bürger und Bürgerlichkeit im 19. Jahrhundert*, ed. Jürgen Kocka (Munich: Deutscher Taschenbuch-Verlag, 1987), 180–205; and Hans Mommsen, "Die Auflösung der Bürgertums seit dem späten 19. Jahrhundert," in idem., 288–315.
82. MacGregor Knox, *To the Threshold of Power, 1922/33: Origins and Dynamics of the Fascist and National Socialist Dictatorships* (Cambridge: Cambridge University Press, 2007), 124.
83. In this respect, see the remarks by Vietinghoff-Scheel at the meetings of the ADV managing committee, 26 November 1921, BA Berlin, R 8048, 133/20; and 12–13 February 1927, BA Berlin, R 8048, 149/78.

6

Continuity and Change on the German Right

The Pan-German League and Nazism, 1918–39

Barry A. Jackisch

In late January 1920 Heinrich Claß met with Adolf Hitler for the first time. Claß, chairman of the Pan-German League (Alldeutscher Verband or ADV) and one of the most influential figures on the postwar *völkisch* Right, traveled to Munich to meet with the radical politician gaining notoriety in local right-wing circles.[1] Their meeting lasted a little over two hours. As Claß recalled, it was not really a "discussion" but rather a two-hour session of Hitler's lectures and rants embellished with fanatical gesticulations. Claß seemed at once shocked and impressed with Hitler's raw political skill and fanatical devotion to the fatherland:

> This man was a political savage . . . [nonetheless] every word that he spoke was absolutely sincere and accurate. This young man had learned well and his powers of perception were solidly grounded in a national, even *völkisch*, worldview. Any problems I might have had with his ideas had primarily to do with the influence of his upbringing and background. On the whole, he represented something totally new in the political life of our *Volk*, and someone from whom we might expect some success in loosening the ties of the working class to the Communist Party.[2]

But two issues continued to bother Claß after his first meeting with the Nazi leader. First, Hitler boldly stated that if he were able to gain a significant foothold among the masses, he would be willing to abandon the basic tenets of his political program later should this prove necessary. Hitler's tactical flexibility shocked Claß's more traditional political sensibilities. As Claß himself expressed it: "Are the ends meant to justify the means?"[3] Secondly, Claß was disturbed by Hitler's unshakable belief in his own powers of persuasion and the way in which he presented himself. Already after the first fifteen minutes of their meeting, Claß became convinced that he was dealing with an absolute hysteric.[4]

While it was entirely possible that this "hysterical eloquence" could have a great impact on the masses, Claß questioned whether or not Hitler really possessed the inherent abilities required of a true statesman.[5]

The meeting between Adolf Hitler and Heinrich Claß marked the beginning of a long and complicated relationship between the Pan-German League and Nazism that, in time, contributed significantly to the dissolution of the non-Nazi Right and the eventual establishment of the National Socialist dictatorship. While historians have referred in broad terms to the significance of Pan-German influence on the development of Nazi ideology, few studies have examined the actual relationship between these two organizations in detail. In reality, ties between the Pan-Germans and the Nazis were not as clear-cut as one might assume based on the two groups' close ideological affinities. Certainly Pan-German ideology—specifically the League's emphasis on racial anti-semitism, German identity based on blood rather than geography, and a paranoid hatred of parliamentary democracy and the political Left in all its forms—significantly influenced the National Socialist world view. However, this did not guarantee political cohesion between the Pan-Germans and the Nazis as political actors in the fractious post-1918 political world.

By stressing broad areas of continuity with the Pan-German League and other elements of the prewar Right, historians have placed the development of Nazi ideology within a longer trajectory of *völkisch* thinking in Germany stretching well back into the Second Reich. In fact, the specific emphasis on the ideological linkage between the Pan-Germans and Nazis emerged quickly in post–World War II attempts to understand the origins of National Socialism. Friedrich Meinecke's *The German Catastrophe* is one early example of this type of argument. In pointing out the general affinities between the Pan-Germans and Nazism, Meinecke posed the following rhetorical question: "Can one doubt any longer that the Pan-Germans and the Fatherland Party are an exact prelude to Hitler's rise to power?"[6] Ideological relationships of this nature have been central to studies that find strong continuity between the Second Reich, the Weimar Republic, and the Third Reich. George Mosse's history of the crisis of German ideology is one example of this approach. While granting that the Pan-German League and Hitler's state were not entirely synonymous, Mosse argues that the ADV exerted considerable ideological influence as the strongest of the *völkisch* organizations after 1918. "Through it [the ADV]," Mosse writes, "volkish ideas found firm footing within the establishment itself; and thus this organization must be ranked with the Youth Movement and the educational system as the chief transmitters of the Germanic ideology from the prewar to the postwar world."[7]

More recently, archivist and historian Rainer Hering has examined the Pan-German League through the lens of Benedict Anderson's theory of the nation as an "imagined community." According to Hering, the Pan-German League prepared the way for racist thinking in modern Germany and, therefore, it represented a significant organizational and ideological constant of the radical nationalist movement stretching from Imperial Germany through the Third Reich.[8] Quoting the well-known German historian Fritz Fischer, Hering concludes that the Third Reich was no accident, or *Betriebsunfall*, but rather the realization of the nation's most extreme historical developments stretching back before 1918, including the radical nationalist vision of the nation espoused by the Pan-German League.[9] But arguments that stress ideological continuity only partly explain the process by which Hitler and the Nazi movement emerged from the contentious, paranoid world of the Weimar Right eventually to destroy the republic and assume dictatorial power in Germany. As this essay will argue, one must also consider the role that real political conflict, sometimes obscured by apparent ideological similarities, within the German radical nationalist movement played in making possible Hitler's ultimate triumph in 1933.

The role of the Pan-German League is particularly important in the conflicts during the Weimar era over the political destiny of the German Right. As the preeminent radical nationalist organization from the pre-1918 period, the ADV sought to reestablish its control over the postwar German Right. In one sense, this meant continuing the Pan-German strategy of establishing political influence through other organizations. One example of this approach in the early Weimar period was the ADV's involvement in the creation of the German Racist Protection and Defense League (Deutschvölkischer Schutz- und Trutzbund or DSTB).[10] The League also pushed for a broader right-wing assault on the Republic by attempting to bring together the disparate elements of the German *völkisch* movement between 1918 and 1924. This strategy featured an early interest in Hitler and the nascent Nazi party. As Claß's comments from his January 1920 meeting with Hitler suggest, many Pan-German leaders viewed Hitler as a valuable agitator, especially among the industrial working class. But because of his upbringing and background, Claß and other Pan-Germans harbored serious reservations about the Nazi leader's long-term prospects as a statesman. This view of Hitler and his party would play an important role in the relationship between these two organizations throughout the Weimar period.

In light of these issues, the relationship between the Pan-Germans and Nazi provides an excellent opportunity to reexamine the nature of the German Right's transformation from the Second to the Third Reich. Far from revealing a relatively clear path of continuity from Wilhelmine radical nationalism through the Weimar Republic to the establishment of the Nazi state in 1933, the relationship between the Pan-Germans and Nazis reveals a complex and sometimes oddly combative history between 1918 and 1939. In examining these developments, this essay builds on Geoff Eley's argument about the contentious and compli-cated transformation of the German Right and Larry Eugene Jones's recent work emphasizing the lack of unity among right-wing forces as an important precondition for the rise and ultimate success of Na-zism.[11] This essay further argues that even among those organizations that espoused similar worldviews conflicts over the leadership of the radical nationalist movement were frequent and significant. The con-flicts that characterized the development of the radical Right in the first decade of the republic's existence helped make possible the Nazi Party's emergence as *the* primary representative of the nationalist opposition between 1930 and 1933. Our understanding of right-wing politics in the Weimar Republic is therefore incomplete if we dismiss these power struggles merely as personal disputes or petty squabbles over minor political fiefdoms. To the contrary, these conflicts—conflicts in which the Pan-German League was often directly involved—reveal the deep divisions that existed within the German Right as it evolved between 1918 and 1933.

From Initial Contact to November 1923

After their first face-to-face meeting in January 1920 Heinrich Claß and Adolf Hitler remained in fairly regular contact through 1923. Specifically, Claß asked fellow Munich Pan-German Dr. Otto Helmut Hopfen to keep him apprised of Hitler's activity. Aside from direct conversations, Claß also received periodic letters with reports and information concerning the Nazi movement. Indeed in the second week of August 1920, Claß re-ceived a detailed letter from Helmut Hopfen regarding Hitler.[12] Hopfen had already heard a number of Hitler's speeches in Munich and found the Nazi leader quite promising. Hitler's demands for universal conscription and his strong anti-French proclamations led Hopfen to suggest to Claß that Hitler might be a good addition to any number of Pan-German meet-ings or programs. Hopfen approached Hitler about a possible speaking arrangement for the Pan-German League. Hitler politely declined, stating, "Such an appearance could be easily misinterpreted by my followers."[13] This was most likely a reference to Hitler's desire to maintain the independence of the Nazi movement and to avoid the appearance that he was simply a tool of the Pan-German League. Nonetheless, Hitler still hoped for some level of cooperation in the form of financial support from the coffers of the Pan-German newspaper, the *Deutsche Zeitung*. As Hopfen recounted to Claß, Hitler requested 1,000 Marks for a proposed fourteen-day speaking trip to Austria in advance of upcoming elections. In a letter dated 18 August 1920, Claß informed Hopfen that the 1,000 Marks would be made available for Hitler's Austria trip.[14]

On his next trip to Munich Claß met with Hitler once again. This time the two men spoke in a side room of the Sterneckerbräu, which at the time doubled as the business office of the Nazi Party. Claß congratulated Hitler on his early successes in Munich and Bavaria and asked if he felt that workers were attending his speeches in any significant numbers. Hitler replied that even though the other parties did everything they could to keep the workers away, the Nazis were making some inroads.[15] The meeting closed with general agreement to Claß's proposal that Helmut Hopfen would cover Hitler and the activities of the Nazi party more closely in the pages of the Pan-German controlled *Deutsche Zeitung*. By January 1921 Claß believed that Hitler was prepared to expand the Nazi movement to northern Germany with significant Pan-German support. This idea was inspired by a meeting between Claß and Hitler at the end of 1920.[16] Perhaps to reassure Claß of his credentials, Hitler brought with him to this meeting a letter of recommendation from Dr. Ernst Pöhner. Pöhner was the Bavarian police director, a staunch supporter of right-wing groups, and one of Claß's trusted acquaintances. Pöhner wrote:

> The bearer of this letter, Herr Hitler, is already known to you from your visit to Munich. I have personally had several long discussions with Hitler and I am convinced that he is an exceptionally bright and capable defender of our common goal. He is an organizational and agitational force of the highest order and is known throughout Bavaria as the best speaker for the National Socialist German Workers' Party. . . . If the necessary financial support can be arranged, Herr Hitler, as he has made clear to me, is prepared to involve himself in northern Germany as well. I wish to recommend Herr Hitler with best regards, and I am confident that he will provide you excellent service.[17]

Pöhner's letter led Claß to believe that Hitler was now prepared to expand his movement into northern Germany. As the de facto head of the northern German *völkisch* movement, Claß could have expected to benefit by combining his established political credentials with Hitler's populist speaking style and charismatic leadership.

In late January 1921 Claß wrote a detailed letter to Dr. Otto Gertung in Nuremberg.[18] Gertung was a member of the board of directors at the MAN works (Maschinenwerke Augsburg-Nürnberg). Claß praised the Nazi movement's successes in Munich and southern Bavaria, particularly its alleged progress in fighting the "Red Terror." Nazi successes were so great, Claß continued, that he had "come to an agreement" with the leaders of the movement to open a new political front in northern Germany. Claß clearly believed at this point that Hitler was sincere in his desire to break out of Bavaria and expand to Berlin.[19] Later that spring Claß began to press Hitler to begin making appearances in Berlin and to establish a formal party office in the nation's capital. In conjunction with these requests, Claß again traveled to Munich and met directly with the Nazi leader. Hitler indicated that he was still prepared, in principle, to attempt the move north. But the costs—Hitler suggested a sum of about 60,000 Marks—would have to be covered in advance.[20] Claß assured Hitler that he would make every effort to raise the money. But this loose arrangement did not hold up for long. Only weeks later, Hitler returned to Berlin and informed Claß that, after careful consideration, he would not be able to make the move north after all. Hitler explained that it would make no sense for him to hold one or more major rallies in Berlin as it would require him to be away from Munich for three weeks or a month in order to start a viable party organization there. He felt he could not afford the time away from Munich because he needed to be there to supervise everything personally. Claß ultimately conceded that their previous plan could not be carried out, but he expressed hope that the Nazi movement would be able to expand to the capital in the very near future.[21]

Seen in the light of broader developments in the Nazi party in the summer of 1921, Hitler's seemingly abrupt decision to break off negotiations over a move to northern Germany becomes much clearer. First, it is entirely possible that Hitler never had any intention of expanding the Nazi movement out from Munich so early on in its development. In this sense, it is possible that he led Claß to believe that this was a possibility primarily to keep all options open, including financial ones, in connection with the Pan-Germans. Secondly, and perhaps more plausibly, if Hitler ever sincerely considered expansion to northern Germany, that plan would have been put off as a result of the Nazi party leadership crisis that developed in the summer of 1921.[22] Although Hitler emerged from this intra-party conflict as a clear victor, it cost valuable time and effort and distracted him from other important party business. This clearly included his negotiations with the Pan-German League.

The relationship between Heinrich Claß and Adolf Hitler was never the same after July 1921. Claß's memoirs indicate that between the summer of 1921 and the summer of 1928 he and Hitler only met directly again twice, once in May 1922 and then again in May 1923. In the meantime, one of Hitler's associates came to Berlin in early 1922 to beg Claß yet again for financial assistance for the *Völkischer Beobachter*.[23] Claß's memoirs indicate that he was able to collect about 30,000 Marks for the *Völkischer Beobachter* from funds controlled by the Pan-German *Deutsche Zeitung*.[24] Claß, however, expressed his growing frustration with the Nazi movement's never-ending demands when he observed: "Never once did we receive a single word [of thanks] for our assistance either from the publisher or from the [Nazi] party."[25]

Despite their increasingly turbulent relationship with Hitler and the Nazi movement, Claß and the Pan-German leadership were not yet ready to distance themselves entirely from Hitler. The Nazi leader's growing stature and potential for the anti-Weimar effort were simply too much to ignore. In May 1922, after learning that Hitler intended to make another visit to Berlin, Claß wrote the Nazi leader and suggested that they should meet again during Hitler's upcoming stay in the capital.[26] Claß even offered to pay for Hitler's round-trip train fare so that they could meet "with a small group of trusted friends to discuss certain issues of utmost importance."[27] The meeting took place at the end of May in connection with Hitler's speech before the Berlin chapter of the highly exclusive National Club of 1919 (Berliner Nationalklub von 1919), a radical right-wing discussion group of which Claß and several other prominent Pan-Germans were charter members. Although Claß's memoirs do not recount any of the details from this meeting, it is likely that it involved the old issue of financial support for the Nazi party. Only six weeks after Hitler's May visit to Berlin, Dr. Emil Gansser, a Nazi supporter and fundraiser, contacted Heinrich Claß concerning money that the Pan-German League had allegedly promised to the Nazi movement but had not yet delivered.[28] According to Gansser's letter, Claß had promised to wire 50,000 Marks to Munich. Whether this money was to come solely from the Pan-German League's coffers or from other sources is unclear. After some confusion regarding the actual status of the funds, the Pan-German League's headquarters sent a letter confirming that the money had been transferred to contacts in the Bavarian Order Bloc (Bayerischer Ordnungsblock).[29]

It is clear from Gansser's correspondence with Claß that Hitler sought funds from the Pan-German League to support the Nazi movement generally, but also more specifically for an increased propaganda campaign to begin in the summer of 1922.[30] However, there is no record of how, if ever, this money reached the Nazi party from the Bavarian Order Bloc. Furthermore, there is no evidence of any direct Nazi response acknowledging final receipt of the funds. As in Claß's previous dealings with Hitler and the Nazi party, it is likely that even this substantial contribution did not warrant a formal statement of thanks from the Nazi party leadership. Hitler's desire to maintain the appearance of his movement's strict independence from all other right-wing groups probably ensured this result. In effect, the Pan-German League and its allies were good enough to provide whatever financial assistance they could muster, but not significant enough to secure any sort of political or personal loyalty from Hitler in return. From this point on there would be no further Pan-German financial assistance for Hitler and the Nazi movement.

Those historians who have stressed the ideological affinities between the Pan-German League and National Socialism have also emphasized this early financial relationship as evidence of strong continuity between the established Right and Hitler's new movement.[31] As a closer examination of the evidence makes clear, however, Pan-German funding for Hitler was actually sporadic and largely ineffective. In reality, the limited Pan-German financial assistance to Hitler's movement was motivated by the League's desire to gain greater control over the Nazi Party as part of a larger Pan-German attempt to destabilize the Republic. Hitler's repeated lack of gratitude for Pan-German assistance and his unwillingness to cooperate with his elders in the radical nationalist movement only further estranged the Pan-German leadership from the Nazi Party. As Hitler's desire to remain independent from the Pan-German League became completely clear, the political connection between the two organizations became increasingly strained.

The Hitler Putsch and its Aftermath

The Pan-German League's already shaky relationship with the Nazi movement deteriorated rapidly in the wake of Hitler's abortive Beer Hall Putsch of November 1923. While Claß and the Pan-German leadership had also considered the possibility of direct, violent action against the government after 1919, they ultimately concluded that it would probably accomplish very little without first creating broader völkisch unity and securing military support.[32] Hitler's poorly organized strike against the Bavarian government only further frustrated the hopes that the Pan-Germans had placed in Hitler's promising political future. In the broader picture, the so-called Beer Hall Putsch was a major turning point in the relationship between the Pan-Germans and the Nazis.

Early on the morning of 9 November 1923 Claß awoke to news of Hitler's actions in the Bürgerbräukeller.[33] Within hours Claß called a meeting of his closest advisors and associates. No one seemed to have any real idea of the true nature of Hitler's move or whether or not it stood any chance of success. While the meeting was still in session, Claß received the most recent issue of the Pan-German *Deutsche Zeitung*. Claß and his colleagues read of the putsch's failure and the showdown on the Odeonsplatz. Claß and fellow Pan-German Paul Bang immediately departed for Munich.[34] Shortly after their arrival Claß and Bang were escorted to the Munich military barracks, where they met with General State Commissar Gustav Ritter von Kahr, Bavarian Reichswehr leader General Otto Hermann von Lossow, and others in charge of the anti-putsch forces.[35] Clearly incensed, Lossow described the debacle at the Bürgerbräukeller and expressed his extreme frustration with Hitler's ill-advised putsch attempt. An exhausted and disgusted Kahr explained to Claß and Bang that after the "holdup" at the Bürgerbräukeller, he was left with no other choice but to suppress the putsch and prevent any further misfortune.[36] Kahr felt no responsibility for the deaths at the Odeonsplatz earlier that day and placed responsibility instead on those who began the "propaganda march" in the first place with full knowledge that Kahr and his ministers would be forced to stop the demonstration.

In the face of public opinion and the very negative light it cast upon Kahr and all of the Bavarian Right, Claß suggested to Kahr that a general amnesty for all parties involved might be the best way to defuse the situation. Much to Claß's dismay, Kahr responded angrily that anyone who had been privy to the "monstrous breach of law" on the evening of 8 November could never have considered protecting these men from punishment. Before parting, Kahr requested that Claß and Bang make it perfectly clear to their northern *völkisch* associates that he and his ministers had been forced to act against the putsch.[37] Claß's meeting with Lossow and Kahr only confirmed to the Pan-German leader the futility of a putsch without sufficient preparation or broader right-wing unity. In Claß's mind, Hitler bore significant responsibility for this disastrous failure and reluctantly backed Kahr and his suppression of the putsch. The League's leaders concluded that the issue simply came down to the maintenance of state authority over total chaos.[38] Perhaps most importantly, the ADV leadership determined that "the salvation of the German Reich can never come out of Bavaria . . . it can and will only be possible from here [Berlin/Prussia]" in a statement that reflected the tension that had already arisen between northern and southern *völkisch* leaders after World War I.[39]

The Pan-German League's press responded quickly to the Beer Hall Putsch fiasco. On 10 November 1923 the *Deutsche Zeitung* ran a lead article simply titled: "Adolf Hitler." The article concluded that Hitler was "finished" as a politician because he lacked the "steel-hard strength" to protect himself from the pitfalls of his career. In the wake of the lost war and the devastating revolution, Hitler seemed to offer a great hope for creating a real "workers' nationalism" that might undermine support for socialism and communism in Germany. However, the article continued, Hitler had succumbed to his own sense of greatness. As the crowds increased at his speeches and his movement grew, he lost touch with his "humble" beginnings. Soon, he found himself caught up in an event that quickly slipped beyond his control. Whatever his motives in acting as he did on 8–9 November may have been, the dreadful outcome of the putsch attempt had, the article concluded, effectively destroyed Hitler's political career.[40]

In the wake of the Hitler Putsch, Pan-German hopes for uniting Germany's radical Right seemed rather bleak indeed.[41] This task would soon become even more difficult in the wake of the sensational Beer Hall Putsch trial in early spring 1924. Hitler used the trial to reinforce his own loyalty to his German fatherland and to assault the "November criminals" for having destroyed the country. He justified his actions on 8–9 November with the assertion that the Weimar government possessed neither the vision nor the resolve to do away with the destructive forces within and outside of Germany that were tearing the Reich apart.[42] Hitler, however, did not direct his rage solely at the Weimar government and its supporters. As an important part of his defense, Hitler also claimed that if what he had committed was high treason, then Heinrich Claß and other members of the Pan-German League should also be tried in as much as they had been planning a similar undertaking in the summer of 1923. In the course of his testimony Hitler asserted that Claß had approached him earlier that summer with plans to institute a three-man directory with Kahr. Moreover, Hitler claimed that his own move against the government was done primarily out of concern that Kahr and his associates were going to strike first and likely fail. Although Claß was never called to testify, he wired the court and published an open letter refuting Hitler's charges.[43]

Hitler's accusations stung Claß and other leading Pan-Germans. What disturbed the Pan-German leader most was not the fact that Hitler publicly accused him of high treason, but rather that Hitler blamed him for sabotaging the putsch by refusing to support it. Claß believed that Hitler intended to deflect attention away from his own decision to act by placing it within the supposedly larger context of right-wing plots against the government. Claß lamented the fact that these charges tarnished the Pan-German League's reputation and further divided the radical nationalist movement.[44] Shortly after the end of the trial and Hitler's conviction, Claß published his final commentary on the affair and refuted each of Hitler's accusations against the Pan-German League and its leadership.[45] "The curtain has fallen on the Munich trial. Let us hope," Claß wrote, "that overwrought emotions subside and that, as a result, those accusations with no basis in fact will cease."[46] By April 1924, however, the damage had been done. The putsch and the subsequent trial dashed the hopes that the Pan-Germans had placed in Hitler as a *völkisch* agitator and mass speaker.[47] More importantly, the unity of the *völkisch* movement for which the Pan-German League had worked since the beginning of the Weimar Republic now seemed out of reach.

In the wake of the putsch trial, Pan-German connections with Hitler's movement virtually ceased for roughly five years. The League's headquarters occasionally received letters between 1924 and 1929 from individual members who tried to encourage the League to resurrect its ties to the Nazi Party. However, these requests produced no substantial change in the League's approach. One example of these failed attempts can be found in the correspondence between Marie Gareis of Nuremburg and the leaders of the ADV and Nazi Party. Gareis wrote several times directly to Hitler, requesting that he meet once more with Claß to resolve their differences. As a result, Claß received a rather coolly worded letter from Rudolf Hess explaining that Hitler was unable to meet with Claß and, in any case, would certainly not rely on "some woman in Nuremberg" to arrange his political affairs. The League in turn requested that Gareis cease her efforts to unite the two leaders.[48] This episode accurately reflected the deteriorating relationship between the League and the Nazi movement in the middle years of the Weimar Republic. It would be some time before the League again turned its attention to Hitler and his party.

From the Young Plan to the Hitler Cabinet

Between the end of Hitler's putsch trial and the right-wing campaign against the Young Plan in 1929, there is no evidence of any meaningful cooperation between the Pan-Germans and Nazis. This can be attributed to several developments. First, the Hitler trial and the *völkisch* infighting that it revealed seemed to stall Pan-German efforts to unite the extreme Right in any further direct action against the Weimar government. Second, the Pan-German League was forced to reevaluate its overall approach to politics and the nature and extent of its influence after 1923–24. After reaching its highest membership total at about 38,000 in 1922, the League's membership declined steadily in the wake of the 1922–23 inflation.[49] This decline in membership and active support forced the ADV leadership to reevaluate its strategy for maintaining Pan-German influence in a more limited capacity within the ranks of the German Right. Finally, the so-called years of stability between 1924 and 1928 also forced the Pan-German League to refocus its efforts in the arena of mainstream party politics. From 1924–28, then, the League made the German National People's Party (Deutschnationale Volkspartei or DNVP) its top priority.

Ultimately, the Pan-German League played an important role in radicalizing the DNVP. The ADV strove to undermine moderate conservatives and pressed the party to adopt an uncompromising radical nationalist stance that ultimately left the DNVP as a junior partner in its negotiations with the explosive Nazi movement after 1929–30.[50] After Alfred Hugenberg's election as DNVP party chairman in 1928, the party's more moderate elements split off either to form new political organizations like the Conservative People's Party (Konservative Volkspartei or KVP), or to return permanently to private life, disgusted with the DNVP's new radical stance.[51] Under Hugenberg's leadership, the DNVP would never again entertain the idea of government participation with any party to its political left as had already happened twice in 1925 and 1927. The DNVP's transformation under Hugenberg's leadership decisively altered the balance of power on the German Right as the leadership of the radical nationalist, anti-Weimar coalition fell into the hands of Adolf Hitler. While Claß, Hugenberg, and their confidants believed that Hitler could be "managed" effectively as one part of a larger nationalist "block," Hitler and his dynamic, expanding party felt differently. As in the Weimar Republic's first years, the Pan-German League and its allies again misjudged Hitler's skill and intentions.

Pan-German leaders believed that only Alfred Hugenberg could salvage the DNVP and turn it into a true anti-democratic, radical nationalist force.[52] As a result, Pan-German machinations helped undermine any lingering hope for a responsible, popular, governmental conservatism in the Weimar Republic. In this regard, the Pan-German League bears significant responsibility for fracturing the German National People's Party and radicalizing conservative politics in the final years of the Weimar Republic. While the DNVP had hardly been a stalwart supporter of the Republic, the loss of any remaining moderate conservatives left Germany's largest conservative party in an extremely difficult position and, in turn, opened the party to a much greater reliance on Nazism between 1930 and 1933. It was in this period that the League again renewed its connections to the Nazi party. Despite the unfavorable impressions of Hitler that the Pan-German leadership had formed in the wake of the abortive Beer Hall Putsch trial, many leading Pan-Germans had by 1929 come to the realization that the newly invigorated Nazi movement could no longer be ignored. Furthermore, the ADV leadership faced increasing pressure from its rank-and-file membership to at least consider the Nazi movement as a possible right-wing ally. The nationalist campaign against the Young Plan initiated in 1929 presented the first real opportunity for the ADV to reestablish contact with the Nazi movement and to push once again for closer cooperation among all right-wing opponents of the Weimar Republic.[53] Rather than developing a new approach to the Nazi movement, however, the ADV simply relied upon its old policy of using Hitler and his party as populist agitators guided by the established political Right, preferably under Pan-German and DNVP leadership.[54]

The ADV's unrealistically paternalistic policy toward National Socialism proved to be even less effective in the face of the deepening national governmental crisis, the controversial policies of Chancellor Heinrich Brüning from 1930 to 1932, and the depression's disastrous impact throughout Germany.[55] While Claß, Hugenberg, and their allies publicly attacked Brüning's policies, Hitler and the Nazis used the same period to reinforce their independence from the established German Right, and gain further support for their own party's policies.[56] The growing conflict between the non-Nazi Right and the NSDAP would become even more intense in the Weimar Republic's final sixteen months. This was also certainly true for the more specific relationship between the Pan-German League and Hitler's movement. The period stretching from the formation of the Harzburg Front in October 1931 until the Nazi triumph in January 1933 witnessed the opening of a nearly unbridgeable rift between the Pan-German League and the Nazi party. By the time of General Kurt von Schleicher's appointment as chancellor in December 1932, many Pan-German leaders remarkably considered the Nazis as a threat that was every bit as dangerous to Germany's future as that posed by the Communists.

The first signs of a renewed conflict between the Pan-Germans and the Hitler movement came at the Harzburg rally in the fall of 1931. The deteriorating economic situation had severely undermined public confidence in the ability of the sitting chancellor Heinrich Brüning to prevent a full-blown economic collapse.[57] The Pan-Germans viewed the policies of the Brüning government as an unmitigated disaster for the German people and welcomed plans for a demonstration of the united German Right against the Brüning cabinet as an opportunity not only to reawaken the spirit of the crusade against the Young Plan but also to send a clear message to Reich President Paul von Hindenberg that the time had arrived for an end to the Brüning government.[58] The ADV leadership hoped that such a demonstration would convince the Reich president that it was time to appoint a new government of national concentration under Hugenberg's leadership that would be vested with emergency powers to save Germany from total collapse. But whatever hopes that Claß and the ADV leadership might have had that the rally at Bad Harzburg on 10–11 October 1931 would lead to a reaffirmation of right-wing unity in the struggle against Weimar were sabotaged by behavior on the part of the Nazi party leader that could only have been described as bizarre.

Claß and several other leading Pan-Germans arrived in Bad Harzburg on 10 October. The main public demonstration, including marches by right-wing paramilitary units, speeches, and the declaration of a joint statement against the Brüning government, was to take place the following day on Sunday, 11 October. As Claß finished a late dinner with other attendees on 10 October, he was called to an emergency "leaders' meeting" to be held at ten o'clock that evening. Claß and his associates moved to the meeting hall only to wait in vain for nearly two hours for Hitler to appear. Finally exasperated with this treatment, DNVP party chairman Hugenberg demanded an explanation for Hitler's absence. Nazi delegates Gregor Strasser and Wilhelm Frick apologized but offered no explanation for their leader's behavior. Instead they informed those present that Hitler now expected several last-minute revisions to the previously agreed-upon joint statement against the Brüning cabinet that was scheduled for release the following day. Shocked by this demand but unwilling to jeopardize the entire gathering, Hugenberg and other right-wing leaders agreed to some minor revisions in tone and style that seemed to satisfy Strasser and Frick.[59]

Hitler's behavior the following day further frustrated and angered the Pan-Germans and representatives of the other non-Nazi organizations that were present at Harzburg. Hitler arrived late to the parade of paramilitary forces that took place that morning and stayed only long enough to review the Nazi Storm Troopers from his car. He abruptly departed before the other paramilitary groups, including the Stahlhelm, had passed the reviewing stand.[60] The Nazi leader then refused to join the midday banquet, later claiming to despise such bourgeois meals while so many of his followers fought on empty stomachs.[61] Finally, Hitler threatened not to speak at the main assembly that was the high point of the rally and that was scheduled to take place later that afternoon. Only as a result of Hugenberg's persuasion did Hitler finally agree to participate. As Claß recalled, the assembly hall that afternoon was torn by a shouting contest featuring "Heil Hitler" and "Heil Hugenberg." "It did not appear," the Pan-German League chairman concluded, "to be a united rally, but rather one of unbridgeable contradictions."[62]

The nationalist movement never overcame the divisions that had manifested themselves so openly at the rally in Bad Harzburg. In the months that followed the relationship between the Nazis and the non-Nazi Right under Hugenberg only deteriorated further as Hitler made clear his party's intent to gain power on its own terms, free from ties to the "old" Right represented by figures like Hugenberg and Claß.[63] In light of these developments, many of the concerns that the Pan-Germans had expressed about Hitler's leadership resurfaced at the end of 1931 and beginning of 1932.[64] Despite the NSDAP's tremendous electoral success in September 1930, the party and its leader could no longer be trusted to support the broad nationalist opposition strategy that the League desired.

Under these circumstances the leaders of the Pan-German League were left with no alternative but to reiterate their support for Hugenberg as the only real leader that could solve Germany's crisis. After the Harzburg fiasco the Pan-Germans could conjure up few other solutions to mend the schism in the increasingly fractured nationalist movement.[65] The ADV's attempts to broker an agreement between the Nazi Party and the DNVP within the broader framework of the national opposition had broken down as a result of inter-party feuding, personal animosities, and differences over strategy and tactics. For the ADV the situation was compounded by the fact that it was losing members at an alarming rate because of the political discord within the German Right and the economic crisis ravaging the country.[66] It was in this increasingly polarized climate that the League confronted the dilemma of the 1932 presidential election.[67]

The breakdown in relations between the Pan-Germans and Nazis between 1931 and 1933 began with Hitler's intransigence and his unwillingness to cooperate fully with other elements of the radical Right at the Harzburg rally in October 1931.[68] After Harzburg Hitler made it increasingly clear that his party was interested in proceeding independently from both Hugenburg's formal attempts to create a more expansive right-wing bloc and from Pan-German efforts to influence the development of the Nazi party with the goal of moderating its allegedly radical socialist elements. Many of the ADV's old concerns about Hitler resurfaced in the wake of the Harzburg rally. Hitler had broken promises on countless occasions to a wide range of groups within the national opposition, and Claß and other Pan-German leaders were now convinced that the Nazi leader was indeed willing to take extreme measures to gain power without cooperation from his elders in the nationalist movement.[69]

The Pan-German League's relationship with the Nazis became even more complicated as a result of the 1932 presidential elections. After long and difficult negotiations in the first two months of 1932, Germany's major right-wing parties failed to reach agreement on a joint candidate to run against the Communist Ernst Thälmann and the sitting president Paul von Hindenburg in the March 1932 presidential elections. The radical Right openly opposed Hindenburg for his support of the Brüning cabinet, yet the divisions that had plagued the Harzburg meeting only months earlier now also prevented Hugenberg, Hitler, and their supporters from agreeing upon a common candidate.[70] As right-wing negotiations floundered, the Nazis announced on 22 February that Adolf Hitler would run for the presidency. Later that evening the DNVP and Stahlhelm announced Theodor Duesterberg as their candidate for the March elections.[71] Once again, Germany's two largest right-wing groups failed to find common ground.

The leaders of the Pan-German League lamented this development as yet another example of the growing division within the ranks of the so-called national opposition.[72] A split candidacy was even worse, ADV leaders argued, when one considered the advantage this would most likely afford the sitting president in his bid for reelection. In spite of Hindenburg's great military service to the nation, the League had come to view him as an abject political failure. The League's relationship with the President had begun to deteriorate already in 1926 when he refused to support Pan-German efforts to appoint Hugenberg head of an emergency government.[73] The ADV's opinion of Hindenburg had declined even further after he signed the Young Plan into law and continued to support the Brüning government with emergency powers in the face of vehement nationalist opposition to the chancellor's policies.[74] Now, to the Pan-German League's deep regret, no single nationalist candidate would even stand against Hindenburg in the March elections.

In the first round of presidential balloting on 17 March 1932 Hindenburg received 49.6 percent of the popular vote and therefore barely missed the absolute majority needed for election. Hitler finished far behind with 30.1 percent of votes cast. Duesterberg, the candidate supported by Hugenberg's DNVP and the conservative veterans' organization known as the Stahlhelm, performed very poorly with only 6.8 percent of the popular vote.[75] In light of these results, Hugenberg decided not to present a nationalist candidate for the second round of balloting that was scheduled to take place on 10 April. Instead, Hugenberg remained neutral and encouraged all of his supporters to do the same.[76] Faced with the choice of supporting Hitler, the Communist candidate Thälmann, or Hindenburg, Claß broke with his trusted ally Hugenberg and authorized League members to support Hitler's candidacy. Claß justified Pan-German support for Hitler by citing the League's freedom of action as a non-party interest group and the need to oppose Hindenburg's candidacy at all costs.[77] Privately, however, Claß believed Hitler stood no realistic chance of defeating Hindenburg. By authorizing Pan-German League members to vote for the Nazi leader, Claß believed that they could safely vent their anger against the current government without actually strengthening the Nazi cause. Claß also felt that he could not ask thousands of ADV members to withhold their votes in the presidential runoff and then solicit their support for the DNVP in the upcoming Prussian state elections that would be taking place on 24 April 1932. In Claß's mind, this decision was a calculated gamble rather than a genuine endorsement of the Nazi leader. As Claß admitted to Hugenberg's close confederate Leo Wegener: "If I wanted to keep my people in line for the Prussian election, . . . then I had to indulge their need to vent their anger and vote in the presidential runoff. [This was] actually harmless because the NSDAP had no chance of winning."[78] Nonetheless, Claß's decision temporarily strained his relations with Hugenberg and provoked dissent within the ADV's own ranks.[79]

Relations between the Pan-German League and the National Socialists deteriorated significantly after the 1932 presidential elections. Between May and December the ADV broke off almost all channels of communication with Hitler's movement as it became clear that the Nazi Party was moving in a direction opposed to the goals of the Claß-Hugenberg axis in the nationalist opposition.[80] Pan-German antipathy toward the NSDAP increased as the Nazis entertained the idea of a "Black-Brown" coalition government in Prussia with the Center Party.[81] At a meeting of the ADV managing committee in September 1932 Claß confided to the League's leadership with a prescience that was remarkable even for him: "Germany has not been in greater danger since the overthrow [of 1918] and today the greatest source of that danger is the NSDAP. One must clearly realize that even a nationalist mass party is still the mass. History demonstrates that a nation can only be prosperous when it is driven into its good fortune by the few [the elite]."[82]

The ADV's opinion of Hitler and the Nazi movement reached its nadir after learning of Nazi cooperation with the Communists in the Berlin transportation strike in the fall of 1932.[83] The Pan-German leadership now believed that Nazism had sold its soul in an all-out quest for political power with disastrous results for the movement. As Claß remarked in December 1932: "I am convinced that the NSDAP is infected with a deadly poison and that this poison can no longer be expelled. I am further convinced that the NSDAP [as a political force] has essentially run its course."[84]

Pan-German misgivings about Nazism did not abate with the creation of the Hitler cabinet on 30 January 1933. Many Pan-German leaders had still not come to terms with the mass demagoguery that had helped catapult the National Socialist movement into power. The ADV's situation report for the first week of February 1933 celebrated the victory of the "nationalist front" and praised Hugenberg for his continuing efforts to bring about a true nationalist coalition.[85] But in celebrating that accomplishment, the ADV downplayed Hitler's role in the events leading to his appointment as chancellor.[86] Privately, Claß and several other Pan-German leaders acknowledged the failure of Pan-German and DNVP efforts to control Hitler. Although Claß was away from Berlin for health reasons at the time of the cabinet's installation, he later said to Hugenberg: "if I had been [in Berlin], I would have clung to you to make sure that you did not go along [with the Hitler cabinet]." Reflecting his deep-seated pessimism regarding the new government, Hugenberg responded, "Now I am a prisoner."[87]

Conclusion

On 15 March 1939 the Gestapo launched coordinated, early morning raids to shut down the Pan-German League's headquarters as well as regional offices across the country. Acting with Hitler's personal approval, the Gestapo brought an end to the Pan-German League's nearly fifty-year history.[88] The official explanation released through the German News Service stated that the League had been shut down and its publications banned in accordance with Article 1 of the 1933 "Law for the Protection of the People and the State."[89] According to private state security documents, the Nazi regime had indeed grown increasingly concerned about the Pan-German League's post-1933 activity. For roughly six years from 1933 until 1939, the Third Reich's security forces tracked the Pan-German League's actions and compiled a detailed record of activities that the Gestapo viewed as potentially threatening to the regime.[90]

It is impossible to determine the extent to which the League might have ever developed as a rallying point for conservative opposition to the Nazi state. Gestapo and other documents, however, suggest that the Nazi leadership believed this might happen and acted quickly to prevent such an occurrence.[91] Although there is no concrete evidence that Pan-German League leaders or their DNVP allies ever even considered specific action against the regime, the Gestapo's reports suggest that the League did express its opposition to the extremes of the Nazi dictatorship through speeches, flyers, and private meetings.

These events in 1939 seem incongruous for several reasons. It is certainly surprising that the Nazi state allowed the Pan-German League to exist at all until 1939. This had in large part to do with the League's non-party status and the apparent similarity between the regime's goals and those of the Pan-Germans. Furthermore, the League's membership had declined significantly by 1933 to between 10,000 and 12,000, was primarily made up of remaining older members, and initially seemed to present no real threat to the Nazi state. Nonetheless, the League's existence in the Third Reich until 1939 and the extensive security reports on its questionable activity constitutes a bizarre final chapter in the strange history of the Pan-German/Nazi relationship that began in 1920.

What, then, can we conclude about the complicated historical connections between these two prominent right-wing groups? Moreover, what does their political relationship reveal about the complex transformation of the German Right in the Weimar period? For decades after the horrors of the Second World War and the Holocaust, historians devoted significant attention to the ideological continuities between the Pan-German League and the Nazi movement. These ideological continuities did indeed exist, and the League bears significant responsibility for exposing sizeable portions of the German middle and upper classes to *völkisch* ideas long before Hitler's rise to power in 1933.[92]

This focus on ideological continuity, however, has obscured several other important lessons about the Pan-German League's relationship with Hitler and the Nazi movement in the Weimar Republic. While the League was an important and early proponent of radical *völkisch* ideology in the pre-1918 period, it was only one of many groups after the war that espoused such ideas. As Geoff Eley has argued, this radical nationalist legacy had in fact become common property of the German Right after the war. This remained, however, primarily an ideological achievement because of the radical nationalist failure to mold the numerous right-wing groups into a coherent, unified, and politically effective force.[93] The checkered relationship between the Pan-Germans and Nazis is a case in point.

In 1932 Heinrich Claß privately acknowledged the fractious nature of right-wing politics and the failure of the non-Nazi Right to mount any meaningful, sustained opposition to the Weimar Republic. Claß observed, "This Republic survives not because of virtuous Republicans, but rather through the mountains of mistakes committed by the nationalists."[94] Although made late in the Republic's history, this revealing comment is especially relevant to the relationship between the Pan-German League and the Nazi movement throughout the Weimar period. The ADV's overconfidence in its ability to control *völkisch* politics after 1918 caused it to misjudge the impact of its actions on the long-term development of the German Right. Claß and the Pan-Germans lamented the nationalist disunity in the wake of Hitler's abortive Beer Hall Putsch. Yet, the League's unrealistic approach to the Nazi movement contributed in significant ways to precisely this outcome. At various critical junctures, the Pan-German League, like many others, simply failed to understand Hitler's true intentions.

Pan-German influence within the DNVP was also an important factor in the League's relationship with Nazism. The Pan-Germans helped insure that a moderate, state-supporting, mass conservative party would not emerge in the final years of the Weimar Republic. In direct response to the ADV's successful campaign on behalf of Alfred Hugenberg's candidacy for the DNVP party chairmanship, moderate conservatives split off from the party and further divided the conservative movement at the precise moment that Nazism was significantly expanding its popular base. While the ADV thus helped to weaken German conservatism, its leaders realized far too late that the Pan-German strategy had also substantially strengthened Hitler's own position in the face of the smaller and significantly less influential DNVP.

In the deeply divided right-wing political landscape of Weimar's final years, Claß and the Pan-Germans finally realized how little control they actually had over the Nazi movement. Conversely, Hitler successfully portrayed his party as the only unified and truly effective force of the nationalist opposition. With the non-Nazi Right in shambles, Hitler's message resonated with German voters in unprecedented ways. Originally hoping to unify the postwar radical nationalist movement, the Pan-German League had instead played an important role in dividing it. This division opened the way for a leader and a movement whose policies would ultimately destroy once and for all the powerful German nation state that Heinrich Claß and the Pan-German League had worked so long to establish.

Notes

1. For a detailed account of the complex right-wing milieu in post–World War I Munich, see Harold Gordon, *Hitler and the Beer Hall Putsch* (Princeton, NJ: Princeton University Press, 1972), esp. 3–184. For an intriguing look at the ties between cultural and political developments in Munich in this period, see also David Clay Large, *Where Ghosts Walked: Munich's Road to the Third Reich* (New York and London: W. W. Norton, 1997). The German Workers' Party (Deutsche Arbeiterpartei) changed its name under Hitler's leadership in February 1920 to the National Socialist German Workers' Party (Nationalsozialistische Deutsche Arbeiterpartei or NSDAP). For further information on the party's early history and Hitler's decisive involvement in it, see Dietrich J. Orlow, *The History of the Nazi Party, 1919–1933* (Pittsburgh, PA: University of Pittsburgh Press, 1969), esp. 1–45.

2. Addendum to volume 2 of Claß's unpublished memoirs, "Wider den Strom," in the unpublished Nachlaß of Heinrich Claß, Bundesarchiv Berlin-Lichterfelde, Bestand N 2368 (hereafter cited as Claß, WdS II-addendum), 3/8–9. These memoirs are a unique source of information concerning Claß's personal contact with Hitler and the early Nazi movement. The section specifically devoted to the Claß-Hitler relationship is located in an addendum at the end of the Claß memoirs. This source, along with numerous documents in the Pan-German League's main archival holdings (Bundesarchiv Berlin, Bestand R 8048, hereafter cited as BA Berlin, R 8048), provides a detailed picture of the relationship between the growing Nazi movement and the Pan-German League that has not been fully appreciated in the historiography. Although Joachim Petzold published an article in

East Germany dealing generally with this topic, it is ideologically colored and fails to draw systematically on the important information contained in the Claß memoirs. See Joachim Petzold, "Claß und Hitler: Über die Förderung der frühen Nazibewegung durch den Alldeutschen Verband und dessen Einfluß auf die Nazi Ideologie," *Jahrbuch für Geschichte* 21 (1980): 247–88. Two other treatments of the Pan-German and Nazi relationship emphasizing strong continuity, again without access to critical documents located at that time in East Germany, are Alfred Kruck, *Geschichte des Alldeutschen Verbandes 1890–1939* (Wiesbaden, 1954); and Brewster Chamberlin, "The Enemy on the Right: The Alldeutsche Verband in the Weimar Republic 1918–1926" (PhD diss., University of Maryland, 1972). Most recently, see an overview of the Pan-German view of Nazism in Rainer Hering, *Konstruierte Nation: der Alldeutsche Verband, 1890 bis 1939* (Hamburg: Christians, 2003), 479–88. On Claß, see the recent biography by Johannes Leicht, *Heinrich Claß 1868–1954. Die politische Biographie eines Alldeutschen* (Paderborn: Schöningh, 2012).

3. Claß, WdS II-addendum, 9.

4. Ibid.

5. Ibid.

6. Friedrich Meinecke, *The German Catastrophe: Reflections and Recollections* (English edition: Boston: Beacon Press, 1963), 30. For a definitive history of the Fatherland Party that disagrees with Meinecke's assessment see Heinz Hagenlücke, *Deutsche Vaterlandspartei. Die nationale Rechte am Ende des Kaiserreiches* (Düsseldorf: Droste, 1997), esp. 13–19 and 408–10.

7. George L. Mosse, *The Crisis of German Ideology: Intellectual Origins of the Third Reich* (New York: Grosset and Dunlap, 1965), 225. Two recent works stress general continuity between pre- and postwar German right-wing thought stretching to National Socialism. In this respect, see Thomas Rohkrämer, *A Single Communal Faith? The German Right from Conservatism to National Socialism* (New York and Oxford: Berg, 2007); and Peter Walkenhorst, *Nation—Volk—Rasse. Radikaler Nationalismus im Deutschen Kaiserreich 1890–1914* (Göttingen: Vandenhoeck & Ruprecht, 2007), esp. 333–42. On specific ideological connections between the Pan-German League and the Third Reich, see Kruck, *Geschichte des Alldeutschen Verbandes*, and Hering, *Konstruierte Nation*.

8. Hering, *Konstruierte Nation*, 9–12, 15.

9. Ibid., 29, 488.

10. For more on the League's role in the creation of the German Racist Protective and Defense League, see Barry A. Jackisch, *The Pan-German League and Radical Nationalist Politics in Interwar Germany, 1918–1939* (Farnham, 2012), 25–29; and Uwe Lohalm, *Völkischer Radikalimus: Die Geschichte des Deutschvölkischen Schutz- und Trutz-Bundes, 1919–1923* (Hamburg: Leibniz Verlag, 1970).

11. See especially Geoff Eley, "Conservatives and Radical Nationalists in Germany: the Production of Fascist Potentials, 1912–1928," in *Fascists and Conservatives: The Radical Right and the Establishment in Twentieth-Century*

Europe, ed. Martin Blinkhorn (London: Unwin Hyman, 1990), 50–70; Larry Eugene Jones, "The Limits of Collaboration: Edgar Jung, Herbert von Bose, and the Origins of the Conservative Resistance to Hitler, 1933–34," in *Between Reform, Reaction, and Resistance: Studies in the History of German Conservatism from 1789 to 1945*, ed. Larry Eugene Jones and James N. Retallack (Providence, RI: Berg Publishers, 1993), 465–501, esp. 468; and most recently Larry Eugene Jones, "German Conservatism at the Crossroads: Count Kuno von Westarp and the Struggle for Control of the DNVP, 1928–30," *Contemporary European History* 18 (2009): 147–77.

12. Hopfen to Claß, 10 August 1920, BA Berlin, R 8048, 392/134–35.
13. Ibid.
14. Claß to Hopfen, 18 August 1920, BA Berlin, R 8048, 392/142.
15. Claß, WdS II-addendum, 10.
16. The records do not indicate whether this December 1920 meeting took place in Berlin or Munich.
17. Pöhner to Claß, 11 December 1920, BA Berlin, R 8048, 258/198. In the typewritten text of the letter, an extra handwritten *t* was added to Hitler's name.
18. Claß to Gertung, 29 January 1921, BA Berlin, R 8048, 258/238.
19. Claß's correspondence with Otto Gertung also included discussions about financial support for Hitler's proposed move north and for the *Völkischer Beobachter*, the recently purchased Nazi newspaper. Hitler's representatives had pressed the Pan-German League for money and Claß, in turn, asked Gertung if he or his company could provide any assistance. In spite of these requests, there is no record of any financial assistance from Gertung or MAN through Claß and his associates for Hitler and the Nazi movement. See Gertung to Claß, 27 February 1921, BA Berlin, R 8048, 258/239; Claß to Tafel, 1 March 1921 and 8 June 1921, BA Berlin, R 8048, 258/240, 243.
20. Claß, WdS II-addendum, 10.
21. Ibid., 11.
22. For this intra-party power struggle and its outcome, see Orlow, *History of the Nazi Party*, 25–45; and Ian Kershaw, *Hitler 1889–1936: Hubris* (New York and London: W. W. Norton, 1998), 160–65.
23. Claß, WdS II-addendum, 11. Claß does not supply the name of Hitler's associate.
24. Ibid.
25. Ibid., 12.
26. Claß to Hittler [*sic*], 11 May 1922, BA Berlin, R 8048, 208/221.
27. Ibid.
28. Gansser to Claß, 21 July 1922, BA Berlin, R 8048, 208/316.
29. ADV leadership committee to Gansser, 26 July 1922, BA Berlin, R 8048, 208/405.
30. Ibid.
31. The two best examples of this interpretation are Chamberlin, "Enemy on the Right," and Petzold, "Claß und Hitler."

32. The abortive 1920 Kapp Putsch in Berlin only reinforced this idea. Claß and the League officially refused to participate in the event because they believed it was poorly planned, not because they were opposed in theory to such a strike. However, several individual Pan-Germans, including prominent League member Paul Bang, were involved. For more on the League's attitude toward the Kapp Putsch, see Jackisch, *Pan-German League*, 33–39.
33. Claß, WdS II-addendum, 27.
34. Ibid.
35. Claß and other Pan-Germans had been in close contact with Kahr and his associates starting in 1920 as part of the League's attempt to gather more information about Hitler, the Nazi movement, and the Bavarian Right. After the French occupation of the Ruhr in January 1923, Claß also discussed with Kahr and Munich police chief Ernst Pöhner the possibility of creating a private army to drive the French out and perhaps turn on the Weimar government itself. Pöhner refused to take any further action without Hitler's full support. Given the poor state of affairs between Hitler and Claß, as well as the far-fetched nature of the plan, the Nazi leader ultimately refused to participate and the entire plan fell apart. See Jackisch, *Pan-German League*, 70–76.
36. Claß, WdS II-addendum, 29.
37. Ibid., 30.
38. Reventlow (ADV executive committee) to Meyer (Leipzig), 22 November 1923, BA Berlin, R 8048, 209/283–84.
39. Ibid., 284.
40. *Deutsche Zeitung*, 10 November 1923, no. 498, 1–2.
41. See the remarkably candid assessment of this problem in Reventlow (ADV executive committee) to Haller-Hallerstein (Augsburg), 3 January 1924, BA Berlin, R 8048, 210/18–18a.
42. For Hitler's speeches at the trial see Eberhard Jäckel and Axel Kuhn, eds., *Hitler: Sämtliche Aufzeichnungen 1905–1924* (Stuttgart: Deutsche Verlags-Anstalt, 1980), 1061–226. For an overall analysis of Hitler's use of the trial, see Kershaw, *Hitler*, 213–16.
43. Claß's open letter appeared in the *Deutsche Zeitung*, 23 March 1924, no. 136, under the title "Justizrat Claß und der Münchener Prozeß: Ein Brief an den Vorsitzenden des Volksgerichts." Claß denied that he had ever given his word to Kahr for a planned move against the government. Taking a legalistic approach, however, Claß never gave the court or the public any indication of the extent to which he had indeed discussed and planned the feasibility of such an operation.
44. Claß, WdS II-addendum, 33.
45. "In eigener Sache. Nachwort zum Münchener Hochverrats-Prozeß," *Alldeutsche Blätter* 19, no. 3 (April 1924): 18–19.
46. Ibid.
47. Claß's low opinion of Hitler's political skills certainly did not improve with the publication of *Mein Kampf*. After reading Hitler's book, Claß

remarked, "Anyone who has read this book and is still not convinced of Hitler's political incompetence is beyond help." See Claß's remarks at a meeting of the ADV managing committee, 4 September 1925, BA Berlin, R 8048, 144/19.

48. This correspondence between Gareis and ADV headquarters stretched from April to June 1925. See BA Berlin, R 8048, 211/146–152, 158–161, 165, 173–179, and 204. See also Hess to Claß, 9 June 1925, BA Berlin, R 8048, 211/185; and ADV headquarters to Gareis, 24 June 1925, BA Berlin, R 8048, 211/204.

49. ADV managing committee, 1–2 December 1928, BA Berlin, R 8048, 156/55–56.

50. For more on the Pan-German League's role in radicalizing the DNVP at the national leadership level and at the local/regional level, see Jackisch, *Pan-German League*, 77–169.

51. For more on the splintering of the DNVP and the formation of the KVP, see Erasmus Jonas, *Die Volkskonservativen 1928–1933. Entwicklung, Struktur, Standort und staatspolitische Zielsetzung* (Düsseldorf: Droste, 1965).

52. For Claß's explanation for the necessity of Hugenberg's leadership of the DNVP and the German Right, see Claß, WdS II, 843.

53. For a history of the Young Plan and its impact on right-wing politics, see Elizabeth Friedenthal, "Volksbegehren und Volksentscheid über den Young Plan und die deutschnationale Sezession" (PhD diss., University of Tübingen, 1957). For the Pan-German League's important role in the anti–Young Plan campaign, see Claß, WdS v. II, pp. 900–908, as well as the correspondence in preparation for the campaign in BA Berlin, R 8048, folders 261–263.

54. Claß praised Hitler and the Nazi party publicly for their apparent willingness to work with all the forces of the anti–Young Plan campaign. Privately, Claß still harbored concerns about Hitler's long-term goals and willingness to work with Hugenberg's DNVP. Nonetheless, by 1929–30, Claß seemed willing to give Hitler another chance and seemed to think that the Nazi Party could be an influential ally if it worked with the nationalist alliance under Hugenberg's leadership. See Claß, WdS v. II-addendum, 37–40.

55. On the Brüning cabinets between 1930 and 1932, see William L. Patch, Jr., *Heinrich Brüning and the Dissolution of the Weimar Republic* (Cambridge: Cambridge University Press, 1998).

56. For the Nazi Party's strategy in the period 1930–32, see Orlow, *History of the Nazi Party*, 185–238.

57. For a more detailed account of the depression in Germany, see Harold James, *The German Slump: Politics and Economics, 1924–1936* (Oxford, 1986).

58. See "Fort mit der Tribut-Regierung!" *Deutsche Zeitung*, 8 June 1930, as well as Claß's remarks before the ADV managing committee, 5 September1931, BA Berlin, R 8048, 167/6–11.

59. Claß, WdS v. II-addendum, 42–45.

60. Leopold, *Hugenberg*, 102, and Kershaw, *Hitler*, 356.

61. Hitler quoted in Kershaw, *Hitler*, 356.

62. Claß, WdS v. II-addendum, 47.

63. Ibid., 48–49. Claß recounts a series of discussions immediately following Harzburg in which Hugenberg described the details of Hitler's petulant behavior at the gathering. Hugenberg also lamented the fact the Hitler failed again on several occasions to keep appointments with him in the months following the Harzburg Front. On the long-term implications of this split, see Larry Eugene Jones, "'The Greatest Stupidity of My Life': Alfred Hugenberg and the Formation of the Hitler Cabinet, January 1933," *Journal of Contemporary History* 27 (1992): 63–87.

64. Claß to Gebsattel, 14 November 1931, BA Berlin, R 8048, 357/366; and Claß to Bongartz, 25 November 1931, BA Berlin, R 8048, 300/219.

65. Claß's remarks at the meeting of the ADV managing committee, 5–6 December 1931, BA Berlin R8048, 168/55–56.

66. Pan-German leaders actually considered proposals for restructuring the League in December 1931, after losing 2,383 members since September of that year. See the lengthy discussion about this issue, ibid., 71–77.

67. For Claß's discussion of this issue, see the minutes of the meeting of the ADV managing committee, 20–21 February 1932, BA Berlin, R 8048, 169/32.

68. Hugenberg and his allies intended the Harzburg Front to serve as a united, nationalist challenge to the Brüning government. Although the meeting produced a manifesto demanding new Reichstag elections and a suspension of emergency legislation, nothing more substantial resulted from it. For more information on the Harzburg Front meeting, see John A. Leopold, *Alfred Hugenberg: The Radical Nationalist Campaign against the Weimar Republic* (New Haven, CT, and London: Yale University Press, 1977), 97–106; and Larry Eugene Jones, "Nationalists, Nazis, and the Assault against Weimar: Revisiting the Harzburg Rally of October 1931," *German Studies Review* 29 (2006): 483–94. For Hitler's erratic behavior at the meeting, see Kershaw, *Hitler*, 356–57.

69. Claß's highly negative assessment of Hitler's behavior at the Harzburg meeting and in the following months is clear in: Claß, WdS II-addendum, 42–49.

70. On the divisions within the German Right over this issue, see Larry Eugene Jones, "Hindenburg and the Conservative Dilemma in the 1932 Presidential Elections," *German Studies Review* 20 (1997): 235–60; and Leopold, *Hugenberg*, 107–21.

71. Jones, "Hindenburg and the Conservative Dilemma," 240–41.

72. Claß to Bongartz, 19 February and 8 March 1932, BA Berlin R 8048, 300/233, 235. See also Claß's remarks at the meeting of the ADV managing committee, 7 May 1932, BA Berlin, R 8048, 170/19. The Pan-German leader was convinced that Hugenberg, not Duesterberg, should have run for the presidency.

73. Between 1926 and 1932 the Pan-German League publicly attacked Hindenburg for allegedly betraying the German people. Claß went so far as to label the president the "executor of the Marxist fulfillment policy."

See Claß, WdS v. II, 909, and his comments at the meeting of the ADV managing committee, 7 September 1928, BA Berlin, R 8048, 155/7–10. Yet despite these repeated public attacks, the Pan-German leadership tried to keep open private channels of communication to Hindenburg through ADV member Prince Otto zu Salm-Horstmar. Oddly, the League hoped they might yet show the president the error of his ways and convince him to dismiss Brüning and appoint a nationalist cabinet before the 1932 presidential elections. Not surprisingly, nothing came of these efforts. For further information, see the minutes of the ADV managing committee, 20–21 February 1932, BA Berlin, R 8048, 169/30–32; and the detailed correspondence, including copies of letters to Hindenburg from Salm-Horstmar in BA Berlin, R 8048, 454/esp. 80–84, 93–94, 123–25.

74. Claß offers a detailed discussion of his organization's deteriorating relationship with Hindenburg in Claß, WdS, II, 906–12.

75. For further information, see Hans Mommsen, *The Rise and Fall of Weimar Democracy* (Chapel Hill, NC, and London: University of North Carolina Press, 1996), 409; and Leopold, *Hugenberg*, 111.

76. On Hugenberg's decision, see Leopold, *Hugenberg*, 111–12.

77. SGA, 7 May 1932, BA Berlin, R 8048, 170/21–22. See also Claß to Bongartz, 19 March 1932, BA Berlin, R 8048, 300/241; and Claß to Gebsattel, 19 March 1932, BA Berlin, R 8048, 357/370–71.

78. Claß to Leo Wegener, 13 April 1932, in the unpublished Nachlaß of Leo Wegener, Bundesarchiv Koblenz, Bestand N 1003, 23/143.

79. Hugenberg was upset with Claß's choice and, according to their mutual friend Reinhold Quaatz, Hugenberg even accused the Pan-German leader of stabbing him in the back. See the entry for 23 March 1932, in *Die Deutschnationalen und die Zerstörung der Weimarer Republik. Aus dem Tagebuch von Reinhold Quaatz 1928–1933*, ed. Hermann Weiß and Paul Hoser (Munich: R. Oldenbourg, 1989), 185.

80. For a complete discussion of this, see the minutes of the ADV managing committee, 9 September 1932, BA Berlin, R 8048, 171/8–12, 15–20.

81. Ibid., 11–12. For the background to these coalition negotiations see: Dietrich Orlow, *Weimar Prussia, 1925–1933: The Illusion of Strength* (Pittsburgh, PA: University of Pittsburgh Press, 1991), 213–24; and Mommsen, *Rise and Fall of Weimar Democracy*, 465–69.

82. Minutes of the ADV managing committee, 9 September 1932, BA Berlin, R 8048, 171/12.

83. *Lageberichte* from 17 November 1932, BA Berlin, R 8048, 551/150–56.

84. Minutes of the ADV managing committee, 10–11 December 1932, BA Berlin, R 8048, 172/43.

85. *Lageberichte* from 1 February 1933, BA Berlin, R 8048, 552/14–15.

86. Ibid., 15. The report praised Hugenberg for his "unforgettable service to Germany." "He [Hugenberg] overcame the bitterness and internal strife in the nationalist camp to push forward a government that Germany needed, a government of the nationalist front."

87. Claß, WdS II-addendum, 50.

88. For the official correspondence approving the Pan-German League's dissolution, see the unpublished records of the Reich Chancellery in the Bundesarchiv Berlin, Bestand R43 II (hereafter cited as BA Berlin, R 43 II), 829–3/5–11.

89. BA Berlin, R 43 II, 829–3/12.

90. For a detailed Gestapo report on the League's meetings, speeches, and rallies throughout Germany and its alleged "anti-governmental" activities, see the file on the Pan-German League copied from the Moscow State Archive (Zentrales Staatsarchiv Moskau, Fond 500-3-569 Alldeutscher Verband) in the records of the Gedenkstätte Deutsche Widerstand, Berlin (hereafter cited as ZSM-ADV), 1–3, 27–44, 139–60. See also the reports on League meetings in Thuringia in the months following Hitler's seizure of power in the unpublished records of the Reich Ministry of the Interior in the Bundesarchiv Berlin, Bestand R 1501, 544/121–29.

91. In this regard see ZSM-ADV, 2–3.

92. Mosse, *Crisis of German Ideology*, 225.

93. Eley, "Conservatives and Radical Nationalists in Germany," 65.

94. Minutes of the ADV managing committee, 7 May 1932, BA Berlin, R 8048, 170/23.

7

WEIMAR'S "BURNING QUESTION"

Situational Antisemitism and
the German Combat Leagues, 1918–33

Brian E. Crim

In December 1925 a patriotic German-Jewish citizen named Bernhard Abraham wrote the Young German Order (Jungdeutscher Orden or Jungdo) with what appeared to be a straightforward question: "Is the Young German Order antisemitic or not?" The Order responded by directing Abraham to several journals in which it addressed the so-called Jewish question.[1] It is doubtful whether Abraham had his question answered satisfactorily even after reading the entire catalog of Young German publications. To be fair, Abraham would have encountered the same inconsistency in similar organizations. The fractious German Right during the Weimar period comprised *völkisch* organizations, traditional conservative parties, and a myriad of combat leagues, or *Wehrverbände*, like the Young German Order. Combat leagues were unique postwar creations that attempted to unify military service and preparedness with political action by translating their constructed memories of the front community, or *Frontgemeinschaft*, into a viable national community, or *Volksgemeinschaft*.[2] Combat leagues covered the ideological spectrum, offering alternative interpretations of the "front" and conceptions of the "nation." Competition for membership was fierce and groups frequently feuded with one another over who should lead the opposition to the Weimar government. The two largest combat leagues were the Stahlhelm, the League of Front Soldiers (Stahlhelm, Bund der Frontsoldaten), and Young German Order. Despite impressive national memberships, the two leading combat leagues were plagued by a generational divide, regional differences, and bitter ideological disputes that hindered their capacity to articulate consistent positions on fundamental issues.

During the Weimar era an organization's stance on the Jewish question, specifically its level of commitment to antisemitism, spoke volumes about that group's worldview. While some organizations never strayed from an unequivocal antisemitic perspective—the National Socialist party (NSDAP), for example—others on the Right practiced "situational" antisemitism. Situational antisemitism was the process by which an organization expressed an opinion or policy concerning Jews in response to internal and external influences. Sometimes these opinions were constructed deliberately, primarily during the latter stages of the Weimar Republic, but most incidents of situational antisemitism reflected an organization's changing priorities resulting from demographics, fluctuating political fortunes, and bitter feuds with rival groups. Such a phenomenon is unsurprising within political parties, but the fact that influential right-wing combat leagues adapted antisemitic rhetoric to satisfy the expectations of others challenges some assumptions concerning antisemitism during the Weimar period. Antisemitism pervaded Weimar politics, but the Right was hardly united when it came to deciding how much importance to attach to the issue. Situational antisemitism as practiced by the Stahlhelm and the Young German Order in particular reveals the ephemeral nature of antisemitic politics in the German Right. Sometimes it was advantageous for a combat league to be virulently antisemitic, especially when it came to attracting younger members or galvanizing opposition to the Weimar government. As Bernhard Abraham noticed, situational antisemitism was reactive and rarely proactive simply because it made sense politically, at least initially.

Situational antisemitism derived from opportunism, pragmatism, and vicious competition in a crowded German Right. The Stahlhelm and the Young German Order were national organizations with an ideologically and regionally diverse membership. Both groups exercised political influence, the Stahlhelm more so, and interacted with established political parties, the military, and especially other combat leagues. Both the Stahlhelm and Young German Order weathered blistering attacks at the hands of the NSDAP. In response to dramatic losses in membership, the Stahlhelm tacked to its right while the Young German Order gambled on the political center. Both groups altered their identities, especially their stances on the Jewish question, because of National Socialist pressure. The Stahlhelm practiced situational antisemitism after acquiring thousands of younger and more radical members in the mid-1920s. Franz Seldte, the first *Bundesführer* and original founder, was largely indifferent to antisemitism, while his rival, second *Bundesführer* Theodor Duesterberg, was a devoted *völkisch* activist and virulent antisemite. Ironically, Seldte joined Hitler's cabinet as minister of labor while Duesterberg dared to oppose Hitler in the 1932 election and spent the Third Reich in silent opposition after it had been revealed that Duesterberg's paternal grandfather was a converted Jew. The Young German Order was the creature of the young lieutenant and Free Corps (Freikorps) commander Artur Mahraun. Mahraun's mercurial personality and independent streak alienated many of his followers and infuriated other combat leagues. Blatantly antisemitic in its early years, the Young German Order lurched from one extreme to the other, repudiating antisemitism in 1930 after forming the German State Party (Deutsche Staatspartei).

Situational antisemitism was in part a legacy of the First World War and the sudden collapse of the German empire. Hubert Mohr's characteristics of modern antisemitism provide insight into why situational antisemitism thrived during the Weimar era. First, Mohr argues, antisemitism is a mental construct, "a collectively shared and fantasized image or 'social myth'" that materializes in a particular social setting. The social myth of the Jew is discursive and discernible in a variety of texts (newspapers, journals, academic writings, speeches, and images). Second and particularly relevant to the postwar period, antisemitism is reductionist, creating "order out of the social confusion of mass society" and providing emotional relief by "blaming the Other, namely the Jews, for the threatened standard of living." Third, Mohr argues that antisemitism is symptomatic of a "crisis of modernization" affecting Western Europe during the nineteenth and twentieth centuries. Consequently, fear of modernity easily transferred to those supposedly benefitting from radical change. Finally, the modern social myth of the Jew does not replace religious anti-Jewish prejudice, but rather "coexists and interacts with the new racist or scientific mythemes." Put simply, "modern societies revitalize old anti-Jewish myths to create a 'New Mythology (of Hate, Prejudice etc.)."[3] German antisemitism reflected the regional diversity of a young and artificially constructed nation. How could one speak of a German national antisemitism in the late nineteenth and twentieth century if the German "nation" was barely a generation old? Antisemitism was capricious and varied in intensity for most of the German empire's existence. The First World War breathed new life into a somewhat peripheral ideology by demolishing the empire and reinvigorating the Jewish question.[4]

Applying Mohr's schema to the combat leagues supports the notion of antisemitism as a "cultural code."[5] Shulamit Volkov argued that antisemitism was a modern ideology that evolved into a "larger semantic space," a vessel for a host of organizations seeking to express a broader vision. By the late nineteenth century, antisemitism was a cultural code for expressing discontent with modernity itself. Germans who found their lives affected by the rapid socio-economic changes associated with industrialization and urbanization were attracted to antisemitism because it offered a comprehensive worldview and an explanatory model. The antisemitic political parties of the late imperial era appeared to come and go with each economic cycle, but antisemitism flourished in the growing constellation of popular and professional associations that often eclipsed formal political parties. Volkov borrows the psychological term "associative merger" to explain how such a simplistic argument reverberated throughout Germany. If you were against the Jews, then you also communicated your rejection of rapid modernization, international socialism, "high finance," or whatever else seemed to be beyond the grasp of the average German to either understand or alter. "The link was made as a matter of course," Volkov argues. "It became part of the prevailing culture."[6] Antisemitism was an easy shorthand for dissatisfaction with one's environment. Consequently, the ideology did not require a significant Jewish population to thrive; the construction of "the Jew" was more potent precisely because it was imaginary.

The *völkisch* movement experienced a revival after the First World War after the so-called war generation became interested in the ideology and matriculated into universities, the combat leagues, and political parties.[7] Always problematic to define even by those who described themselves as devotees, *völkisch* ideology was a combustible mix of ideas including extreme nationalism, racial antisemitism, and a belief in a hierarchical social order rooted in a mystical past.[8] The *völkisch* movement embraced antisemitism as a cultural code by advocating eugenics, social and racial hygiene, a return to agrarian social structures, aggressive imperialism (especially in Eastern Europe), and a rejection of all forms of internationalism.[9] Antisemitic parties before the First World War were too fragmented to be effective until they merged with *völkisch* groups capable of integrating antisemitism into a broader agenda.[10] Given the diversity of thought within the movement, one can argue that *völkisch* thinkers and activists also practiced situational antisemitism. *Völkisch* advocate Paul Hartig defined the ideology as the "affirmation of the Germanic race and of belonging to the Germanic blood kinship with all the resulting conclusions and duties of that philosophy of life" and secondly the "unconditional physical and mental rejection of everything foreign," especially "everything Jewish."[11] Hartig and others preferred to promote the idea of "racial renewal" over what they derided as "*Radauantisemitism*," or simple and vulgar antisemitic rhetoric.[12] *Völkisch* groups spoke of correcting the corrosive influence of the "Jewish spirit" on German society while denying they were antisemitic. These distinctions were fanciful and unconvincing to most critics, but it is worth noting that self-proclaimed *völkisch* organizations distanced themselves from antisemitism.

Bringing an end to the Weimar Republic, derisively known in some circles as the "in-between Reich" (*Zwischenreich*) or "*Judenrepublik*," was a shared goal of the right-wing combat leagues. The preferred method of its removal was yet another subject of debate, but associations hoping to avoid being banned by the Weimar authorities after the November 1923 coup attempt towed the line and generally eschewed "putschist" politics. The combat leagues undermined the authority of the Weimar government and were responsible for continuous violence, but they seldom posed an existential threat to the republic after 1923. A recent regional study of Weimar political violence suggests that most activity was "small violence" aimed at controlling the street. Violence was symbolic, often theatrical, and another arena in which the combat leagues competed with one another for influence.[13] However, paramilitary groups such as the Free Corps and the combat leagues normalized the notion of violence as a form of political expression as well as targeting Jews and Bolsheviks as internal and external enemies.[14] In the end, the NSDAP captured the streets and a significant portion of the electorate by promoting a *völkisch* worldview and an unequivocal stance on the Jewish question while the situational anti-Semites limped into obscurity or surrendered to their ambitions and adjusted accordingly.

The Stahlhelm: A House Divided

The Stahlhelm formed during the height of the 1918 November Revolution when Imperial Army captain Franz Seldte and seven other returning veterans met in the basement of Seldte's small factory in Magdeburg. The Stahlhelm evolved into an influential political force despite contending with internal divisions and external competitors envious of the combat league's growing national organization. A dynamic alternative to the mainstream parties, the Stahlhelm militarized bourgeois political activism in the wake of the First World War by appealing to the remnants of civilian militias, demobilized veterans, and disgruntled National Liberals and conservatives who had a hard time making sense of a strange political environment.[15] As the largest combat league the Stahlhelm occupied two worlds—first, it passed for a traditional veterans' organization with benign connections to political parties and, second, it was a paramilitary organization that regularly participated in illicit and street violence designed to subvert the Weimar government and outmaneuver competing combat leagues.[16] These sometimes conflicting aims exacerbated the Stahlhelm's evolving identity crisis and contributed to its ambiguous relationship with the important ideological questions of the day.

The Stahlhelm's inability to achieve internal unity allowed rival organizations to lure away disaffected members and degrade its vision of a national community built on the "front spirit." The relationship between the two *Bundesführers*, the founder Franz Seldte and Theodor Duesterberg, who was elected second *Bundesführer* in April 1923, was complicated and never entirely cordial. Volker Berghahn aptly described Seldte as "a classic product of the Wilhelmine era."[17] The November Revolution and impending civil war motivated Seldte to form an organization of veterans intent on restoring "law and order" beginning with his home town of Magdeburg. A short biography of Seldte written soon after being named the Third Reich's labor minister claimed he was raised in a rural setting, a fact that prevented him from turning to liberalism and materialism.[18] Apparently Seldte's true biography of running the family factory and voting for the National Liberals did not adequately reflect National Socialist values. Duesterberg was seven years older than Seldte and a career officer in the Imperial Army. A major by 1914, Duesterberg held influential positions throughout the war, even serving as an aide to the German delegation during the Treaty of Versailles proceedings. Duesterberg was one of the founding members of the archconservative German National People's Party (Deutschnationale Volkspartei or DNVP) and a Stahlhelm member since December 1919. Duesterberg transformed the Halle chapter into a competing branch of the Stahlhelm, dividing the Stahlhelm into what Berghahn framed as competing wings—"Seldte Evolutionism" vs. "Duesterberg Radicalism."[19] While Seldte tolerated working under the confines of the Weimar government, at least temporarily, Duesterberg's wing used more extreme rhetoric and appealed to an increasingly younger and more radical membership.

The Stahlhelm's two-headed power structure and competition from other combat leagues transformed its ambivalent stance on antisemitism from a peripheral concern into a major liability. The Stahlhelm certainly embraced the coded language of antisemitism from the outset, but internal and external pressures beginning in the mid-1920s required ever more definitive statements on the Jewish question. As early as 1921 the Stahlhelm defined "front soldier" as simply an individual who served six months in a frontline unit during the First World War. The Stahlhelm's handbook clarified that only men of "German origin," that is, *deutschstämmige,* could be members, although this was equally vague.[20] Consequently, dozens of Jews joined the Stahlhelm without issue. Some Stahlhelm officers recognized the potential for future trouble by noting that the organization would have a difficult time being considered a legitimate voice of opposition if it allowed Jewish members.[21] Seldte was content to ignore the issue, correctly assuming that most Jews would probably avoid a combat league that seemed to be hostile to their interests. Seldte claimed to see "neither Jews or non-Jews, but Stahlhelm people." Duesterberg, on the other hand, declared the issues of membership and antisemitism a "burning question."[22]

The controversy surrounding the Stahlhelm's adoption of an "Aryan paragraph" reveals the depth of the divide between the group's two wings and marks the beginning of its experience with situational antisemitism. Seldte was less interested in defending the handful of Jewish members in the Stahlhelm than he was in preventing Duesterberg's growing *völkisch* bloc from further infiltrating his organization by forcing an explicit ban on Jews. Seldte was engaged in the unenviable task of supplicating vocal extremists in his own group while ensuring that the Stahlhelm remained a legitimate organization with tangible political influence. Seldte's goal was to avoid being labeled a *völkisch* organization and risk bringing unwanted attention from the Weimar government. With every ban of a combat league or right-wing group linked to anti-government violence, most of which occurred in the aftermath of assassinations of Weimar politicians and the failed Hitler putsch, the Stahlhelm's membership swelled with young radicals sympathetic to Duesterberg's agenda. The Stahlhelm debated the Aryan paragraph for two years before deciding to exclude Jews officially. In March 1924 the Stahlhelm added the sentence "Jews cannot be accepted into the Stahlhelm" to its constitution. The accompanying statement explained that the Stahlhelm struggled for four years on behalf of the German race and its future, adding that "the feeling of being a German must be made as holy a right as can be" and that "influences from foreign races" should no longer play a role in German society. Moreover, while the Stahlhelm declared that it "has nothing to do with any of the antisemitic groups or *völkisch* parties," it was clear Duesterberg's desire to create "*völkisch* national pride" eclipsed Seldte's conservatism. The

Stahlhelm, the statement continued, was interested in establishing antisemitic credentials and supporting the *völkisch* agenda without abandoning aspirations of becoming a broad-based nationalist movement.[23] In a letter to a Jewish critic of the Aryan paragraph, the Stahlhelm stated disingenuously that it avoided the term *"völkisch"* because it implied partisanship. The letter also admitted that "it is not known whether individual chapters honored the Aryan paragraph."[24] Given the number of unwelcome "discoveries" that plagued the Stahlhelm in later years, many chapters in fact ignored the policy. Most Jews who joined the Stahlhelm before 1924 left after the adoption of the Aryan paragraph.

The Stahlhelm's antisemitic rhetoric was generally uninspired and hardly original. The essential message reveals elements of Volkov's cultural code—Jews embodied all that was flawed in the Weimar Republic, serving as surrogates for internationalism and other forces of national degeneration. An essay written by a Stahlhelm chapter leader described capitalism in Germany as "your enemy." But capitalism for foreigners was not an enemy, "especially when it is in Jewish hands." The author claimed that international capitalism benefitted Germany's enemies and undermined the Fatherland. Linking Jews with internationalism was a trademark of coded antisemitic discourse.[25] A 1926 article in its daily newspaper entitled "Where does the enemy stand?" provides one of the Stahlhelm's few definitive statements on the Jewish question. The anonymous author wrote that "the vast majority of Jews are our decisive enemies" because they corrupted the state and Germany's economic life. Jews embodied a degenerate "shop keeper spirit (*Händlergeist*)" and were enemies of everything the Stahlhelm represented. Still, in keeping with the Stahlhelm's unwillingness to align itself completely with antisemites, the article concluded that Jews were among Germany's enemies, but not the primary threat.[26] The Stahlhelm leadership, including Duesterberg, believed more radical groups made the mistake of attacking Jews personally when the Right should focus on eliminating Jewish "ideals" and "spirit." In other words, participating in the *Radauantisemitismus* of boorish anti-Semites tarnished the Stahlhelm's reputation and frightened potential middle class supporters. The Stahlhelm was seemingly confident in its internal positions on race, although these positions varied from chapter to chapter. One internal memo stated that, "it is self-understood that in a future state elements from foreign races, such as Jews and others who in the course of history have spread non-Aryan blood within the state . . . will have no role."[27] The Stahlhelm used antisemitism to critique broader social problems. This brand of situational antisemitism considered excessive

Jewish influence as symptomatic of cultural and moral decline. Building a national community grounded in soldierly values reverses the decline and solves the Jewish question simultaneously.

The most revealing insight into the Stahlhelm's deliberations on the Jewish question ironically originated from Jews themselves. Jewish citizens forced the Stahlhelm to confront its inconsistent positions on race and challenged its claim to embody a potential national community derived from the front community. When Stahlhelm officials answered critics, which was infrequently, their responses exposed their ambivalence and confusion concerning their own Aryan paragraph. As this correspondence reveals, outsiders were sometimes more aware of situational antisemitism than the organization practicing it. Max Senator, a Jewish doctor who served with distinction during the First World War, wrote numerous letters demanding an explanation for the Stahlhelm's Aryan paragraph. Senator could not understand why men who were "not pure-blooded in the *völkisch* sense" were excluded, especially when someone like himself volunteered for front duty and served all four years, won the Iron Cross (First and Second Class) and a medal for sustaining injury, converted to Protestantism, loved Prussia and the Hohenzollerns, and condemned the November Revolution. Given all this, Senator asked, "How is the Stahlhelm united behind the concept of front community if personalities like me are rejected?"[28] In another letter to the Stahlhelm's political department, Senator decried the hypocrisy of the Stahlhelm calling itself the "Association of Front Soldiers" when it excluded decorated Jewish veterans. Senator recalled that the "true Front" accepted him, commenting that no one ever asked him if he was "pure-blooded" on the battlefield.[29] The lowly Stahlhelm official responsible for answering Senator was respectful, as ordered, but the response was riddled with clichés and obfuscations.[30] The Stahlhelm admitted that many Jews served at the front and did their duty (a fact they denied elsewhere), but its reasons for excluding Jews were sound—Jews were leaders of the November Revolution, dominated the economy, which was in shambles, and the immigration of *Ostjuden* threatened the *völkisch* principles on which the German nation stood. Furthermore, the Jewish presence in government was tantamount to the "domination by a foreign race." However, the letter to Senator noted, the Stahlhelm did not screen applicants who may have been half-Jews or had Jewish blood, a truth that undermined the Stahlhelm in later years. The Stahlhelm conceded the tragedy of its own logic to Senator—although many Jews were patriotic, excluding Jews from the future nation was necessary for Germany's survival.[31]

The frequency of inquiries from mostly outraged Jewish citizens burdened local chapters who seemed equally confused by the policy. A memo from the Landesverband Westmark to the Neuweid chapter apologized for the discomfort of answering the correspondence, especially because "individual cases" of Jewish bravery and honorable service made the Aryan paragraph difficult to explain. The memo referenced the Seldte-Duesterberg split when justifying the policy, noting that the absence of a strong stance on race threatened "comradeship and unity."[32] In other words, the benefits of enunciating antisemitic positions outweighed the liabilities. When a Jewish veteran by the name of Julius Bentz asked about the reasons for adopting an Aryan paragraph, the answering Stahlhelm official was surprisingly honest, citing "strong political pressure" within the patriotic movement. The official added that he agreed that many Jewish veterans served admirably. Still, Bentz was advised to join the National Association of Jewish Front Soldiers (Reichsbund jüdischer Frontsoldaten or RjF).[33] Another concerned Jewish veteran, Dr. Richard Kantorowicz, ridiculed the Stahlhelm's contradictory statements on race and accused Seldte of acting for political reasons, which is something the Stahlhelm more or less admitted to itself and others. Kantorowicz concluded the letter venomously: "You don't think Jews find Germany's struggle for the inner and external freedom as meaningful as every other German? Then, Mr. Seldte, you don't know any German Jews! Then, Mr. Seldte, you were not together with any Jewish comrades at the Front!"[34] Of course, Seldte was with Jewish comrades at the front, but this inconvenient truth was a liability in the postwar context.

The Stahlhelm's internal debates contributed to its situational antisemitism, but external pressure was probably more responsible. The competition in the German Right for membership and influence was so great that a group's insufficient attention to antisemitism impaired its ability to attract and retain members. The Stahlhelm was obviously vulnerable on the issue and moved to its Right to avoid the drain of members elsewhere, principally to the NSDAP. An intermittent partner and fellow traveler among the combat leagues, the NSDAP's growing strength influenced the Stahlhelm's discourse on a number of issues. The NSDAP used antisemitism as a weapon against its competitors, and let there be no doubt, the Stahlhelm was competing in several areas — membership, interpreting the memory of the war experience for political ends, and framing responses to the Weimar political system. The influx of radical members attracted to Duesterberg's *völkisch* perspective facilitated the NSDAP's future success in siphoning off Stahlhelm members. The truth was never a concern, just the fear that rumors of Jewish members or of perceived laxness on the "burning question" would be enough to force the venerable Stahlhelm on the defensive. For example, the Stahlhelm was horrified when a Jewish newspaper incorrectly reported that a Düsseldorf businessman held an honorary membership in the Stahlhelm while simultaneously belonging to the RjF. The Stahlhelm released a statement exclaiming that "absolutely none of it was true!"[35] More interesting than its heated response was the Stahlhelm's suspicion that the NSDAP spread the rumor. In July 1927, nearly a year before the article appeared in print, the NSDAP published names of those it believed were Jews in the Stahlhelm. Rather than reject the premise or ignore the charge, the Stahlhelm investigated the names and reaffirmed publicly its Aryan paragraph.[36] A few years later when the Koblenz chapter reported that they had a "problematic" member, a Catholic married to a Jew, the Stahlhelm regional command reminded the chapter of the Aryan paragraph and cautioned that "our enemies would be given a point of attack" if the member was discovered.[37] In every instance the Stahlhelm seemed unconcerned about the charges until they were made public. Situational antisemitism involves acting to satisfy the expectations of others. The "enemy" was also an occasional friend—the NSDAP.

The cycle of accusation and recrimination culminated in the "Case Eichbaum" during the summer of 1932. The incident began when twenty members of the Magdeburg chapter resigned after they learned that one of their comrades was an ethnic Jew who converted to Christianity. Aside from revealing an increase in racial thinking within the Stahlhelm on the eve of the Third Reich, the incident revealed the extent to which the organization calibrated its position in response to the rising tide of National Socialism. The Weimar chapter reported to its regional office that the true significance of Case Eichbaum was the apparent impotence of Stahlhelm leadership in the face of the NSDAP propaganda. "Weimar is a Nazi fortress," the report noted, and that competing with the NSDAP was more difficult there than anywhere else. The memo further warned that the resignations would have negative repercussions for chapters already struggling to retain members. "The Stahlhelm is being watched sharply by the Nazis, and every mistake, every weakness, will be used and made public. Case Eichbaum, the basic meaning of which is the Jewish Question, will be used strongly to show the irresponsibility of the *Bundesführer* [Seldte]." After acknowledging that the Weimar chapter was "regrettably in sharp conflict with the Nazis," the report warned that the Stahlhelm must avoid further

incidents that would weaken its position.[38] The NSDAP was not immune to situational antisemitism, especially during an election year,
but its positions were clear and its members energized. The Stahlhelm
was reactive and rarely proactive when it came to enunciating positions
on race, at least since the 1924 debates on the Aryan paragraph. The
NSDAP sensed a weakness and exploited it to great effect.

The Stahlhelm's situational antisemitism originated with Franz
Seldte's relative indifference to the issue and the resulting disunity over
the future direction of the combat league. Theodor Duesterberg was the
anti-Semite and architect of the Aryan paragraph, a fact that did little to
mitigate the firestorm over the revelation that the second *Bundesführer*
had a Jewish grandfather. Duesterberg joined the political fray in 1932
by running for president as the "Front soldier's candidate," which was
a moniker most believed belonged to the incumbent and beloved old
Field Marshal Paul von Hindenburg. The news broke during the campaign and the NSDAP press skewered Duesterberg, whose candidacy
harmed Hitler's own campaign. Seldte decided to stand by Duesterberg to preserve the appearance of unity, but Duesterberg was so successful in recruiting *völkisch* members to the Stahlhelm that many of
them could not stomach the thought of someone with Jewish ancestry
leading it.[39] In a strained effort to retain Duesterberg in the organization
while preserving the Stahlhelm's antisemitic credentials, some members gave Duesterberg options that dozens of other "tainted" members
never had. One member suggested that Duesterberg submit a sworn
statement to the effect that he had no business connections, relatives, or
any relationship with Jews whatsoever. Duesterberg would also have
to prove that he and his relatives fought in all of Germany's wars. Allowing these loopholes for him but no one else was the height of hypocrisy, but in the end Duesterberg was helpless once the NSDAP had
him in its sights. For years Duesterberg used antisemitism to outmaneuver Seldte and push the Stahlhelm further into the *völkisch* bloc. The
Stahlhelm was mortally wounded by the revelations about its second
Bundesführer, cementing its status as a junior partner to the NSDAP and
setting the stage for its absorption into National Socialist organizations
during the Third Reich.

The Young German Order: The *Völkisch* Middle?

The Young German Order was founded by former Imperial Army lieutenant and Free Corps commander Artur Mahraun. Born in 1890 from

an East Prussian family, Mahraun was raised to value the Prussian military tradition and its Protestant roots. Like Franz Seldte, Mahraun gathered some of his men and organized a local response to the November Revolution. The experience served as the catalyst for his political activism during the Weimar era.[40] Mahraun created the Young German Order in his hometown of Kassel in 1920 with the goal of achieving a synthesis of Prussia and Weimar. In this *Volksstaat*, James Diehl writes, "the Prussian principle of leadership would be combined with the democratic *bündisch* concepts derived from the German youth movement."[41] Supremely confident and armed with an attractive message for younger veterans, Mahraun was a prolific author and inspirational public speaker. Whereas the Stahlhelm had difficulty controlling its message because of the Seldte-Duesterberg split, the Young German Order was Mahraun's organization through and through. However, Mahraun was prone to contradicting himself on subjects ranging from foreign policy to antisemitism. Most senior advisors were loyal to Mahraun to the end, although a number of chapter leaders broke away during one of Mahraun's many shifts in policy and created a small rival organization. The Order's shifting attitude toward Jews is a textbook case of situational antisemitism precisely because it hinged on one man—Mahraun. At first glance, Mahraun appears as a craven political opportunist, willing to abandon core beliefs in exchange for greater acceptance by the center. The German Right was crowded and Mahraun always found ways to differentiate the Young German Order from other combat leagues. The Young German Order issued blistering attacks on Jews and the "Jewish spirit," but its antisemitism acted as a cultural code for Mahraun's fear of the "degenerate forces" of plutocracy, international capitalism, materialist socialism, and generally any form of internationalism.[42] Hardly an opportunist, Mahraun was virtually excommunicated from the *völkisch* Right for appealing to the center and, in part, casting off antisemitic rhetoric precisely when other combat leagues embraced it as a core belief. As Weimar's political fortunes changed, so too did Mahraun's use, or disuse, of antisemitism. In the end, Mahraun miscalculated and most of his members abandoned him and the utopian *Volksstaat* for the more tangible *Volksgemeinschaft* of the NSDAP.

Mahraun wrote frequently on the Jewish question throughout the 1920s, directly linking his conception of the state to the defeat of Jewry: "Our goal is the destruction of the Jewish worldview and its replacement with German-Christian civil and communal life."[43] As a self-proclaimed *völkisch* organization, the Young Germans explicitly denied membership to Jews. Unlike the Stahlhelm, there was no serious internal debate on the ramifications of adopting an Aryan paragraph, nor did the Young German Order struggle with ambivalence. Mahraun wrote in 1924: "Today we find ourselves in a proper race war between Germans and Jews and this race war includes all political questions important to the German Fatherland." He cited Jews' excessive influence in the German state, their poisoning of German religion, their control of "high finance," the press, and the dangers posed by the *Ostjuden*.[44] In a lengthy speech to Young German members, Mahraun articulated his plan to attract workers away from a labor movement dominated by Marxists and controlled by "international Jewry." Mahraun then proudly declared the Young German Order a *völkisch* organization because it fought for the German race and the reconquest of the nation and state from "the influence of Jewry." He concluded the speech by identifying "Jewish domination" and party democracy as the primary obstacles to the *Volksstaat*. Also in 1924, the *Jungdeutsche* newspaper published a series of articles entitled "Jewish Domination." The series is a remarkable think piece on the Jewish question and demonstrates the Order's intellectual investment in antisemitism. The first article equated Jews with party politics and plutocracy and lamented the United States' entry on to the world stage, linking America to a campaign of "world democratization" managed by "international Jewry." In the second installment, the *Jungdeutsche* detailed how Jews exercised power in other countries, concluding that Jews controlled most banks and succeeded in turning Christians against each other. The final article entertained grand conspiracy theories of Jewish world domination through various means, including the League of Nations. In a truly ironic twist, the Young Germans described the German Democratic Party (Deutsche Demokratische Partei or DDP), their future partner in the founding of the German State Party, as a leading Jewish organization responsible for subjugating Germany to a Jewish agenda.[45]

The Young Germans viewed the "destruction of the Jewish worldview" as the spiritual victory of German ideals over Jewish ones, not the physical destruction or even removal of Jews from Germany. The Young German leadership appeared to fear Jewish power, which it associated with all manner of internationalism. Heinrich von Stadtbrück asked how wise it was to agitate against Jews when they controlled the economy and could therefore exact a painful revenge against veterans.[46] An essay on the failings of German Christianity argued that Jews exercised an immoral influence of everyday German life. The author asked why Germany had spent two thousand years spreading Christianity and the lessons of the New Testament only to be forced to "make room for the Old Testament."[47] Young German publications argued that the German race's strength was its nation state while Jews suffered the fate of a rootless existence. As one author noted: "The Fatherland of Jews is other Jews."[48] In an article entitled "The Jewish Colonies in Soviet Russia" the *Jungdeutsche* declared that the long-standing Zionist aim of establishing a Jewish state was accomplished by the Bolshevik Revolution. The article was sympathetic toward reports of pogroms in Russian villages, seeing it as a logical response to Jewish domination of the cities.[49] Continuing this theme of "Judeo-Bolshevism," a Young German journal published a cartoon depicting a stereotypical Jewish figure in Berlin communicating to communist thugs in Moscow. The Jew, dressed as a capitalist complete with a top hat, conspires with his Bolshevik partners: "First blood must flow, then you'll get your Rubels again."[50] One would expect such discourse in National Socialist publications, but the Young German Order was clearly invested in an antisemitic worldview, at least initially.

The origins of the Young German Order's situational antisemitism concerned its falling out with the German Right. The acrimonious relationship began in the early 1920s after the Young Germans advocated rapprochement with France, a move that alienated other combat leagues and marked Mahraun as a rebellious and unreliable member of the opposition to the Weimar Republic.[51] The Young Germans initially cooperated with the Stahlhelm where there was mutual interest, such as attracting workers from the Social Democrats, but the rivalry over turf and members defined the relationship. The Stahlhelm's close relationship with media mogul and DNVP chairman Alfred Hugenberg irreparably harmed the relationship. Mahraun called Franz Seldte a good and brave man, but lamented his opportunism for throwing his weight behind Hugenberg, the very face of plutocracy the Young Germans hoped to undo.[52] It is clear Mahraun was not privy to the Stahlhelm's internal politics since it was Duesterberg who pushed for a closer relationship with the Hugenberg and the DNVP.[53] Seldte, on the other hand, thought Mahraun was a hopeless romantic whose flights of fancy endangered the Right's unity.[54] As early as 1925, key figures in the German Right recognized the Young German Order as a maverick organization, calling Mahraun a "pest" and plotting to strip members away from the organization or change its leadership.[55] Most of the discord between the Young German Order and the rest of the German Right had little to do with antisemitism. If anything, the Young German Order and its most vocal critic, the NSDAP, shared a similar perspective on antisemitic politics. Claudia Koonz notes the NSDAP pursued "ethnic fundamentalism" during elections and generally avoided ugly antisemitic rhetoric to appeal to a larger audience.[56] However, disagreements and feuds seemingly unrelated to the Jewish question invited challenges over which organization was more pure when it came to antisemitism. Rival groups used the same coded antisemitic discourse against each other as they did against powerful socio-economic forces linked to "international Jewry."

The abortive November 1923 putsch was a decisive moment for Mahraun and the Young German leadership and their relationship with the *völkisch* movement. Fearing a government backlash, the Young Germans quickly condemned the action and sought to distance itself from the recklessness of the "Munich circle." Although some in the Munich chapter supported the putsch and participated in antisemitic violence, Weimar authorities investigating the Order believed the organization considered the putsch counterproductive.[57] Mahraun used situational antisemitism to lambast the NSDAP and others for their crude antisemitism and putschist tactics while still managing to criticize Jewish influence on a "higher level." Mahraun rejected what he called the "Munich antisemitism" of Hitler and Erich Ludendorff because it had destructive consequences, but quickly added he was not pro-Jewish. His concern was that such radical antisemitism could unite Jews against Germans and make life even more challenging. "The expulsion of Jews is a utopia," wrote Mahraun. It was unrealistic, not undesirable. Mahraun cautioned against a "false antisemitism" grounded in violence and simplistic rhetoric. The Young German newspapers attacked Hitler and Ludendorff for being reactionary and not revolutionary in their ideology, accusing them of "un-German" tactics more reminiscent of Rome than heroic Germany. The Order appealed to its youthful image and labeled the Munich circle as backward and dangerous for a future Germany where young people exercised greater influence.[58] Having already weathered numerous attacks from erstwhile allies, Mahraun criticized the *völkisch* movement in 1928 for falling under the influence of *Radauantisemitismus*.[59] Mahraun used essentially the same language as those he called the Munich circle, but couched it in constructive terms. The Jewish stranglehold on the German state necessitated a "positive" solution to the Jewish question, which Mahraun maintained was ultimately "a German Question."[60] Walking this discursive tightrope only succeeded in alienating both his *völkisch* flank and the more mainstream organizations Mahraun hoped to include in his future political endeavors.

The Young German Order seemingly abandoned its worldview in 1930 when it merged with the left-liberal German Democratic Party to form the German State Party. For a group that railed against political parties and castigated the Stahlhelm and others for maintaining links to parties to then join forces with a mainstream political party was senseless to many. Moreover, the DDP included several prominent Jews and enjoyed Jewish support in elections. The Young Germans sold the State Party as an attempt to tap into the "positive activism of the political middle" and change the image of the centrist parties from the refuge of old men to the natural home of dynamic young people.[61] The Young Germans now portrayed the Weimar Republic as an imperfect and primitive form of the *Volksstaat*. Mahraun justified the creation of the State Party to his more skeptical base as an attempt to force the government to evolve and circumvent fascism and communism, both of which were gaining strength in Weimar elections.[62] Buying into the system confused and outraged a significant number of Young German members and incensed others on the Right. One former Young German recalled in 1979: "Honestly, I did not feel that great about the State Party. The thing just came too quickly and caused problems for me in the village, especially among the Stahlhelm and Nazis." The member noted that his chapter used to call the State Party the "*Spaßpartei*," or "joke party."[63] It is clear that the Young German leadership never consulted the rank and file, and the negative reaction from members highlighted the growing ideological distance between the organization's leadership and its increasingly radical membership. The Young Germans could not express utopian principles grounded in *völkisch* ideology while simultaneously aligning itself with a centrist political party.

The transition to the State Party instigated a particularly ugly episode of situational antisemitism. The Young Germans were attacked by their rivals for being soft on Jews and criticized by its new ally, the DDP, for being too antisemitic. Mahraun was forced to craft a new stance that appeased no one, mostly because it was completely disingenuous. In the article "My Position Regarding Jewry," Mahraun recast the Young German Order as a mainstream organization interested in a "live and let live" policy regarding Jewish citizenship. Mahraun suggested Jewish groups pursue their own path while the Young German Order maintained its *völkisch* principles. Mahraun stated that the Young Germans would continue to work for a Christian-German state while partnering with the DDP in the State Party. Mahraun's revised stance on antisemitism was essentially that Jews could enjoy equal rights in the new Germany so long as they accepted the Christian-German nature of the *Volksstaat*.[64] Senior Young German leader Kurt Pastenaci claimed that the Young German movement was not antisemitic despite some evidence to the contrary. "We are not antisemitic, but pro-German," Pastenaci wrote, adding that cooperation with Jews was possible outside of the Order, but that the Order itself remained strictly a "community of blood."[65] Mahraun stressed that the Young German Order would remain an independent organization with an Aryan paragraph, although Jews were welcome in the State Party.[66] The DDP discussed privately its concern for retaining Jewish voters in light of its partnership with the Young Germans.[67] The Young German Order, on the other hand, experienced a dramatic loss of membership soon after forming the State Party. A former chapter leader wrote that he could not stomach the State Party because it represented a betrayal of the Young German Order's race consciousness. To cooperate with Jews was treachery, the disaffected chapter leader wrote, and an insult to the martyrs of the *völkisch* movement.[68] If its own members resented the trend toward engagement with Weimar, the Young German Order's enemies smelled blood in the water.

The NSDAP assailed the Young Germans for their role in founding the State Party, focusing most of its attention on Mahraun and his situational antisemitism. Predictable headlines like *"Judenpartei"* appeared in its papers, and the NSDAP mocked Mahraun for talking like a professional antisemite as leader of the Young German Order, but behaving like a philosemite since founding the State Party.[69] The NSDAP deployed the same sort of tactics it used against the Stahlhelm—attack your rivals' antisemitic credentials, imply the leadership is influenced by Jews, and appeal to the organization's disgruntled base. Alfred Rosenberg wrote a pamphlet cataloging Mahraun's Jewish connections, all of which were vague and somehow connected to the Young German Order's French policy.[70] Following the logic of the cultural code, linking Mahraun to rapprochement with an enemy was the equivalent of equating him to Jewry. The Young German Order countered the charge by confirming Mahraun's "Nordic blood" and attacking the NSDAP for its "Roman fascism."[71] The Young Germans defended themselves against antisemitic attacks by challenging their opponents' own antisemitic credentials. One article in the Young German press scoffed at Hitler for claiming to a *New York Times* reporter that he was not antisemitic and respected Jews' legal rights. The Young Germans also denounced Joseph Goebbels for implying in his journal *Angriff* that there was potential for cooperation between the Soviet Union and Germany, accusing him of aligning with "Jewish dictators" in Russia."[72] The Young

Germans charged the NSDAP press with employing the same "divide and conquer" strategy Jews used to conquer Germany. Like the Stahlhelm, the Young German Order was eclipsed by the more dynamic and ideologically consistent NSDAP, an entity unencumbered by internal disputes or accusations of situational antisemitism.

The Stahlhelm and Young German Order in the Third Reich

The National Socialist euphemism for eradicating opposition and dissolving competing loyalties to the party was *Gleichschaltung*, a word that translates into "coordination," "integration," "bringing into line," or, more accurately, "Nazification."[73] The NSDAP began "coordinating" their *völkisch* and nationalist comrades before 1933. The Stahlhelm and Young German Order limped into the Third Reich with a combination of hope and despair—hope that the long-awaited *Volksgemeinschaft* would finally come to fruition and despair that they would be on the outside looking in. The Stahlhelm was clearly the stronger of the two combat leagues, but after a few months of criticizing the new regime Franz Seldte recognized the inevitability of a Nazi state and subsumed the Stahlhelm under Nazi leadership on 27 April 1933, and accepted the position of minister of labor. The Stahlhelm officially merged with the SA in July of 1933 and reluctantly assumed the name "SA Reserve I." Other combat leagues formed the "SA Reserve II."[74] With Duesterberg marginalized after the revelation about his grandfather and a brief imprisonment during the Night of the Long Knives and Seldte co-opted into the new regime, Hitler transformed the Stahlhelm into a National Socialist veterans' organization of dubious value.

A significant number of Stahlhelm members resented the erasure of their identity and institutional memory at the hands of the emboldened new regime. A Stahlhelm acquaintance of Viktor Klemperer encapsulated the spirit of resistance and pride when he told him, "Don't be surprised if you meet me in the Stahlhelm uniform with a Swastika armband. I have to—and as a member of the Stahlhelm I am, after all, something better and different from an SA man, and deliverance will come from the Stahlhelm."[75] Sensing this disloyalty in several local chapters, the SA continued to slander and undermine the Stahlhelm presence to justify "coordination." National Socialist investigators sought examples of Stahlhelm disobedience. Some reports accused the Stahlhelm of harboring communists and suggested that it may even be capable of sabotage.[76] And, just as it did during the Weimar era, the NSDAP used antisemitism to sow discord within the Stahlhelm and challenge its legitimacy as a true German organization. Although Stahlhelm newspapers mimicked National Socialist antisemitic discourse and publicized the boycott against Jewish businesses, the SA in particular accused the Stahlhelm of being soft on Jews. The SA implied that the Stahlhelm still harbored Jews, a fact that necessitated the takeover.[77] The old slander of the Weimar years still served a function during the Third Reich.

In contrast to the Stahlhelm, the Young German Order had a short lifespan under the Third Reich. The Young German Order, by virtue of Artur Mahraun's past statements and its role in the creation of the State Party, was already suspect in the eyes of the new regime. Immediately after Hitler's appointment the Young German leadership declared: "It is self-understood that the Young German Order is the new national opposition." In an article entitled, "Germany Awake!" a play on the NSDAP's famous campaign slogan, Mahraun declared, "the Young German Order is the only national movement that did not give in to the Munich school."[78] He continued by accusing the NSDAP of usurping power and betraying Germany. Another article described the Nazi leadership principle, or *Führerprinzip*, as an abomination and proof that the NSDAP was "czarist" and bent on an imperial reign not unlike ancient Rome.[79] The Young German press also chastised Seldte for accepting a cabinet position and accused him of forsaking the "Front spirit" in favor of the "tyranny of parties," a criticism the Stahlhelm had leveled against the Young German Order only months before.[80] The Nazi regime certainly took notice and issued a lengthy report chronicling the Order's troubled past with the NSDAP. The report noted Mahraun's critical stance on the 1923 putsch, the inherent evil of the French policy, and the dramatic reversal on the Jewish question. The Nazi report acknowledged that the Young German Order was one of the first combat leagues to promote racial considerations, but the organization succumbed to Jewish influence after forming the State Party. The author concluded that the Young German Order and NSDAP shared many views, but the former's continued existence threatened the smooth consolidation of the Third Reich.[81] After months of less than subtle criticism of the regime, the Young German Order was officially banned and Mahraun arrested briefly in July 1933.

For all of its criticism of the regime, the Young German Order seemed to revert to its original antisemitic worldview, although it still insisted on distinguishing its own antisemitism from that of the NSDAP's. The Young Germans supported the boycott of Jewish businesses in April 1933, but asked why the new regime chose not to root out individuals

214 • Brian E. Crim

with "Jewish spirit" in addition to blood. The Order also supported leg-islation directed at removing Jews from the civil service and professions, policies Mahraun advocated in multiple publications throughout the 1920s.[82] The primary difference between the antisemitism of the Young German Order and that of the NSDAP was the former's focus on destroy-ing Jewish "influences" in German society. Jews themselves were practi-cally irrelevant in this construct. The Young Germans seemed to accuse the Third Reich of perpetuating the very degenerate forces it supposedly despised. The Young Germans celebrated excluding Jews and certainly considered it necessary, but so too was eliminating plutocracy, capital-ism, and preventing Italian-style fascism from taking root on German soil. The advent of National Socialism failed to resolve what the Young Germans considered the true nature of the Jewish question.

Situational antisemitism was the function of a fluid and complex po-litical environment. The notion that the German Right was steeped in antisemitism is a simplistic interpretation. Fixating on how to express a position on antisemitism or gauging how friends and enemies would receive that position was not synonymous with privileging antisemi-tism over other aspects of one's worldview. Some groups truly were obsessed with racial issues, others more interested in co-opting the coded language of antisemitism to denounce hostile social and cultural forces. Antisemitic politics during the Weimar era highlighted some of the divisions in the ideologically diverse Right, specifically between the *völkisch* bloc and more traditionally conservative organizations. At-titudes toward race and antisemitism were hardly unanimous. Large combat leagues like the Stahlhelm and Young German Order contended with internal divisions while competing for political influence in the marketplace of ideas. Bernhard Abraham, the Jewish citizen whose in-quiry introduced this chapter, asked if the Young German Order was truly antisemitic. A better question directed at the German Right might have been: How antisemitic are you, and under what circumstances?

Notes

1. "Anfrage eines Juden" and "Antwort an den Juden," *Der Kämpfer für Christentum und Deutschtum*, 1 January 1926, Bundesarchiv Koblenz, Zeitsgeschichtliche Sammlung 1 (hereafter cited as BA Koblenz, ZSg 1), 128/57.
2. James M. Diehl, *Paramilitary Politics in Weimar Germany* (Bloomington: Indiana University Press, 1977), 93–96, 169–75. Diehl identifies the combat leagues as military associations prior to 1924, arguing that the more

militarized and radical associations changed tactics and became more overtly political after the failed Hitler putsch.

3. Hubert Mohr, "Remarks on 'The Jew' as a Social Myth and Some Theoretical Reflections on Anti-Semitism" in *Antisemitismus, Paganismus, Völkisch Religion*, ed. Herbert Cancik and Uwe Puschner (Munich: Saur, 2004), 1–11.

4. Odel Heilbronner, "From Antisemitic Peripheries to Antisemitic Centres: The Place of Antisemitism in Modern German History," *Journal of Contemporary History* 35 (2000): 559–76, 560–64.

5. Shulamit Volkov, "Antisemitism as a Cultural Code: Reflections on the History and Historiography of Antisemitism in Imperial Germany," *Leo Baeck Institute Yearbook* 23 (1978): 25–46.

6. Shulamit Volkov, *Germans, Jews, and Antisemites* (Cambridge: Cambridge University Press, 2006), 73–108.

7. Michael Wildt's impressive collective biography of the leadership of the Reich Security Main Office notes that a number of the leading figures, including Reinhard Heydrich and Werner Best, were active in *völkisch* politics as students. See Wildt, *Generation des Unbedingten. Das Führungskorps des Reichssicherheitshauptamtes* (Hamburg: Hamburger Edition, 2002). Ulrich Herbert's biography of Werner Best also describes the attraction of *völkisch* ideology to the generation born at the turn of the twentieth century. Too young to serve in the war, but mature enough to participate in *völkisch* political activism, members of this "war generation" filled the ranks of the SS. See Ulrich Herbert, *Best: Biographische Studien über Radikalismus. Weltanschauung und Vernunft 1903–1989* (Bonn: Dietz, 1996).

8. Uwe Puschner, "Völkisch Plädoyer für einen 'engen' Begriff," in *"Die Erziehung zum deutschen Menschen." Völkische und nationalkonservative Erwachsenbildung in der Weimarer Republik*, ed. Paul Ciupke, et al. (Essen: Klartext Verlagsgesellschaft, 2007), 53–66. Puschner argues that the *völkisch* movement was successful in linking anti-Semitism to anti-Bolshevism, a precedent for Hitler's conception of "Judeo-Bolshevism."

9. Stefan Breuer, "Gescheiterte Milieubildung: Die Völkischen im deutschen Reich," in *Völkische Religion und Krisen der Moderne. Entwürfe "arteigener" Glaubenssysteme seit der Jahrhundertwende*, ed. Stefanie v. Schnurbein and Justus H. Ulbricht (Würzburg: Königshausen und Neumann, 1996), 996–1012.

10. Werner Bergmann, "Völkischer Antisemitismus im Kaiserreich," in *Handbuch zur Völkischen Bewegung" 1871–1918*, ed. Uwe Puschner, Walter Schmitz, and Justus H. Ulbricht (Munich: Saur, 1996), 449–63, 461.

11. Quoted in Uwe Puschner, "Anti-Semitism and German Voelkisch Ideology," *Antisemitismus, Paganismus, Völkisch Religion*, ed. Cancik and Puschner, 55–64. Puschner notes that *völkisch* activists disagreed over the importance of antisemitism to the movement. Theodor Fritsch represented the extreme antisemitic wing of the movement, while Friedrich Lienhard preferred to promote "Germanism" over anti-Jewish rhetoric.

12. Puschner, "Anti-Semitism and German Voelkisch Ideology," 58.

13. Dirk Schumann, *Political Violence in the Weimar Republic, 1918–1933: Fight for the Streets and Fears of Civil War*, trans. by Thomas Dunlap (New York and Oxford: Berghahn Books, 2009), 312.
14. See Robert Gerwarth, "The Central European Counter-Revolution: Paramilitary Violence in Germany, Austria and Hungary after the Great War," *Past and Present* (2008): 175–209, 200. Gerwarth sees the wave of counter-revolutionary violence as a prelude to the Third Reich's genocidal campaign against "Judeo-Bolshevism."
15. Peter Fritzsche, *Rehearsals for Fascism: Populism and Political Mobilization in Weimar Germany* (New York: Oxford University Press, 1990), 166.
16. James Diehl traces the Stahlhelm's growth as follows: 2,000 in 1919–20; 100,000 by 1924; 500–600,000 in the mid-1920s; and 750,000 after 1933. See Diehl, *Paramilitary Politics*, 293–97.
17. Volker R. Berghahn, *Der Stahlhelm. Bund der Frontsoldaten, 1918–1935* (Düsseldorf: Droste, 1966), 26.
18. Wilhelm Kleinau, *Franz Seldte. Ein Lebensbericht* (Berlin,1933), 8.
19. Berghahn, *Stahlhelm*, 69.
20. Stahlhelm, Bundesamt, Rundschrieben Nr. 87, 18 September 1928, in the unpublished records of the Stahlhelm, Bundesarchiv Berlin-Lichterfelde, Bestand R 72 (hereafter cited as BA Berlin, R 72), 273/3.
21. Vorschläge betr. Neuorganisation des "Stahlhelms," 26 November 1921, BA Berlin, R 72, 4/258–61.
22. Quoted in Berghahn, *Stahlhelm*, 65–66.
23. Meeting of the Stahlhelm executive committee, 11 May 1926, BA Berlin, R 72, 5/99–147. See in particular the five-point proposed resolution attached to the communiqué of 11 May 1926, BA Berlin, R 72, 5/151–52.
24. Letter to Dr. Karl Scherer, 11 June 1926, BA Berlin, R 72, 113/155–56.
25. "Die inneren Beziehng zwischen der Weimarer Verfassung und dem Versailler Diktat," BA Berlin, R 72/4, 181.
26. "Wo steht der Feind?" *Der Stahlhelm*, 14 March 1926, BA Berlin, R 72, 348/92.
27. Letter to Karl Böhlke, 3 May 1926. BA Berlin, R 72, 71/45–46.
28. Senator to Duesterberg, 12 June 1929, BA Berlin, R 72, 273/18–20.
29. Senator to the political division of the Stahlhelm's national office, 18 August 1929, BA Berlin, R 72, 273/16.
30. Wagner to v. Wedel, 3 August 1929, BA Berlin, R 72, 273/15.
31. Stahlhelm to Senator, 27 December 1928, BA Berlin, R 72, 273/6–7.
32. Letter to Kreis Neuweid from Landesverband Westmark des Stahlhelm, 2 January 1931, BA Berlin, R 72, 273/32.
33. Bentz to Wagner, 28 December 1931, and response, 11 January 1932, BA Berlin, R 72, 113/33–35.
34. Engel to Seldte, 6 July 1932, BA Berlin, R 72,273/41.
35. "Gerlach's jüdischer Kommerzienrat," 22 January 1928, BA Koblenz, ZSg 1–88/5, 4.
36. Letter to the Stahlhelm, Landesverband Industriegebiet, 4 July 1927, BA Berlin, R 72, 78/96.

37. Letter from Meyer (Kreis Neuwied) to the Koblenz district organization of the Stahlhelm, 18 December 1931, BA Berlin, R 72, 273/30.

38. Letter from the Stahlhelm's Thuringian district organization to the regional organization for central Germany (Landesverband Mitteldeutschland), 20 June 1932, BA Berlin, R 72, 273/22–23.

39. Berghahn, *Stahlhelm*, 239–40.

40. "Die Politik Artur Mahrauns: Ihre tieferend Gründe und Endziele," n.d., in the unpublished records of the Jungdeutscher Orden, Bundesarchiv Berlin-Lichterfelde, Bestand R 161 (hereafter cited as BA Berlin, R 161), 9.

41. Diehl, *Paramilitary Politics*, 97–98. A welcome new contribution on the Jungdo's political thought is Clifton Ganyard, *Artur Mahraun and the Young German Order: An Alternative to National Socialism in Weimar Political Culture* (Lewistown, NY, 2008).

42. See Artur Mahraun, *Gegen Getarnte Gewalten. Weg und Kampf einer Volksbewgung* (Berlin: Jungdeutscher Verlag, 1928), for a programmatic outline of the Young German worldview and Mahraun's perspective on his frequent conflicts with the Right.

43. Mahraun, "Jungdeutsch-völkische Politik," *Der Jungdeutsche*, 26 January 1924, BA Koblenz, ZSg 1–128/56.

44. Mahraun, "Fortsetzung unserer Auseinandersetzung mit den Deutschen Juden," *Der Jungdeutsche*, 26 July 1924, BA Koblenz, ZSg 1–128/56.

45. "Judenherrschaft I, II, III," *Der Jungdeutsche*, 28–30 October 1924, BA Koblenz, ZSg 1–128/56.

46. Stadtbrück, "Die Kirchenväter und die Juden," *Der Jungdeutsche*, 8 October 1924, BA Koblenz, ZSg 1–128/56.

47. Untitled essay, BA Koblenz, Zsg 1–128/7 (27).

48. Huchzermeyer, "Jungdeutscher Orden und Rassenfrage," *Jahrbuch des Jungdeutschen Ordens 1925* (Berlin: Jungdeutscher Verlag, 1925), 20–21, in BA Koblenz, Zsg 1–128/20.

49. "Die Judenkolonien in Sowjetrussland," *Der Jungdeutsche*, 10 April 1926, BA Koblenz, Zsg 1–128/56.

50. *Der Staatsbürger*, Bd. 1, Heft 1, BA Koblenz, ZSg 1–128/1.

51. Count Rüdiger von der Goltz, chairman of the United Patriotic Leagues of Germany (Vereinigte Vaterländische Verbände Deutschlands or VVVD), accused the Young German Order of treason because of the so-called French policy. In 1926 Goltz declared that "a greater danger than our enemies is disunity." See the text of a speech he delivered, 1 September 1926, in Goltz's unpublished Nachlaß, Bundesarchiv Militärarchiv Freiburg (hereafter cited as BA-MA Freiburg, NL Goltz), 10. Mahraun outlined the French policy in *Der nationale Friede am Rhein* (Berlin: Jungdeutscher Verlag, 1926).

52. Young German chancellor Otto Bornemann was embroiled in a libel case with Hugenberg after writing a series of exposes on his "plutocratic" and "authoritarian" methods. Bornemann also derided the Stahlhelm for attaching its fate to his fortune. See Bornemann, "Hugenberg, Der Herr über Presse und Film," *Der Jungdeutsche*, 21 September 1930, BA Koblenz, ZSg 1–128/56.

53. Mahraun, *Gegen Getarnte Gewalten*, 206.

54. Hermann, "Romantik des Frontgeschlechtes," *Der Jungdeutsche*, 17 October 1929.

55. Comment by Berger at a discussion of presidential candidates at a meeting of right-wing parties and patriotic organizations, 30 April 1925, in the unpublished Nachlaß of Friedrich von Gayl, Bundesarchiv Koblenz, 23.

56. Claudia Koonz, *The Nazi Conscience* (Cambridge, 2003), 26.

57. "Bericht über den Verlauf der am 7 November 1923, abends 8 Uhr in Grossen Saal des Kriegsvereinhauses veranstalten Kundgebung des Jungdo Bruderschaft Gross-Berlin," in the unpublished records of the Reich ministry of interior, Bundesarchiv Berlin-Lichterfelde, Bestand R 1501, 113266b/40.

58. Otto Bornemann, "Die Wahrheit über München," *Der Jungdeutsche*, 8 December 1923, BA Koblenz, ZSg 1–128/56.

59. Artur Mahraun, *Das Jungdeutsche Manifest. Volk gegen Kaste und Geld, Sicherung des Friedens durch Neubau der Staaten* (Berlin: Jungdeutscher Verlag, 1928), 22.

60. Mahraun, *Gegen Getarnte Gewalten*, 220.

61. "Die Erste Presse-Konferenz," *Der Jungdeutsche*, 11 September 1930, BA Koblenz, ZSg 1–128/56.

62. "Es sprechen die Führer der Deutschen Staatspartei," *Der Jungdeutsche*, 11 September 1930, BA Koblenz, ZSg 1–128/56.

63. Werner Wolf, "Die Geschichte der Bruderschaft Mainz/Rhein des Jungdeutschen Ordens," in the unpublished records of the Jungdeutscher Order, BA Berlin, R 161, 42.

64. Mahraun, "Meine Stellung zum Judentum," *Der Jungdeutsche*, 6 August 1930, BA Koblenz, ZSg 1–128/56.

65. Kurt Pastenaci, "Gegensätze in der Deutschen Staatspartei?" *Der Meister* 5, no. 12 (September 1930): 545–52, BA Koblenz, Zsg 1–128/59.

66. Volksnationale Reichsvereinigung, *Der erste Reichsvertretertag am 5. und 6. April 1930* (Berlin: Jungdeutscher Verlag, 1930), BA Koblenz, Zsg 1–128/40.

67. In this respect, see the minutes of the executive committee of the German State Party, 12 June 1932, in the unpublished records of the Deutsche Demokratische Partei /Deutsche Staatspartei, Bundesarchiv Berlin-Lichterfelde, Bestand R 45 III, 50/70–94.

68. Mobius, "Als Jungdeutscher kann ich nicht mehr Mahraun wählen" (1930), BA Berlin, R 161, 8.

69. "Als Hochmeister Antisemit; als 'Reichsvorsitzender' Philosemit—Das Bekenntnis einer edlen Seele," *Völkischer Beobachter*, 2 March 1930, BA Berlin, R 161, 8.

70. "Abrechnung mit Mahraun," *Der Jungdeutsche*, 24 September 1926, BA Koblenz, ZSg 1–128/56.

71. "Der 'Jude' Mahraun," *Der Jungdeutsche*, 4 August 1931, BA Koblenz, ZSg 1–128/56.

72. "Goebbels und Moskau," *Der Jungdeutsche*, 25 August 1928, BA Koblenz, ZSg 1–128/56.

73. Ian Kershaw, *The Nazi Dictatorship: Problems and Perspectives of Interpretation* (London, 1993), 135, and Koonz, *Nazi Conscience*, 73.
74. Berghahn, *Stahlhelm*, 256–72.
75. Victor Klemperer, *I Shall Bear Witness: The Diaries of Victor Klemperer, 1933–1941*, trans. Martin Chalmers (London, 1998), 27.
76. Letter from Gauleiter der Kurmarck to Reichskanzler Adolf Hitler, 16 January 1934, BA Berlin, R 43 II, 1202/146–56.
77. Article in *Der SA Mann*, 27 April 1935, and "Kampf gegen Staatsfeinde," *Magdeburger Zeitung*, 27 August 1935, BA Berlin, R 72, 488.
78. Mahraun, "Deutschland Erwache!" *Der Jungdeutsche*, 1 February 1933, BA Koblenz, ZSg 1–128/56.
79. "Führerprinzip und Selbstverwaltung," *Der Jungdeutsche*, 17 August 1933, BA Koblenz, ZSg 1–128/56.
80. Pastenaci, "Volk über rechts und links," *Der Jungdeutsche*, 2 February 1933, BA Koblenz, ZSg 1–128/58.
81. "Die Politik Artur Mahrauns: Ihre tieferen Gründe und Endziele," BA Berlin, R 161, 9.
82. "Nur Juden?" and "Gegen die Überfremdung," *Der Jungdeutsche*, 27 April 1933, BA Koblenz, ZSg 1–128/56.

8

ANTISEMITISM AND THE JEWISH QUESTION IN THE POLITICAL WORLDVIEW OF THE CATHOLIC RIGHT

Ulrike Ehret

This chapter examines the discussion of the Jewish question and the image of the Jew on the Catholic Right by using examples from the publications and correspondence of some of its leading representatives. The essay argues that the Catholic Right's profoundly religious worldview of a God-given organic order did not allow the traditional Christian "solution" to the Jewish question, namely the conversion of Jews to Christianity. Furthermore, right-wing Catholics saw Jews less as a religious community than as an alien, even racially distinct people that undermined German culture and threatened German national unity. Still, their proposed "solution" to the Jewish question was partly Christian in that they sought to promote a Christian national education and the constitution of a Christian corporative state. This, in turn, would have revoked unconditional Jewish Emancipation and ultimately excluded Jews from German society. This chapter argues that the Catholic Right did not simply tolerate the antisemitism of the German National People's Party (Deutschnationale Volkspartei or DNVP) and National Socialism as an inconvenient flaw of the nationalist movement, but that it was an integral factor in the Catholic Right's embrace of the *völkisch* movement.

Small in numbers and caught between the nationalist conservatism of the largely Protestant DNVP and the social conservatism of the Catholic Center Party, the Catholic Right has not figured prominently in the political histories of Imperial and Weimar Germany. Klaus Breuning and Horst Gründer, who provided an early overview of the Catholic Right, its organization, and its worldview and publications, acknowledge a certain affinity between the worldview of the Catholic Right and National Socialism, in particular in their desire to revive a German Reich. Yet they are cautious to portray the Catholic Right as a precursor to National Socialism.[1] According to Breuning and Gründer, the Jew hatred of the Catholic Right was neither racist nor was it the driving force in their flirtation with National Socialism.[2] This view has since been challenged by more recent work on the Catholic Right. Christoph Hübner shows in his analysis of one of the Right's most well-known journals, *Die Gelben Hefte*, that many Catholics on the Right used hostile racial images of Jews in their writings and publications.[3] Larry Eugene Jones goes even further when he claims that the Catholic Right not only helped pave the way for Hitler, but that they did so out of conviction and not as part of a strategy of containment. Jones addresses the virulent antisemitism of influential individuals on the Catholic Right as a factor in their attraction to National Socialism.[4] His studies on the Westphalian Catholic nobility and the Reich Catholic Committee of the DNVP combine the worldview of the Catholic Right with their political history and institutional and personal affiliations in such a way that the relation between ideology and political commitment becomes more obvious.[5]

In light of recent research, the chief significance of the Catholic Right did not lie in its *Standespolitik* as nobles or in its party politics as members of the DNVP, but in its ability to create an alternative network for nationalist-minded Catholics who were likewise repelled by the anti-Catholicism of *völkisch* groups and the coalition between the Center Party and the SPD. Fewer than 50 percent of the Catholic electorate voted for the Center Party in the 1920s, a percentage that improved slightly in 1928 under the more conservative leadership of Ludwig Kaas.[6] Catholics, like other Germans, chose to support those parties that promised to represent their increasingly diverse interests beyond the limits of solely Catholic or ecclesiastic concerns. Furthermore, considering that the future of the Weimar Republic depended on the decisions of a few "undemocratic conservatives"[7] in 1932 and 1933, among them fellow travelers of the Catholic Right such as Franz von Papen, the DNVP's man within the Center,[8] the worldview and antisemitism of the Catholic Right remains important in any enquiry into the early acquiescence of Christian conservatives to the National Socialist regime.

The antisemitism of the Catholic Right was certainly the most virulent form of Jew hatred among Catholics in Weimar Germany. Over the last decades research into Catholic antisemitism has shown that anti-Jewish sentiments and rhetoric were dependent on the place of Catholics in national politics. In the case of Imperial Germany, Catholic antisemitism is best seen in the context of German nation building, where Catholic antisemitism was part of the attempt to craft a cohesive cultural identity and political union among German Catholics in the face of a dominant Protestant (Prussian) national discourse.[9] For the postwar period, Anthony Kauders and Oded Heilbronner have convincingly shown that in the diverse and polarized world of Weimar politics, the propensity to anti-Jewish views and rhetoric depended not necessarily on Catholic dogma but rather on a person's commitment to a political and cultural milieu as well as on the general political infrastructure and culture of a region.[10]

In contrast to the traditional ambivalence that most Catholics displayed toward Jews (Christian charity and protection against allegedly malign Jewish influences), there was little ambivalence in the treatment of the Jewish question by the Catholic Right. National unity and the reconciliation between the Christian confessions was their priority. Their conviction that Germany suffered under the contemporary, almost Biblical, struggle between "Christian" values and "Jewish" influences left little room for Christian charity toward Jews. Unlike Olaf Blaschke's Catholic ultramontanes of the nineteenth century, these Catholic nationalists sought to defend and unify not Catholic and Church interests but those of a Christian-conservative nation.[11]

The Catholic Right: Aim, Organization, and Worldview

The Catholic Right was united in its opposition to the newly founded democratic German republic and in its desire to forge a German national community, or *Volksgemeinschaft*, based on a corporative organic society and crowned by a German monarch. The immediate aim was to strengthen German Christian conservatism that had become even more deeply divided after the war and had only recently found a new political home in the DNVP.[12] Its previous political home, the Center Party, had been a pillar of prewar conservatism but had "betrayed" conservative ideals in the eyes of the Catholic Right when it supported the democratic republic. Worse still, it cooperated with the Right's political and ideological opponents, the Social Democrats and liberals. The longterm aim of the Catholic Right was to heal the historic confessional schism in Germany to forge a national community. Its dream envisaged an end to the young democracy and a return to a monarchical or authoritarian political structure and conservative Christian values.

Although at times it has seemed as if the Catholic Right was a heterogeneous group, it is easily identifiable in terms of its social and regional background. The majority of national conservative Catholics belonged to the social elites of Imperial and Weimar Germany, the nobility, and educated middle class. They were landowners, high-ranking civil servants, and academics. There were a few entrepreneurs and members of the lower clergy, but no manual workers. Geographically, the Reich Catholic Committee was represented in most regions of Germany but found its key support in the Catholic diaspora regions of Prussia, in particular in Westphalia, Berlin, Silesia, but also in Catholic Bavaria.[13]

The organizational home of the Catholic Right was the Reich Catholic Committee of the DNVP (Reichskatholikenausschuß der Deutschnationalen Volkspartei or RKA), established on 25 October 1920 by Baron Engelbert von Landsberg-Velen from an old and distinguished Westphalian noble family.[14] Other well-known members of the RKA included the highly decorated artillery general Max von Gallwitz and the former mayor of Cologne and DNVP representative in the Prussian Landtag, Max Wallraf, as well as the historian Martin Spahn.[15] The creation of the RKA was an alternative to the foundation of a completely new party, an endeavor that had already failed in the attempt to establish the nationalist Christian People's Party (Christliche Volkspartei) to the right of the Center Party.[16] The RKA might have delivered the organizational backbone to Catholic and national politics, but it was not the only platform for the Catholic Right. Following the conservative tradition of *Sammlungspolitik*, DNVP Catholics were keen to maintain a network of like-minded Christians that stretched across class and confessional divisions. Those reluctant to commit to a political party, like the brothers Hermann and Ferdinand von Lüninck, turned toward voluntary and paramilitary associations such as the peasant leagues and the Stahlhelm.[17] They nevertheless assisted the RKA in election campaigns, supported its publications, and petitioned the Catholic bishops in favor of the RKA. It was the preferred political commitment of Catholic nobles of the Right as it fitted both their dislike of parliamentary democracy and their understanding of the nobility's traditional paternalistic role in society. Further contacts within the network of the Catholic Right included links to the Christian Trade Unions, the Benedictine monastery of Maria Laach whose members voted for the DNVP from 1924 on, and the Young Conservatives around Heinrich von Gleichen and Arthur Moeller van den Bruck, as well as organizations on the paramilitary Right such as the Stahlhelm and the Young German Order (Jungdeutscher Orden).[18]

The RKA set out to win support for the DNVP votes among conservative Catholics who still supported the Center Party and petitioned the Catholic bishops to support their political cause. In matters of political day-to-day routine the RKA and its satellites supported DNVP policies. For their political activities Catholics of the Right relied on their status and on a number of publications that sought to promote internal cohesion within the DNVP and to strengthen the national conservative network in general.[19] Amongst these publications was the RKA organ, the *Katholisches Korrespondenzblatt* (1921–26; later revived as the *Katholische Führerbriefe*, 1932–33), edited by Johannes Pritze and Paul Lejeune-Jung, the latter a former Center Party politician who subsequently served as deputy chairman of the RKA.[20] More ambitious in its reach and intellectual claim was *Die Gelben Hefte*, successor to the well-known learned Catholic journal *Historisch-Politische Blätter*, edited by Max Buchner.[21] Most of their own publications struggled financially and never reached a mass audience outside the German nationalist camp. Yet writers and publicists of the Catholic Right had a range of media at their disposal that reached beyond the boundaries of DNVP party lines. Pritze, for example, supported Eduard Stadtler's young conservative journal *Das Gewissen* and Heinrich Klinkenberg and Martin Spahn's *Das Deutsche Volk*, sharing authors and mailing lists of subscribers to the *Korrespondenzblatt*.[22] Support for the Catholic Right and its publication also came from the right wing of the Center Party. Wilhelm Reinermann, secretary of the Association of Catholic Journeymen (Kolpingsverein), edited *Das Deutsche Volk*.[23]

The RKA was most successful in its early years between 1920 and 1924 when it expanded geographically, opening chapters in Silesia, Westphalia, the Rhineland, Baden, Saxony, East Prussia, and Bavaria.[24] It also managed to persuade the DNVP leadership to nominate more Catholics as DNVP election candidates resulting in ten Catholic deputies among the 107 German nationalist Reichstag representatives in 1924.[25] The RKA eventually broke apart in 1929 over the Prussian Landtag's vote on whether to accept the Prussian Concordat with the Vatican. Alfred Hugenberg, chairman of the DNVP from 1928, had demanded absolute loyalty to the DNVP party line and its rejection of the Prussian Concordat. While this would suggest that the confessional divide within the DNVP could ultimately not be overcome, this callous disregard of Catholic interests within the DNVP prompted most of the "old nationalists" to resign from the RKA and later from the party itself. These included among others Engelbert von Landsberg, Paul Lejune Jung, Max Wallraf, Max Buchner, Kurt Ziesché, and Max von Gallwitz.[26] For nationalists closer to the "young conservatives" like Martin Spahn, however, Hugenberg had proven his leadership qualities and served the party's main aim of forging a united national conservative front.[27]

The Catholics who stood on the Right were not "lesser Catholics" as they have been portrayed in Catholic historical writing.[28] To be sure, they certainly did not belong to the Center Party; in fact their entire raison d'être was opposition to the Center Party and its policies and ideals. Yet this did not diminish their commitment to the Catholic faith or their loyalty to Rome as the spiritual and organizational center of Catholicism. The Catholic Right might no longer have been "Catholic" in their politics, but "Catholic" was their religious commitment. Their worldview, too, was anchored in a religious frame of reference to Catholic values and ideals.

Catholics on the Right had conserved many characteristics of an eighteenth- and nineteenth-century Catholic conservative worldview whose foundation was set by God's authority and the principles of natural law. According to these principles, mankind lived in a God-given order where everybody had a predestined place in a corporative society. All secular authority was consequently derived from God's majesty and was exercised through institutions that had developed through history, not from human covenants and certainly not from popular sovereignty. Man's task was to maintain this divine order.[29] The ideal social polity in the eyes of the Catholic Right was the premodern corporative order of small communities governed by the traditional elite of guild masters, aristocracy, and the Church. The crowning temporal authority lay in a hereditary monarchy or a charismatic leader figure.[30] Like their ancestors, the Catholic Right in Weimar Germany consequently fought what they perceived as outgrowth of the "ideas of 1789": materialistic liberalism and its more modern variants in socialism and democracy. Yet in contrast to nineteenth-century ultramontane and integralist Catholics, they were *kleindeutsch* German nationalists. If the Catholic Right in Weimar dreamed of a new Reich, it was a version of the Second German Reich of Bismarck, not a Catholic Reich in a federation with the Habsburg Empire, which was to Max Buchner the "grave of [their] national hopes."[31]

Antisemitism was an integral part of the worldview of the Catholic Right. Considering that the Catholic Right included aging barons of the rural and industrial Catholic aristocracy, academics, and higher civil servants as well as "young conservatives" like Martin Spahn and Eduard Stadtler, it is not surprising that the anti-Jewish sentiments voiced at meetings or elaborated in publications ranged from nineteenth century theories of the Judeo-Masonic conspiracy to the racial characterizations of Jews. The minutes of the 1923 meeting of the Catholic Westphalian aristocracy illustrate the breadth of anti-Jewish beliefs among the Catholic Right ranging from a trust in the veracity of the "Protocols of the Elders of Zion" to the view that Jewry and Germandom were ultimately incompatible. Count Franz von Galen, who chaired the meeting, and his brother Clemens von Galen, future bishop of Münster, participated in this meeting, as did Martin Spahn and Franz von Papen. After presentations on the theme of "*Volkstum,* Jewry and Freemasonry," the minutes summarized the participants' view on the Jewish question in three points. First, the accusations of the "Protocols" were deemed plausible because of their "inner truth," their confirmation through recent events, and the fact that Jews had sought to obstruct their distribution.[32] Second, the assimilation of Jewry and Germandom along Anglo-Saxon lines was held to be impossible, because the German nature ("*die bodenständige, nationale, produktivarbeitende Einstellung*") was intrinsically contrary to the "Jewish spirit." Third, fighting Jewry did not contradict Catholic principles; on the contrary, "since Christ's death the Jews are the rejected people, God's scourge, the main representatives of materialism, decomposition, of anti-Christendom."

Two years later Count Otto Westphalen spoke on national self-defense at another gathering of the Catholic nobility.[33] Westphalen warned against the growing influence of Jews in Germany and urged the state to take measures against those *Fremdkörper* who sought to destroy it:

> I count among the *Fremdrassen* that refuse to assimilate, for example, the Jews. The state has the right, with reservations, not to treat them as full citizens, to impose restrictions on their political rights, their freedom of residence, their choice of a profession, and so on, just as the medieval state had done with the approval of the Church. . . . However, the presupposition for such a *Sonderbehandlung* of those *Fremdkörper* who are not willing to assimilate is that the state will not incorporate them violently and against their will.[34]

In an afterthought Westphalen also urged to protect the people against the influence of immoral modern fashion and dances.[35]

The tendency to project almost everything that seemed modern and uncontrollable onto "the Jews" only to end in a grandfatherly protest against modern dances still had its roots in a recognizable worldview. If the foundation of the Catholic Right's worldview was a religiously heightened belief in Germandom, at its heart lay the conviction that Germany found itself in a Biblical struggle between good and evil, between Christian values and materialism, between the old order and socialism. In many publications of the Catholic Right these conflicts were epitomized by the struggle between Christianity and Jewry. Max Buchner turned this Manichean view of the world into the heart of his journal, *Die Gelben Hefte.* In the introduction to its first edition from 1924, Buchner argued that the modern world was divided between the "Christian-patriotic battlefront," the Catholic parties, and a third "front, which in political terms was democracy . . . and in spiritual terms mainly Jewry, liberalism and freemasonry."[36]

The religious assumptions that lay at the heart of such views of the Jewish question were still quite noticeable, and religious references were common "explanations" why modern Jews had become the alleged source of liberalism, materialism, and national decay. Among these, the charge of Jewish deicide was common, whereas passages from Christian scripture, papal pronouncements, and ecclesiastic publications also served to support the claim that Jews were a threat to the Christian world.[37] Yet for many of the Catholics who identified themselves with the Right, their interpretation of the Jewish question profoundly influenced their political commitments.

Antisemitism in the Political Game of Christian-National Politics

The parentage of the DNVP and a commitment to Catholicism were apparent in the 1920 program of the Reich Catholic Committee. The program, along with an introductory letter signed by Baron Engelbert von Landsberg, was sent to the Papal Nuncio Eugenio Pacelli and the German Catholic episcopate. The letter highlighted the importance of the Jewish question to the policies of the Catholic Right. At the same time, the RKA committed itself to the principle of Christian charity as long as this was not detrimental to the interests of the nation.[38]

> [The] most important task of the present lies in the maintenance and revival of the Christian nationalist idea, particularly among the masses that have been seduced by socialism. This task determines at the same time our stance towards the Jewish question. While we acknowledge the law of Christian charity that excludes no one, we are not prepared to concede to an alien and international people either secret or public political influence that exceeds their numbers by far, that threatens our cultural identity, and that does not usually contribute to a Christian national education (*Volkserziehung*).[39]

The most detailed discussion of the Jewish question together with a clear political pledge to the DNVP was published six years later by the Breslau professor in theology and, according to Breuning, "the most influential mind of the Catholic Right,"[40] Kurt Ziesché. At this time, the DNVP found itself on the opposition bench again after it had left the coalition government of Chancellor Hans Luther in protest against the signing of the Locarno treaties. Ziesché's book *Das Königtum Christi in Europa,* which was published in 1926 with the imprimatur of the diocese of Regensburg, amounted to an intellectual and political manifesto of the Catholic Right. It was an attempt to position the Catholic Right within the spectrum of Catholic and conservative politics in Weimar Germany outside the Center Party. Unlike other political manifestos, this statement was firmly rooted in a religious worldview. In Ziesché's opinion, the forces of history were driven by the eternal and fundamental antagonism between "true Jewry" and "true Christendom" where one was to be the "ruin [*Vernichtung*]" of the other.[41] To corroborate his claim, Ziesché explained how Jews from the time of the French Revolution had emerged as victors of this struggle and came to dominate science, politics, the economy, public opinion, and "socialism."[42] In Ziesché's eyes, the key to confronting the chaos and problems of modern society was to assure that Christendom would win over Jewry in this Biblical struggle. He consequently called on all conservative Catholics to support the Catholic Right in defense against the left-leaning Center Party and "Jewish influences."[43]

Ziesché's political manifesto was clear. The place of the Catholic Right was not with the "Jewified" Center Party but with the largely Protestant DNVP: "Catholics of the Right in Germany are *völkisch*," Ziesché argued. "The *völkisch* idea must not to be neglected, even if its abuse can end in the surrogate religion of nationalism."[44] Ziesché was aware of the DNVP's deeply ingrained anti-Catholic sentiments and the small faction of radical anti-clerics within the party. For the sake of a unified Christian front Ziesché tolerated their excessive nationalism but cautioned against any hope to establish a "German religion" that claimed to be more German than a "Jewified Christendom."[45]

The Catholic Right identified with the *völkisch* Right not solely because of their radical nationalism and Christian values. Equally important was their exclusionary antisemitism. To the Catholic Right the DNVP seemed less "Jewified" than the Center Party, their previous political home, and more determined to deal with the Jewish question than any democratic party. The limits of the Right's antisemitism were consequently set less by religious sentiments than by political considerations, that is, its long-term aim of a Christian-national revival and the short-term changes in national politics and the DNVP's role therein.

The link between political events and the frequency and intensity of the antisemitic hostility in the publications of the Catholic Right is most clearly seen in the pages of contemporary newspapers, as in this case the *Katholisches Korrespondenzblatt*. In the summer of 1923, when rumor was ripe of a renewed attempt at a nationalist coup d'état, an event that most leading Catholics of the Right whole-heartedly supported,[46] the *Korrespondenzblatt* expressed its sympathy with the *völkisch* Right and in particular with the nationalists in Bavaria on a number of occasions.[47] At the same time, the number of anti-Jewish statements in the paper increased from previous years, as did articles that discussed the Jewish question in detail. These contributions called for a more assertive stance against the alleged dominance of Jews in Germany than the "healthy antisemitism" the Catholic Church allowed.[48] The *Korrespondenzblatt* also invited Chaplain Joseph Roth to elaborate on his thoughts on "Catholicism and the Jewish Question" in three lengthy installments. Roth later joined the Nazi regime's Ministry of Church Affairs but at the time was an active, yet radical member of the clergy of the Archdiocese of Munich-Freising.[49] In great detail, Roth argued that Catholics could be antisemites without renouncing Catholic charity and universalism, because antisemitism was an act of self-defense. Catholics should also begin to see Jews as an alien race whose characteristics were determined by race and blood, because only racial antisemitism had so far led the most effective struggle against Jewry. According to Roth, this contradicted neither Catholic charity nor Catholic universalism that embraced all races. If a race stood for immorality as Jews did, then it was Catholic duty to oppose this race.[50] However, Catholics should not follow the Swastika and mob law or publish "petty tasteless antisemitic tracts."[51] Roth ultimately preferred a "religious policy" toward Jews that "would eliminate [*ausschalten*] them from German public life . . . not out of hatred toward Jews, but out of the love for Christian religion and morals."[52]

Such a focus on the Jewish question at the time was not a coincidence. The editors of the *Korrespondenzblatt* purposefully and carefully designed the content of the RKA newspaper to provide a compelling showcase for the aims and policies of the Catholic Right. The publication of lengthy discussions of the Jewish question in 1923 was very much an integral part of it. Johannes Pritze, who edited the *Katholische Korrespondenzblatt*, sought to represent "in politics the religious and cultural interests of German Catholicism through the [DNVP]."[53] In his eyes, nothing less than the fate of the fatherland was at stake. Pritze commissioned most of the contributions from other national conservative Catholics. If necessary, the topic as well as the political intention of the articles was often set out in advance by the editors.[54] Opinions conflicting with their political line, for example from conservative but Center Party Catholics, were published with a brief introduction by the editor clarifying their "erroneous" ways.[55] Neither the treatment of the Jewish question by Roth nor any other anti-Jewish remark in the paper required a clarifying introduction by the editor.

Verbal and physical attacks on Jews increased noticeably in summer and autumn 1923 along with the more self-confident activism of the *völkisch* Right and a wave of antisemitic news coverage. The wave broke in the abortive Hitler Putsch in November 1923 and subsided shortly thereafter when the democratic parties, including the Center Party, moved to restrain the use of antisemitism on their platforms.[56] The DNVP also muted antisemitism in its rhetoric in the campaign for the December 1924 Reichstag elections as it faced the prospect of entering national government. The party upheld this restraint as long as it was part of center-right coalition governments, but returned to its open and radical antisemitism in 1932 as it found itself in competition with the more popular NSDAP. Yet the DNVP's antisemitism was not a mere rhetorical ploy in their political game. Nor did it solely serve as a "communicative bridge" to the *völkisch* Right, as Stephan Malinowski suggests in the case of the German nobility.[57] Most representatives of the conservative Right subscribed to an antisemitism that hoped to diminish Jewish influence in German society. Even Count Kuno von Westarp, chairman of the DNVP from 1926 to 1928, who has been seen as an upright traditionalist among Weimar conservatives, found F. K. Günther's theses on Jews as an "alien race" generally convincing.[58] The intensity of antisemitic comments in the publications of the Catholic Right might have varied depending on contemporary events, yet antisemitism never vanished. Max Buchner inaugurated the Right's new academic journal, the *Gelben Hefte*, in 1924, roughly at the same time when the DNVP party leaders moved to soften their party's public expressions of anti-Jewish hatred. Christoph Hübner, who has analyzed the content of the *Gelben Hefte*, shows that antisemitism was a regular component of its articles. Furthermore, a racial definition of Jews was becoming increasingly common in the pages of the *Gelben Hefte* beginning in the late 1920s.[59]

The private correspondence of DNVP Catholics attests to the same continuity of antisemitic prejudices. For example, in a letter to the editors of *Das Deutsche Volk*, the newspaper of the Catholic student union, the Ring of German Catholics (Ring deutscher Katholiken), Martin Spahn emphasized the importance of antisemitism to the success of the German nationalist cause and described the form and function the Ring's antisemitism should take in the following words:

> I see the fight against the excessive domination of Jewry as one of our main objectives. We have to be antisemites, both as Christians and as Germans; it cannot be ignored that especially Jewry putrefies our religion and our patriotic ideals in every respect. We must, however, insist that the nature of today's antisemitism evolves into a more idealistic form. Today it is mainly based on race hatred and hostility. As long as it remains that way, it is something negative and cannot create positive values. We have to distinguish ourselves sharply from the rabid *Hakenkreuzlertum* [of the racist Right] and develop our attitude towards Jewry into a positive Christianity and Germandom.[60]

Only four months later Spahn elaborated upon his idea of the Jewish question in a letter to Susanne Thomas, his secretary who came from a Jewish background. Here Spahn rejected the notion that the Jewish question was a "spiritual question" as his secretary had suggested but emphasized instead the distinct racial character that Jewry had developed over a long period of time. Spahn felt that the distinctive Jewish character had become so strong that the difficult relation between Jews and Germandom could no longer be ignored.[61] Spahn assured Susanne Thomas that not the entire Jewish race worked against Germandom. Jews who "cling to their race with all their might" or those who were "truly devoted to becoming part of the German people" were not part of a Jewish-German struggle.[62]

Racial antisemitism also found an institutional home in the Political College (Politisches Kolleg), an academy for Christian-nationalist education and think tank directed by Spahn. Originally founded by "young conservatives" around Heinrich von Gleichen, Spahn moved the Political College ever closer to the DNVP with the intent to turn it into the party's academy.[63] The nationalist education at the Political College was essentially *völkisch* and antisemitic with lectures on "Race, People, State" by Count Ernst zu Reventlow, offering courses on "World Revolution and *Völkisch* Policy," or on "The Jewish Question in the Light of Racial Disintegration," based on the writings of the forefathers of racial antisemitism: Paul de Lagarde, Julius Langbehn, Houston Stewart Chamberlain, and Eugen Dühring.[64]

Around the same time that Martin Spahn had urged Catholic students to be antisemitic, the "old nationalist" Max Buchner rejected pogroms and violence against Jews. Yet he insisted that no one should forget that a small Jewish minority "with their not quite harmless racial characteristics" could not be allowed to rule over Christians. Hence,

one ought to strive to eliminate or exclude Jews from German public life.[65] Five years later Buchner declined the opportunity to speak
against the anti-Jewish violence that he apparently deplored.[66] Buchner declined an invitation from the Association for the Defense against
Antisemitism (Verein zur Abwehr des Antisemitismus) to speak at
one of their public meetings in May 1930. He explained that an ongoing struggle against Jewish domination was robbing German public
life of its most treasured values. This struggle, he believed, should be
fought with fair means, not with rabid Jew baiting. However, Buchner expressed his sympathy for the "strong anti-Jewish wave that runs
through the greater part of our people." In Buchner's view the anti-
Jewish measures of the past, as well as the current antisemitic rhetoric
and action, were justified and pardonable because they arose out of
self-defense.[67]

The Catholic Right believed in the need to solve the Jewish question. This was central to their worldview and influenced their political
choices and activities. More importantly, the anti-Jewish hostility of the
Catholic Right failed to address what was the most fundamental difference between Christian and *völkisch* or racial antisemitism, namely,
the possibility of Jewish conversion to Christianity. The leaders of the
Catholic Right had little patience with traditional Augustinian theology that saw in Jews witnesses to God's revelations who ought to be
protected and converted, not persecuted. True to the religious premises
of their own worldview and their view of the Jewish question, the "solution" of the Catholic Right was also Christian. It was not the promise
of conversion but that of a corporative state and organic society that
would secure Christian control over culture, economy, and government and ultimately over the alleged "Jewish influences" in German
society.[68] Conversion was a possibility, yet it was a conversion to the
German nation or German Christian culture not to Catholicism that the
Catholic Right expected.

For Ferdinand von Lüninck and a number of like-minded Catholics
the gap between them and the NSDAP eventually closed in June 1931
when they openly identified with the aims of the party in a letter sent to
Bishop Kaspar Klein of Paderborn, a move not tolerated by the Catholic
bishops.[69] It was not just Hitler's anti-Marxism and nationalism that
was so appealing to these nobles. They also accepted National Socialist
anti-Jewish measures as a remedy for the nation's problems: "Likewise,
the relentless fight against the unhealthy dominance of Jewry in our
political, economic and cultural life must be embraced because everywhere where the forces of decomposition have asserted themselves in

past and present, they have been headed by the Jewish element, the 'Element of Decomposition.'"[70] Later, in his capacity as provincial president of Westphalia in Hitler's Germany, Ferdinand von Lüninck faithfully implemented the April 1933 Law for the Restoration of the Civil Service against those whom he had always perceived as the usurpers of the German people, namely Center Party Catholics and the political Left as well as Jews. With a similar devotion to his administrative duties, Lüninck actively supported the expropriation of Jewish wealth and assets as part of the regime's Aryanization program.[71]

The efforts of the Catholic Right to rebuild Christian conservatism in alliance with the Protestant DNVP were already failing by the time Ferdinand von Lüninck turned toward National Socialism in 1931. The majority of the "founding fathers" of the RKA had resigned, while the Committee itself, now led by Hugenberg's supporter Julius Doms and under the spiritual tutelage of Martin Spahn, became a passive part of the party. Supporting National Socialism seemed to be the most feasible way to forge a conservative nationalist front to Ferdinand von Lüninck in 1931. Other Catholics of the Right, including Spahn, Eduard Stadtler, Hans Bernhard Gisevius, and Edmund Forschbach, reluctantly followed Lüninck's path two years later, after Hugenberg's DNVP had failed to impose its leadership on the *völkisch* coalition.[72]

Catholic Responses to the Catholic Right and its Antisemitism

The Reich Catholic Committee and its satellite organizations were determined to draw more people to their cause, but their direct political influence was very limited as long as Weimar Germany's governments remained democratic. For years, the *Gelben Hefte* struggled financially. Even after its finances stabilized from 1932 onward, the journal's readership was fairly modest, never achieving a circulation of more than 2,000.[73] Spahn's attempt to advance nationalist education and thought through the Political College barely survived until 1933 on ever diminishing resources.[74] By 1931 the inroads the RKA had hoped to make for right-wing Catholics into the DNVP remained little more than faint paths. Hübner estimates that 11.9 percent of those who belonged to the DNVP were Catholics and that 8.6 percent of Germany's Catholic electorate voted for the DNVP.[75] Disputes with the DNVP leadership under Alfred Hugenberg over a concordat between the Holy See and Prussia, however, did much to weaken the RKA and effectively marginalized it within the party after 1928.[76]

On a political level there was no love lost between the Catholic Right and the Center Party. In the years before 1929—after that date the Center Party began to concentrate on its opposition to the NSDAP—Center Party campaign appeals left no doubt that Catholics were not to support the DNVP because the party placed Germandom before Christendom and the DNVP's Reich Catholic Committee, "bound to Protestant structures," did not stand for Catholic interests.[77] The Center Party's criticism of the racism and antisemitism of the Young German Order and DNVP was sharp.[78] However, consistent with the Center's traditional policies on Jewry and Judaism, many of its attacks on the extreme Right interpreted *völkisch* antisemitism as an intrinsically "religious question" and consequently primarily condemned its anti-clericalism and *völkisch* attacks on the Catholic Church rather than on German Jews.[79] The Center's sister party in Bavaria, the Bavarian People's Party (Bayerische Volkspartei or BVP), condemned *völkisch* antisemitism later than the Center and with much less fervor, something that was scarcely surprising in light of the fact that the Bavarian DNVP, the Bavarian Middle Party (Bayerische Mittelpartei or BMP), was the junior partner in every BVP government from the Bavarian Landtag election of June 1920 onward.

The leadership of the Catholic Church in Germany also turned a cold shoulder to the DNVP Catholics. Throughout Weimar Germany the chairman of the German bishops' conference, Cardinal Adolf Bertram of Breslau, resisted all attempts on the part of the Catholic Right to elicit public support of the German episcopacy. Although the bishops saw in the Right's antisemitism mainly an instrument to bridge the anti-clerical element of the *völkisch* movement, as represented by Erich Ludendorff, with the nationalism of the Catholic Right,[80] the bishops nevertheless consistently criticized *völkisch* and paramilitary organizations such as the Stahlhelm and the Young German Order until the Nazi seizure of power in 1933.[81] This meant that the clergy and lay Catholics were not supposed to join either of these associations or the NSDAP. The bishops could also obstruct the political activity of the Catholic Right by barring their diocesan priests from sitting in the DNVP parliamentary delegations in the Reich or individual German states.[82] The support the Catholic Right received from the Church's extensive ecclesiastical structure was consequently more indirect and local. Anti-Jewish publications by renowned Catholic journals such as the *Historisch-Politische Blätter* or publishing houses such as the Bonifatius Druckerei in Paderborn were welcome sources of anti-Jewish quotations, better still if these publications bore the imprimatur of the local bishop and thus enjoyed ecclesiastic approval to print.[83] The work of the Catholic Right was further encouraged by the explicit support of Abbot Ildefons Herwegen of Maria Laach, an invitation by Bishop Wilhelm Berning of Osnabrück, and the sympathetic ear of Arnold Josef Rosenberg, the general curate of the diocese of Paderborn.[84] In 1932 DNVP Catholics finally made their first inroads into Catholic associations loyal to the Center when they were invited to organize their own workshops and speakers at the seventy-first annual German Catholic Congress in Essen. [85]

DNVP Catholics might not have gained significant political weight among Catholic voters, yet it was successful in tapping into the contemporary yearning for national unity and grandeur, with the result that Catholic youth, students, and academics began to loosen their ties to the organizations of political Catholicism.[86] Indeed, throughout the Weimar Republic members of the Center Party and its affiliated associations such as the People's Association for Catholic Germany (Volksverein für das katholischen Deutschland) filed anxious reports on a Catholic public that seemed to be moving away from the Center, but particularly in those regions where the Catholic Right was most active.[87] For example, in the summer of 1931 the Stahlhelm succeeded in generating considerable Catholic support for its referendum to force the dissolution of the Prussian Landtag in areas like Trier and Koblenz.[88] The campaign for the dissolution of the Prussian Landtag also found strong support from right-wing Catholics who in their campaign literature complained that there was a strong Jewish influence in the state parliament.[89] Other Catholic strongholds such as Breslau, Lower and Upper Silesia, the lower left bank of the Rhine, and the Hunsrück were also reported to have been receptive to *völkisch* propaganda. The report from the People's Association report did not see the reason for this rebellion in mere party-politicking by Center voters, but thought that their alienation was more fundamental, that ordinary Catholics had refused their support for "ideological reasons."[90]

The opinion of ordinary Catholics, where documented, confirms the observations of the People's Association. In the critical years 1931–32, the Center's previous collaboration with the SPD and the perceived threat of Bolshevism often persuaded individual Catholics that their interests were best served by nationalist parties.[91] Again, the Right's antisemitism was not just tolerated but often seemed to have been part of its attraction. An example of this was a factory director in Kiel. Furious at the criticism of National Socialism by the local priest, he complained in April 1932 to Bishop Berning that "Hindenburg was promoted by the anti-clerical Social Democracy, the Jews of the democratic parties whose ancestors had crucified Christ, and the Catholic Center. . . . Hitler [on the other side] is the candidate of all national and truly social-minded Germans [including many loyal Catholics]."[92]

Conclusion

The antisemitism expressed across the network of the Catholic Right was an amalgam of Christian, cultural, and social-Darwinist anti-Jewish sentiments and reflects its commitment to Catholicism and discontent with the political and economic changes in Germany since before the turn of the century. Those Catholics who had joined or sympathized with the DNVP also subscribed to a party that promoted *völkisch* and exclusionary antisemitism even if as individuals they did not always share the radical antisemitism they found in the publications of the DNVP's Catholic faction. Their antisemitism was more than a "communicative bridge" across the denominational divide in order to form a Christian national front. It was central to a worldview that saw a fundamental struggle between Christian and Jewish forces in the modern world. Furthermore, to many Catholics, this belief was a guide in their political choices and activities. In their willingness to exclude Jews from German society, the antisemitism of the Catholic Right was considerably more radical than the anti-Jewish sentiments expressed by the Center Party or the German bishops. While the latter were still wary of excessive nationalism, the Catholic Right lived to enhance nationalist sentiments among German Christians. In contrast to the older generation of national conservative Catholics, the nation was supreme in the eyes of the younger "new nationalist" of the Catholic Right. Everything else, including the interests of the Catholic Church, was subordinate to national unity and valor. The radicalism of their antisemitism was a consequence of a nationalism that longed for the rebirth of a Christian and united Germany. Their "solutions" to a Jewish question ultimately did not differ much from the measures of the medieval Catholic Church that sought to segregate Jews and Christians and keep the former isolated from Christian society. Yet postwar Germany was not medieval Europe, and the Catholic Right's "solution" to the Jewish problem was not encouraged either by the hierarchy of the Catholic Church in Germany or by the German Center Party, both of which accepted Jewish emancipation as a fait accompli.

Within the spectrum of German politics it was only the *völkisch* movement, the DNVP, and ultimately the NSDAP that promised to deliver the national unity and an energetic approach to their Jewish question that the Catholic Right demanded.

Notes

This chapter is a modified version of a section of chapter 4 in Ulrike Ehret, *Church, Nation and Race: Catholics and Antisemitism in Germany and England, 1918–1945* (Manchester: Manchester University Press, 2012).

1. Horst Gründer, "Rechtskatholizismus im Kaiserreich und in der Weimarer Republik unter besonderer Berücksichtigung der Rheinlande und Westfalen," *Westfälische Zeitschrift* 134 (1984): 107–55, here 154–55; Klaus Breuning, *Die Vision des Reiches. Deutscher Katholizismus zwischen Demokratie und Diktatur 1929–1934* (Munich: Hueber Verlag, 1969), 179–212, 321.

2. Gründer, "Rechtskatholiken," 153. On the antisemitism of the Catholic Right, see 147, and Breuning, *Vision*, 99–113.

3. Christoph Hübner, "National-konservatives Denken im deutschen Katholizismus der Weimarer Zeit: Die 'Gelben Hefte' 1924 bis 1933" (MA thesis, University of Erlangen, 2000).

4. Larry Eugene Jones, "Catholic Conservatives in the Weimar Republic: The Politics of the Rhenish-Westphalian Aristocracy, 1918–1933," *German History* 18 (2000): 60–85, here 85.

5. Larry Eugene Jones, "Catholics on the Right: The Reich Catholic Committee of the German National People's Party, 1920–1933," *Historisches Jahrbuch* 126 (2006): 221–67.

6. Jones, "Catholics," 221.

7. Michael Mann, *Fascists* (New York: Cambridge University Press, 2004), 77.

8. For von Papen's own description of his politics, see Gründer, "Rechtskatholiken," 150. On Papen's role within the Catholic Right and German politics, see Larry Eugene Jones, "Franz von Papen, the German Center Party, and the Failure of Catholic Conservatism in the Weimar Republic," *Central European History* 38 (2005): 191–217; and Jones, "Catholic Conservatives," 71–72, as well as his more recent article, "Franz von Papen, Catholic Conservatives, and the Establishment of the Third Reich, 1933–34," *The Journal of Modern History* 83 (2011): 272–318.

9. For further information, see Olaf Blaschke, *Katholizismus und Antisemitismus im Deutschen Kaiserreich* (Göttingen: Vandenhoeck & Ruprecht, 1997); Helmut Walser Smith, *German Nationalism and Religious Conflict. Culture, Ideology, Conflicts, 1870–1914* (Princeton, NJ: Princeton University Press, 1994); Helmut Walser Smith and Chris Clark, eds., *Protestants, Catholics and Jews in Germany 1800–1914* (Oxford: Berg Publishers, 2001); David Blackbourn, "Roman Catholicism, the Centre Party and Antisemitism

in Imperial Germany," in *Hostages of Modernisation: Studies on Modern Antisemitism 1870–1933/39*, ed. Herbert A. Strauss, 2 vols. (Berlin: de Gruyter, 1992–93), 1:107–28.

10. See Anthony Kauders, *German Politics and the Jews: Düsseldorf and Nuremberg, 1910–1933* (Oxford: Oxford University Press, 1996); and Oded Heilbronner, "The Role of Nazi Antisemitism in the Nazi Party's Activity and Propaganda: A Regional Historiographical Study," *Leo Baeck Institute Yearbook* 35 (1990): 397–439.

11. Blaschke, *Katholizismus*, 266.

12. On German conservatism and the radical Right, see Geoff Eley, *Reshaping the German Right. Radical Nationalism and Political Change after Bismarck* (New Haven, CT: Yale University Press, 1980); and Larry Eugene Jones and James Retallack, eds., *Between Reform, Reaction and Resistance. Studies in the History of German Conservatism from 1789–1945* (Oxford: Berg Publishers, 1993).

13. Jones, "Catholics," 226.

14. Ibid., 228–29.

15. Ibid., 240. Martin Spahn (1875–1945), son of the respected former Center Party chairman Peter Spahn, had been professor of modern history in Strasbourg before 1918, and a Center politician before he joined the DNVP in 1921. See Jones, "Catholics," 235, as well as the biographical study by Gabriele Clemens, *Martin Spahn und der Rechtskatholizismus in der Weimarer Republik* (Mainz: Matthias Grünewald, 1983), 172–73.

16. On the attempt of Baron Hermann von Lüninck to set up the short-lived Christian People's Party, see Jones, "Catholics," 227–28.

17. Hübner, *National-konservatives Denken*, 13–14; Jones, "Catholic Conservatives," 65.

18. Ehret, *Church, Nation, and Race*, 121. On Maria Laach, see Richard Faber, "Politischer Katholizismus. Die Bewegung von Maria Laach," in *Religions- und Geistesgeschichte der Weimarer Republik*, ed. Hubert Cancik (Düsseldorf: Patmos Verlag, 1982), 136–58.

19. Pritze's statement on the activities and aims of the RKA and *Korrespondenzblatt*, 14 March 1923, in unpublished records of the DNVP, Bundesarchiv Berlin-Lichterfelde, Bestand R 8005 (hereafter cited as BA Berlin, R 8005), 482.

20. Jones, "Catholics," 231. I would like to thank Larry Jones for pointing me toward the diverse publications of the Catholic Right.

21. A historian by training, Buchner was full professor for medieval and Bavarian history at the University of Würzburg from 1926 and was made *Ordinarius* of the history department at the University of Munich in 1936. Buchner managed to elicit the approval of the Jesuit *Die Stimmen der Zeit*. In this respect, see Buchner's unpublished Nachlaß, Bundesarchiv Koblenz (hereafter cited as BA Koblenz, NL Buchner), 118. See also Peter Herde, "Max Buchner (1881–1941) und die politische Stellung der Geschichtswissenschaft an der Universität Würzburg 1925–1945," in *Die Universität Würzburg in den Krisen der ersten Hälfte des 20. Jahrhunderts.*

Biographisch-systematische Studien zu ihrer Geschichte zwischen dem Ersten Weltkrieg und dem Neubeginn 1945, ed. Peter Baumgart (Würzburg: Schöningh, 2002), 183–251, 205–6.

22. Pritze to the DNVP Kreisverein Brunzlau, 1 February 1926, BA Berlin, R 8005, 482/119. On *Das deutsche Volk,* see Hübner, *National-konservatives Denken,* 29.

23. On Reinermann, see Wieland Vogel, *Katholische Kirche und Nationale Kampfverbände in der Weimarer Republik* (Paderborn: Schöningh, 1989), 145.

24. Jones, "Catholics," 233.

25. Ibid., 238.

26. Ibid., 252, 256.

27. Hübner, *National-konservatives Denken,* 110.

28. Rudolf Lill, "Deutsche Katholiken und die Judenverfolgung in der Zeit von 1850–1933," in *Kirche und Synagoge,* ed. Karl Heinrich Rengstorf and Siegfried Kortzfleisch, 2 vols. (Stuttgart: Klett, 1968), 370–420, here 400.

29. For example, see Hermann von Lüninck, "Die katholische Staatsordnung," in *Katholische Politik,* no. 1, Cologne, March 1924, 12–20, here 16. For an excellent summary of their worldview, see Hübner, *National-konservatives Denken,* 40–49.

30. Ferdinand von Lüninck, "Praktische Möglichkeiten der Verwirklichung einer organischen Staats- und Gesellschaftsordnung unter den heutigen Rechts- und Wirtschaftsverhältnissen," *Katholische Politik,* no. 3, Cologne, January 1925, 33–34.

31. Buchner, quoted in Hübner, *National-konservatives Denken,* 40.

32. All the following quotations are taken from "Bericht über den nationalpolitischen Kursus für den rheinisch-westfälischen katholischen Adel in Willibaldessen, 23–25 April 1923," in the unpublished Nachlaß of Martin Spahn, Bundesarchiv Koblenz (hereafter cited as BA Koblenz), 177. See also Jones, "Catholic Conservatives," 68.

33. Otto von Westphalen, "Die Aufgaben des Staates und die Grenzen der Staatsgewalt," *Katholische Politik,* no. 3, Cologne, January 1925, 45–71, esp. 45–47.

34. Ibid., 56–57.

35. Ibid., 60.

36. Buchner's inauguration speech celebrating the launch of the *Gelben Hefte* in June 1924, BA Koblenz, NL Buchner, 128.

37. For example, see Kurt Ziesché, *Das Königtum Christi in Europa,* (Regensburg: G. J. Manz, 1926), 3. See also Westphalen, "Aufgaben," 55, as well as the article "Judenfrage," *Katholisches Korrespondenzblatt,* 17 February 1923, no. 7.

38. See the letter from the Reich Catholic Committee to Papal Nuncio Eugenio Pacelli, n.d. (most likely August 1920). in the Schorlemer-Archiv des Westfälisch-Lippischen Landwirtschaftsverbandes, Münster. This is also mentioned in Jones, "Catholics," 230.

39. Ibid.

40. Breuning, *Vision,* 104.

41. Ziesché, *Königtum*, 14.

42. Ibid., 4–5, 72.

43. Ibid., 20–22, 122–25.

44. Ibid., 58, 61.

45. Ibid., 11.

46. Ferdinand von Lüninck led the Westphalian League (Westfalenbund) and later the Westphalian branch of the paramilitary, right-wing Stahlhelm after the two organizations merged in 1924. Martin Spahn, too, supported the nationalist attempts to overthrow the republic by Wolfgang Kapp and General Walther von Lüttwitz in 1920 and Adolf Hitler in November 1923. For further details, see Jones, "Catholic Conservatives," 143–44. On Spahn, see Clemens, *Martin Spahn*, 161–62.

47. For example, see *Katholisches Korrespondenzblatt*, 19 May 1923, no. 20, and 21 July 1923, no. 29.

48. Felix Joseph Klein (Bonn), "Zur Judenfrage," *Katholisches Korrespondenzblatt*, 17 February 1923, no. 7.

49. On Roth, see Kevin Spicer, *Hitler's Priests: Catholic Clergy and National Socialism* (Dekalb, IL: University of Northern Illinois Press, 2008), 93–100; and Raimund Baumgärtner, "Vom Kaplan zum Ministerialrat. Josef Roth—eine nationalsozialistische Karriere," in *Politik—Bildung—Religion. Hans Maier zum 50. Geburtstag*, ed. Theo Stammen et al. (Paderborn: Schöningh, 1996), 221–34. See also Heike Kreutzer, *Das Kirchenministerium im Gefüge der nationalsozialistischen Herrschaft* (Düsseldorf, 2000), 161–82.

50. Roth, "Katholizismus und Judenfrage," *Katholisches Korrespondenzblatt*, 28 April 1923, no. 17.

51. Ibid., 12 May 1923, no. 19.

52. Ibid., 5 May 1923, no. 18.

53. Pritze summarizing the achievements of the *Korrespondenzblatt* in the same, 7 April 1923, no. 14.

54. For example, see the letter to Otto Fischer, Breslau, 18 May 1926, BA Berlin, R8005, 482/4.

55. For example, see the *Katholisches Korrespondenzblatt*, 24 March 1923, no. 12.

56. Ehret, *Church, Nation, and Race*, 131–32.

57. Stephan Malinowski, *Vom König zum Führer. Sozialer Niedergang und politische Radikalisierung im Deutschen Adel zwischen Kaiserreich und NS-Staat* (Berlin: Akademie-Verlag, Frankfurt: Fischer, 2003).

58. Stephan Malinowski, "Kuno Graf von Westarp—ein missing link im preussischen Adel," in *"Ich bin der letzte Preuße": Der politische Lebensweg des konservativen Politikers Kuno Graf von Westarp (1864–1945)*, ed. Larry Eugene Jones and Wolfram Pyta (Cologne, Weimar, Vienna: Böhlau, 2006), 9–33, here 18.

59. Hübner, *National-konservatives Denken*, 54–56.

60. Spahn to the Ring of German Catholics, 2 February 1925, BA Koblenz, NL Spahn, 185.

61. Spahn to Susanne Thomas, 13 June 1925, BA Koblenz, NL Spahn, 115.

62. Ibid.

63. Berthold Petzinna, "Das Politische Kolleg. Konzept, Politik und Praxis einer konservativen Bildungsstätte in der Weimarer Republik," in *Die Erziehung zum deutschen Menschen. Völkische und nationalkonservative Erwachsenenbildung in der Weimarer Republik*, ed. P. Ciupke (Essen: Klartext, 2007), 101–11, here 102, 105.

64. Ehret, *Church, Nation, and Race*, 134.

65. Buchner, *Gelben Hefte* 2 (1925–26): 332–71, 368, quoted in Hübner, *Nationalkonservatives Denken*, 116.

66. Buchner declined because he felt used by the Association as a negative target, and because his participation at such an event would lead to misunderstandings within the *völkisch* movement. Buchner to the Association in Defense against Antisemitism, 21 May 1930, BA Koblenz, NL Buchner, 32.

67. Ibid.

68. Ziesché, *Königtum*, 75. See also the minutes of the conference "Bericht über den nationalpolitischen Kursus für den rheinisch-westfälischen katholischen Adel in Willibaldessen, 23–25 April 1923," BA Koblenz, NL Spahn, 177.

69. The following quotes are taken from a letter to Bishop Klein, Paderborn, from Baron v. Elverfeldt, Graf Wilhelm Droste zu Vischering, Barons v. Schorlemer-Overhagen, Reinhard v. Brenken, v. Fürstenberg-Körtlinghausen, v. Lüninck-Ostwig, 1 June 1931. They asked Bishop Klein to withdraw the hierarchy's ban on the Stahlhelm and the NSDAP and its support for the Center Party. For further details, see Jones, "Catholic Conservatives," 79.

70. Jones, "Catholic Conservatives," 79.

71. Karl Teppe, "Ferdinand von Lüninck 1888–1944," in *Zeitgeschichte in Lebensbildern. Aus dem deutschen Katholizismus des 19. und 20. Jahrhunderts*, ed. Jürgen Aretz, Rudolf Morsey and Anton Rauscher, vol. 8 (Mainz: Grünewald, 1997), 41–53, here 50–51.

72. Jones, "Catholics," 265.

73. Dieter Weiß , "Katholischer Konservatismus am Scheideweg—Die 'Historisch-Politischen Blätter' und die 'Gelben Hefte,'" in *Konservative Zeitschriften zwischen Kaiserreich und Diktatur. Fünf Fallstudien*, ed. Hans-Christof Kraus (Berlin: Duncker & Humblot, 2003), 97–115, here 108–109.

74. Clemens, *Martin Spahn*, 168. For an overview of the history and work of the Politische Kolleg see Petzinna, "Kolleg," 102–19.

75. Hübner, *National-konservatives Denken*, 20.

76. Gründer, "Rechtskatholiken," 147; Jones, "Catholics," 222.

77. Grebe, *Zentrum und die deutschen Katholiken*, Flugschriften der Deutschen Zentrumspartei (n.p. [Berlin], 1924), in Geheimes Staatsarchiv Berlin (hereafter cited as GStA Berlin), XII Hauptabteilung, Zeitgeschichtliche Sammlung, III, Nr. 37.

78. For example, see the Center Party flyer 1924, "Sozialpolitik. Zentrumspartei und andere Parteien. 5. Die Deutschvölkischen," by Joseph Andre

(Stuttgart), GStA Berlin, XII, III, 37, as well as the Center pamphlet on the Young German Order, GStA Berlin, XII, III, 38.

79. Grebe, *Zentrum und die deutschen Katholiken*. See also Georg Schreiber, ed., *Grundfragen der Zentrumspolitik. Ein politisches Handbuch in Frage und Antwort* (Berlin, 1924), 155, 176, in GStA Berlin, XII, III, 38.

80. Bertram and Cardinal Schulte of Cologne to the Fulda Bishops Conference, 24 January 1924, in the Historisches Archiv des Erzbistums Köln, Ge n 23.11, 2.

81. Minutes of Diocesan Conference, Freiburg, 17–19 August 1932, in the Erzbischöfliches Archiv Freiburg, B2–56/2. On the relationship between the hierarchy and the Young German Order, see Vogel, *Nationale Kampfverbände*, 45.

82. See the reference to Bertram's objections to the candidacies of Ziesché and Wolff in the minutes of the RKA meeting, 10 March 1929, BA Koblenz, NL Spahn, 177. Consider, too, the notion that Bertram was too lenient, in a letter from Kalthoff to Spahn, 1 December 1926, BA Koblenz, NL Spahn, 177.

83. For example, see "Etwas mehr Klarheit" and "Solche Schriften gehören auf den Markt." *Katholisches Korrespondenzblatt*, 27 January 1923, no. 4. For the quote from the *Historisch-Politische Blätter*, *Katholisches Korrespondenzblatt*, 28 April 1923, no. 17.

84. In a letter to Martin Spahn in 1924, Alfred Möllers reported on his meeting with Rosenberg and that he had "met with the general curate's complete sympathy for the struggle against Jewish influence which also affects the Center press today." Möllers to Spahn, 14 November 1924, BA Koblenz, NL Spahn, 177.

85. It was only a partial victory in as much as the speakers at the public assemblies were still exclusively from the Center or Bavarian People's Party. Similarly, no DNVP Catholics were represented on the Central Committee of the Catholic Congress. See *Katholische Führerbriefe*, 1 (September 1932), 6. See also Clemens, *Martin Spahn*, 173.

86. Clemens, *Martin Spahn*, 173. For a similar observation, see the lecture by Bishop Berning of Osnabrück, "Radikale Strömungen bei der studierenden Jugend," Fulda, 1931, Bistumsarchiv Osnabrück (hereafter cited as BA Osnabrück), 04–61–00–11.

87. Minutes of the meeting of the Bavarian chapter of the People's Association for a Catholic Germany, 12 April 1925, in the unpublished records of the People's Association for a Catholic Germany, Bundesarchiv Berlin, Bestand R 8115 I (hereafter cited as BA Berlin R 8115 I), 125/232. See also the work of Derek Hastings, who demonstrates the popularity of nationalist thought and the considerable Catholic sympathies in Bavaria for the early National Socialist movement and the DNVP. See Derek Hastings, "How Catholic was the Early Nazi Movement? Religion, Race and Culture in Munich, 1919–1924," *Central European History* 36 (2003): 383–433, esp. 401–31, and 428, n.137.

88. The Stahlhelm Landesverband Westmark was founded in summer 1930 to replace the dissolved Stahlhelm Industriegebiet und Rheinland. The decision to conduct a referendum to force the dissolution of the Prussian Landtag was announced by the Stahlhelm's national leadership in October 1930, and officially registered with the Prussian government in February 1931. For further details, see Joachim Tautz, *Militärische Jugendpolitik in der Weimarer Republik. Die Jugendorganisation des Stahlhelm, Bund der Frontsoldaten: Jungstahlhelm und Scharnhorst, Bund deutscher Jungmannen* (Regensburg: Roderer, 1998), 422, n.225.

89. "Aufruf rechtsgerichteter Katholiken zum Volksbegehren: An die katholischen Deutschen in Preußen!" as well as the minutes of the meeting of the RKA, 16 March 1931, BA Koblenz, NL Spahn, 177.

90. Letter from Kohlen to Wrede (People's Association for a Catholic Germany), 1 June 1931, BA Berlin, R 8115 I, 90.

91. For letters in support of the Stahlhelm, Young German Order, and the right-wing Catholics, see Erzbischofliches Archiv Paderborn (EBAP), XVIII, 23 — Vaterländische Verbände. See also the letters from Kommerzienrat Carl Bödiker, the Prussian general counsel, Hamburg, to Berning, 29 November 1932, BAO, 04–61–00–7, and Wilhelm Hübsch (Mühlheim-Ruhr) to Konrad Algermissen (People's Association for a Catholic Germany), 19 September 1931, Stadtarchiv Mönchen-Gladbach, Nachlaß Algermissen, 15/7/1.

92. Letter from Kiel to Bishop Berning, 14 April 1932, BAO, 04–62–32.

9

Eugenics and Protestant Social Thought in the Weimar Republic

Friedrich von Bodelschwingh and the Bethel Institutions

Edward Snyder

In 1931 Friedrich von Bodelschwingh, one of Germany's foremost Protestant theologians and director of the Bethel Institutions in Bielefeld from 1910 until his death in January 1946, met with leading members of the Inner Mission (Innere Mission), an umbrella organization of Protestant social-welfare providers, in the town of Treysa to discuss the place of eugenics—or the idea of selective breeding—in Protestant-run institutions. At the conclusion of the conference the group formally articulated a position that not only embraced eugenics, but also approved the implementation of surgical sterilization within the institutions of the Inner Mission. As such, the conference's conclusions not only represented the general attitude of most German Protestants to eugenics, but also foreshadowed the position many would take on early Nazi eugenic legislation like the Law for the Prevention of Hereditarily Diseased Offspring (Gesetz zur Verhütung erbkranken Nachwuchses).

Like many of his colleagues within the Inner Mission, Bodelschwingh was a staunch conservative nationalist who was disillusioned by the outcome of World War I and the newly founded Weimar Republic. As director of the Bethel Institutions, Bodelschwingh was troubled not only by the rising costs of caring for the disabled but feared that the immense human cost of the war, combined with the dramatic expansion of the welfare state in the Weimar Republic, threatened the health of the national body. Eugenics, he believed, would help organizations like the Inner Mission to rein in exploding health care costs and combat the demographic challenges that Germany faced as a result of the war. Yet, while many German Protestants certainly agreed with Bodelschwingh's enthusiasm for eugenics, their support was far from unanimous. Among those who dissented were former missionaries from Bodelschwingh's own Bethel institutions, which specialized in the care of people with epilepsy and mental illnesses. As disciples of Bodelschwingh's famous father who bore the same name, the missionaries firmly believed in the effectiveness of therapeutic measures like work therapy, or *Erziehung zur Arbeit*, that formed the core of their work in German East Africa before the war. Believing that mental illness was just as much a corruption of the soul as it was a medical disease, the Bethel missionaries were highly skeptical of scientific solutions like eugenics because they failed to address the spiritual component of care.

Through the lens of Friedrich von Bodelschwingh and the Bethel institutions, this chapter will examine Protestant attitudes toward eugenics during the Weimar era. Specifically, it will explore how Protestants not only came to embrace eugenics, but also how they developed a position that was largely in agreement with early Nazi policies. It will also argue that the war, more than any other single factor, was responsible for shaping Protestant social welfare policies from 1919 to 1933. By and large conservative and nationalistic, German Protestants were deeply troubled by Germany's defeat in World War I and remained highly suspicious of the Weimar Republic and the institutionalized welfare state that followed in the wake of its founding. Eugenics, in this sense, promised to restore a fallen Germany to its place among the *Kulturnationen* of Europe while simultaneously functioning as a prophylactic that would limit further damage resulting from Weimar welfare initiatives. In this respect, the concerns that troubled men like Bodelschwingh were not all that dissimilar from those of the *völkisch* Right of the 1920s.[1] Furthermore, many Protestant social workers had vivid memories of suffering during the war, as they were unable to acquire the resources they needed to care for the sick and needy. Concerned about reliving this nightmare, they looked positively on eugenic measures like sterilization as a way to eliminate future generations of people in need.

Not all Protestants, however, were as enthusiastic about eugenics as Bodelschwingh and his colleagues in the Inner Mission. This chapter argues that in order to better understand the complex history of Protestant social welfare during the Weimar Republic, one must also examine the contributions of returning missionaries after the war. In the case of the Bethel Institutes—officially known as the v. Bodelschwinghsche Stiftungen Bethel, but more commonly referred to as the Anstalt Bethel—they acted as a sharp contrast to Bodelschwingh and other leading members of the Inner Mission.[2] Largely insulated from the traumatic war experience of those who remained in Europe, they continued to articulate a vision of social welfare based almost exclusively

on the ideas of Bodelschwingh's late father.[3] Specifically, they emphasized the importance of the work ethic, familial bonds, and notions of
responsibility. Using their access to Bethel's extensive public relations
apparatus, they produced a flood of promotional material to respond to
the infiltration of modern science at Bethel. This essay thus argues that
while support for eugenic policies was an important aspect of Weimar
conservatism, it was by no means universal. By examining the attitudes
of Protestant missionaries returning from overseas, this chapter also
questions the assertions of recent contributions to the historiography of
German imperialism that the colonies served as a laboratory of modernity.[4] While the colonial experience certainly encouraged many individuals to experiment with ideas like eugenics, the Bethel missionaries
also showed that the colonies could insulate individuals from processes
back in Europe.

Eugenics at Bethel before 1918

Although eugenics did not gain serious credence in Protestant circles
until after 1918, it had already established itself as a legitimate subject of scientific inquiry by the turn of the century. The term was first
coined by the British statistician Francis Galton in 1881 and grew out of
a larger interest in racial science during the late nineteenth century. By
the turn of the century eugenics had gained widespread academic acceptance in the scholarly community with the creation of professional
associations and journals devoted to its propagation.[5] By the end of the
nineteenth century, leading eugenicists across Europe and the United
States were coming out in support of a compulsory sterilization law. In
1892 one physician had even taken it upon himself to perform surgical sterilization at his local clinic, and there were recorded incidents of
American institutions in Kansas and Indiana where mass sterilization
had been performed in the late 1890s and early 1900s.[6]

Bethel, for its part, was certainly not insulated from these conversations. While he was initially silent on the question of eugenics, Bodelschwingh nevertheless displayed a strong interest in modern science
and professionalization. Upon his father's death in 1910, he made it
very clear that Bethel would be more receptive to modern ideas than it
had been under the elder Bodelschwingh. In an administrative report
from 1910 the younger Bodelschwingh, as the new head of the Bethel
Institutions, proclaimed, "the institutions for the scholarly investigation
and interpretation of the wealth of materials collected in our institute

should be greatly expanded."[7] To this end he hired a number of new physicians, some of whom expressed interest in exploring the possible benefits of eugenic measures. In 1910 he hired Walter Steinbiss to serve as the new head physician at Waldlabor, one of Bethel's institutions. Steinbiss arrived at Bethel as an outspoken advocate of euthanasia, the most extreme of eugenic measures.[8] According to Hermann Feldmann, another Bethel physician who gave Steinbiss a tour of the community, euthanasia came up repeatedly as the two visited the institutions:

> As we left Ophra, Dr. Steinbiss remarked: "Do you realize, colleague, that we do not need this house. One or two spoonfuls of hydrocyanic acid [Blausäure] would suffice." . . . Dr. St[einbiss] further observed . . . that the treatment of the sick, particularly those sheltered at Bethel, did not concern him, that he was a pathological anatomy and could not suppress the thought whenever he saw a sick person: "hopefully I will be soon getting your brain."[9]

Steinbiss's musings only served to horrify Feldmann and his colleagues, demonstrating that eugenics was still sufficiently surrounded by taboo to prevent any serious discussion of adopting it at Bethel. It was not until after the war that eugenics would begin to gain serious traction within Bethel and other Protestant circles.

More than any other factor, it was World War I that changed the attitudes of German Protestants on eugenics. Although Bethel's leaders had tried to prepare for the war by making the community as self-sufficient as possible, not even the best planning could overcome the state's incompetence.[10] From the high point of the war in 1916 through the postwar revolutions, Bodelschwingh estimated that over three hundred people died each year at Bethel as a result of starvation. By comparison, he estimated that between 1925 and 1928 an average of only ninety-two residents died each year of similar causes despite a significant increase in the number of patients within the community.[11] Furthermore, as he later noted, the food shortages primarily found "its first victims precisely among the sickest and the weakest."[12] As a result of this merciless brutality, the leaders of the Bethel Institutions began to reassess eugenics in the years after the war as a way to prevent the repeat of such a catastrophe. As Karl Bonhoeffer, a noted Berlin psychiatrist and the father of the Protestant resistance hero Dietrich Bonhoeffer, wrote in 1920, the suffering caused by the war radically transformed the way in which welfare providers not only cared for the ill, but altered the way they conceived of humanity.[13] Rather than stretch further already thin supplies of food with the result that everyone had to suffer, social workers began to wonder whether or not it would be more humane to deny the severely disabled aid so that healthier individuals would have a better chance of survival. For the social workers at Bethel, it meant that eugenics was no longer a taboo subject.

Eugenics at Bethel during the Weimar Era

Even though on the surface eugenics appeared to contradict the Inner Mission's goal of providing religiously motivated care, it neverthe-less offered a convenient opportunity for its leaders to embrace the in-creased demands for social welfare during the Weimar era while trying to remain true to their own ideals. Bethel, for example, was renowned for its use of work therapy as a tool for social welfare. Bodelschwingh firmly believed that by teaching the mentally disabled to work consis-tently and efficiently to the best of their abilities he could mitigate the negative effects of their illnesses and reintegrate them into mainstream society. In the same vein, Bodelschwingh argued that the reason disaf-fected migrant workers found themselves on the margins of society was because they lacked the discipline to hold a steady job. Work therapy would not only help them to establish roots in a single community but also transform them into loyal Protestant supporters of a conservative-led state. Under the leadership of Bodelschwingh's father, work therapy formed the foundation of every initiative at Bethel; from its institutions for epilepsy, to its worker colonies for impoverished migrant workers, all the way to its mission in the German colony in East Africa.[14] Yet by the 1920s, the viability of this philosophy came under increasing pres-sure as Bethel's leadership experienced more and more difficulty in re-cruiting professional physicians and financing the community's various initiatives. In order to attract qualified physicians and remain competi-tive with the better-paying state-run institutions, Bethel needed to dem-onstrate its commitment to modern medicine and health care. Toward this end, Bodelschwingh embraced modern psychiatry, specifically *Re-formpsychiatrie,* and the model of preventative treatment, or what Bodel-schwingh called *Aktivere Krankenbehandlung.* Developed by Hermann Simon, a psychiatrist in the nearby city of Gütersloh, the therapy pre-scribed activity such as outdoor physical labor as a treatment for mental illness.[15] This model was particularly appealing to Bodelschwingh not only because it meshed well with the Bethel milieu, but also because it scientifically justified the core aspect of Bethel's mission.

The only problem with the Simon model was that it failed to ad-dress the issue of spiraling costs, as social welfare providers would still be responsible for the care of future generations. Yet, when coupled with eugenic measures such as sterilization and limits on marriage, the work ethic once again became financially feasible. As Hans-Walter Schmuhl, one of the preeminent authorities on therapeutic practices in the Weimar Republic and the Protestant reaction to Nazi eugenic policies, has noted: "The eugenic prophylactic was designed to get at the root of mental illness and to eradicate it in successive generations."[16] Schmuhl has even gone so far as to highlight the psychiatric reforms of the 1920s as the primary factor that opened the door for Protestants like Bodelschwingh to think realistically about the benefits of eugenics. Yet while psychiatric reforms like the Simon model undoubtedly molded Bodelschwingh's perception of eugenics, they formed only part of the larger puzzle. Far more influential was the crisis of faith that many German Protestants experienced after 1918. As both J. R. C. Wright and Klaus Scholder emphasize, German Protestants, like most conservatives, were both "shocked" and devastated by the outcome of the war.[17] They had invested themselves so heavily in the conflict and its outcome, identifying "the German cause with the will of God" to the point that "a German victory was made to seem virtually the fulfilment of divine righteousness."[18] The defeat confronted Protestants with a series of major questions as they sought to explain how Germany had lost a conflict that it seemed destined to win.

Not surprisingly, a large number of German Protestants turned to apocalyptic predictions of doom for Germany's future and channeled their frustration into a deep mistrust, and in some cases visceral hatred, for the new Weimar state. For their own part, the leaders of the Inner Mission focused their rage almost exclusively on the expanded nature of Weimar social welfare. As staunch nationalists, they were deeply concerned by the secular character of the republic and feared that its social welfare programs would only push religion even further from the public sphere. For example, one of Weimar's most significant achievements was the dramatic expansion and bureaucratization of the old Empire's social welfare programs. On the face of it, this should have been something that a person like Bodelschwingh would have applauded. Among other things, the Weimar government emphasized education and on-the-job training, or *Ausbildung*—something that Bodelschwingh and other Protestants, in theory at least, supported.[19] Yet he could not see past the secular nature of the aid, believing that it would do nothing to effect genuine improvement in the condition of the mentally ill and so-called deviant individuals unless there were religious strings attached to the way in which it was administered.

Although the leaders of the Inner Mission were dismayed by the Weimar state's administration of social welfare, as staunch nationalists they were even more concerned about the demographic impact of the war. Like many social welfare advocates across Europe, Bodelschwingh firmly believed that the human cost of the conflict made any victories in the war pyrrhic at best: "You can easily see what a catastrophic development lies ahead if things continue as they have thus far. . . . To be sure, it is true that the war has left a deep cut [in the German nation]. It called the competent and those who were physically useful at the front and let them die, while those who were physically and mentally of no use stayed home."[20] Unless Germany immediately addressed this catastrophic imbalance by preventing the "feeble minded [*schwachsinnige*]" or "inferior types [*Minderwertige*]" from reproducing, it risked falling back to the "front of subhumans [*Front der Untermenschen*]."[21]

For sure, Bodelschwingh and his colleagues in the Inner Mission were extremely pessimistic about Weimar's ability to meet these challenges. Yet they also lacked confidence in their own ability to administer social aid effectively. With a greater number of individuals turning to social welfare institutions for care and with the depletion of their resources as a result of the postwar economic crises, directors like Bodelschwingh became quickly overwhelmed and consumed by a deep sense of foreboding. While Bodelschwingh continued to paint an optimistic picture of life at Bethel in his solicitations for private donations, the speeches he gave before closed audiences were notably darker and filled with despair:

> We have 2,200 epileptics at Bethel, and day in and day out there are not two minutes when one of our charges does not collapse with a loud cry. And if you should participate on Sunday in our religious services, you would experience for yourself that time and time again how we are startled by one of these cries of death [*Todeschreie*] to remind us that we live in a place where sickness, pain, suffering, misery, and guilt all come together.[22]

No longer did Bodelschwingh celebrate the poor and sick who came to Bethel in search of assistance. Rather, he emphasized the burden they placed on the institution and bemoaned their presence as a constant reminder of the miserable state in which Bethel seemed to find itself. Already devastated by the collapse of the monarchy and the inexplicable defeat in 1918, the aftermath of the war was simply too much for Protestant leaders like Bodelschwingh to absorb. They simply found themselves overwhelmed by the demands of caring for so many people with so few resources.

Of course, these concerns were also not limited to Bodelschwingh and his associates at Bethel. Beginning in 1930 Hans Harmsen, one of the leading and most influential figures in the Central Committee for the Inner Mission (Central-Ausschuß der Inneren Mission), voiced similar concerns as he sought to shape his organization's policy agenda.[23] Deeply concerned about the demographic impact of the war on Germany's population, Harmsen argued: "Earlier the procreation of asocially inferior elements of the population would always be balanced by that of socially valuable, productive families. . . . [But today] an abundance of children is mostly characteristic of drunkards, psychopaths, those without inhibitions, and asocial elements."[24] At the same time, Harmsen also held Weimar's social welfare apparatus responsible for exacerbating the problem by directing resources to those most in need rather than to individuals whom he deemed of higher genetic stock. Instead of trying to restore the quality of the population, Weimar welfare "predominantly serves inferior elements," leading "to a danger for the preservation of a healthy national substance."[25] To counter this tendency, Harmsen used his influence within the Inner Mission to advocate a "radical reorientation" in the mission of Protestant social welfare.[26]

By the end of the 1920s many Protestant leaders had begun to give serious consideration to the adoption of surgical sterilization and genetically motivated marriage counseling within the institutions of the Inner Mission. Some even went so far as to express open support for eugenics. In the process, their rhetoric described these policies as the key to victory in the life-and-death struggle for the health of the German national body. As Young-Sun Hong has asserted, Protestants were particularly attracted to the idea of "supra-individual entities" like the *Volk*.[27] For them, the *Volk* was an organic body created by God, and therefore it deserved the same amount of care as the individuals who composed it. If some of these people were diseased and were thus hurting the greater *Volk*, social welfare providers needed to find a way to eliminate the infection. For this reason, Protestant leaders favored measures like sterilization over so-called positive eugenic measures—that is, policies that encouraged reproduction among specific groups.[28]

Bodelschwingh first voiced his public support for eugenics at a speech he gave to the Lutheran Academic Society (Evangelischer Akademikerschaft) in Lübeck in 1929. The speech touched upon each of the Inner Mission's major concerns and contended that after ten years of Weimar social welfare policies, the German *Volk* stood at a major crossroads that would determine its ultimate fate: "As a barometer for the signs of degeneration of our nation we are reminded time and time again that the number of the weak, the sick, the spiritually broken, and the inferior types continue to grow. . . . For it is inherent in the times in which we live that the misery caused by the war has become more and more visible through modern welfare work and has thus come out of hiding into the public limelight."[29] These factors, Bodelschwingh continued, had led to a noticeable increase in the number of mentally and physically disabled individuals over the course of the previous decade, a development that cast doubt on Germany's future. Yet, thanks to eugenics, which had "announced itself as a savior in our Fatherland" the institutions of the Inner Mission could work to reverse this tide.[30] Bodelschwingh marveled at how selective breeding practices had resulted in a "remarkable development" in the overall quality of plant and animal populations. If the leaders of the Inner Mission were genuinely serious about rescuing Germany from what he saw as the brink of demographic disaster, Bodelschwingh concluded, they needed to seriously contemplate implementing eugenic measures in their institutions.

Ideally Bodelschwingh sought to accomplish this at Bethel in a way that did not undermine the influence of the Bethel philosophy. However, he found himself increasingly preoccupied with a myriad of responsibilities and deteriorating health. As a result Bodelschwingh delegated a significant amount of authority to Gustav Dietrich, the deeply ambitious head of the worker colonies. Always concerned about enhancing his own power within Bethel, Dietrich managed to establish himself as Bodelschwingh's unofficial ambassador by the end of the decade. He represented Bethel at major conferences, such as the Conference of Experts for Eugenics of the Inner Mission (Fachkonferenz für Eugenik der Inneren Mission) in 1932 and at the Main Assembly of the German Associations of Travelers' Welfare (Hauptversammlung der deutschen Wandererfürsorgeverbände) in 1933 and was increasingly responsible for hiring decisions at the institution.[31] Most notably, he had a significant role in the hiring of head physicians Carl Schneider (1930–33) and Werner Villinger (1934–39), both of whom would play integral roles in laying the groundwork for the implementation of eugenic policies at Bethel.[32]

Bodelschwingh was particularly enamored with Villinger, whom he had originally tried to recruit in 1930 to serve as Bethel's head physician. During the 1920s Villinger served as an advising psychiatrist at the Raue Haus in Hamburg, which had been established by the Inner Mission's founder Johann Hinrich Wichern, and had authored several pieces expressing support for eugenic measures like sterilization. As Bethel's head physician, Villinger established himself as a leading voice at Inner Mission conferences on questions of eugenics.[33] While Bodelschwingh was more interested in Villinger's service at the Raue Haus as a sign that the psychiatrist would also pass muster with the Bethel milieu than in his opinions on eugenics, Villinger's appointment at Bethel would nevertheless have ominous consequences for Bethel during the Third Reich. Along with Dietrich, who quickly became an enthusiastic Nazi and ardent supporter of the German Christians, Villinger would be primarily responsible for implementing the 1934 sterilization law.[34]

By the time Harmsen had called for the Treysa conference on eugenics in 1931, Bodelschwingh had refined and expanded his position on surgical sterilization. In contrast to his earlier speech in Lübeck, he used this opportunity to provide a theological justification for eugenics. Here he insisted "that the God-given functions of the body have to stand in absolute obedience [to the principle] that if this or that member might lead to evil and to the destruction of God's kingdom, the possibility or obligation that it be eliminated exists."[35] In other words, if a mental illness caused someone to commit an action that harmed the national body, one had an obligation to do whatever necessary to prevent that person from continuing his harmful actions. Bodelschwingh continued that he would "agree, though with uneasiness . . . if sterilization were acknowledged as a necessary expedient. I would see it as a duty and in conformity with the will of Jesus."[36] But, as Young-Sun Hong has observed, it was not uncommon for Protestant social welfare providers to understand mental illness as a divine punishment for sin.[37] Decades earlier professional physicians had accused Bodelschwingh's of harboring similar views. In this sense, one could see the younger Bodelschwingh's attitudes as a logical extension of his father's belief about the origin of mental illness. His position was the perfect combination of his father's traditional philosophy and his own interest in modern science.

Ultimately, the results of the Treysa conference were compiled in a resolution outlining the position of the Inner Mission on questions related to eugenics. While the document strictly rejected euthanasia and eugenically motivated abortion, it strongly advocated surgical sterilization. Echoing the concerns of the conference's participants, the declaration clearly stated that the economic crises had created a scenario where the Inner Mission no longer had the resources to meet the challenges it faced. With this in mind, the participants at Treysa believed that sterilization would reduce their future financial burden by reducing the number of patients. Even more noteworthy, however, was the religious justification the resolution provided for surgical sterilization.

Parroting Bodelschwingh's speech almost verbatim, the resolution insinuated that mental illness was a form of sin and that social welfare providers thus had a moral obligation to eradicate it at its root:

> For the Holy Gospel does not demand the unconditional integrity of the body [*die unbedingte Unversehrheit des Leibes*]. Should its God-given functions lead in this or that member of the whole to evil or to the destruction of God's kingdom, there exists not just the right but the moral duty of charity toward others [*Nächstenliebe*] to sterilize, a responsibility that not only the current but also future generations have imposed upon us.[38]

By providing material and theological arguments in favor of sterilization, the Treysa resolution provided Protestant social reformers with the justification they needed to implement eugenic policies—and eventually the Nazi law for compulsory sterilization—within their own institutions.[39] Thus, many of the Inner Mission's leaders were not pressured by the regime to act against their own conscience. Bodelschwingh's concerns about the law had nothing to do with the act of sterilization itself, but rather with the involuntary nature of the law. Therefore, rather than protest the law itself, Bodelschwingh concentrated his energy overwhelmingly on convincing candidates for sterilization to consent voluntarily.[40]

The Bethel Missionaries and Opposition to Eugenics

While a significant number of Protestants in the Inner Mission embraced measures like sterilization as the silver bullet solution for all of their fears and concerns during the Weimar era, this consensus was far from unanimous. At Bethel returning missionaries from East Africa were among the most vocal opponents of eugenic practices. Trained largely under the elder Bodelschwingh, they firmly believed that the best therapies for mental and psychological disabilities were a combination of work therapy and spiritual care. Eugenics was at best a partial solution because it focused exclusively on the biological component of the illness. Furthermore, as the missionaries also pointed out, eugenics promised only to eliminate future generations of the mentally disabled. It did nothing to care for individuals who were already suffering.

While in East Africa, the Bethel missionaries had made the philosophy of the elder Bodelschwingh the foundation of their mission work.[41] They were particularly proud of their initiative at Lutindi, a former refuge for the freed children of slaves that they transformed into the colony's first modern center for mental illness.[42] Upon returning to Bielefeld in 1918, however, they were deeply troubled by the increased interest in modern science among Bethel's leaders. As the Bethel mission inspector Walter Trittelvitz wrote: "We build beautiful institutions, we organize the care of the sick, we undertake social initiatives, but in the process we forget about God's empire. Although one heals the external damage, one overlooks the deepest and innermost damage."[43] Missionaries like Trittelvitz felt that they could not in good conscience support something that was at best a partial solution. As far as they were concerned, work therapy and religious faith were the elements that defined Bethel in the years before World War I. To abandon them would be to forsake the legacy of Bethel's founder and inspiring spirit.

The primary reason why the missionaries remained so skeptical of eugenics and devoted to the elder Bodelschwingh's philosophy was because of their experience during the war. While they certainly had experienced their own trauma in Africa, they had a markedly different experience than that of their colleagues back in Germany. Whereas those who had remained in Germany had to cope with devastating shortages and witness unimaginable suffering, the missionaries did not have to navigate these issues until they finally arrived back in Europe as prisoners of war.[44] An examination of the personal letters missionaries sent to their families indicates that the suffering they experienced never brought them to the point where they would question their devotion to the concept of work therapy. For example, the wife of one missionary complained that she suffered from a headache and back pain because the Belgians made her sit on a suitcase instead of a chair.[45] Other missionaries complained about a lack of variety in their food, or a shortage of reading material.[46] If nothing else was clear, it was that the missionaries in East Africa did not suffer to the same extent as their counterparts in Europe. Unlike their colleagues in Bielefeld, the Bethel missionaries had never been prompted by their wartime experiences to fundamentally question the viability of the Bodelschwingh philosophy.

Upon returning to Bethel, the majority of missionaries chose to work in Bethel's vast public relations network, known as the Dankort. They preferred to work there, as opposed to becoming a parish pastor, because the Dankort would permit them to leave easily once the British allowed them to return to Africa. At the same time, public relations work was also conducive to what the missionaries referred to as their home mission, or *Heimatsmission*.[47] Even though they had lost their communities in Africa, the Bethel missionaries continued to think of themselves first and foremost as missionaries. They were particularly concerned about what they saw as an increase in secularization and modernization, especially in the field of social welfare. The missionaries worried that modern medicine and science had superseded religion and work therapy as the primary methods of social welfare delivery. They therefore used their position in the Dankort to defend both their understanding of social welfare as well as the legacy of their mentor, the elder von Bodelschwingh.

As "Bethel's open window to the outside world," the Dankort produced a wide variety of promotional material about Bethel and its various initiatives.[48] In this sense, the missionaries exercised control over the publicity of Bethel and played a major role in shaping the public image of Bethel. In order to counteract the growing influence of modern science at the institution, the missionaries made sure to portray Bethel as a community that still believed in the importance of work therapy as the core aspect of effective social welfare. For example, in an advertisement entitled "Ein Großbetrieb der Nächstenliebe," Trittelvitz demonstrated his remarkable talent for embracing modern themes to defend traditional ideas by portraying Bethel as a traditional enclave in a modern, industrial city: "There is only one large-scale enterprise [*Großbetrieb*] that in its essence is without parallel in Germany or the entire world. That is the enterprise of charity in Bethel near Bielefeld. This unique undertaking is all the more noteworthy because it shows how in the field of social welfare the broad-minded vision of organization has to work together with loving attention to detail if real help is to be achieved."[49] While Bielefeld may not have had the massive steel plants of Essen and Dortmund or the sprawling coal mines of Bochum, it was nevertheless home to the largest center of social welfare in Germany and, by extension, had a unique place in a larger global network. Despite its location in the heart of a modern industrial city, Trittelvitz stressed that Bethel's success did not result from modern ideas like eugenics. Even though Bethel employed the services of seventeen physicians, "only 7 percent of our patients are healed."[50] Most people who came to Bethel, Trittelvitz explained, remained at the community for the remainder of their lives, even with the treatment provided by modern medicine. The primary task of Bethel, Trittelvitz insisted, was "the care of the spiritually and mentally ill" for as long as they lived in the community.[51] For Trittelvitz, the work ethic and religion rather than ideas like eugenics constituted the core of the social welfare philosophy at Bethel.

In addition to shorter advertisements and pamphlets, the Dankort also produced several book-length literary tours of the Bethel community. Like the shorter pamphlets, the longer books were particularly effective because they were widely distributed and allowed the missionaries to shape Bethel's public image in a way that was easy for the average reader to comprehend. To this end, they heavily promoted aspects of the community that demonstrated the importance of work therapy while deemphasizing the role of modern science. Nowhere is this more evident than in Gerhard Jasper's *Wege durch Bethel*.[52] After a tour of the Dankort, Jasper guided his readers to the buildings Nazareth and Sarepta, centers for training social welfare workers. As he described the importance of social welfare at Bethel, Jasper noted how ideas like work therapy and responsibility were core components of the institution's social philosophy and that students would have learned of their importance while attending classes in these buildings. Once they had completed their studies, these students would then go on to influence the missions of other organizations, encouraging them too to adopt ideas like work therapy. "A large number of those," Jasper explained, "are also in the service of the Bethel mission in East Africa. How varied are their branches of work: care of the sick and infirm, work with young women in need of training . . . schools for artisans, household training, and so on."[53] For Jasper linking the training of social workers with the Mission was key because he believed that it would endow traditional forms of social welfare with legitimacy in the eyes of the reader, particularly in so far as schools like those at Nazareth and Sarepta had come under heavy attack in the early twentieth century from professional physicians intent on introducing modern medicine at religious institutions.[54]

Throughout his tour of Bethel Jasper repeatedly evoked the theme of work therapy. After departing Nazareth and Sarepta, he introduced his readers to Bethel's artisan quarter, or *Handwerkerviertel*, the neighborhood where Bethel's social welfare workers would implement the ideas they had learned under Bodelschwingh's tutelage.[55] As he guided readers into the various workshops on the street, Jasper's commentary underscored the importance the missionaries attached to work therapy in contrast to their rejection of modern medicine. Nowhere was this more eloquently expressed than in the following passage from Jasper's book: "Whoever goes down into the artisans' street and peers into the workshops will quickly see the bustling creativity that prevails here, all of which only confirms Father Bodelschwingh's contention that work is the best medicine for those who are ill. Whoever is sick and can work often knows even better than those who are healthy how to appreciate work as a gift of God."[56] The way in which Jasper invoked Bodelschwingh's legacy was particularly noteworthy insofar as it demonstrated that despite the emergence of modern ideas like eugenics and psychiatry work therapy was still central to Bethel's greater mission.

Jasper's depiction of work therapy at Bethel stood in sharp contrast to his assessment of the place of modern science in the community's mission. As he took his readers by Mara, Bethel's modern center for the care of epilepsy, Jasper only noted that the building contained "examination rooms for neurological investigations, a private laboratory, and so on." Perhaps most indicative of the scorn with which Jasper held modern science was his dismissive comment that to the missionaries the building's true importance lay in the "facilities for water treatment that were to be found in the basement."[57] In contrast to the great lengths with which Jasper had described the importance and legacy of work therapy at Bethel, this brief encounter with Mara was the only time the reader encountered modern, scientific Bethel on Jasper's tour.

In addition to their written publications, the Bethel missionaries also relied heavily upon visual imagery to make their argument. While in Africa they had become particularly adept at using photographs and visual imagery to describe their activities and capture the attention of audiences back in Europe. After the war they not only continued to use images as a significant aspect of their home mission but they also explored the potential of film, an emerging technology about which most German Protestants were still skeptical.[58] At a time when many Protestants focused on film's potential for corruption, the Bethel missionaries understood it as a novelty that they could use to increase the size of their audiences.[59] By using film they hoped to attract the interest of curious people who otherwise would have taken little interest in Bethel. With this in mind they established a film service at Bethel and produced a number of films that not only promoted the Bethel institutions but also a variety of other Protestant initiatives.[60]

The films that the missionaries produced about Bethel all stressed the importance of work therapy as an aspect of social welfare at the same time that they minimized the role of modern medicine in the life of the Bethel institutions. Typically, the missionaries showed their films as part of a larger event in which the audience also heard a brief lecture and contextualization from one of the missionaries. These lectures always emphasized the importance of work therapy over science within the community.[61] While the missionary speaker acknowledged the medical establishment, he limited the scope of its work to caring only for the "bodily welfare [*leibliche wohl*]" of the patients.[62] Ultimately, as the missionary explained to his audience, the purpose of Bethel's existence was to "serve the sick. To create work and a home for those who were ill was the wish of Father Bodelschwingh. . . . He taught us to use the least force [*die kleinste Kraft*]; he saw every sick person as a co-worker."[63] As in the case of the Dankort's literary efforts, the film lectures constituted a key element of what the missionaries conceived as their people's mission, or *Volksmission*, because it afforded them the opportunity to portray Bethel in a light that reflected their agenda and their understanding of the institution.

The films themselves only reinforced the themes from the introductory lectures. For example, the film *Aus dem Leben eines Fallsüchtigen* told the story of Walter Beckmann, a non-functioning alcoholic discovered by a group of children. When the village's pastor discovered Beckman, he sent one of the children to Bethel to ask for help. Naturally, the institution was more than willing to accept Beckman and treat his alcoholism in accordance with Bodelschwingh's use of work therapy. In the words of the film's synopsis: "Several years later we find Walter in the cabinet maker's workshop, his friend in the tailor's shop. They are confirmed [in the Lutheran faith] and want to learn the craft of an artisan."[64] Separated from alcohol and taught a proper work ethic, Beckmann had once again become a productive member of the community. At no point did the film discuss modern scientific ideas like eugenics as a possible solution for combating alcoholism.

The films were an unqualified success, as large audiences gathered not only to learn more about Bethel but also—and probably more likely—to experience the novelty of film. Yet as the technology advanced, the missionaries came under more pressure to develop a new, more modern film to continue drawing large audiences. Like the earlier films, the new film would serve as an integral aspect of the home mission by highlighting ideas important to the missionaries, such as work therapy. Unlike the earlier films, however, the new film would be even more direct in its rejection of eugenics as a social welfare tool.

One of the early drafts of the new film *Durch Liebe zum Glauben* clearly emphasized these points. It told the story of a young man named Karl, who was studying to become a pastor. One day Karl came home to tell his parents: "I have studied and studied, but science has torn my Bible to pieces and taken my faith."[65] Horrified by his attitude, Karl's mother concluded that the only way to rescue Karl was to send him to Bethel. Upon arriving at Bethel, one of the first buildings the pro-science Karl visited was Patmos, a modern center for the treatment of epilepsy and mental illnesses. As the film depicted images of the institution, the director of Patmos approached Karl with the observation: "These feeble-minded children are for themselves and others nothing but a burden. Would it not be better if one put a painless end to their lives?"[66] Taken aback by the director's blunt assessment of the child, Karl turned to a deaconess and asked for clarification, as he could not believe what he had just heard. The manuscript then read: "In a state of shock the nurse pressed the child to herself and responded violently with a defensive gesture."[67] All of this took place under a heading entitled "Euthanasia" and was clearly intended by the film's authors as a blunt unequivocal rejection of Bethel's medical establishment.

The missionaries' indictment of the medical community only grew stronger as the tour progressed. This time Karl observed several social workers from Nazareth caring for a patient who was bedridden. The film specifically noted that they had to feed the patient and then physically lift him on to a bed. Disgusted by what he observed, the medical director once again commented: "These brutish types really no longer have any purpose."[68] This time, however, one of the deacons overheard the director and reacted with a clear rebuttal of the medical establishment: "Father Bodelschwingh says: 'When our patients are there for no other purpose, they still have the task to teach us love and patience.'"[69] While the medical director remained unimpressed, Karl took the message to heart and declared that he had found his calling and wanted to move to Bethel where he could become a social worker and care for the sick.

In this manuscript the missionaries at the Dankort could not have been any clearer in their assessment of Bethel's medical community. When confronted by the crude candor of the medical director, the supposedly pro-science Karl was stunned. Unlike earlier films that had promoted ideas like work therapy while only alluding to the flaws of eugenics, the new film directly confronted modern science and its potential flaws. To the audience the doctors were a distant, isolated segment of the community. Yet while such a depiction may have accurately reflected the attitudes of the missionaries, it did not serve well as propaganda for Bethel. In an attempt to portray the Bethel institutions in a primarily positive light, the final version of the film all but wrote the doctors and modern science out of the script. The original manuscript, on the other hand, provided a clear indication of what the missionaries at Bethel thought of modern science and its fascination with eugenics as a solution to the social and moral crises of the postwar world.

Conclusion

The Bethel mission is vital to understanding how and why German Protestants came to embrace eugenics during the Weimar era. The postwar activities of the missionaries demonstrated that they were not, as Sebastian Conrad has suggested,[70] part of a process of radicalization that culminated in the racially grounded social welfare policies of the Third Reich. To the contrary, the Bethel missionaries remained insulated from scientific forms of racism in Africa and returned to Germany in 1918 deeply disturbed by the amount of influence modern science gained within the Bethel institutions.

To be sure, not everyone returned from the colonies as insulated as the Bethel missionaries, and Africa did not always reinforce traditional beliefs like work therapy. Francis Galton was heavily influenced by his trip to South Africa, and other missionaries were much more open-minded than their Bethel counterparts to the possibilities of eugenics.[71] Yet, the Bethel mission was important precisely because of its uniqueness. It clearly showed that the colonies were not always exotic spaces from which Europeans returned fundamentally different from how they had been before they left. The missionaries from Bethel returned in 1918 with just as strong a belief in traditional methods of social welfare, like work therapy, as when they initially departed for Africa. Africa was not always a laboratory of modernity in which Europeans experimented with new ideas before implementing them in Europe.

The postwar activities of the Bethel missionaries thus shed new light on the development of Protestant social welfare during the Weimar Republic and reveal how the colonial experience influenced postwar debates over eugenics. As the case of the Bethel missionaries clearly demonstrates, individuals returning from the colonies actively shaped Protestant social welfare policies as they urged Protestants to implement traditional practices like work therapy and opposed modern scientific advances like eugenics. Therefore, the Bethel mission not only requires historians to reassess the relationship between Africa and Europe, but also to examine how the colonies influenced processes, like social welfare, that appeared to be firmly rooted in the western world. Although numerous studies have already situated German social welfare within a larger European (or Western) context, no one has yet to discuss how the non-Western world participated in these processes.[72] If anything, the example of Bethel demonstrates the glaring need for a new, transnational study of German social welfare.

Ultimately, the case of Bethel shows that those Protestants who remained in Germany during the war became the staunchest advocates of eugenics during the Weimar era. The suffering produced by the privations of war combined with the shock of Germany's defeat to leave German Protestants completely devastated. For them, the war produced a crisis of faith that led them to question the principles and philoso-phies they had held so dear before 1914. The result was that many of these ideas, such as work therapy, lost much of the luster as Protestants searched for new ideas that would help Germany both regain the pres-tige it lost through the war and prevent such devastation from happen-ing again. To this end, eugenics appeared to be the perfect, silver-bullet solution to many of Germany's postwar social and moral crises. Those who spent the war years outside of continental Europe, on the other hand, did not suffer to the same degree as their colleagues back home. The missionaries in East Africa never suffered to the extent that they began to question their faith in the effectiveness of work therapy. There-fore, when they returned to Europe in 1918, they saw no reason for the community to deviate from traditional methods of social welfare and felt especially compelled to defend those ideas against the claims of modern science. In their minds, the growing popularity of eugen-ics at Bethel was another troubling sign of the postwar decline in reli-gious faith and importance of the church. In this sense, their campaign against eugenics represented less of a moral objection than a defense of the status quo.

Finally, the support Protestants expressed for eugenics during the Weimar era is noteworthy because of the way in which it laid the groundwork for the eventual collaboration between the Inner Mission and the Nazi regime on the question of surgical sterilization. Having already declared their support for sterilization in Treysa, many Protes-tant institutions, including Bethel, were more than willing to help the Nazis implement their compulsory sterilization law in 1934.[73] Protes-tant social welfare providers, therefore, were not pushed into imple-menting Nazi sterilization, but were very often willing accomplices.

Notes

1. Paul Weindling, *Health, Race and German Politics Between National Unification and Nazism, 1870–1945* (Cambridge and New York: Cambridge University Press, 1993), 402. See also Sheila Faith Weiss, *Race Hygiene and National Efficiency: The Eugenics of Wilhelm Schallmayer* (Berkley: University of California Press, 1987), 149–53; and Hans-Walter Schmuhl, *The Kaiser Wilhelm Institute for Anthropology, Human Heredity and Eugenics: Crossing Boundaries* (Dordrecht: Springer, 2008), 47–55.
2. For further information on Bethel and its initiatives, see Matthias Benad, ed., *Bethels Mission (1). Zwischen Epileptischenpflege und Heidenbekehrung* (Bielefeld: Luther Verlag, 2001); Matthias Benad and Kerstin Winkler, eds.,

Bethels Mission (2). Bethel im Spannungsfeld von Erweckungsfrommigkeit und öffentlicher Fürsorge (Bielefeld: Luther Verlag, 2001); and Matthias Benad and Vicco von Bülow, eds., *Bethel Mission (3). Mutterhaus, Mission und Pflege* (Bielefeld: Luther Verlag, 2003)

3. For a concise biography of the elder Friedrich von Bodelschwingh, see Hans-Walter Schmuhl, *Friedrich von Bodelschwingh* (Hamburg: Rohwolt, 2005).

4. For example, see Sebastian Conrad, *Globalisierung und Nation im Deutschen Kaiserreich* (Munich: C. H. Beck, 2006), 74–123.

5. Eric D. Weitz, *A Century of Genocide: Utopias of Race and Nation* (Princeton, NJ: Princeton University Press, 2003), 38–39; and Peter Weingart, Jürgen Kroll, and Kurt Bayertz, *Rasse, Blut und Gene. Geschichte der Eugenik und Rassenhygiene in Deutschland* (Frankfurt: Suhrkamp, 1988), 199–205.

6. Hans-Walter Schmuhl, *Rassenhygiene, Nationalsozialismus, Euthanasie. Von der Verhütung zur Vernichtung "lebensunwerten Lebens" 1890–1945* (Göttingen: Vandenhoeck & Ruprecht, 1987), 99.

7. Bodelschwingh, "Verwaltungsbericht 1910," in the Hauptarchiv der v. Bodelschwingschen Stiftungen Bethel, Bielefeld (hereafter cited as HA Bethel), 2/91–21.

8. Hans-Walter Schmuhl, *Ärzte in der Anstalt Bethel 1870–1945* (Bielefeld: Bethel-Verlag, 1998), 24–25.

9. Denkschrift Dr. Feldmann, 8 February 1910, HA Bethel, 1/c 18h.

10. For more on starvation and German food policy, see Avner Offer, "The Blockade of Germany and the Strategy of Starvation, 1914–1918," in *Great War, Total War: Combat and Mobilization on the Western Front, 1914–1918*, ed. Roger Chickering and Stig Förster (New York: Cambridge University Press, 2000), 169–88.

11. Friedrich von Bodelschwingh, *Saat und Segen in der Arbeit von Bethel. Ein Rückblick auf die Zeit seit dem Tode des Anstaltsvaters* (Bethel bei Bielefeld: Verlagshandlung der Anstalt Bethel, 1932), 9.

12. Ibid., 32.

13. "Jahreshauptversammlung des Deutschen Vereins für Psychiatrie in Hamburg am 27. und 28. Mai 1920," *Allgemeine Zeitschrift für Psychiatrie* 76 (1920–21): 600.

14. For further information on the concept of work therapy and the worker colonies, see Ewald Frie, *Wohlfahrtsstaat und Provinz. Fürsorgepolitik des Provinzialverbandes Westfalen und des Landes Sachsen 1880–1930* (Paderborn: Ferdinand Schöningh, 1993); Matthias Benad and Hans-Walter Schmuhl, ed., *Bethel-Eckardtsheim: Von der Gründung der ersten deutschen Arbeiterkolonie bis zur Auflösung als Teilanstalt (1882–2001)*, (Stuttgart: W. Kohlhammer, 2006), 428–37; Karl Heinrich Pohl, *Zwischen protestantischer Ethik, Unternehmerinteresse und organisierter Arbeiterbewegung. Zur Geschichte der Arbeitsvermittlung in Bielefeld von 1887 bis 1914*, Bielefelder Beiträge zur Stadt- und Regionalgeschichte, vol. 8 (Bielefeld: Stadtarchiv und Landesgeschichtliche Bibliothek, 1991); and Jürgen Scheffler, "Der Anstalt Bethel und die 'Brüder von der Landstraße.' Anstaltsdiakonie und

Wohlfahrtspflege am Beispiel der Wandererfürsorge," in *Bethels Mission (2): Bethel im Spannungsfeld von Erweckungsfrömmigkeit und öffentlicher Fürsorge. Beiträge zur Geschichte der v. Bodelschwinghschen Anstalten Bethel*, ed. Matthias Benad and Kerstin Winkler (Bielefeld: Luther-Verlag, 2001), 197–224.

15. See Hermann Simon, *Aktivere Krankenbehandlung in der Irrenanstalt* (Berlin: de Gruyter, 1929); as well as Angela Grütter, *Hermann Simon. Die Entwicklung der Arbeits- und Beschäftigungstherapie in der Anstaltspsychiatrie. Eine biographische Betrachtung* (Herzogenrath: Murken-Altrogge, 1995).

16. Schmuhl, *Ärzte in der Anstalt Bethel*, 33.

17. J. R. C. Wright, *"Above Parties": The Political Attitudes of the German Protestant Church Leadership, 1918–1933* (London and New York: Oxford University Press, 1974), 49–50.

18. Klaus Scholder, *The Churches and the Third Reich, Volume One: Preliminary History and the Time of Illusions, 1918–1934* (Philadelphia: Fortress Press, 1988), 6.

19. See Detlev J. K. Peukert, *The Weimar Republic: The Crisis of Classical Modernity* (New York: Hill and Wang, 1989), 129–46; Christoph Sachße and Florian Tennstedt, *Geschichte der Armenfürsorge in Deutschland*, vol. 2: *Fürsorge und Wohlfahrtspflege 1871–1929* (Stuttgart: W. Kohlhammer, 1988), 68–217; and Young-Sun Hong, *Welfare, Modernity, and the Weimar State, 1919–1933* (Princeton, NJ: Princeton University Press, 1998).

20. Bodelschwingh, "Lübecker Vortrag," 1929, HA Bethel, 2/91–16.

21. Ibid.

22. Ibid.

23. For further information on Harmsen, see Sabine Schleiermacher, *Sozialethik im Spannungsfeld von Sozial- und Rassenhygiene.: Der Mediziner Hans Harmsen im Centralausschuss für die Innere Mission* (Husum: Matthiesen Verlag, 1998).

24. Hans Harmsen, "Grundsätzliches unserer Arbeit: Bevölkerungspolitische Neuorientierung unserer Gesundheitsfürsorge," *Gesundheitsfürsorge: Zeitschrift der evangelischen Kranken- und Pflegeanstalten* 5 (1931): 3–4.

25. Ibid., 4.

26. Ibid., 4.

27. Hong, *Welfare, Modernity, and the Weimar State*, 256–57.

28. On the differences between positive and negative eugenics, see Wilhelm Schalmayer, *Vererbung und Auslese in ihrer sozioligischen und politischen Bedeutung. Preisgekrönte Studie über Volksentartung und Volkseugenik* (Jena: G. Fischer, 1910). See also Weiss, *Race Hygiene and National Efficiency*, 86–89.

29. Bodelschwingh, "Vortrag in Lübeck über Fragen der Eugenik," 1929, HA Bethel, 2/91–16, 22, reprinted in Anneliese Hochmuth, *Spurensuche. Eugenik, Sterilisation, Patientenmorde und die v. Bodelschwinghschen Anstalten Bethel 1929–1945*, ed. Matthias Benad (Bielefeld: Bethel Verlag, 1997), 215–26.

30. Ibid.

31. Hans-Walter Schmuhl, "30. Eckardtsheim und der Nationalsozialismus (1931–1941)," in *Bethel-Eckardtsheim: Von der Gründung der ersten deutschen Arbeiterkolonie bis zur Auflösung als Teilanstalt (1882–2001)*, ed. Matthias

Benad and Hans-Walter Schmuhl (Stuttgart: W. Kohlhammer, 2006), 455–89, 459. See also Hochmuth, *Spurensuche*, 8–10.
32. Although he appeared skeptical of eugenics and racial hygiene before 1933, Carl Schneider had nevertheless written articles on the topic before arriving at Bethel in 1930. In 1930 Schneider transferred to the University of Heidelberg as an instructor of psychiatry and neurology, where he wrote on the relationship between work therapy and eugenics. Later Schneider became deeply involved in the T-4 Program that involved the Nazi murder of the physically and mentally handicapped and even returned to Bethel in 1941 as part of a selection commission. For an example of Schneider's writing, see Carl Schneider, *Behandlung und Verhütung der Geisteskranken* (Berlin: J. Springer, 1939).
33. Schmuhl, *Ärzte in der Anstalt Bethel*, 83.
34. Despite his support for sterilization Villinger remained cool toward euthanasia. When Bethel himself was threatened by the T-4 Program, Villinger served as a trusted contact for Bodelschwingh as the pastor sought to protect Bethel. For more on the German Christians, see Doris Bergen, *Twisted Cross: The German Christian Movement in the Third Reich* (Chapel Hill: University of North Carolina Press, 1996).
35. "Beitrag F. v. Bodelschwingh," in the Protokol der Fachkonferenz für Eugenik I, in the Archiv des diakonischen Werkes der Evangelischen Kirche in Deutschland, Berlin, CA/G 1800/1, 85. See also Schleiermacher, *Sozialethik*, 230–31.
36. Ibid.
37. Hong, *Welfare, Modernity and the Weimar State*, 256–57.
38. "Die Treysaer Resolution des Central-Ausschusses für Inner Mission (1931)," in *Eugenik, Sterilisation, "Euthanasie"*, 106–10. See also "Niederschrift über die Beratungen der Fachkonferenz für Eugenik vom 18.-20. Mai 1931 in Treysa," HA Bethel, 2/38–144.
39. For further information on the churches and Nazi era eugenics, see Kurt Nowak, *"Euthanasie" und Sterilisierung im "Dritten Reich". Die Konfrontation der evangelischen und katholischen Kirche mit dem Gesetz zur Verhütung erbkranken Nachwuchses und die "Euthanasie"-Aktion* (Halle: Niemeyer, 1977).
40. Schmuhl, *Ärzte in der Anstalt Bethel*, 36.
41. Although based in Bethel, the official name of the mission was the Protestant Mission to German East Africa (Evangelische Mission nach Deutsch-Ostafrika). It was not known officially as the Bethel Mission until 1922.
42. See Albert Diefenbacher, *Psychiatrie und Kolonialismus. Zur "Irrenfürsorge" in der Kolonie Deutsch-Ostafrika* (Frankfurt: Campus-Verlag, 1985); and Hildegard Waltenberg, *Lutindi, die Stadt auf dem Berge* (Bielefeld: H. Waltenberg, 1997).
43. Trittelvitz, "Eine grundlegende Freude," *Bote von Bethel* 130 (1927): 2–16.
44. For further information on the domestic experience in World War I, see Roger Chickering, *Imperial Germany and the Great War, 1914–1918* (New York: Cambridge University Press, 1998), 99–103, 140–46.

45. "Zur Lage der ostafrikanischen Missionare im Gefangenen-Lager Saintes. Ergänzung," 1917, HA Bethel, 2/51–9.
46. "Die Lage der gefangenen Missionare aus Ostafrika im Gefangenen Lager Saintes. Ergänzung," 1917, HA Bethel, 2/51–9.
47. Rundschreiben von Trittelvitz, 14 June 1926, HA Bethel, 2/37–10, 8.
48. Gerhard Jasper, *Wege durch Bethel* (Bethel bei Bielefeld: Verlaghandlung der Anstalt Bethel, 1934), 3–4.
49. Trittelvitz, "Ein Großbetrieb der Nächstenliebe," n.d., HA Bethel, 2/37–22.
50. Ibid.
51. Ibid.
52. Not only was Gerhard Jasper a former missionary, but in 1926 he became the head of the *Dankort* as well. Missionaries like Trittelvitz considered Jasper's appointment particularly important because it cemented the mission's control over the office.
53. Jasper, *Wege durch Bethel*, 6.
54. Hans-Walter Schmuhl, *Ärzte in der Westfälischen Diakonissenanstalt Sarepta 1890–1970*, ed. Matthias Benad (Bielefeld: Bethel-Verlag, 2001), 7–14.
55. Jasper, *Wege durch Bethel*, 9.
56. Ibid., 9.
57. Ibid., 11.
58. Heiner Schmitt, *Kirche und Film. Kirchliche Filmarbeit in Deutschland von ihren Anfängen bis 1945* (Boppard am Rhein: Harald Boldt, 1979), 21.
59. Trittelvitz to Heienbrok, 27 November 1920, HA Bethel, 2/37–32.
60. Schmitt, *Kirche und Film*, 123. See also Beschlussnotiz, 25 April 1922, HA Bethel, 2/37–32.
61. "Kurze Einleitungsworte zum Bethelfilm," n.d. (ca. 1922–24), HA Bethel, 2/37–36.
62. Ibid.
63. Ibid.
64. "Feierstunden mit beweglichen Lichtbildern aus dem Leben und der Arbeit der Bodelschwinghschen Anstalten in Bethel bei Bielefeld," n.d., HA Bethel, 2/37–33.
65. "Durch Liebe zum Glabuen. Wie ein Verirrter in Bethel den Weg fand," n.d., HA Bethel, 2/37–36, 4.
66. Ibid., 12.
67. Ibid., 13.
68. Ibid., 14.
69. Ibid., 14.
70. Conrad, *Globalisierung und Nation*, 121–23. See also Sebastian Conrad, "'Eingeborenenpolitik' in Kolonie und Metropole. 'Erziehung zur Arbeit' in Ostafrika und Ostwestfalen," in *Das Kaiserreich transnational: Deutschland in der Welt, 1871–1914*, ed. Sebastian Conrad and Jürgen Osterhammel (Göttingen: Vandenhoeck & Ruprecht, 2004), 107–28.
71. For example, see Francis Galton, *Narrative of an Explorer in Tropical South Africa* (New York: Ward, Lock and Co., 1889), 140. See also Nicholas W. Gillham, *A Life of Sir Francis Galton from African Exploration to the Birth*

of Eugenics (New York and Oxford: Oxford University Press, 2001); For more in general on the relationship between colonization and eugenics in Germany, see Pascal Grosse, *Kolonialismus, Eugenik und bürgerliche Gesellschaft in Deutschland, 1850–1918* (New York: Campus Verlag, 2000).

72. For example, see E. P. Hennock, *The Origin of the Welfare State in England and Germany, 1850–1914: Social Policies Compared* (New York: Cambridge University Press, 2007); and Gerhard A. Ritter, *Sozialversicherung in Deutschland und England. Entstehung und Grundzüge im Vergleich* (Munich: C. H. Beck, 1983).

73. For further information, see Jochen-Christoph Kaiser, *Sozialer Protestantismus im 20. Jahrhundert: Beiträge zur Geschichte der Innern Mission 1914–1945* (Munich: R. Oldenbourg, 1989), 316–90; Kurt Nowak, *"Euthanasie" und Sterilisierung im "Dritten Reich." Die Konfrontation der evangelischen und katholischen Kirche mit dem Gesetz zur Verhütung erbkranken Nachwuchses und der "Euthanasie"-Aktion* (Halle [Salle]: VEB Max Niemeyer Verlag, 1977), 91–105; and Hans-Walter Schmuhl, *Rassenhygiene, Nationalsozialismus, Euthanasie. Von der Verhütung "lebensunwerten Lebens" 1890–1945* (Göttingen: Vandenhoeck & Ruprecht, 1987).

 10

CARL SCHMITT AND THE WEIMAR RIGHT

Joseph W. Bendersky

For decades it had been widely assumed that Carl Schmitt "exercised a powerful influence over the right-wing critics of the Republic."[1] Schmitt, certainly one of Weimar's most eminent conservative thinkers, expressed ideas that appreciably affected the entire intellectual climate of the era. He definitely held a place of distinction in any Weimar discourse in political and legal theory. However, his relationship to the German Right is as complex and differentiated as that side of the cultural, intellectual, and political spectrum is widely and significantly diverse. It was an identification and association that varied over time and was as much personal and biographical as it was intellectual. Importantly, it only reached the stage of political involvement in the final phase of the republic starting in 1930, and even then it did not entail an engagement with party politics. Indeed, Schmitt's relationship with important segments of the Weimar Right was often one of mutual disregard, disagreement, and critical animosity.[2] Such negative perceptions were no doubt, in part, a result of his Catholic religious and intellectual heritage as well as judgments of him as a Catholic partisan, even though the link between his political ideas and Catholicism was also quite tenuous. Nonetheless, despite the challenge they present, it is precisely such complexities that make Schmitt such an intriguing figure for historical discussion and analysis.

The most obvious affinities between Schmitt and other conservatives emanated from their shared sensibilities on fundamental assumptions about human nature and modern society. From early adulthood, Schmitt displayed an intellectual, as well as deeply emotional, *Weltschmerz* and proclivity toward cultural pessimism. His own intense personal insecurity further heightened such sentiments. The young Schmitt was constantly beleaguered by a "horrible *Angst* of men and the world." At several points, this tormented "self-destructive *Angst*" brought him to the brink of suicide. The deeply Catholic Schmitt found no solace in religion no matter how much he prayed; reading Dostoevsky and Kierkegaard only compounded his despondency.[3] Although Schmitt first publicly projected such cultural pessimism in his wartime book *Theodor Däublers "Nordlicht"*, his diaries reveal such ubiquitous sentiments long before the catastrophe that began in 1914. Still clinging to the presumed universal norms and eternal values of Catholic spiritualism, he lamented the relativistic world of nineteenth-century positivism created by scientific materialism and a capitalism that spawned a culture celebrating the selfish pursuit of money and pleasure. In his mind, these incessant trends, together with an increasingly dominating technological existence, were destroying the inherent value of the human being and the meaning of existence itself.[4]

Yet even here both Schmitt's Rhenish Catholicism, and the peculiar personal vantage point from which he perceived such trends, separated him from a substantial number of conservative groups and segments of German society. For in addition to moral relativism and materialism, he rebuked Protestantism and the neo-Kantian idealism then challenging the dominant positivism. He similarly decried "racial mysticism" and "Wagnerism" often associated with *völkisch* conservative circles.[5] His distinctiveness was most evident during World War I, where he displayed none of the nationalism typical of the German Right. Quite the contrary, his recently disclosed strong anti-war diary entries showed a complete disassociation from the early nationalistic euphoria and subsequently a hostility toward the justifications and rationalizations for that war. Concerned for the welfare of his Slavic wife, Pawla Dorotić, he expressed his sympathy for the French, Italians, and Russians, while manifesting virulent condemnation of bourgeois society and "Prussian militarism," all of whom he felt were far more barbarous than the Slavs. He raged against a "loathsome war," as something "crazy" that could not be justified by economics or "*Vaterland*." He depicted his service in military intelligence in Munich as slavery within a Prussian institution that crushed the individual. A future icon of statism, the young Schmitt recoiled from the Prusso-German state as a cynical machine and purveyor of a militarism, a "grizzly monster" responsible for the useless deaths of thousands of German soldiers.[6] Schmitt's anti-Prussianism persisted into the 1920s, as he expressed his great relief at leaving the University of Greifswald for the less Prussian and more compatible Rhineland cultural milieu of Bonn.[7]

Schmitt's "war experience," to the extent that one can actually call it that since he never served at the front, certainly separated him from those National Revolutionaries such as Ernst Jünger who in the 1920s transformed that "heroic struggle" into an existential political ideology that not only contributed to the increasing militarization of German political life but contained the seeds of a militant assault on the Weimar Republic.[8] And contrary to many later interpretations of him, Schmitt would never romanticize war; even in his later starkly realistic analyses and commentaries on power and international struggles among states, he considered war a ghastly affliction to be avoided except as the ultima ratio.[9] Moreover, though romanticism was an important source for some German conservatives, it was never a foundation for Schmitt's thinking. Rather than expressing his own romantic sentiments, his *Politische Romantik*, written toward the end of the war, was a devastating critique of the political dimensions of the Romantic movement.[10] At the same time, the young Schmitt also rejected the more traditional power political stance of adherents of the realist school of thought such as Erich Kaufmann, to whom the "greatest social ideal is a victorious war."[11] As late as 1917, though conceding the realistic need to reconcile power and morality, Schmitt still asserted the "primacy of *Recht* over *Macht*."[12]

Into the early 1920s, Schmitt remained a conservative Catholic, not in theological dogma or political engagement but essentially in cultural and intellectual identity. Although he delivered papers before Center Party groups, he was primarily associated with intellectual circles centered around Catholic publications such as *Hochland* and *Germania*. To him, Catholicism stood as a spiritual and humanizing bulwark of eternal moral values against liberal capitalism and socialism that was reducing human life to a "process of production and consumption."[13] He also drew inspiration from pre-1848 reactionary Catholic thinkers such as Donoso Cortes, Louis de Bonald, and Joseph de Maistre, which helps explain misconceptions of Schmitt as a romantic reactionary.[14] However, Schmitt took from them not a philosophy of reactionary politics but insights into the crisis of the modern world. Like the Church, they offered some solace from his cultural pessimism. Nonetheless, while clearly reflecting a Catholic perspective, he was simultaneously affecting the broader conservative climate by critiquing mass society and lamenting the loss of traditional values. In this respect, Schmitt not only reflected cultural pessimism, he became an important instrument in perpetuating such pessimism in German intellectual life. His highly regarded publications certainly popularized it within Catholic circles, and probably beyond.

As Schmitt weaned himself from such close Catholic identification in the late 1920s, his intellectual affiliations with fundamental principles of conservative realism became more precisely enunciated. Unfortunately, despite an abundance of new revelatory documentation this crucial transformation in Schmitt's thinking is yet to be adequately explained. It is clear, however, that his Catholic neo-idealism faded as his entire political philosophy came to rest upon a Hobbesian anthropological foundation excluding the universal moral norms he had so passionately articulated and defended in his youth. He moved from the religious notion of man as evil to one reminiscent of the Hobbesian state of nature, noting that "all genuine political theories presuppose man to be . . . a dangerous and dynamic being."[15] As he remarked, "In a good world among good people, only peace, security, and harmony would prevail. Priests and theologians are here just as superfluous as politicians and statesmen." He no longer promoted the Catholic Church, representing eternal values, as a potential arbiter among worldly powers. Declaring "higher law" an "empty phrase," he doubted that universal morality, including that based upon natural law or reason, could serve as a basis for politics. In the absence of an agreement on standards or of an arbiter to decide what constitutes in the real world such ideals as justice and morality, political groups seize these universal principles to advance their own cause and undermine that of their opponents. He did not deny that deeply held values and ideals existed but saw them as emanating from a pluraverse of culturally diverse groups that often clashed and competed with each other. His political world was one in which "concrete human groupings fight with other concrete human groupings in the name of justice, humanity, order, or peace." For Schmitt, the "intense and extreme antagonism" rising from these culturally divergent economic, religious, moral, and national groups creates a situation in which existentially different "others" and "strangers" confront each other as friends and enemies.[16]

Within this Schmittian version of political realism the centrality of the state was one of the most pronounced commonalities with Weimar conservatives. In his writing, the institution of the state was no longer the oppressive "Moloch" he had lamented during the war. Long entrenched in conservative thinking since Hegel, the sovereign state remained, to Schmitt, the institution of both necessity and deliverance. In the Hobbesian world of recurrent enmity, only the state could guarantee order, peace, and stability. It alone provided security against external and internal enemies; it was the prerequisite for all other aspects of economic, cultural, and political life. Until the end of his life, he advanced the state as the decisive political authority within society.[17] Most of his Weimar works, in fact, related directly to the origin, nature, and exercise of state power. The long-term legacy of his state thinking is clearly evident in the founding of the journal *Der Staat* by young conservative jurists affiliated with Schmittian circles in the Federal Republic.[18]

To Schmitt, the sovereign state was the pivotal political institution "not because it dictates omnipotently or levels all other units, but because it decides and can therefore within itself hinder all other antagonistic associations. Where it exists, the social conflicts of individuals and social groups can be decided in such a manner that order, i.e., a normal situation remains."[19] But modern mass democracy, particularly as practiced in Weimar, was making it increasingly difficult for the state to perform this role because no consensus existed on the basic foundations of society, economics, or politics. Weimar was a patchwork of irreconcilable principles and promises, in which the aspirations of one side threatened the very existence of the other (capitalism vs. socialism; individual rights vs. collective rights; proletarian triumph vs. bourgeois survival; legitimacy vs. illegitimacy of the constitutional order). These fundamental antagonisms manifested themselves through *Interessenparteien* and *Weltanschauungsparteien*, thereby magnifying the problems of the state. Instead of loose associations seeking support from a broad spectrum of the electorate, Weimar parties were tightly organized exclusive entities representing specific economic interests or ideologies. From a natural plurality of interests and associations, Weimar had degenerated into a *Parteienstaat*, where class and party interests prevailed over the welfare and security of the country. Majority coalition governments were usually tenuous, often paralyzed. A majority coalition customarily used all legal means at its disposal to sustain itself in power while condemning the political activity of its opponents. Reducing parliament to "a poor façade" for "rule by parties and vested economic interests," these parties also usurped, exploited, and undermined the traditional legitimacy, authority, and power of the state.[20]

Although Schmitt's preference for the traditional state over the parliamentarian *Parteienstaat* was well suited for the mindset of Germany's anti-republican Right, it was nevertheless problematic for right-wing political parties. His critique of parties applied as much to the German People's Party (Deutsche Volkspartei or DVP), the German National People's Party (Deutschnationale Volkspartei or DNVP), and even the Catholic Center (Deutsche Zentrumspartei) as it did to the Social Democrats, the Communists, and the Nazis. In 1926 Schmitt privately confided his "almost continual fear [of how] the German Right and Left pursue their politics."[21] Two years later, his classic study *Constitutional Theory* implicitly contested the constitutionality of certain reactionary proposals by the DNVP and other right-wing organizations to establish a more conservative/authoritarian upper house of parliament and to weaken the no-confidence provision of Article 54. The first, he asserted, violated the principle of democratic equality and the second would undermine a foundation of the constitutional system by disrupting the balance of power between executive and legislative branches.[22]

Similarly, Schmitt's critique of liberalism, while broadly bolstering the conservative intellectual and political assault on the republic, manifested a certain hostility toward the economic interests and politics of a substantial portion of the German Right, especially the DVP, DNVP, and large industrial organizations. Though certainly standing with a free economy and private property, he consistently displayed contempt for a capitalist value system promoting the utilitarian pursuit of money and profit. To him, this was a hallmark of a spiritually and humanly valueless materialism. Among his criticisms of liberalism was that it attempted to treat everything, including politics, like an economic or business relationship. The emphasis on the primacy of economics that liberal capitalists shared with Marxists only accelerated trends in which modern society reduced the human being to the pursuit of economic interests, overshadowing and in so doing obliterating those moral, psychological, and spiritual qualities that constituted the vital essence of human life and experience. Liberal capitalism further weakened the state by "subjugating it to economics."[23]

Nationalism, a core ideological sentiment and political foundation of the Right, was an equally complex aspect of Schmitt. From his earliest years, his intellectual orientation, like his personal affiliations and preferences, was quite cosmopolitan, drawing inspiration from French, Russian, and Spanish culture and their intelligentsia. He married two Serbs, and found Italy and Spain alluring. He neither shared the chauvinistic euphoria of the early stages of World War I, nor succumbed to the mounting wartime nationalist psychology fed by the increasing sacrifices demanded and propaganda campaigns. Before the end of Weimar, one never finds him extolling the virtues of Germanness or Germandom. Yet he was a nationalist. The distortions of Germans and their culture in foreign wartime propaganda disturbed him greatly, as did Versailles.[24] To Schmitt, the French were Germany's oppressor, an attitude inflamed by what he witnessed as a professor at the University of Bonn during the occupation of the Rhineland and in particular by the French military incursion into the Ruhr in 1923. He warned that unfulfilled naïve expectations about Germany's entry into the League of Nations might only result in the "perpetuation of its defeat," the "completion of its enormous and unprecedented surrender of its arms," and consequent "surrender of its rights."[25] He later published an edited work entitled *Positionen und Begriffe im Kampf mit Weimar-Genf-Versailles 1923–1939*.[26] And his friend-enemy theory was more relevant to international relations and conflicts than it was even to domestic politics, as the former embodied implicit warnings against Germany's loss of "political freedom and political independence." The lack of will to engage in politics, like hopes of unilateral disarmament and reducing conflicts to economic competition, would not, he wrote, eliminate risks of political struggle: "Only a weak people will disappear."[27]

Moreover, behind the rhetoric and ideals of supposed peaceful economic interrelationships, Schmitt detected the deceitful continuation of power politics in pursuit of traditional national interests. Here he shared the anti-Wilsonian, anti-Americanism of nationalist conservative intellectuals such as the historian Hans Rothfels and the head of the University of Kiel's Institute for World Economy, Andreas Predöhl. To Schmitt, increasing American economic penetration worldwide, particularly in Germany, represented the most modern form of imperialism. While appearing apolitical in legal, linguistic, and moral justification, this new form of imperialism, with its "elastic and extendible" principles, resulted in the indirect, though no less decisive, hegemonic domination of the United States. He saw US manipulation of the League, the Kellogg-Briand Treaty outlawing war, and Germany's status as a debtor state, a "beggar in rags," as prime examples of a "slyness and Machiavellianism" America used to elevate itself to the ultimate arbiter of what constituted disarmament, the right of intervention or non-intervention, and war. Schmitt warned the Germans against succumbing not to direct military conquest but being seduced by foreign concepts of what was rightful, especially in the area of international law. Instead of being neutral and universal principles, the concepts promoted by the United States were in actuality "instruments of a foreign power." Perhaps "more dangerous than military oppression and economic exploitation" would be for Germany to allow itself to be "morally disarmed" by disingenuous concepts of rights and international law.[28]

The common domestic enemy of Schmitt and the Right was Marxism. That ideological movement threatened a multitude of cherished conservative values and institutions—religion, social and economic status, national identity, and the state. Indeed, while Schmitt often criticized the bourgeoisie of which he was a part, Marxists sought its very elimination. He feared both the rationalist version of orthodox Marxism culminating in the dictatorship of the proletariat as well as the irrationalist version of direct action typical of Georges Sorel's *Reflections on*

Violence and syndico-anarchists Schmitt associated with the powerful motivating force of myth.[29] He had also early identified Mussolini's fascism as propelled by the irrational "force of myth," but until the Nazi electoral breakthrough in 1930, Schmitt's enemy stood on the left. Like his encounters with the French, he had experienced "bolshevism" first hand as an officer in Munich in 1919.[30] Until the end of his life, he retained vivid images of the leftist violence and its subsequent suppression by the army and Free Corps during the short-lived Bavarian Soviet Republic. With respect to Marxism, Schmitt's inherent personal insecurity, the peculiar historical consciousness that reinforced it, and the press of contemporary historical events coalesced into a distinct political orientation. Always anxiety ridden, Schmitt's affinity with Hobbes led him back to the insecurity, violence, and destruction of the age of religious warfare before the seventeenth-century European state system established order through the *Jus Publicum Europaeum*.[31] Memories of 1919 Munich and subsequent communist revolts of the early republic, revived by radical leftist activities during Weimar's final phase, affected his politics and scholarship on the subject. As in the past, now, too, only the state could provide the necessary protection and stability.

Of all state institutions, Schmitt persistently identified the Weimar president as the pivotal one. Schmitt classified the president as a *pouvoir neutre*, a neutral force above fratricidal political parties. A president's constitutional oath obligated him to guarantee the Weimar constitution, as well as to defend the German state and keep it functioning if the Reichstag was paralyzed due to the lack of a majority or if anti-democratic forces acquired a Reichstag majority. Schmitt interpreted the presidency as one of Weimar's greatest sources of popular democratic legitimacy because it was the only office directly elected by the people instead of party-controlled lists. Moreover, his seven-year term offered governmental stability, whereas habitually collapsing party coalitions often left the Reichstag in disarray. Following his oath to uphold the constitution, a president also had the authority to counterbalance a paralyzed party-dominated Reichstag by direct democratic appeal to the people through referenda and new elections.[32]

Article 48 embodied some of the most important authority a president possessed. It granted him extraordinary power in an *Ausnahmezustand*, a situation of exceptional crisis, to temporarily suspend parts of the constitution and intervene with the armed forces. Schmitt defined these powers very broadly and opposed new laws limiting such presidential authority. He argued that a president needed such flexibility to meet unforeseen crises; he could also suspend various constitutional rights so long as he did not violate the essence of the constitution or the rights of the Reichstag, government, or president. Such actions were merely temporary measures, not laws; they could not suspend, alter, or destroy the existing constitutional order. The check on the abuse of such power was the Reichstag's right to rescind emergency decrees.[33] While most jurists opposed this latitudinarian interpretation, the father of the Weimar constitution, Hugo Preuss, agreed with Schmitt.[34]

After Paul von Hindenburg's election as Reich president in 1925, the German Right began to embrace the idea of a strong president exercising his prerogatives on behalf of the German state. But to Schmitt, the president was neither an *Ersatzkaiser* standing above the other institutions of government nor a force that would undermine democracy, turning the country back down a reactionary authoritarian path as some on the Right envisioned. A country can have "a sovereign dictatorship or a constitution," he wrote, "one excludes the other." Even in an *Ausnahmezustand*, one could not "abrogate" or "revise the constitution," or "transform the republic into a monarchy."[35] Schmitt had, in fact, developed the core of his theory of presidential power before Hindenburg was even a candidate in 1925. He subsequently elaborated these basic premises in a series of books and articles. In *Constitutional Theory*, he also emphasized the "inviolability of the constitution." Only the German people acting as a "constitutional granting power" had established a "constitutional democracy," and only that people through a similar act of sovereign decisionism could change the fundamental bases and essence of the legal and political order they had created. Individual constitutional provisions might be temporarily suspended by the president under Article 48, or revised by a two-thirds Reichstag majority under Article 76, but neither such actions could alter the fundamental essence of the existing Weimar order instituted in 1919.[36]

In 1926 Hindenburg's office, supported by the Weimar Right, clearly invoked Schmittian arguments to thwart leftist and democratic party efforts to limit presidential power under Article 48. And certain critics, such as the Social Democratic jurist Hermann Heller, identified Schmitt with radical conservative writers such as Vilfredo Pareto, a charge Schmitt rebuffed with indignation. In reality, the German Right virtually neglected Schmitt throughout the 1920s, while those sympathetic to the republic proved quite receptive to his ideas. The democratic German Academy for Politics (Deutsche Hochschule für Politik) published his *Concept of the Political*, among his most controversial works. Republican political writers such as Waldemar Gurian, a Catholic, and Sigmund Neumann, a democrat, adopted his friend-enemy thesis; Robert

Michels and Karl Mannheim employed his critique of parliamentary government; and Karl Loewenstein called the latter an "ingenious treatise." That work, Loewenstein wrote, "is so rich in fruitful and profound ideas" that it constituted the "strongest contribution to the subject." Moritz Julius Bonn called Schmitt to Berlin in 1928 as a professor at the Handelshochschule. Otto Kirchheimer and Franz Neumann, Social Democratic activists, both of whom later become prominent political thinkers, worked with Schmitt until 1933.[37]

Schmitt became more closely associated with the Weimar Right, intellectually, personally, and politically in Berlin around 1930. He still maintained individual connections with Catholic intellectuals such as Romano Guardini and Paul Adams, editor of *Germania*, but Schmitt was certainly not an advocate of political Catholicism. And he resisted persistent efforts by various Catholic circles to entice him into a leadership role in their organizations.[38] The radical conservative intellectual circles that now took an intense interest in Schmitt were those without political party affiliations. They shared Schmitt's critique of the *Parteienstaat*, which they sought to replace with a vaguely envisaged authoritarian "New State." Consistent with his long-standing emphasis upon stability and consistent with his well-established constitutional interpretations contrary to such revolutionary objectives, Schmitt never became an advocated for the "New State." Nonetheless, journals such as *Der Ring*, *Der Kunstwart*, and *Die Tat* began giving Schmitt's publications and lectures exposure among the right. Ignoring the fundamental, often complex, arguments in Schmitt, writers such as Hans Zehrer, Horst Grüneberg, and others used his ideas as malleable formulations to legitimize and promote their goals of eliminating parliamentary government and establishing a post-capitalistic economy and post-democratic society.[39] This transformation and misappropriation was almost immediately apparent to Ludwig Feuchtwanger, Schmitt's long-time Jewish friend and publisher. Feuchtwanger noted his "deep revulsion" that the radical Right was "claiming" and "popularizing [Schmitt's writing] in the worst possible manner."[40]

Yet Schmitt was partially responsible for this identification, as he was personally associating with several prominent representatives of the radical Right. Most notable were Wilhelm Stapel and Albert Erich Günther, editors of *Deutsches Volkstum*; the flamboyant advocate of a militant national revolution, Ernst Jünger; and Jünger's friend Hugo Fischer, editor of the *Blätter für Philosophie*.[41] Schmitt definitely enjoyed socializing with such men and commiserating together about contemporary crises. All relished their intellectual discourses. Mutual admiration was often offset by strong disagreement, even distrust. Jünger's enthusiasm over Schmitt's friend-enemy thesis was the beginning of an often close, sometimes chilly, life-long friendship. Still, the gap between Schmitt's defense of the existing state and Jünger's ideas on total mobilization into a worker-soldier state was immense. Schmitt never thought Jünger's visions could, or should, ever materialize and redeem Germany. Schmitt foresaw, in fact, a Nazi misuse of Jünger's movement before they then cast him aside.[42]

Linked in certain respects by their concerns over a multitude of modern problems as manifested in Weimar, Stapel and Schmitt were equally concerned about the rise of National Socialism and feasible means of dealing with this powerful movement. Schmitt's recently disclosed life-long antisemitism also provided a common sentiment with Stapel. And both men supported the presidential system as a necessary counterweight to a paralyzed parliamentary system. On the other hand, Schmitt never shared Stapel's vision of a Protestant Christian nationalist state toward which the presidential system would pave the way.[43] Schmitt's diaries from 1930 to 1934 do reveal a vehement intensification of his antisemitism at the end of the Weimar Republic. At times he lashed out against Jewish influence in German culture and politics. To him, however, Jews constituted one problematic group among many, including Social Democrats and the Center Party. Most of these private harangues were reserved for Jewish colleagues and critics who he felt had launched unjustified assaults against him, his theories, and his students. His criticisms of Jews were never systematic, and his undeniable, often crudely expressed antisemitism remained inconsistent and contradictory, much in the manner in which he defamed non-Jews. During this period of heightened antisemitism, he retained often intimate relationships with the Jewish Eisler family, as well as with particular colleagues such as Erwin Jacobi, Albert Hensel, Ludwig Feuchtwanger, and his student Otto Kirchheimer. In the very midst of this heightened antisemitism, his diary entries reveal great admiration for Leo Strauss personally and intellectually. For example, Schmitt supported Strauss's application for a Rockefeller Fellowship, as he had earlier helped Kirchheimer's academic advancement. None of Schmitt's antisemitic sentiments were reflected in his political and legal theory. Nor can one explain his studies in terms of his attitudes toward Jews or any fear of their influence. In fact, his political and legal analyses were often lauded, even shared and internalized, by Jewish friends, publishers, students, and colleagues.[44]

In terms of a personal and working relationship Schmitt was closer by far to Georg Eisler and Jacobi than he was to Stapel. Indeed, while Schmitt considered Stapel a congenial publicist with whom he could have candid political discussions, Stapel had serious reservations about the amorality and cultural relativism inherent in Schmitt's political ideas. Stapel cautioned those too easily enamored with Schmitt's thought, describing him as "a brilliant intellect, but a dangerous novice. At bottom, a nihilist who doesn't believe in anything."[45] He was, Stapel wrote, a "disbelieving Catholic" unwilling to give up his Catholicism, a man whom the Centrists around party chairman Ludwig Kaas and the Jesuits allegedly hated because of his nationalism. Nonetheless, Stapel still found Schmitt a "highly interesting and significant phenomenon," and the two would remain confidants as part of the conservative subculture during the Nazi years.[46]

Ultimately, Schmitt only published three articles in the journals of the radical Right. Two of these unequivocally rejected any elimination or radical transformation of the existing political and legal order; and the third warned against granting National Socialists an electoral majority.[47] "I would not," he wrote in 1930, "consider any fundamental constitutional reform at this time," cautioning against "incalculable and dangerous experiments."[48] And while using Schmitt's ideas to assault the republic, even Hans Zehrer of *Die Tat* believed that Schmitt and the Social Democratic jurist Hermann Heller "both hold open the way back, perhaps because they themselves see no new goal."[49] It was the installation of the presidential system under Centrist Heinrich Brüning in 1930 that first brought Schmitt into the sphere of right-wing politics. Formerly his prolific writing had generally contributed to the intensity of political discussions and intellectual controversies that characterized Weimar culture. Now his works would be read, discussed, and used in governmental circles and would affect policy decisions. Schmitt and his works would become an integral dimension of the political and ideological debates over the presidential system. Two of his most significant works, *Der Hüter der Verfassung* and *Legalität und Legitimität*, provided significant theoretical legal justification and practical political legitimation of the kind of presidential power, especially the reliance upon Article 48, exercised by Hindenburg through the chancellorships of Brüning, Papen, and Schleicher. His role, however, always remained secondary as a behind-the-scenes adviser and public advocate. Standing outside the true inner circles of various political coteries making decisions, he was consulted—and his ideas used and disregarded—depending upon the changing political strategies and personal whims of those in power.[50]

In 1929, shortly before the presidential system was conceived, Schmitt elaborated on his long-standing theory of presidential power in an article on the defender of the constitution, a preliminary sketch of his *Hüter der Verfassung*.[51] Its arguments caught the attention of Otto Meissner and Erich Zweigert, two state secretaries soon involved in justifying and administering Hindenburg's presidential cabinets.[52] As Brüning's policies evolved toward authoritarian assertions of presidential power in the spring of 1930, his government relied upon the constitutional theory of Walter Jellinek and Schmitt to justify remaining in office after a vote of no confidence. By July, the government had solicited a *Gutachten* in which Schmitt confirmed the constitutionality of issuing emergency economic decrees under Article 48, an interpretation shortly upheld by the German supreme court.[53]

While supporting Brüning, Schmitt never established a close personal relationship with him. Instead, he became a confidant within the circles around the decisive figure in the presidential system, General Kurt von Schleicher. Beginning in 1929, Schmitt had befriended Johannes Popitz, a highly respected state secretary in the Reich finance ministry. A Schleicher supporter, Popitz would hold similar positions in the Third Reich before being executed in 1944 as a conspirator in the plot to assassinate Hitler. Popitz popularized Schmitt's critique of the *Parteienstaat* and his theory of the president as a "neutral force" above parties whose exercise of emergency powers was both democratic and necessary to defend the constitution.[54] In early 1931, Schmitt began an equally long relationship with two of Schleicher's innermost confidants, Majors Erich Marcks and Eugen Ott. They would be his most important conduits to Schleicher, and Schmitt remained in regular contact with them until 1933. Marcks read Schmitt's *Die Diktatur, Der Hüter der Verfassung*, and *Legalität und Legitimität*. His own publications echoed Schmitt's arguments on Weimar parties and the presidency in an *Ausnahmezustand*. Marcks promoted Schmitt's ideas within the government and favored their popularization among the broader public.[55] Likewise, impressed by Schmitt, Ott would later as military attaché to Japan assist in the dissemination of Schmitt's works among academic and political circles in that country.[56]

One of the clearest indications that Schmitt had not penetrated the innermost center of the true political decision makers was Papen's Prussian coup of 20 July 1932. Papen's dismissal of the Prussian government and declaration of martial law in that state took Schmitt completely by surprise.[57] Nonetheless, that action thrust Schmitt into the national limelight. The government commissioned Schmitt, Erwin Jacobi, and Carl Bilfinger to prepare and argue the Reich's case before the supreme court, with Schmitt publishing articles to justify the legality and necessity of this takeover. In addition to the political maneuvering of the various litigants, the debates and publicity leading up to, during, and in the aftermath of the trial Prussia vs. Reich to a large extent focused on the political and constitutional theories Schmitt had been advancing for years. In the courtroom and the press, jurists, journalists, and political activists praised and chastised his ideas on presidential authority, generally as defender of the constitution, and specifically as commissarial dictator under Article 48 in the current *Ausnahmezustand*. The debate cascaded beyond the arguments in his *Legalität und Legitimität* and *Hüter der Verfassung* into the broader political context of the necessity of the president to distinguish friend from enemy in defense of state and constitution against, on the one hand, a legal seizure of power by anticonstitutional parties and, on the other, the breakdown of the essential machinery of state due to the paralyzed *Parteienstaat*.[58]

The notion that in public life and politics perception is reality certainly pertained to Schmitt's predicament in 1932. The intellectual radical Right claimed him as its own. *Deutsches Volkstum, Der Ring*, and *Die Tat* extolled the wisdom and necessity of his theories, thereby confirming the worst suspicions and fears of liberals and leftists that Schmitt was indeed politically promoting, and theoretically legitimizing, an anti-democratic assault on the very fundamental principles and existence of the republic.[59] To the liberal *Vossische-Zeitung*, he sought an end to parliamentary government through a presidential dictatorship. The *Neue Blätter für den Sozialismus* lambasted Schmitt's friend-enemy thesis as an amoral doctrine of the domination of the powerful, asserting that in a democracy it is the people, not an authoritarian president, who were entrusted with the defense of the constitution. *Die Weltbühne* now proclaimed him the *Kronjurist* of the anti-democratic Reich government.[60] Nonetheless, the latest research and recent illuminating documentation from his unpublished *Nachlaß*, especially his private diaries, substantiate that Schmitt was attempting to stabilize the German state in a precarious situation rather than seeking the abrogation of the constitution in favor of a rightist dictatorship or a reactionary transformation of Weimar.[61]

Schmitt was, in fact, totally unsympathetic to Papen's plans for exploiting the Prussian crisis to institute an authoritarian regime through reactionary constitutional reform. Since the 1920s, he was the only prominent jurist who had consistently held that the constitution was immune to fundamental change in its basic character through parliamentary amending authority under Article 76. In *Legalität und Legitimität* he had made it categorically clear that the exceptional powers of the president "were intended as a check on certain abuses of the parliamentary system, and therefore were meant to save the system, but were not intended to establish some new kind of state."[62] In other public venues, he had continually argued that the country needed a stable government before proceeding with fundamental changes. At the onset of the presidential system, he stated he "would not consider any fundamental constitutional change at this time," warning against "incalculable and dangerous experiments." During the crisis of 1932, he again wrote there was not "much latitude for great constitutional experiments." Instead, the "government should utilize all constitutional means . . . at its disposal."[63]

Perhaps the most important witness to Schmitt's motives and intentions during this final crisis of Weimar was Ernst Rudolf Huber, later one of Germany's most respected constitutionalists. Schmitt had personally selected Huber to assist him on constitutional matters related to the plans and activities of the presidential government. With clarity and detail, Huber has recounted that Schmitt had no grand plans for the transformation of the Weimar political and legal system. Schmitt remained highly skeptical of the "premature constitutional projects of the conservatives and right-liberals." He certainly was not seeking a transition to a Third Reich, as he considered the National Socialists a danger to traditional German state and society; his comments about Hitler were decidedly "derogatory." Schmitt was preoccupied with, and focused solely upon, the extreme dangers of the immediate situation, attempting only to prevent the suicide of the Weimar Republic. Neither was the "goal the creation of a military dictatorship, but the reestablishment of orderly conditions under which one could then out of necessity again return to a civilian constitution."[64]

To these ends, Schmitt had been engaged by the presidential government to draw up the constitutional justifications and details for the legal implementation of plans for declaring a state of emergency, or *Staatsnotstandsplan*. The plan was conceived in the aftermath of the NSDAP and KPD gaining a Reichstag majority in the July 1932 elections, which held out the likelihood of the total paralysis of the constitutional and political system. These anti-constructional parties could exploit this majority to legally prevent the establishment of any government through a no-confidence vote of any chancellor or cabinet; at the same time, they could foil the current rule by presidential emergency decrees under Article 48 by rescinding any measures instituted under that provision. To Schmitt, these democratic elections and a completely neutral legal interpretation of the constitution had set the stage for the possibility of the entire breakdown of the Weimar system due to a totally paralyzed government, civil war, or the seizure of power through revolution or legal acquisition of the NDSAP or KPD, both determined to destroy not just Weimar but much of the traditional German state and society. The *Staatsnotstandsplan* would institute a presidential emergency government for the period of time necessary to reestablish public order and the beginnings of economic recovery. In the interim, the paralyzed Reichstag would be dissolved without calling for new elections until order was restored and a change in the political and psychological climate held out the prospect of a functioning party system. The plan also included the concentration of police and military power in the presidential government, and for the suppression of the Communist and Nazi parties. In early 1933, then chancellor Schleicher, having failed to garner support for a grand coalition strategy for political unity and economic reconstruction, revived the *Staatsnotstandsplan*. However, by that point Schmitt felt the situation was so precarious that the most efficacious political and legal strategy was not dissolving the Reichstag without new elections. Instead, he advocated a constitutional ploy by which the Reich president would continue his emergency government without recognizing a Nazi-Communist majority vote of no confidence in the cabinet on the grounds that this was merely an obstructionist political tactic designed to paralyze and ultimately destroy the constitutional system. In Schmitt's interpretation, such obstructionist negative majorities violated the intent of Article 54 governing votes of no confidence. To Schmitt, presidential power, now constitutionally justified by *"ratione necessitates,"* remained the key to the survival of Weimar. Although Schmitt still worked closely with Marcks and Ott, by this time Schleicher no longer consulted him. And when Hindenburg rejected Schleicher's attempt to finally institute the *Staatsnotstandsplan*, Schmitt's efforts to provide a constitutional strategy for salvaging what was left of Weimar and thwart a Nazi acquisition of power came to naught.[65]

Instead of impeding an NSDAP triumph, the presidential system had, in the end, facilitated the transition to Hitler's dictatorship by increasingly conditioning the country to authoritarian government. It would be Schmitt's involvement with the presidential system that drew him into initial collaboration with the Nazis. In April 1933 two prominent conservatives in the new Hitler government, Papen and Popitz, the latter his trusted friend, enlisted Schmitt to help draft the *Reichsstatthaltergesetz*, the law that led to the Nazification of state governments.[66] Ironically, this very same conservative identification subsequently undermined Schmitt's position in the Third Reich. Within a few years, the Nazis purged him from party offices and publicly chastised him for not being a true National Socialist. To them, he was conservative to the core. They condemned him as a purveyor of traditional Hegelian ideas on state and society and of reactionary political Catholicism, both inhibiting their grandiose plans for the transformation of Germans and Germany.[67]

His rejection by the Nazis notwithstanding, Schmitt's activities and publications as the figurehead Nazi *Kronjurist* made him thereafter a universal pariah in most political and intellectual circles. And the integral corollary to such condemnation of him was his reputation as a member of the radical Right who had worked prodigiously to undermine Weimar democracy. But Schmitt had never endeavored to intellectually subvert Weimar; and his relationship to Weimar conservatism was complex and vacillating. Indeed, while never a Center Party partisan, he often identified with Catholics, among the staunchest supporters of Weimar. And he stayed aloof from rightist political parties such as the DNVP and DVP, parties about which he had strong reservations. Postwar associations of him with those intellectuals who identified themselves as disciples of the "Conservative Revolution" were likewise misplaced. Although he had personal and intellectual relationships with figures such as Jünger and Stapel, he never shared their visions of a post-Weimar society nor had any confidence they could succeed in such pursuits. In fact, works on the radical intellectual and revolutionary Right written at the end of Weimar did not identify Schmitt with these movements.[68] When Jünger's assistant Armin Moehler first introduced the term "Conservative Revolution" after World War II, Schmitt always doubted the very concept and was wary of identifying himself with it.[69] Moreover, his political and legal ideas, including his devastating critiques of parliamentary government and the *Parteienstaat*, had found a broad Weimar audience extending from moderate Jewish democrats to socialists. Since the Schmitt renaissance of the 1990s, his Weimar works have once again been recognized for their scholarly erudition, insights, originality, and realism by a broad spectrum of political and intellectual circles around the world.

Nonetheless, if one considers Schmitt's work and influence in terms of a broader cultural *Gestalt*, they clearly contributed to an intellectual, psychological, and political climate favorable to the Weimar Right. While he perceived his critiques of Weimar's ills as diagnostic, and others later recognized them as incisive analyses of that system's deficiencies, the general thrust of his works rarely corresponded to the progressive hopes and promises of many of those who had established Weimar and had such high expectations for it. His anthropological pessimism and starkly realistic portrayal of a political world of friends and enemies, like his assaults on liberalism and hostility to Marxism, added fortifying scholarly credibility to the reservations many Germans had about a liberal-democratic republic. While reinforcing such doubts, he simultaneously provided the Right with penetrating and alluring ideas easily integrated into their mindset.

Although the Right tended to neglect Schmitt until around 1930, and then would often misunderstand, distort, and misuse his ideas, his very concepts and terminology lent themselves to such popularized adoption and adaptation. Long before rightist intellectuals and those political figures initiating the presidential system turned specifically to Schmitt's works and advice, his ideas had already become part of the political culture, coinage, and atmosphere of Weimar. Concepts such as the *Parteienstaat* and presidential dictatorship, with or without attribution to Schmitt, had become integral to the political discourses and uncompromising ideological confrontations of that era. It was not the scholarly sophistication and validity of his analyses, nor his actual intentions for the presidential system, that mattered but the overall negative psychological effect they had on the political mood.

Many future assessments and judgments of Schmitt's conservative stance in Weimar would likewise ignore his fundamental concepts and the intricacies of his ideas, as well as his actual political positions and activities. They focused instead on this overall perception of him as anti-democratic right-wing enemy of the republic. During his interrogations of Schmitt at Nuremberg, prosecuting attorney Robert Kempner rebuked his claims to scholarly freedom of expression: "Did you sermonize for 30 years in order to bring about the ideal of democracy?" On the contrary, Kempner charged: "Didn't you enthusiastically welcome the dictatorship as the fulfillment of your scholarly dreams?" Kempner then stated bluntly that "we will not allow democracy to be attacked with the apparent means of democracy." Alluding to the arguments in his *Legalität und Legitimität* that a democracy did not have the right to commit suicide, Schmitt responded, "The finest articulation of precisely that concept originated with me." Not only did Schmitt's reference have no credibility with Kempner, but the prosecutor had no idea to what Schmitt was actually referring.[70] Schmitt's complicated experiences with Weimar conservatism had been superseded by a despicable reputation lacking both nuance and historical accuracy.

Notes

1. For one of the earliest versions of this perspective see Charles E. Frye, "Carl Schmitt's Concept of the Political," *The Journal of Politics* 28 (1966): 818–30.
2. The literature on Schmitt is now so enormous that complete bibliographies would require volumes. For the most up-to-date references, see Reinhard Mehring, *Carl Schmitt: Aufstieg und Fall* (Munich: C. H. Beck, 2009), 583–98; and Andreas Koenen, *Der Fall Carl Schmitt. Sein Aufstieg zum "Kronjuristen des Dritten Reiches"* (Darmstadt: Wissenschaftliche Buchgesellschaft, 1995), 863–946.
3. Carl Schmitt, *Tagebücher. Oktober 1912 bis Februar 1915*, ed. Ernst Hüsmert (Berlin: Akademie Verlag, 2003), 43, 96, 145, 157–59, 185; and Carl Schmitt, *Die Militärzeit 1915 bis 1919. Tagebuch Februar bis Dezember 1915. Aufsätze und Materialien*, ed. Ernst Hüsmert and Gerd Giesler (Berlin: Akademie Verlag, 2005), 43, 57, 102, 152.
4. Schmitt, *Tagebücher*, ed. Hüsmert, 64, 91, 267. See also Carl Schmitt, *Theodor Däublers "Nordlicht." Drei Studien über die Elemente, die Geist, und die Aktualität des Werkes* (Munich: G. Müller, 1916).
5. Schmitt, *Militärzeit*, 95, 152, 176.
6. Schmitt, *Tagebücher*, ed. Hüsmert, 175, 209–10, 243, 285; idem., *Militärzeit*, 24, 70, 94, 89, 91, 94, 99, 105–6, 130.
7. Schmitt to Moritz Julius Bonn, 16 June 1922, in Bonn's unpublished Nachlaß, Bundesarchiv Koblenz (hereafter cited as BA Koblenz, NL Bonn), 49.
8. On right-wing intellectuals, often identified as Conservative or National Revolutionaries, see Kurt Sontheimer, *Antidemokratisches Denken in der Weimarer Republik. Die politischen Ideen des deutschen Nationalismus zwischen 1918 und 1933* (Munich: Nymphenburge Verlagshandlung, 1962); Martin Greiffenhagen, *Das Dilemma des Konservatismus in Deutschland* (Munich: R. Piper, 1971); Klemens von Klemperer, *Germany's New Conservatism: Its History and Dilemma in the Twentieth Century* (Princeton, NJ: Princeton University Press, 1972); Armin Mohler, *Die Konservative Revolution in Deutschland, 1918–1932. Ein Handbuch*, 2nd ed. (Darmstadt: Wissenschaftliche Buchgesellschaft, 1972); and Walter Struve, *Elites against Democracy: Leadership Ideals in Bourgeois Political Thought in Germany, 1890–1933* (Princeton, NJ: Princeton University Press, 1973); as well as Jeffrey Herf, *Reactionary Modernism: Technology, Culture, and Politics in Weimar and the Third Reich* (New York: Cambridge University Press, 1984); and Jerry Z. Muller, *The Other God that Failed: Hans Freyer and the Deradicalization of German Conservatism* (Princeton, NJ: Princeton University Press, 1987).

9. Carl Schmitt, *The Concept of the Political*, trans. George Schwab (Chicago: University of Chicago Press, 2007), 48–49.

10. Carl Schmitt, *Politische Romantik* (Munich: Duncker & Humblot, 1919).

11. See Erich Kaufmann, *Das Wesen des Völkerrechts und die Clausula rebus sic stantibus. Rechtsphilosophische Studie zum Rechts-, Staats- und Vertragsbegriff* (Tübingen: J. C. B. Mohr, 1911), 146.

12. Carl Schmitt, "Recht und Macht," *Summa. Eine Vierteljahresschrift*, 4 vols. (Hellerau: Hellerauer Verlag, 1917–18), 1:37–52, reprinted in *Militärzeit*, 432–44.

13. Carl Schmitt, *Römisches Katholizismus und Politische Form*, 2nd ed. (Munich: Theatiner Verlag, 1925). See also Joseph W. Bendersky, *Carl Schmitt: Theorist for the Reich* (Princeton, NJ: Princeton University Press, 1983), 49–54. For an unsuccessful attempt to portray Schmitt as essentially a political theological thinker see Koenen, *Der Fall Schmitt*.

14. Carl Schmitt, *Political Theology: Four Chapters on the Concept of Sovereignty*, trans. George Schwab (Chicago: University of Chicago Press, 1985), 53–66.

15. Schmitt, *Concept of the Political*, 52, 61, 65–67.

16. Ibid., 26–37, 65–67.

17. Carl Schmitt, "Die legale Weltrevolution. Politischer Mehrwert als Prämie auf juristic Legalität und Superlegalität," *Der Staat* 21 (1978): 321–39.

18. Mehring, *Carl Schmitt*, 525.

19. Schmitt, *Concept of the Political*, 19–20, 29–33, 43–52.

20. Carl Schmitt, *The Crisis of Parliamentary Democracy*, trans. Ellen Kennedy (Cambridge, MA: MIT Press, 1985), 1–17, 20.

21. Schmitt to Bonn, 17 June 1926, BA Koblenz, NL Bonn, 50.

22. Carl Schmitt, *Constitutional Theory*, trans. Jeffrey Seitzer, (Durham, NC: Duke University Press, 2008,), 320, 366.

23. Schmitt, *Tagebücher*, ed. Hüsmert, 64, 91. See also Schmitt, *Römischer Katholizismus*, 24; and idem., *Concept of the Political*, 70–73.

24. Schmitt, *Militärzeit*, 183–399, 539–62; Schmitt, *Concept of the Political*, 73.

25. Carl Schmitt, *Die Kernfrage des Völkerbundes* (Berlin: Dummler, 1926), 82.

26. Carl Schmitt, *Positionen und Begriffe im Kampf mit Weimar—Genf—Versailles 1923–1939* (Hamburg: Hanseatischer Verlags-Anstalt, 1940).

27. Schmitt, *Concept of the Political*, 52–53, 78.

28. Carl Schmitt, "USA. und die völkerrechtlichen Formen des modernen Imperialismus," in *Die Vereinigten Staaten von America* (Köningsberg, 1933), 117–142.

29. Schmitt, *Crisis of Parliamentary Democracy*, 51–76; and *Concept of the Political*, 37–38, 63–64, 74.

30. Mehring, *Carl Schmitt*, 114–15.

31. Carl Schmitt, *The Nomos of the Earth in the International Law of the Jus Publicum Europaeum*, trans. G. L. Ulmen (New York: Telos Press, 2003), 140–71.

32. Carl Schmitt, *Der Hüter der Verfassung* (Tübingen: J. C. P. Mohr, 1931), 16, 32–33, 40, 88–89, 132, 158–59.

33. Carl Schmitt, "Die Diktatur des Reichspräsidenten nach Artikel 48 der Weimarer Verfassung," Anhang in *Die Diktatur. Von den Anfängen des modernen Souveränitätsgedanken bis zum proletarischen Klassenkampf*, 4th ed. (Berlin: Duncker & Humblot, 1978), 213–59.
34. Hugo Preuss, "Reichsverfassungsmässige Diktatur," *Zeitschrift für Politik* 13 (1924): 101.
35. Schmitt, "Die Diktatur," 238–42.
36. Schmitt, *Constitutional Theory*, 20–29, 77, 104–12.
37. Bendersky, *Carl Schmitt*, 60–63, 71–73, 91–95. Karl Loewenstein, *Minderheitsregierung in Großbritannien. Verfassungsrechtliche Untersuchungen zur neuesten Entwicklung des britischen Parlamentarismus* (Munich: J. Schweitzer, 1925), 1.
38. For further information, see Koenen, *Der Fall Carl Schmitt*, 25–221, and Bendersky, *Carl Schmitt*, 140–41.
39. See Mehring, *Carl Schmitt*, 245–80, and Bendersky, *Carl Schmitt*, 132–35.
40. Mehring, *Carl Schmitt*, 269.
41. Ibid., 269–70. The intriguing relationship between Schmitt and Hugo Fischer has not been adequately explored. Such a study is problematic because the extant correspondence is one sided and does not contain Schmitt's letters to match Fischer's detailed, quite revealing ones. In this respect, consult Schmitt's unpublished Nachlaß, Nordrhein-Westfälischen Hauptstaatsarchiv, Düsseldorf, Bestand RW 265 (hereafter cited as NRWHStA Düsseldorf, NL Schmitt), 3564–624.
42. Franz Blei, "Ein deutsches Gespräch," *Neue Schweizer Rundschau* 7, no. 7 (July 1932): 518–33. See also Bendersky, *Carl Schmitt*, 136.
43. On Stapel, see Heinrich Kessler, *Wilhelm Stapel als politischer Publizist. Ein Beitrag zur Geschichte des konservativen Nationalismus zwischen den beiden Weltkriegen* (Nuremberg: Spindler, 1967), 147–49.
44. See Carl Schmitt, *Tagebücher 1930–1034*, ed. Wolfgang Schuller and Gerd Giesler (Berlin: Akademie Verlag, 2010). Schmitt's antisemitism is one of the most controversial, yet to date most inadequately explained, aspects of his politics. The intense personal antisemitism revealed by his private notes and diaries have led scholars such as Raphael Gross, *Carl Schmitt und die Juden. Eine deutsche Rechtslehre* (Frankfurt: Suhrkamp, 2000), to make the erroneous claim that the core of Schmitt's legal thought was to construct a legal theory as a bulwark against Jewish influence. The recent study by Mehring (see n. 2), based upon the most extensive examination of Schmitt's papers, clearly refutes this assertion but nevertheless fails to address this complex question adequately.
45. Stapel to Kolbenheyer, 27 September 1931, cited in Siegfried Lokatis, "Wilhelm Stapel und Carl Schmitt—Ein Briefwechsel," *Schmittiana. Beiträge zu Leben und Werk Carl Schmitts*, ed. Piet Tommissen 6 (1996): 27–108, here 42–43.
46. Stapel to Kolbenheyer, 11 June 1933, cited in Lokatis, "Stapel und Schmitt," 48–49.
47. Carl Schmitt, "Eine Warnung vor falschen politischen Fragestellungen," *Der Ring* 3, no. 48 (30 November 1930): 844–45; idem., "Zur politischen

Situation in Deutschland," *Der Kunstwart* 44, no. 4 (October 1930–September 1931): 253–56; and idem., "Legalität und gleiche Chance politischer Machtgewinnung," *Deutsches Volkstum* 14, no. 7 (July 1932): 557–64.

48. Schmitt, "Zur politischen Situation in Deutschland," 255.
49. Hans Zehrer, "Der Weg in das Chaos. Enthüllungen, Skandale, Sensationen," *Die Tat* 21, no. 8 (November 1929): 568.
50. Mehring, *Carl Schmitt*, 281–82.
51. Carl Schmitt, "Der Hüter der Verfassung," *Archiv des öffentlichen Rechts*, Neue Folge 16 (March 1929): 161–237.
52. Mehring, *Carl Schmitt*, 281–82; Bendersky, *Carl Schmitt*, 118–19.
53. Carl Schmitt, "Verfassungsrechtliche Gutachten über die Frage, ob der Reichspräsident befugt ist, auf Grund des Art. 48 Abs. 2 RV. Finanzgesetzvertretende Verordnungen zu erlassen" (28 July 1930), in the unpublished records of the Reichskanzlei, Bundesarchiv Berlin-Lichtenfelde, Bestand R 43 I (hereafter cited as BA Berlin, R 43 I), 1870/286–310.
54. Mehring, *Carl Schmitt*, 281–82. See also Wolfram Pyta and Gabriel Seiberth, "Die Staatskrise der Weimarer Republik im Spiegel des Tagebuchs von Carl Schmitt," *Der Staat* 38 (1999): 429–32; and Bendersky, *Carl Schmitt*, 113–17.
55. See Schmitt-Erich Marcks correspondence, NRWHStA Düsseldorf, NL Schmitt, RW 265, 9024–33. See also Erich Marcks, "Staat und Wehrmacht," *Wissen und Wehr. Monatshefte der deutschen Gesellschaft für Wehrpolitik und Wehrwissenschaften* 11, no. 2 (February 1930): 65–82; and "Reich, Volk, und Reichswehr," *Wissen und Wehr* 12, no. 1 (January 1931): 1–12.
56. See Schmitt-Eugen Ott correspondence, NRWHStA Düsseldorf, NL Schmitt, RW 265, 10741–46.
57. Mehring, *Carl Schmitt*, 289.
58. In this respect, see ibid., 290–99; Pyta and Seiberth, "Carl Schmitts Tagebuch als Spiegel," 428–48; and Bendersky, *Carl Schmitt*, 154–66.
59. See the 1932 issues of *Deutsche Volkstum*. See also Hans Zehrer, "Revolution oder Restauration?" *Die Tat* 24, no. 5 (Aug. 1932): 353–93; and Albrecht Erich Günther, *Was wir von Nationalsozialismus erwarten: Zwanzig Antworten* (Heilbronn: E. Salzer, 1932), 82–98.
60. "Auseinandersetzung mit Carl Schmitt," *Vossische Zeitung*, 11 September 1932, no. 437. See also Georg Quabbe, "Die Interpretation des Ausnahmezustandes—Ein staatsrechtlicher Leitfaden für Diktaturbeflissene," *Vossische Zeitung*, 11 September 1932, no. 437. In a similar vein, see Reinhold Aris, "Politik und Ethik: Kritische Anmerkungen zu Carl Schmitts politischer Theories," *Neue Blätter für den Sozialismus* 3, no. 10 (October 1932): 542–48; and idem., "Krisis der Verfassung: Die gegenwartige Situation," *Neue Blätter für den Sozialismus* 3, no. 1 (January 1932): 19–29; and Thomas Eck, "Das Volk als Hüter der Verfassung," *Neue Blätter für den Sozialismus* 3, no. 7 (July 1932): 347–55.
61. See Mehring, *Carl Schmitt*, 289–302, and Pyta and Seiberth, "Carl Schmitts Tagebuch als Spiegel," 423–28.
62. Carl Schmitt, *Legalität und Legitimität* (Munich: Duncker & Humblot, 1932), 89.

63. Carl Schmitt, "Gesunde Wirtschaft im starken Staat," *Mitteilungen des Vereins zu Wahrung der gemeinsamen wirtschaftlichen Interessen in Rheinland und Westfalen*, No. 1, Heft 21 (23 November 1932), 30–31.

64. Ernst Rudolf Huber, "Carl Schmitt in der Reichskrise der Weimarer Endzeit" and "Aussprache," in *Complexio Oppositorum: Über Carl Schmitt*, ed. Helmuth Quaritsch (Berlin: Duncker & Humblot, 1988), 33–70.

65. Lutz Berthold, *Carl Schmitt und der Staatsnotstandsplan am Ende der Weimarer Republik* (Belin, 1999). See also Mehring, *Carl Schmitt*, 287–92, 299–304; Wolfram Pyta and Gabriel Seiberth, "Die Staatskrise der Weimarer Republik im Spiegel des Tagebuchs Carl Schmitt—2. Teil," *Der Staat* 38 (1999): 594–610; and Bendersky, *Carl Schmitt*, 183–91.

66. Mehring, *Carl Schmitt*, 304–7, 319–58; Bendersky, *Carl Schmitt*, 195–218.

67. Mehring, *Carl Schmitt*, 378–79; Bendersky, *Carl Schmitt*, 219–42.

68. In this respect, see Walter Gerhart [Waldemar Gurian], *Um des Reiches Zukunft. Nationale Wiedergeburt oder politische Reaktion?* (Freiburg im Breisgau: Herder, 1932); Sigmund Neumann, *Die deutschen Parteien. Wesen und Wandel nach dem Kriege* (Berlin: Junker und Dünnhaupt, 1932); and Eugen Schmahl, *Der Aufstieg der nationalen Idee* (Stuttgart et al.: Union Deutsche Verlagsgesellschaft, 1933).

69. Mohler, *Die Konservative Revolution*, 76, 83. See also Schmitt to Forsthoff, 7 July 1970, in *Briefwechsel Ernst Forsthoff-Carl Schmitt 1926–1974*, ed. Dorothee Mussgnug, Reinhard Mussgnug, and Angela Reinthal (Berlin: Akademie Verlag, 2007), 310.

70. Interrogation of Professor Karl [*sic*] Schmitt by R. M. W. Kempner, 11 April 1947, in the Robert M. W. Kempner Papers, US Holocaust Memorial Museum Archives, Washington, DC, RG 71–0005.05, Prosecution Case Books, Case XI, Box 187. On Schmitt's argument that anti-constitutional parties should not be granted the "equal chance" to acquire power legally and that liberal democracies should not commit political suicide by allowing them to do so, see *Legalität und Legitimität*, 28–61.

 Contributors

Joseph W. Bendersky is professor of German History at Virginia Commonwealth University and book review editor for *Holocaust and Genocide Studies*. He is the author of *Carl Schmitt: Theorist for the Reich* (1983); *The "Jewish Threat": Anti-Semitic Politics of the U.S. Army* (2000); *A Concise History of Nazi Germany* (2014); and has published a translation of Schmitt's *On the Three Types of Juristic Thought* (2004). His recent articles include: "Carl Schmitt's Path to Nuremberg: A Sixty-Year Reassessment" (2007); "Panic: The Impact of Gustav Le Bon's Crowd Psychology on U.S. Military Thought" (2007); and "Dissension in the Face of the Holocaust: The 1941 American Debate over Antisemitism" (2010). He is currently continuing his research on various aspects of Carl Schmitt's life and theories.

Brian E. Crim is associate professor of History at Lynchburg College in Virginia. He has published on modern German history, most significantly "Terror from the Right: Revolutionary Terrorism and the Failure of the Weimar Republic" (2007) and "'Our Most Serious Enemy': The Specter of Judeo-Bolshevism in Germany, 1918–1923" (2011). He is currently in the process of completing a book-length manuscript tentatively titled *"A Most Serious Enemy": Antisemitism in the German Military Community, 1914–1938*.

Ulrike Ehret is a lecturer in modern European History at the University Erlangen-Nuremberg. She has published extensively on Catholicism, fascism, and anti-Semitism, including her recent book *Church, Nation and Race: Catholics and Antisemitism in Germany and England* (Manchester: Manchester University Press, 2012). She is currently working on a research project on the relationship between political radicalism and popular opinion and their effect upon democratic politics in interwar Europe.

Daniela Gasteiger is currently a research assistant and doctoral candidate in the Department of Modern and Contemporary history at

Ludwig-Maximilians-Universität in Munich. She studied history and art history at the Johannes-Gutenberg-University in Mainz and the Sorbonne and received her Masters of Arts at the Ludwig-Maximilians-Universität in Munich in 2005. Her research interests cover the history of the World War I, Weimar Germany, and political conservatism. For her doctoral dissertation she is preparing a biography of Count Kuno von Westarp (1864–1945) with support from the Deutsche Forschungsgemeinschaft.

Rainer Hering is director of the Landesarchiv Schleswig-Holstein and teaches Modern History and Archival Science at the Universities of Hamburg and Kiel. His extensive publications include *Konstruierte Nation. Der Alldeutsche Verband 1890 bis 1939* (Hamburg: Christians, 2003) and other publications on the Pan-German League as well as a number of articles and essays on different aspects of the history of the Lutheran Church in modern German history. He is also a specialist on the history of Hamburg and Schleswig-Holstein.

Björn Hofmeister received his PhD from Georgetown University in 2012 and is currently a Postdoctoral Fellow at the History Department of Free University Berlin. He is co-editor of *Kaiserreich und Erster Weltkrieg 1871–1918. Geschichte in Quellen und Darstellung*, 5th ed. (Stuttgart: Reclam, 2010); and *Gelehrtenpolitik, Sozialwissenschaften und akademische Diskurse in Deutschland im 19. und 20. Jahrhundert* (Stuttgart: Steiner, 2006). His currently revising his doctoral dissertation "Between Monarchy and Dictatorship: Radical Nationalism and Social Mobilization of the Pan-German League, 1914–1939" for publication and is preparing a scholarly edition of *Heinrich Claß. Politische Erinnerungen des Vorsitzenden des Alldeutschen Verbandes 1915–1933/36.*

Barry A. Jackisch received his PhD from the State University of New York at Buffalo in 2000 and is currently associate professor of European History at the University of St. Francis in Fort Wayne, Indiana. He is author of the recently published book *The Pan-German League and Radical Nationalist Politics in Interwar Germany, 1918–1939* (Farnham: Ashgate, 2012) and has presented and published extensively on various aspects of the German Right in the Weimar Republic. He is currently working on a book-length manuscript in the field of city planning and urban environmental history tentatively entitled *The Nature of Berlin: Green Space and Germany's Capital City, 1870–1990.*

Larry Eugene Jones is professor of Modern European and German History at Canisius College in Buffalo, New York, and is author of *German Liberalism and the Dissolution of the Weimar Party System, 1918–1933* (Chapel Hill, NC, and London: University of North Carolina Press, 1988). He co-edited with James Retallack *Between Reform, Reaction, and Resistance: Studies in the History of German Conservatism from 1789 to 1945* (Providence, RI, and Oxford: Berg Publishers, 1993); and more recently with Wolfram Pyta *"Ich bin der letzte Preuße": Der politische Lebensweg des konservativen Politikers Kuno Graf von Westarp (1864–1945)* (Cologne, Weimar, and Vienna: Böhlau Verlag, 2006). He is currently preparing a monograph for Cambridge University Press on the 1932 presidential elections.

Wolfram Pyta is director of the Historical Institute at the University of Stuttgart. He has published widely on a range of topics in modern German history, including *Gegen Hitler und für die Republik. Die Auseinandersetzungen der deutschen Sozialdemokratie mit der NSDAP in der Weimarer Republik* (Düsseldorf, 1989); and *Dorfgemeinschaft und Parteipolitik 1918–1933. Die Verschränkung von Milieu und Parteien in den protestantischen Landgebieten Deutschlands in der Weimarer Republik* (Düsseldorf, 1996). His most recent monograph is his authoritative *Hindenburg. Herrschaft zwischen Hohenzollern und Hitler* (Berlin, 2007).

Edward Snyder recently received his PhD from the University of Minnesota and is a visiting assistant professor at St. Olaf College in Northfield, Minnesota. His dissertation, "Work not Alms: The Bethel Mission to East Africa and German Protestant debates over Eugenics, 1880–1933," examines the attitudes of German Protestants to eugenics with specific focus on the influence of returning missionaries from Africa. His research interests include the relationship between religion and imperialism and the anti-Nazi resistance in the Third Reich.

Selected Bibliography of New and Standard Works on the History of the German Right, 1918–33

Abelshauser, Werner. "Gustav Krupp und die Gleichschaltung des Reichsverbandes der Deutschen Industrie, 1933–1934." *Zeitschrift für Unternehmensgeschichte* 47 (2002): 3–26.

———. *Ruhrkohle und Politik. Ernst Brandi 1875–1937*. Essen: Klartext, 2009.

Abraham, David. "Constituting Bourgeois Hegemony: The Bourgeois Crisis of Weimar Germany." *Journal of Modern History* 51 (1979): 417–37.

Allen, William Sheridan. *The Nazi Seizure of Power: The Experience of a Single Town, 1922–1945*. New York: Franklin Watts, 1984.

Aretin, Karl Otmar. "Der bayerische Adel. Von der Monarchie zum Dritten Reich." In *Bayern in der NS-Zeit. Herrschaft und Gesellschaft in Konflikt*, ed. Martin Broszat, Elke Fröhlich, and Anton Großmann, 6 vols., 3:513–67. Munich: R. Oldenbourg, 1977–83.

———. "Die bayerische Regierung und die Politik der bayerischen Monarchisten in der Krise der Weimarer Republik 1930–1933." In *Festschrift für Hermann Heimpel zum 70. Geburtstag am 19. September 1971*, ed. Max-Planck-Institut für die Geschichte, 205–37. Göttingen: Vandenhoeck & Ruprecht, 1971.

Auerbach, Hellmuth. "Vom Trommler zum Führer. Hitler und das nationale Münchner Bürgertum." In *Irrlicht im leuchtenden München? Der Nationalsozialismus in der Hauptstadt der Bewegung*, ed. Björn Mensing and Friedrich Prinz, 67–91. Regensburg: Friedrich Pustet, 1991.

Baranowski, Shelley. "Conservative Elite Anti-Semitism from the Weimar Republic to the Third Reich." *German Studies Review* 19 (1996): 525–37.

———. "Continuity and Contingency: Agrarian Elites, Conservative Institutions and East Elbia in Modern German History." *Social History* 12 (1987): 285–308.

———. "Convergence on the Right: Agrarian Elite Radicalism and Nazi Populism in Pomerania, 1928–33." In *Between Reform, Reaction, and Resistance: Studies in the History of German Conservatism from 1789 to 1945*, ed. Larry Eugene Jones and James Retallack, 407–32. Providence, RI, and Oxford: Berg, 1993.

———. *The Sanctity of Rural Life: Nobility, Protestantism, and Nazism in Weimar Prussia*. New York and Oxford: Oxford University Press, 1995.

Barth, Boris. *Dolchstoßlegenden und politische Desintegration. Das Traume der deutschen Niederlage im Ersten Weltkrieg 1914–1933.* Düsseldorf: Droste, 2003.

Baumann, Carl-Friedrich. "Fritz Thyssen und der Nationalsozialismus." *Zeitschrift des Geschichtsvereins Mühlheim a.d. Ruhr* 70 (1988): 139–54.

Beck, Hermann. "Between the Dictates of Conscience and Political Expediency: Hitler's Conservative Alliance Partner and Antisemitism during the Nazi Seizure of Power." *Journal of Contemporary History* 41 (2006): 611–40.

———. "Konflikte zwischen Deutschnationalen und Nationalsozialisten während der Machtergreifung." *Historische Zeitschrift* 292 (2011): 645–80.

———. *The Fateful Alliance: German Conservatives and Nazis in 1933. The* Machtergreifung *in a New Light.* New York and Oxford: Berghahn Books, 2009.

Becker, Bert. "Revolution und rechte Sammlung. Die Deutschnationale Volkspartei in Pommern 1918/19." In *Geist und Gestalt im historischen Wandel. Facetten deutscher und europäischer Geschichte. Festschrift für Siegfried Bahne,* 211–30. Münster, New York, Munich, and Berlin: Waxmann, 2000.

Behrens, Beate. *Mit Hitler zur Macht. Aufstieg des Nationalsozialismus in Mecklenburg und Lübeck 1922–1933.* Rostock: Neuer Hochschulschriftenverlag, 1998.

Bendersky, Joseph W. *Carl Schmitt: Theorist for the Reich.* Princeton, NJ: Princeton University Press, 1983.

Berding, Helmut. *Moderne Antisemitsmus in Deutschland.* Frankfurt: Suhrkamp, 1988.

Berghahn, Volker R. "Die Harzburger Front und die Kandidatur Hindenburgs für die Reichspräsidentenwahlen 1932." *Vierteljahrshefte für Zeitgeschichte* 13 (1965): 64–82.

———. *Der Stahlhelm: Bund der Frontsoldaten 1918–1935.* Düsseldorf: Droste, 1966.

———. "Das Volksbegehren gegen den Youngplan und die Ursprünge des Präsidialregimes 1928–1930." In *Industrielle Gesellschaft und politisches System. Beiträge zur politischen Sozialgeschichte. Festschrift für Fritz Fischer zum siebzigsten Geburtstag,* ed. Dirk Stegmann, Bernd Jürgen Wendt, and Peter-Christian Witt, 431–46. Bonn: Verlag Neue Gesellschaft, 1978.

Bergmann, Werner. "Völkischer Antisemitismus im Kaiserreich." In *Handbuch zur "Völkischen Bewegung" 1871–1918,* ed. Uwe Puschner, Walter Schmitz, and Justus H. Ulbricht, 449–63. Munich: Saur, 1996.

Bernd, Hans Dieter. "Die Beseitigung der Weimarer Republik auf ‚legalem' Weg: Die Funktion des Antisemitismus in der Agitation der Führungsschicht der DNVP." PhD diss., Fernuniversität Hagen, 2004.

Berthold, Lutz. *Carl Schmitt und der Staatsnotstandsplan am Ende der Weimarer Republik.* Berlin: Duncker & Humblot, 1999.

Bessel, Richard. "The 'Front Generation' and the Politics of Weimar Germany." In *Generations in Conflict: Youth Revolt and Generation Formation in Germany, 1770–1968,* ed. Mark Roseman, 121–36. Cambridge: Cambridge University Press, 1995.

———. *Political Violence and the Rise of Nazism: The Storm Troopers in Eastern Germany, 1925–1934.* New Haven: Yale University Press, 1984.

Bloxham, Donald, and Gerwarth, Robert, eds. *Political Violence in Twentieth-Century Europe.* Cambridge: Cambridge University Press, 2011.

Bösch, Frank. *Das konservative Milieu. Vereinskultur und lokale Sammlungspolitik in ost- und westdeutschen Regionen (1900–1960)*. Göttingen: Wallstein Verlag, 2002.
———. "Militante Geselligkeit. Formierungsformen der bürgerlichen Vereinswelt zwischen Revolution und Nationalsozialismus." In *Politische Kulturgeschichte der Zwischenkriegszeit 1918–1939*, ed. Wolfgang Hardtwig, 151–82. Göttingen: Vandenhoeck & Ruprecht, 2005.
Breitman, Richard. "On German Social Democracy and General Schleicher 1932–33." *Central European History* 9 (1976): 352–78.
Breuer, Stefan. *Anatomie der konservativen Revolution*. Darmstadt: Wissenschaftliche Buchgesellschaft, 2003.
———. *Grundpositionen der deutschen Rechten 1871–1945*. Tübingen: Edition Diskord, 1999.
———. *Ordnungen der Ungleichheit. Die deutsche Rechte im Widerstreit ihrer Ideen 1871–1945*. Darmstadt: Wissenschaftliche Buchgesellschaft, 2001.
———. *Die radikale Rechte in Deutschland 1871–1945. Eine politische Ideengeschichte*. Ditzingen: Reclam, 2010.
———. *Die Völkischen in Deutschland. Kaiserreich und Weimarer Republik*. Darmstadt: Wissenschaftliche Buchgesellschaft, 2008.
Breuning, Klaus. *Die Vision des Reiches. Deutscher Katholizismus zwischen Demokratie und Diktatur 1929–1934*. Munich: Hueber Verlag, 1969.
Bruendel, Steffen. *Volksgemeinschaft oder Volksstaat. Die "Ideen von 1914" und die Neuordnung Deutschlands im Ersten Weltkrieg*. Berlin: Akademie Verlag, 2003.
Busche, Raimund von dem. *Konservatismus in der Weimarer Republik. Die Politisierung des Unpolitischen*. Heidelberg: C. Winter, 1998.
Carsten, F. L. *The Reichswehr and Politics 1918 to 1933*. Oxford: Oxford University Press, 1966.
Cary, Noel D. "The Making of the Reich President, 1925: German Conservatism and the Nomination of Paul von Hindenburg." *Central European History* 23 (1990): 179–204.
Chamberlin, Brewster. "The Enemy on the Right. The Alldeutscher Verband in the Weimar Republic 1918–1926." PhD diss., University of Maryland, 1972.
Chickering, Roger. "Political Moblization and Associational Life: Some Thoughts on the National Socialist Workers' Club (e.V.)." In *Elections, Mass Politics, and Social Change in Modern Germany: New Perspectives*, ed. Larry Eugene Jones and James Retallack, 307–28. Cambridge: Cambridge University Press, 1992.
———. *We Men Who Feel Most German: A Cultural Study of the Pan-German League 1886–1914*. Boston: Allen and Unwin, 1984.
Childers, Thomas. "The National Socialist Mobilisation of New Voters: 1928–1933." In *The Formation of the Nazi Constituency, 1919–1933*, ed. Thomas Childers, 202–31. Totowa, NJ: Croon Helm, 1986.
———. *The Nazi Voter: The Social Foundations of Fascism in Germany, 1919–1933*. Chapel Hill, NC, and London: University of North Carolina Press, 1983.
———, ed. *The Formation of the Nazi Constituency, 1919–1933*. Totowa, NJ: Croon Helm, 1986.
Clemens, Gabriele. *Martin Spahn und der Rechtskatholizismus in der Weimarer Republik*. Mainz: Matthias Grünewald, 1983.

Conrad, Horst. "Stand und Konfession. Der Verein der katholischen Edelleute. Teil 2: Die Jahre 1918–1949." *Westfälische Zeitschrift* 159 (2009): 91–154.

Conze, Eckart. "'Only a Dictator Can Help Us Now': Aristocracy and the Radical Right in Germany." In *European Aristocracies and the Radical Right, 1918–1939*, ed. Karina Urbach, 129–47. Oxford: Oxford University Press, 2007.

———. *Von deutschem Adel. Die Grafen von Bernstorff im 20. Jahrhundert*. Stuttgart: Deutsche Verlags-Anstalt, 2000.

Crim, Brian E. "From *Frontgemeinschaft* to *Volksgemeinschaft*: The Role of Antisemitism within the German Military and Veteran Community, 1916–1938." PhD diss., Rutgers University, 2003.

———. "'Our Most Serious Enemy': The Specter of Judeo-Bolshevism in Germany, 1918–1923." *Central European History* 44 (2011): 624–41.

Diehl, James M. *Paramilitary Politics in Weimar Germany*. Bloomington: Indiana University Press, 1977.

———. "Von der 'Vaterlandspartei' zur 'nationalen Revolution': Die 'Vereinigten Vaterländischen Verbände Deutschlands (VVVD)' 1922–1932." *Vierteljahrshefte für Zeitgeschichte* 33 (1985): 617–39.

Dimitrios, Alexander. *Weimar und der Kampf gegen "rechts." Eine politische Biographie*. 4 vols. Ulm: Verlag Dr. Paul Schulz, 2009.

Dörr, Manfred. "Die Deutschnationale Volkspartei 1925 bis 1928." PhD diss., Universität Marburg, 1964.

Dressel, Guido. *Der Thüringer Landbund—Agrarischer Berufsverband als politische Partei in Thüringen 1919–1933*. Weimar: Wartburg Verlag, 1998.

Eglau, Hans Otto. *Fritz Thyssen. Hitlers Gönner und Geisel*. Berlin: Siedler, 2003.

Ehret, Ulrike. "Catholics and Antisemitism in Germany and England, 1918–1939." PhD diss., University of London, 2006.

Eley, Geoff. "Conservatives and Radical Nationalists in Germany: The Production of Fascist Potentials, 1912–1928." In *Fascists and Conservatives: The Radical Right and the Establishment in Twentieth-Century Europe*, ed. Martin Blinkhorn, 50–70. London: Unwin Hyman, 1990.

———. *Reshaping the German Right: Radical Nationalism and Political Change after Bismarck*. New Haven, CT, and London: Yale University Press, 1980.

Endres, Rudolf. "Der Bayerische Heimat- und Königsbund." In *Land und Reich/ Stamm und Nation. Probleme und Perspektiven bayerischer Geschichte. Festgabe für Max Spindler zum 90. Geburtstag*, ed. Andreas Kraus, 4 vols., 3: 415–36. Munich: Bayerische Akademie der Wissenschaften / Kommission für bayerische Landesgeschichte, 1984.

Erger, Johannes. *Der Kapp-Lüttwitz Putsch. Ein Beitrag zur deutschen Innenpolitik 1919/20*. Düsseldorf: Droste, 1967.

Faber, Richard. "Politischer Katholizismus. Die Bewegung von Maria Laach." In *Religions- und Geistesgeschichte der Weimarer Republik*, ed. Hubert Cancik, 136–58. Düsseldorf: Patmos Verlag, 1982.

Falter, Jürgen. "Der Aufstieg der NSDAP in Franken bei den Reichstagswahlen 1924–1933. Ein Vergleich mit dem Reich unter besonderer Berücksichtigung landwirtschaftlicher Einflußfaktoren." *German Studies Review* 9 (1986): 319–59.

———. *Hitlers Wähler*. Munich: C. H. Beck, 1991.

————. "The Two Hindenburg Elections of 1925 and 1932: A Total Reversal of Voter Coalitions." *Central European History* 23 (1990): 225–41.

Falter, Jürgen, and Zintl, Reinhard. "The Economic Crisis of the 1930s and the Nazi Vote." *Journal of Interdisciplinary History* 19 (1988): 55–85.

Feldman, Gerald D. "Der 30. Januar und die politische Kultur von Weimar." In *Die deutsche Staatskrise 1930–1933*, ed. Heinrich August Winkler, 263–76. Munich: R. Oldenbourg, 1992.

————. "Paul Reusch and the Politics of German Heavy Industry, 1908–1933." In *People and Communities in the Western World*, ed. Gene Brucker, 2 vols., 2:293–31. Homewood, IL: Dorsey Press, 1979.

————. "Right-Wing Politics and the German Film Industry: Emil Georg Stauss, Alfred Hugenberg und die UFA, 1917–1933." In *Von der Aufgabe der Freiheit. Politische Verantwortung und bürgerliche Gesellschaft im 19. und 20. Jahrhundert. Festschrift für Hans Mommsen zum 5. November 1995*, ed. Christian Jansen, Lutz Niethammer, and Bernd Weisbrod, 219–30. Berlin: Akademie Verlag, 1995.

Fischer, Fritz. *Bündnis der Eliten. Zur Kontinuität der Machtstrukturen in Deutschland 1875–1945*. Düsseldorf: Droste, 1979.

Flemming, Jens. "Die Bewaffnung des 'Landvolks'. Ländliche Schutzwehren und agrarischer Konservatismus in der Anfangsphase der Weimarer Republik." *Militärgeschichtliche Mitteilungen* 26 (1979): 7–36.

————. "Großagrarische Interessen und Landarbeiterbewegung. Überlegungen zur Arbeiterpolitik des Bundes der Landwirte und des Reichslandbundes in der Anfangsphase der Weimarer Republik." In *Industrielles System und politische Entwicklung in der Weimarer Republik. Verhandlungen des Internationalen Symposiums in Bochum vom 12.–17. Juni 1973*, ed. Hans Mommsen, Dietmar Petzina, and Bernd Weisbrod, 745–62. Düsseldorf: Droste, 1974.

————. "Konservatismus als 'nationalrevolutionäre Bewegung'. Konservative Kritik an der Deutschnationalen Volkspartei 1918–1933." In *Deutscher Konservatismus im 19. und 20. Jahrhundert. Festschrift für Fritz Fischer*, ed. Dirk Stegmann, Bernd-Jürgen Wendt, and Peter-Christian Witt, 295–331. Bonn: Verlag Neue Gesellschaft, 1983.

————. "Landarbeiter zwischen Gewerkschaften und 'Werkgemeinschaft'. Zum Verhältnis von Agrarunternehmern und Landarbeiterbewegung in der Anfangsphase der Weimarer Republik." *Archiv für Sozialgeschichte* 14 (1974): 351–418.

————. *Landwirtschaftliche Interessen und Demokratie. Ländliche Gesellschaft, Agrarverbände und Staat 1890–1925*. Bonn: Verlag Neue Gesellschaft, 1978.

————. "Landwirtschaftskammer und ländliche Organisationspolitik in der Rheinprovinz, 1918–1927. Ein Beitrag zur Vorgeschichte der 'Grünen Front'." In *Von der Reichsgründung bis zur Weimarer Republik*, ed. Kurt Düwell and Wolfgang Köllmann, 2:314–32. Wuppertal, 1984.

————. "Zwischen Industrie und christlich-nationaler Arbeiterschaft. Alternativen landwirtschaftlicher Bündnispolitik in der Weimarer Republik." In *Industrielle Gesellschaft und politisches System. Beiträge zur politischen Sozialgeschichte. Festschrift für Fritz Fischer zum 70. Geburtstag*, ed. Dirk Stegmann, Bernd Jürgen Wendt, and Peter-Christian Witt, 259–76. Bonn: Verlag Neue Gesellschaft, 1978.

Föllmer, Moritz, and Meissner, Andrea. "Ideen als Weichensteller? Polyvalenz, Aneignung und Homogenitätsstreben im deutschen Nationalismus 1890–1933." In *Ideen als gesellschaftliche Gestaltungskraft im Europa der Neuzeit*, ed. Lutz Raphael and Heinz-Elmar Tenorth, 313–26. Munich: R. Oldenbourg, 2006.

Frech, Stefan. *Wegbereiter Hitlers? Theodor Reismann-Grone. Ein völkischer Nationalist (1863–1949)*. Paderborn: Schöningh, 2009.

Friedenthal, Elizabeth. "Volksbegehren und Volksentscheid über den Young Plan und die deutschnationale Sezession." PhD diss., Universität Tübingen, 1957.

Friedrich, Norbert. *"Die christlich-soziale Fahne empor!" Reinhard Mumm und die christlich-soziale Bewegung*. Stuttgart: W. Kohlhammer, 1997.

———. "'National, Sozial, Christlich'. Der Evangelische Reichsausschuß der Deutschnationalen Volkspartei in der Weimarer Republik." *Kirchliche Zeitgeschichte* 6 (1993): 290–311.

Fritzsche, Peter. "Between Fragmentation and Fraternity: Civic Patriotism and the Stahlhelm in Bourgeois Neighborhoods during the Weimar Republic." *Tel Aviver Jahrbuch für deutsche Geschichte* 17 (1988): 123–44.

———. "Breakdown or Breakthrough? Conservatives and the November Revolution." In *Between Reform, Reaction, and Resistance: Studies in the History of German Conservatism from 1789 to 1945*, 299–328. Providence, RI, and Oxford: Berg Publishers, 1993.

———. *From Germans into Nazis*. Cambridge, MA: Harvard University Press, 1998.

———. *Rehearsals for Fascism: Populism and Political Mobilization in Weimar Germany*. New York and Oxford: Oxford University Press, 1990.

———. "Der Deutsche Reichskriegerbund Kyffhäuser 1930–1934. Politik, Ideologie und Funktion eines 'unpolitischen' Verbandes." *Militärgeschichtliche Mitteilungen* 36 (1984): 57–76.

Funck, Marcus. "Schock und Chance. Der preßische Militäradel in der Weimarer Republik zwischen Stand und Profession." In *Adel und Bürgertum in Deutschland II. Entwicklungslinien und Wendepunkte im 20. Jahrhundert*, ed. Hans Reif, 127–71. Berlin: Akademie Verlag, 2001.

Ganyard, Clifton. *Artur Mahraun and the Young German Order: An Alternative to National Socialism in Weimar Political Culture*. Lewistown, NY: Edward Mellen Press, 2008.

Gemein, Gisbert Jörg. "Politischer Konservativismus am Rhein und in Westfalen in der Weimarer Zeit am Beispiel der Deutschnationale Volkspartei." In *Rheinland-Westfalen im Industriezeitalter. Beiträge zur Landesgeschichte des 19. und 20. Jahrhunderts*, ed. Kurt Düwell and Wolfgang Köllmann, vol. 3: *Vom Ende der Weimarer Republik bis zum Land Nordrhein-Westfalen*, 62–75. Wuppertal: Peter Hammer, 1984.

Gerwarth, Robert. "The Central European Counter-Revolution: Paramilitary Violence in Germany, Austria and Hungary after the Great War." *Past and Present* 200 (2008): 175–209.

Gerwarth, Robert, and Horne, John. "Vectors of Violence: Paramilitarism in Europe after the Great War, 1917–1923." *Journal of Modern History* 83 (2011): 489–512.

————, eds. *War in Peace: Paramilitary Violence in Europe after the Great War*. Oxford: Oxford University Press, 2012.

Gessner, Dieter. *Agrardepression und Präsidialregierungen in Deutschland 1930–1933. Probleme des Agrarkonservatismus am Ende der Weimarer Republik*. Düsseldorf: Droste, 1977.

————. *Agrarverbände in der Weimarer Republik. Wirtschaftliche und soziale Voraussetzungen agrarkonservativer Politik vor 1933*. Düsseldorf: Droste, 1976.

Götz von Olenhusen, Irmtraud. "Vom Jungstahlhelm zur SA: Die junge Nachkriegsgeneration in den paramilitärischen Verbänden der Weimarer Republik." In *Politische Jugend in der Weimarer Republik*, ed. Wolfgang R. Krabbe, 146–82. Bochum: Universitätsverlag Brockmeyer, 1993.

Granier, Gerhard. *Magnus von Levetzow. Seeoffizier, Monarchist und Wegbereiter Hitlers. Lebensweg und ausgewählte Dokumente*. Boppard am Rhein: Harald Boldt, 1982.

Greiffenhagen, Martin. *Das Dilemma des Konservatismus in Deutschland*. Munich: R. Piper, 1971.

Gründer, Horst. "Rechtskatholizismus im Kaiserreich und in der Weimarer Republik unter besonderer Berücksichtigung der Rheinlande und Westfalen." *Westfälische Zeitschrift* 134 (1984): 107–55.

Hagenlücke, Heinz. *Deutsche Vaterlandspartei. Die nationale Rechte am Ende des Kaiserreiches*. Düsseldorf: Droste, 1997.

Hartwig, Edgar. "Zur Politik und Entwicklung des Alldeutschen Verbandes von seiner Gründung bis zum Beginn des 1. Weltkrieges, 1891–1914." PhD diss., Friedrich Schiller Universität Jena, 1966.

Hastings, Derek. "How Catholic was the Early Nazi Movement? Religion, Race and Culture in Munich, 1919–1924." *Central European History* 36 (2003): 383–433.

Haus der Geschichte Baden-Württemberg, ed. *Adel und Nationalsozialismus im deutschen Südwesten*. Karlsruhe: G. Braun Buchverlag, 2007.

Heilbronner, Oded. "From Antisemitic Peripheries to Antisemitic Centres: The Place of Antisemitism in Modern German History." *Journal of Contemporary History* 35 (2000): 559–76.

————. "The Role of Nazi Antisemitism in the Nazi Party's Activity and Propaganda: A Regional Historiographical Study." *Leo Baeck Institute Yearbook* 35 (1990): 397–439.

————. "The German Right: Has It Changed?" *German History* 21 (2003): 541–61.

Heinsohn, Kirsten. "Das konservative Dilemma und die Frauen. Anmerkungen zum Scheitern eines republikanischen Konservatismus in Deutschland 1912 bis 1930." In *"Ich bin der letzte Preuße": Kuno Graf von Westarp und die deutsche Politik (1900–1945)*, ed. Larry Eugene Jones and Wolfram Pyta, 77–107. Cologne, Weimar, and Vienna: Böhlau, 2006.

————. *Konservative Parteien in Deutschland 1912 bis 1933. Demokratisierung und Partizipation in geschlechterhistorischer Perspektive*. Düsseldorf: Droste, 2010.

————. "'Volksgemeinschaft' als gedachte Ordnung. Zur Geschlechterpolitik in der Deutschnationalen Volkspartei." In *Geschlechtergeschichte des Politischen. Entwürfe von Geschlecht und Gemeinschaft im 19. und 20. Jahrhundert*, ed. Gabriele Boukrif et al., 83–106. Münster: LIT Verlag, 2002.

Hempe, Mechthild. *Ländliche Gesellschaft in der Krise. Mecklenburg in der Weimarer Republik.* Cologne, Weimar, and Vienna: Böhlau, 2002.

Herbert, Ulrich. *Best: Biographische Studien über Radikalismus. Weltanschauung und Vernunft 1903–1989.* Bonn: Dietz, 1996.

Herbst, Ludolf. *Hitlers Charisma. Die Erfindung eines deutschen Messias.* Frankfurt: S. Fischer, 2010.

Herde, Peter. "Max Buchner (1881–1941) und die politische Stellung der Geschichtswissenschaft an der Universität Würzburg 1925–1945." In *Die Universität Würzburg in den Krisen der ersten Hälfte des 20. Jahrhunderts. Biographisch-systematische Studien zu ihrer Geschichte zwischen dem Ersten Weltkrieg und dem Neubeginn 1945,* ed. Peter Baumgart, 183–251. Würzburg: Schöningh, 2002.

Herf, Jeffrey. *Reactionary Modernism: Technology, Culture, and Politics in Weimar and the Third Reich.* New York: Cambridge University Press, 1984.

Hering, Rainer. *"Dem besten Steuermann Deutschlands": Der Politiker Otto von Bismarck und seine Deutung im radikalen Nationalismus zwischen Kaiserreich und "Drittem Reich."* Friedrichsruh: Otto-von-Bismarck Stiftung, 2006.

———. "'. . . eine sehr sympathische Stellung.' Der Kyffhäuser-Verband der Vereine Deutscher Studenten und der Alldeutsche Verband." In *125 Jahre Vereine Deutscher Studenten. 1881–2006,* vol. 1: *Ein historischer Rückblick,* ed. Marc Zirlewagen, 25–43. Bad Frankenhausen: Akademischer Verein Kyffhäuser, 2006.

———. "Eliten des Hasses. Der Alldeutsche Verband in Hamburg 1892 bis 1939." *Hamburger Arbeitskreis für Regionalgeschichte Mitteilungen* 43 (2005): 44–69.

———. "'Es ist verkehrt, Ungleichen Gleichheit zu geben.' Der Alldeutsche Verband und das Frauenwahlrecht." *Ariadne* 43 (2003): 22–29.

———. "Juden im Alldeutschen Verband?" In *Aus den Quellen. Beiträge zur deutschjüdischen Geschichte. Festschrift für Ina Lorenz zum 65. Geburtstag,* ed. von Andreas Brämer, Stefanie Schüler-Springorum, and Michael Studemund-Halévy, 291–300. Munich and Hamburg: Dölling und Galitz, 2005.

———. *Konstruierte Nation. Der Alldeutsche Verband 1890–1939.* Hamburg: Christians, 2003.

———. "'Parteien vergehen, aber das deutsche Volk muß weiterleben': Die Ideologie der Überparteilichkeit als wichtiges Element der politischen Kultur im Kaiserreich und in der Weimarer Republik." In *Völkische Bewegung—Konservative Revolution—Nationalsozialismus. Aspekte einer politisierten Kultur,* ed. Walter Schmitz und Clemens Vollnhals, 33–43. Dresden: Thelem, 2005.

———. "Radikaler Nationalismus zwischen Kaiserreich und 'Drittem Reich' am Beispiel der Alldeutschen Blätter." In *Das konservative Intellektuellenmilieu in Deutschland, seine Presse und seine Netzwerke (1890–1960),* ed. Michel Grunewald and Uwe Puschner in collaboration with Hans Manfred Bock, 427–43. Bern: Peter Lang, 2003.

Hertzman, Lewis. *DNVP: Right-Wing Opposition in the Weimar Republic, 1918–1924.* Lincoln: University of Nebraska Press, 1963.

———. "The Founding of the German National People's Party, November 1918–January 1919." *Journal of Modern History* 30 (1958): 24–36.

Hildebrand, Daniel. *Landbevöklerung und Wahlverhalten. Die DNVP im ländlichen Raum Pommerns und Ostpreußens 1918–1924.* Hamburg: Verlag Dr. Kovac, 2004.

Hiller von Gaertringen, Friedrich. "'Dolchstoß'-Diskussion und 'Dolchstoßlegende' im Wandel von vier Jahrzehnten." In *Geschichte und Gegenwartsbewußtsein. Festschrift für Hans Rothfels zum 70. Geburtstag,* ed. Waldemar Besson and Friedrich Hiller von Gaertringen, 122–60. Göttingen: Vandenhoeck & Ruprecht, 1963.

———. "Die Deutschnationale Volkspartei in der Weimarer Republik." *Historische Mitteilungen* 9 (1996): 169–88.

———. "Die Deutschnationale Volkspartei." In *Das Ende der Parteien 1933,* ed. Erich Matthias and Rudolf Morsey, 541–562. Düsseldorf: Droste, 1960.

———. "Die konservative Preußen und die Weimarer Republik." In *Preußen. Nostalgischer Rückblick oder Chance zu historischer Aufarbeitung. Referate im Rahmen eines Symposiums an der Rheinisch-Westfälischen Technischen Hochschule Aachen anläßlich der Berliner Preußen-Ausstellung 1981,* ed. Francesca Schnizinger and Immo Zapp, 52–69. Ostfildern: Scripta Mercaturae Verlag, 1984.

———. "Zur Beurteilung des 'Monarchismus' in der Weimarer Republik." In *Tradition und Reform in der deutschen Politik. Gedenkschrift für Waldemar Besson,* ed. Gotthard Jasper, 138–86. Frankfurt: Propyläen, 1976.

Hoegen, Jesko von. *Der Held von Tannenberg. Genese und Funktion des Hindenburg-Mythos.* Cologne: Böhlau, 2007.

Hoepke, Klaus Peter. "Die Kampffront Schwarz-Weiß-Rot. Zum Scheitern des national-konservativen 'Zähmungs'-Konzepts an den Nationalsozialisten im Frühjahr 1933." *Fridericiana. Zeitschrift der Universität Karlsruhe* 36 (1984): 34–52.

Hofmeister, Björn. "Between Monarchy and Dictatorship: Radical Nationalism and Social Mobilization of the Pan-German League, 1914–1939." PhD diss., Georgetown University, 2012.

Hofstett, Anke. "Der 'Stahlhelm. Bund der Frontsoldaten' und der Nationalsozialismus." In *Nationalsozialismus und Erster Weltkrieg,* ed. Gerd Krumeich, 191–206. Essen: Klartext, 2010.

Holzbach, Heidrn. *Das "System Hugenberg". Die Organisation bürgerlicher Sammlungspolitik vor dem Aufstieg der NSDAP.* Stuttgart: Deutsche Verlags-Anstalt, 1981.

Hömig, Herbert. *Brüning: Kanzler in der Krise der Republik. Eine Weimarer Biographie.* Paderborn: Schöningh, 2001.

Horn Wolfgang. *Führerideologie und Parteiorganisation in der NSDAP.* Düsseldorf: Droste, 1972.

Hubatsch, Walther. *Hindenburg und der Staat. Aus den Papieren des Generalfeldmarschalls und Reichspräsidenten von 1878 bis 1934.* Göttingen: Musterschmidt-Verlag, 1966.

Hübner, Christoph. "National-konservatives Denken im deutschen Katholizismus der Weimarer Zeit: Die 'Gelben Hefte' 1924 bis 1933." MA thesis, University of Erlangen, 2000.

Hürter, Wilhelm. *Wilhelm Groener. Reichswehrministerium am Ende der Weimarer Republik (1928–1932).* Munich: R. Oldenbourg, 1993.

Ishida, Yuji. *Jungkonservative in der Weimarer Republik. Der Ring-Kreis 1928–1933.* Frankfurt: Peter Lang, 1988.

Jackisch, Barry A. "Kuno Graf von Westarp und die Auseinandersetzung über Locarno. Konservative Außenpolitik und die deutschnationale Parteikrise 1925." In *"Ich bin der letzte Preuße": Kuno Graf von Westarp und die deutsche Politik (1900–1945),* ed. Larry Eugene Jones and Wolfram Pyta, 147–62. Cologne, Weimar, and Vienna: Böhlau, 2006.

———. *The Pan-German League and Radical Nationalist Politics in Interwar Germany, 1918–39.* Farnham: Ashgate, 2012.

Jasper, Gotthard. *Die gescheiterte Zähmung. Wege zur Machtergreifung Hitlers 1930–1934.* Frankfurt: Suhrkamp, 1986.

Jochmann, Werner. "Die Ausbreitung des Antisemitismus." In *Deutsches Judentum in Krieg und Revolution 1916–1923. Ein Sammelband,* ed. Werner E. Mosse, 409–510. Tübingen: J. C. B. Mohr, 1971.

John, Jürgen. "Zur politischen Rolle der Großindustrie in der Weimarer Staatskrise. Gesicherte Erkenntnisse und strittige Meinungen." In *Die deutsche Staatskrise 1930–1933. Handlungsspielräume und Alternativen,* ed. Heinrich August Winkler, 215–38. Munich: R. Oldenbourg, 1992.

Jonas, Erasmus. *Die Volkskonservativen 1928–1933. Entwicklung, Struktur, Standort und staatspolitische Zielsetzung.* Düsseldorf: Droste, 1963.

Jones, Larry Eugene. "Adolf Hilter and the 1932 Presidential Elections: A Study in Nazi Strategy and Tactics." In *Von Freiheit, Solidarität und Subsolidarität — Staat und Gesellschaft der Moderne in Theorie und Praxis. Festschrift für Karsten Ruppert zum 65. Geburtstag,* ed. Markus Raasch and Tobias Hirschmüller, 549–73. Berlin: Duncker & Humblot, 2013.

———. "Between the Fronts: The German National Union of Commercial Employees from 1928–1933." *Journal of Modern History* 48 (1976): 462–82.

———. "Carl Friedrich von Siemens and the Industrial Financing of Political Parties in the Weimar Republic." In *Von der Aufgabe der Freiheit. Politische Verantwortung und bürgerliche Gesellschaft im 19. und 20. Jahrhundert. Festschrift für Hans Mommsen zum 5. November 1995,* ed. Christian Jansen, Lutz Niethammer, and Bernd Weisbrod, 231–46. Berlin: Akademie Verlag, 1995.

———. "Catholic Conservatives in the Weimar Republic: The Politics of the Rhenish-Westphalian Aristocracy, 1918–1933." *German History* 18 (2000): 60–85.

———. "Catholics on the Right: The Reich Catholic Committee of the German National People's Party, 1920–33." *Historisches Jahrbuch* 126 (2006): 221–67.

———. "Crisis and Realignment: Agrarian Splinter Parties in the Late Weimar Republic, 1928–1933." In *Peasants and Lords in Modern Germany. Recent Studies in Agricultural History,* ed. Robert G. Moeller, 198–232. Boston: Allen & Unwin, 1986.

———. "Edgar Julius Jung: The Conservative Revolution in Theory and Practice." *Central European History* 21 (1990): 142–74.

———. "Franz von Papen, Catholic Conservatives, and the Establishment of the Third Reich, 1933–1934." *The Journal of Modern History* 83 (2011): 272–318.

———. "Franz von Papen, the German Center Party, and the Failure of Catholic Conservatism in the Weimar Republic." *Central European History* 38 (2005): 191–217.

———. "German Conservatism at the Crossroads: Count Kuno von Westarp and the Struggle for Control of the DNVP, 1928–30." *Contemporary European History* 18 (2009): 147–77.

———. "'The Greatest Stupidity of My Life': Alfred Hugenberg and the Formation of the Hitler Cabinet, January 1933." *Journal of Contemporary History* 27 (1992): 63–87.

———. "Hindenburg and the Conservative Dilemma in the 1932 Presidential Elections." *German Studies Review* 20 (1997): 235–60

———. "Kuno Graf von Westarp und die Krise des deutschen Konservativismus in der Weimarer Republik." In *"Ich bin der letzte Preuße": Kuno Graf von Westarp und die deutsche Politik (1900–1945)*, ed. Larry Eugene Jones and Wolfram Pyta, 109–46. Cologne, Weimar, and Vienna: Böhlau, 2006.

———. "Nationalists, Nazis, and the Assault against Weimar: Revisiting the Harzburg Rally of October 1931." *German Studies Review* 29 (2006): 483–94.

———. "Nazis, Conservatives, and the Establishment of the Third Reich, 1932–34." *Tel Aviver Jahrbuch für deutsche Geschichte* 23 (1994): 41–64.

———. "The Limits of Collaboration: Edgar Jung, Herbert von Bose, and the Origins of the Conservative Resistance to Hitler, 1933–34." In *Between Reform, Reaction, and Resistance: Studies in the History of German Conservatism from 1789 to 1945*, ed. Larry Eugene Jones and James N. Retallack, 465–501. Providence, RI, and Oxford: Berg Publishers, 1993.

Jones, Larry Eugene, and Pyta, Wolfram, eds. *"Ich bin der letzte Preuße": Kuno Graf von Westarp und die deutsche Politik (1900–1945)*. Cologne, Weimar, and Vienna: Böhlau, 2006

Jones, Larry Eugene, and Retallack, James, eds. *Between Reform, Reaction and Resistance. Studies in the History of German Conservatism from 1789–1945*. Providence, RI, and Oxford: Berg Publishers, 1993.

Kaiser, Jochen-Christoph. *Sozialer Protestantismus im 20. Jahrhundert: Beiträge zur Geschichte der Innern Mission 1914–1945*. Munich: R. Oldenbourg, 1989.

Kasten, Bernd. "Deutschnationale Führungsschichten und der Aufstieg der NSDAP in Mecklenburg-Schwerin 1930–1933." *Mecklenburgische Jahrbücher* 115 (2000): 233–57.

———. *Herren und Knechte. Gesellschaftlicher und politischer Wandel in Mecklenburg-Schwerin 1867–1945*. Bremen: Edition Temmen, 2011.

Kauders, Anthony. *German Politics and the Jews: Düsseldorf and Nuremberg, 1910–1933*. Oxford: Oxford University Press, 1996.

Keinemann, Friedrich. *Vom Krummstab zur Republik. Westfälischer Adel unter preußischer Herrschaft*. Bochum: Brockmeyer, 1997.

Kempner, Claudia. *Das "Gewissen" 1919–1925. Kommunikation und Vernetzung der Jungkonservativen*. Munich: R. Oldenburg, 2011.

Kennedy, Ellen. *Constitutional Failure: Carl Schmitt in Weimar*. Durham, NC: Duke University Press, 2004.

Kershaw, Ian. *Hitler 1889–1936: Hubris*. New York and London: W. W. Norton, 1998.

Kiiskinen, Elina. *Die Deutschnationale Volkspartei in Bayern (Bayerische Mittelpartei) in der Regierungspolitik des Freistaats während der Weimarer Zeit*. Munich: C. H. Beck, 2005.

Kissenkoetter, Udo. *Gregor Straßer und die NSDAP*. Stuttgart: Deutscher Verlags-Anstalt, 1978.

Kittel, Manfred. "'Steigbügelhalter' Hitlers oder 'stille Republikaner'? Die
Deutschnationalen in neuer politikgeschichtlicher und kulturalistischer
Perspektive." In *Geschichte der Politik. Alte und neue Wege*, ed. Hans-Christof
Kraus and Thomas Nicklas, 201–35. Munich: R. Oldenbourg, 2007.

————. "Zwischen völkischem Fundamentalismus und gouvernementaler
Taktik. DNVP-Vorsitzender Hans Hilpert und die bayerischen Deutschnationalen." *Zeitschrift für bayerische Landesgeschichte* 59 (1996): 849–901.

Klausa, Ekkehard. "Vom Bündnispartner zum 'Hochverräter'. Der Weg des
konservativen Widerstandskämpfer Ferdinand von Lüninck." *Westfälische
Forschungen* 43 (1993): 530–71.

Klein, Klein. "Zur Vorbereitung der faschistischen Diktatur durch die deutsche
Großbourgeoisie (1929–1933) ." *Zeitschrift für Geschichtswissenschaft* 1 (1953):
872–904.

Kleine, George H. "Adelsgenossenschaft und Nationalsozialismus." *Vierteljahrshefte für Zeitgeschichte* 26 (1978): 100–43.

Koenen, Andreas. *Der Fall Carl Schmitt. Sein Aufstieg zum "Kronjuristen des Dritten Reiches"*. Darmstadt: Wissenschaftliche Buchgesellschaft, 1995.

Kolb, Eberhard. *Was Hitler's Seizure of Power on January 30, 1933, Inevitable?* With
a comment by Henry Ashby Turner, Jr. Washington, DC: German Historical
Institute, 1997.

Kolb, Eberhard, and Pyta, Wolfram. "Die Staatsnotstandsplanung unter den
Regierungen Papen und Schleicher." In *Die deutsche Staatskrise 1930–1933.
Handlungsspielräume und Alternativen*, ed. Heinrich August Winkler, 155–82.
Munich: R. Oldenbourg, 1992.

Koshar, Rudy. *Social Life, Local Politics, and Nazism: Marburg, 1880–1945*. Chapel
Hill: University of North Carolina Press, 1986.

Krabbe, Wolfgang. "Die Bismarckjugend der Deutschnationalen Volkspartei."
German Studies Review 17 (1994): 9–32.

————. *Die gescheiterte Zukunft der ersten Republik. Jugendorganisationen bürgerlicher Parteien im Weimarer Staat*. Opladen: Westdeutscher Verlag, 1995.

Kratzsch, Gerhard. *Engelbert Reichsfreiherr von Kerckerinck zur Borg. Westfälischer Adel zwischen Kaiserreich und Weimarer Republik*. Münster: Aschendorff, 2004.

Krebs, Willi. "Der Alldeutsche Verband in den Jahren 1918–1939 — ein politisches
Instrument des deutschen Imperialismus." Phil. diss., Berlin [DDR], 1970.

Kruck, Alfred. *Geschichte des Alldeutschen Verbandes 1890–1939*. Wiesbaden:
Franz Steiner, 1954.

Krüger, Gerd. *"Treudeutsch allewege!" Gruppen, Vereine und Verbände der Rechten
in Münster (1887–1929/30)*. Münster: Aschendorff, 1992.

————. "Von den Einwohnerwehren zum Stahlhelm. Der nationale Kampfver-
band 'Westfalenbund e.V.' (1921–1924)." *Westfälische Zeitschrift* 147 (1997):
405–32.

Kuropka, Joachim, "Aus heißer Liebe zu unserem Volk und zu underer hl.
Kirche. Franz Graf von Galen als Politiker." *Oldenburger Jahrbuch* 107 (2007):
101–25.

Langer, Peter. *Macht und Verantwortung. Der Ruhrbaron Paul Reusch*. Essen: Klartext, 2012.

———. "Paul Reusch und die 'Machtergreifung'." *Mitteilungsblatt des Instituts für soziale Bewegungen. Forschungen und Forschungsberichte* 28 (2003): 157–202.

———. "'v. Gilsa an Reusch (Oberhausen)': Wirtschaftsinteressen und Politik am Vorabend der Großen Krise." In *Abenteuer Industriestadt. Oberhausen 1874–1999. Beiträge zur Stadtgeschichte*, ed. Stadt Oberhausen, 2 vols., 2:103–24. Oberhausen: Laufen, 2001

Leicht, Johannes. *Heinrich Claß 1868–1953. Die politische Biographie eines Alldeutschen*. Paderborn: Schöningh, 2012.

Lensing, Helmut. "Der Christlich-Soziale Volksdienst in der Grafschaft Bentheim und im Emsland. Die regionale Geschichte einer streng protestantischen Partei in der Endphase der Weimarer Republik." *Emslandische Geschichte* 9 (2001): 63–132.

Leopold, John A. *Alfred Hugenberg: The Radical Nationalist Campaign against the Weimar Republic*. New Haven, CT, and London: Yale University Press, 1977.

———. "The Election of Alfred Hugenberg as Chairman of the German National People's Party." *Canadian Journal of History* 7 (1972): 149–71

Levy, Richard S. *The Downfall of the Anti-Semitic Parties in Imperial Germany*. New Haven, CT, and London: Yale University Press, 1975.

Liebe, Werner. *Die Deutschnationale Volkspartei 1918–1924*. Düsseldorf: Droste, 1956.

Lob, Brigitte. *Albert Schmitt O.S.B. in Grüsssau und Wimpfen. Sein kirchengeschichtliches Handeln in der Weimarer Republik und im Dritten Reich*. Cologne and Weimar: Böhlau, 2000.

Lohalm, Uwe. *Völkischer Radikalismus. Die Geschichte des Deutschvölkischen Schutz- und Trutz-Bundes 1919–1923*. Hamburg: Leibniz-Verlag, 1970.

Malinowski, Stephan. "'Führertum' und 'Neuer Adel.' Die Deutsche Adelsgenossenschaft und der Deutsche Herrenklub in der Weimarer Republik." In *Adel und Bürgertum in Deutschland II. Entwicklungslinien und Wendepunkte im 20. Jahrhundert*, ed. Heinz Reif, 173–211. Berlin: Akademie Verlag, 2001.

———. "Kuno Graf von Westarp — ein *missing link* im preußischen Adel. Anmerkungen zur Einordnung eines untypischen Grafen." In *"Ich bin der letzte Preuße": Kuno Graf von Westarp und die deutsche Politik (1900–1945)*, ed. Larry Eugene Jones and Wolfram Pyta, 9–32. Cologne, Weimar, and Vienna: Böhlau, 2006.

———. "Vom blauen zum reinen Blut. Antisemitischer Adelskritik und adliger Antisemitismus 1871–1944." *Jahrbuch für Antisemitismusforschung* 12 (2003): 147–69.

———. *Vom Königtum zur Führer. Sozialer Niedergang und politische Radikalisierung im deutschen Adel zwischen Kaiserreich und NS-Staat*. Berlin: Akademie Verlag, 2003.

———. "'Wer schenkt uns wieder Kartoffeln?' Deutscher Adel nach 1918 — eine Elite?" In *Deutscher Adel im 19. und 20. Jahrhundert. Büdinger Forschungen zur Sozialgeschichte 2002 und 2003*, ed. Günther Schulz and Markus A. Denzel, 503–37. St. Katharinen: Scripta Mercaturae, 2004.

Marx, Christian. *Paul Reusch und die Gutehoffnungshütte. Leitung eines deutschen Großunternehmens*. Göttingen, 2012.

Matthiesen, Helga. *Greifswald in Vorpommern. Konservatives Milieu im Kaiserreich, in Demokratie und Diktatur 1900–1990*. Düsseldorf: Droste, 2000.

Matzerath, Horst, and Henry A. Turner. "Die Selbstfinanzierung der NSDAP 1930–1932." *Geschichte und Gesellschaft* 3 (1977): 59–92.

Mayer, Karl J. "Kuno Graf von Westarp als Kritiker des Nationalsozialismus." In *"Ich bin der letzte Preuße": Kuno Graf von Westarp und die deutsche Politik (1900–1945)*, ed. Larry Eugene Jones and Wolfram Pyta, 190–216. Cologne, Weimar, and Vienna: Böhlau, 2006.

McElligott, Anthony. *Rethinking the Weimar Republic: Authority and Authoritarianism 1916–1936*. New York: Bloomsbury, 2014.

Mehring, Reinhard. *Carl Schmitt: Aufstieg und Fall. Eine Biographie*. Munich: C. H. Beck, 2009.

Mergel, Thomas. "Führer Volksgemeinschaft und Maschine." In *Politische Kulturgeschichte der Zwischenkriegszeit 1918–1939*, ed. Wolfgang Hardtwig, 91–127. Göttingen: Vandenhoeck & Ruprecht, 2005.

———. *Parlamentarische Kultur in der Weimarer Republik. Politische Kommunikationen, symbolische Politik und Öffentlichkeit im Reichstag*. Düsseldorf: Droste, 2002.

———. "Das Scheitern des deutschen Tory-Konservatismus. Die Umformung der DNVP zu einer rechtsradikalen Partei 1928–1932." *Historische Zeitschrift* 276 (2003): 323–68.

Merkenich, Stephanie. *Grüne Front gegen Weimar. Reichs-Landbund und agrarischer Lobbyismus 1918–1933*. Düsseldorf: Droste, 1998.

Meyhoff, Andreas. *Blohm & Voss im "Dritten Reich." Eine Hamburger Großwerft zwischen Gescäft und Politik*. Hamburg: Christians, 2001.

Mohler, Armin. *Die Konservative Revolution in Deutschland, 1918–1932. Ein Handbuch*. 2nd ed. Darmstadt: Wissenschaftliche Buchgesellschaft, 1972.

Mohr, Hubert. "Remarks on 'The Jew' as a Social Myth and Some Theoretical Reflections on Anti-Semitism." In *Antisemitismus, Paganismus, Völkisch Religion*, ed. Herbert Cancik and Uwe Puschner, 1–11. Munich: Saur, 2004.

Möhring, Peter. "Ferdinand Freiherr von Lüninck." *Westfälische Lebensbilder* 17 (2005): 60–102.

Mommsen, Hans. "Fritz-Dietlof Graf v.d. Schulenburg und die preußische Tradition." *Vierteljahrshefte für Zeitgeschichte* 22 (1984): 213–39.

———. "Die Illusion einer Regierung ohne Parteien und der Aufstieg der NSDAP." In *Demokratie in der Krise. Parteien im Verfassungssystem der Weimarer Republik*, ed. Eberhard Kolb and Walter Mühlhausen, 113–39. Munich: R. Oldenbourg, 1997.

———. "Die nationalsozialistische Machteroberung: Revolution oder Gegenrevolution?" In *Europäische Sozialgeschichte. Festschrift für Wolfgang Schieder*, ed. Christof Dipper. Lutz Klinkhammer, and Alexander Nützenadel, 41–56. Berlin: Duncker & Humblot, 2000.

———. "Heinrich Brünings Politik als Reichskanzler: Das Scheitern eines politischen Alleingangs." In *Wirtschaftskrise und liberale Demokratie. Das Ende der Weimarer Republik und die gegenwärtige Situation*, ed. Karl Holl, 16–45. Göttingen: Vandenhoeck & Ruprecht, 1978.

————. "Regierung ohne Parteien. Konservative Pläne zum Verfassungsumbau am Ende der Weimarer Republik." In *Die deutsche Staatskrise 1930–1933. Handlungsspielräume und Alternativen*, ed. Heinrich August Winkler, 1–18. Munich: R. Oldenbourg, 1992.

————. "Staat und Bürokratie in der Ära Brüning." In *Tradition und Reform in der deutschen Politik. Gedenkschrift für Waldemar Besson*, ed. Gotthard Jasper, 81–137. Frankfurt: Propyläen, 1976.

————. *Die verspielte Freiheit. Der Weg der Republik von Weimar in den Untergang 1918 bos 1933*. Berlin: Propylaen, 1989.

Mosse, George L. *The Crisis of the German Ideology: Intellectual Origins of the Third Reich*. New York: Grosset & Dunlap, 1964.

————. "Die deutsche Rechte und die Juden." In *Entscheidungsjahr 1932. Zur Judenfrage in der Endphase der Weimarer Republik*, ed. Werner E. Mosse, 184–216. Tübingen: J. C. B. Mohr, 1966.

Müller, Andreas. *"Fällt der Bauer, stürzt der Staat." Deutschnationale Agrarpolitik 1928–1933*. Hamburg: Herbert Utz Verlag, 2003.

Müller, Hans Peter. "Antisemitismus im Königreich Württemberg zwischen 1871 und 1914." *Jahrbuch des Historischen Vereins für Württembergisch Franken* 86 (2002): 547–83.

————. "Die Bürgerpartei/Deutschnationale Volkspartei (DNVP) in Württemberg 1918–1933. Konservative Politik und die Zerstörung der Weimarer Republik." *Zeitschrift für Württembergische Landesgeschichte* 61 (2002): 374–433.

————. "Die Deutsche Vaterlandspartei in Württemberg und ihre Erbe. Besorgte Patrioten oder Rechtsideologen?" *Zeitschrift für Württembergische Landesgeschichte* 59 (2000): 217–45.

————. "Landwirtschaftliche Interessenvertretung und völkisch-antisemitische Ideologie. Der Bund der Landwirte/Bauernbund in Württemberg 1895–1918." *Zeitschrift für Württembergische Landesgeschichte* 53 (1994): 263–300.

————. "Sammlungsversuche *charaktervoller Konservativer*. Die Volkskonservativen in Württemberg 1930–1932." *Zeitschrift für Württembergische Landesgeschichte* 64 (2005): 339–54.

————. "Wilhelm Bazille. Deutschnationaler Politiker, württembergischer Staatspräsident." *Lebensbilder aus Baden-Württemberg* 21 (2005): 480–517.

————. "Wilhelm Vogt. Württembergischer Bauernbundpolitiker und bäuerlicher Standesvertreter im Kaiserreich und in der Weimarer Republik 1854–1938." *Lebensbilder aus Baden-Württemberg* 18 (1994): 395–417.

Muller, Jerry Z. *The Other God that Failed: Hans Freyer and the Deradicalization of German Conservatism*. Princeton, NJ: Princeton University Press, 1987.

Müller, Markus. *Die Christlich-Nationale Bauern- und Landvolkpartei 1918–1933*. Düsseldorf: Droste, 2001.

Müller, Sven Oliever. *Die Nation als Waffe und Vorstellung. Nationalismus in Deutschland und Großbritannien im Ersten Weltkrieg*. Göttingen: Vandenhoeck & Ruprecht, 2002.

Neebe, Reinhard. *Großindustrie, Staat und NSDAP 1930–1933. Paul Silverberg und der Reichsverband der Deutschen Industrie in der Krise der Weimarer Republik*. Göttingen: Vandenhoeck & Ruprecht, 1981.

————. "Unternehmerverbände und Gewerkschaften in den Jahren der großen Krise 1929–33." *Geschichte und Gesellschaft* 9 (1983): 302–30.

―――. "Die Industrie und der 30. Januar 1933." In *Nationalsozialistische Diktatur 1933–1945. Ein Bilanz*, ed. Karl Dietrich Bracher, Manfred Funke, and Hans-Adolf Jacobsen. Bonn: Bundeszentrale für Politische Bildung, 1983.

Nowak, Kurt. "Die evangelischen Kirchenführer und das Präsidialsystem: Konfessionelle Politik im Spannungsfeld von authoritärem Staatsgeist und kirchenbehördlicher Pragmatik (1930–1932)." In *Die deutsche Staatskrise 1930–1933. Handlungsspielräume und Alternativen*, ed. Heinrich August Winkler, 19–38. Munich: R. Oldenbourg, 1992.

Ohnezeit, Maik. *Zwischen "schärfster Opposition" und dem "Willen zur Macht." Die Deutschnationale Volkspartei (DNVP) in der Weimarer Republik 1918–1928.* Düsseldorf: Droste, 2012.

Opitz, Günther. *Der Christlich-soziale Volksdienst. Versuch einer protestantischen Partei in der Weimarer Republik.* Düsseldorf: Droste, 1969.

Orlow, Dietrich. *The History of the Nazi Party: 1919–1933.* Pittsburg, PA: University of Pittsburgh Press, 1969.

Overy, R. J. "'Primacy Always Belongs to Politics': Gustav Krupp and the Third Reich." In *War and Economy in the Third Reich*, R. J. Overy, 119–43. Oxford: Oxford University Press, 1994.

Patch, William L., Jr. *Heinrich Brüning and the Dissolution of the Weimar Republic.* Cambridge: Cambridge University Press, 1998.

―――. "Heinrich Brüning's Recollections of Monarchism: The Birth of a Red Herring." *The Journal of Modern History* 70 (1998): 340–70.

Peters, Michael. *Der Alldeutsche Verband am Vorabend des Ersten Weltkrieges (1908–1914). Ein Beitrag zur Geschichte des völkischen Nationalismus im spätwilhelminischen Deutschland.* Frankfurt and New York: Peter Lang, 1996.

Petzinna, Berthold. "Das Politische Kolleg. Konzept, Politik und Praxis einer konservativen Bildungsstätte in der Weimarer Republik." In *Die Erziehung zum deutschen Menschen. Völkische und nationalkonservative Erwachsenenbildung in der Weimarer Republik*, ed. P. Ciupke, 101–11. Essen: Klartext, 2007.

―――. *Erziehung zum deutschen Lebensstil. Ursprung und Entwicklung des jungkonservativen "Ring"-Kreises 1918–1933.* Berlin: Akademie Verlag, 2000.

Petzold, Joachim. *Franz von Papen. Ein deutsche Verhängnis.* Munich and Berlin: Buchverlag Union, 1995.

Peukert, Detlev J. K. *The Weimar Republic: The Crisis of Classical Modernity.* New York: Hill and Wang, 1989.

Plumbe, Werner. "Der Reichsverband der Deutschen Industrie und die Krise der Weimarer Wirtschaft." In *Herausforderungen der parlamentarischen Demokratie. Die Weimarer Republik im europäischen Vergleich*, ed. Andreas Wirsching, 129–56. Munich: R. Oldenbourg, 2007.

Pomp, Rainer. "Brandenburgischer Landadel und die Weimarer Repulik. Konflikte um Oppositionsstrategien und Elitenkonzepte." In *Adel und Staatsverwaltung in Brandenburg im 19. und 20. Jahrhundert. Ein historischer Vergleich*, ed. Kurt Adamy and Kristina Hübener, 185–218. Berlin: Akademie Verlag, 1996.

―――. *Bauern und Grossgrundbesitzer auf ihrem Weg ins Dritte Reich. Der Brandenburgische Landbund 1919–1933.* Berlin: Akademie Verlag, 2011.

Pyta, Wolfram. *Dorfgemeinschaft und Parteipolitik 1918–1933. Die Verschränkung von Milieu und Parteien in den protestantischen Landgebieten Deutschlands in der Weimarer Republik*. Düsseldorf: Droste, 1996.

———. *Hindenburg. Herrschaft zwischen Hohenzollern und Hitler*. Munich: Siedler, 2007.

———. "Paul von Hindenburg als charismatischer Führer der deutschen Nation." In *Charismatische Führer der deutschen Nation*, ed. Frank Möller, 109–47. Munich: R. Oldenbourg, 2004.

———. "Vernunftrepublikanismus in den Spitzenverbänden der deutschen Industrie." In *Vernunftrepublikanismus in der Weimarer Republik. Politik, Literatur, Wissenschaft*, ed. Andreas Wirsching and Jürgen Eder, 87–108. Stuttgart: Franz Steiner Verlag, 2008.

———. "Verfassungsumbau, Staatsnotstand und Querfront: Schleichers Versuche zur Fernhaltung Hitlers von der Reichskanzlerschaft August 1932 bis Januar 1933." In *Gestaltungskraft des Politischen. Festschrift für Eberhard Kolb*, ed. Wolfram Pyta and Ludwig Richter, 173–97. Berlin: Duncker & Humblot, 1998.

———. "Das Zerplatzen der Hoffnung auf eine konservative Wende. Kuno Graf von Westarp und Hindenburg." In *"Ich bin der letzte Preuße". Der politische Lebensweg des konservativen Politikers Kuno Graf von Westarp (1864–1945)*, ed. Larry Eugene Jones and Wolfram Pyta, 163–87. Cologne, Weimar, and Vienna: Böhlau, 2006.

Pyta, Wolfram, and Seiberth, Gabriel. "Die Staatskrise der Weimarer Republik im Spiegel des Tagebuchs Carl Schmitt." *Der Staat* 38 (1999): 423–48, 594–610.

Rasch, Manfred. "Über Albert Vögler und sein Verhältnis zur Politik." *Mitteillungsblatt des Instituts für soziale Bewegungen. Forschungen und Forschungsberichte* 28 (2003): 127–56.

Reeken, Dietmar von. "National oder nationalsozialistisch? Eine Fallstudie zum Verhältnis von Stahlhelm und NSDAP im Emden 1932 bis 1935." In *Ostfriesland zwischen Republik und Diktatur*, ed. Herbert Reyer, 201–38. Aurich: Ostfriesische Landschaft, 1998.

Reif, Hans. "Antisemitismus in den Agrarverbänden Ostelbiens während der Weimarer Republik." In *Ostelbische Agrargesellschaft im Kaiserreich und in der Weimarer Republik. Agrarkrise—junkerliche Interessenpolitik—Modernisierungsstrategien*, ed. Heinz Reif, 378–411. Berlin: Akademie Verlag, 1994.

———, ed. *Adel und Bürgertum in Deutschland II. Entwicklungslinien und Wendepunkte im 20. Jahrhundert*. Berlin: Akademie Verlag, 2001.

Retallack, James. "Anti-Semitism, Conservative Propaganda, and Regional Politics in Late Nineteenth Century Germany." *German Studies Review* 11 (1988): 377–403.

———. *The German Right, 1860–1920: Political Limits of the Authoritarian Imagination*. Toronto: University of Toronto Press, 2006.

———. *Notables of the Right: The Conservative Party and Political Mobilization in Germany, 1876–1918*. Boston: Unwin Hyman, 1988.

Ribhegge, Wilhelm. *Konservative Politik in Deutschland. Von der Französischen Revolution bis zur Gegenwart*. Darmstadt: Wissenschaftliche Buchgesellschaft, 2009.

Richardi, Hans-Günter. *Hitler und seine Hintermänner. Neue Fakten zur Frühge-schichte der NSDAP.* Munich: Süddeutscher Verlag, 1991.

Roder, Hartmut. *Der christlich-nationale Deutsche Gewerkschaftsbund (DGB) im politisch-ökonomischen Kräftefeld der Weimarer Republik.* Frankfurt, Bern, and New York: Peter Lang, 1986.

Roth, Karl Heinz. "Franz von Papen und der Faschismus." *Zeitschrift für Ge-schichtswissensschaft* 51 (2003): 589–625.

Ruge, Wolfgang. "Die 'Deutsche Allgemine Zeitung' und die Brüning-Regie-rung. Zur Rolle der Großbourgeoisie bei der Vorbereitung des Faschismus." *Zeitschrift für Geschichtswissenschaft* 16 (1968): 19–53.

———. *Hindenburg: Porträt eines Militaristen.* Cologne: Paul-Rugenstein, 1981.

Rütters, Peter. "Der Deutschnationale Handlungsgehilfen-Verband (DHV) und der Nationalsozialismus." *Historisch-politische Mitteilungen* 16 (2009): 81–108.

Sauer, Bernhard. "Freikorps und Antisemitismus in der Frühzeit der Weimarer Republik." *Zeitschrift für Geschichtswissenschaft* 56 (2008): 5–29.

Scheck, Raffael. *Alfred von Tirpitz and German Right-Wing Politics, 1914–1930.* Atlantic Highlands, NJ: Humanities Press, 1998.

———. "German Conservatism and Female Political Activism in the Early Wei-mar Republic." *German History* 15 (1997): 34–55.

———. *Mothers of the Nation: Right-Wing Women in Weimar Germany.* Oxford and New York: Berg Publishers, 2004.

———. "Zwischen Volksgemeinschaft und Frauenrechten: Das Verhältnis re-chtsbürgerlicher Politikerinnen zur NSDAP 1930–1933." In *Nation, Politik und Geschlecht. Frauenbewegungen und Nationalismus in der Moderne*, ed. Ute Planert, 234–49. Frankfurt and New York: Campus Verlag, 2000.

Schildt, Axel. *Konservatismus in Deutschland. Von den Anfängen im 18. Jahrhundert bis zur Gegenwart.* Munich: C. H. Beck, 1998.

———. *Militärdiktatur mit Massenbasis? Die Querfrontkonzeption der Reichswehr-führung um General von Schleicher am Ende der Weimarer Republik.* Frankfurt and New York: Campus Verlag, 1981.

Schmitz, Walter, and Vollnhals, Clemens, eds. *Völkische Bewegung—Konservative Revolution—Nationalsozialismus. Aspekte einer politisierten Kultur.* Dresden: Thelem, 2005.

Schmuhl, Hans-Walter. *Rassenhygiene, Nationalsozialismus, Euthanasie. Von der Verhütung zur Vernichtung "lebensunwerten Lebens" 1890–1945.* Göttingen: Vandenhoeck & Ruprecht, 1987.

Schrenck-Notzing, Caspar von, ed. *Stand und Probleme der Erforschung des Kon-servatismus.* Berlin: Duncker und Humblot, 2000.

Schulz, Gerhard. "Der 'Nationale Klub von 1929' zu Berlin. Zum politischen Verfall einer Gesellschaft." *Jahrbuch für die Geschichte Mittel- und Ostdeutsch-lands* 11 (1962): 207–37.

———. "Reparationen und Krisenproblemen nach dem Wahlsieg der NSDAP 1930. Betrachtungen zur Regierung Brüning." *Vierteljahrschrift für Sozial- und Wirtschaftsgeschichte* 67 (1980): 200–22.

———. *Zwischen Demokratie und Diktatut. Verfassungspolitik und Reichsreform in der Weimarer Republik.* 3 vols. Berlin: de Gruyter, 1987–92.

Schumann, Dirk. *Political Violence in the Weimar Republic, 1918–1933: Fight for the Streets and Fears of Civil War,* trans. by Thomas Dunlap. New York and Oxford: Berghahn Books, 2009.

Schwarzmüller, Theo. *Zwischen Kaiser und "Führer." Generalfeldmarschall August von Mackensen. Eine politische Biographie.* Paderborn: Schöningh, 1996.

Seiberth, Gabriel. *Anwalt des Reiches. Carl Schmitt und der Prozess "Preußen contra Reich" vor dem Staatsgerichtshof.* Berlin: Duncker & Humblot, 2000.

Sneeringer, Julia. *Winning Women's Votes: Propaganda and Politics in Weimar Germany.* Chapel Hill, NC, and London: University of North Carolina Press, 2002.

Sontheimer, Kurt. *Antidemokratisches Denken in der Weimarer Republik. Die politischen Ideen des deutschen Nationalismus zwischen 1918 und 1933.* Munich: Nymphenburger Verlagshandlung, 1962.

Stark, Gary D. *Entrepreneurs of Ideology: Neoconservative Publishers in Germany 1890–1933.* Chapel Hill: University of North Carolina Press, 1981.

———. "Der Verleger als Kulturunternehmer: Der J. F. Lehmanns Verlag und Rassenkunde in der Weimarer Republik." *Archiv für Geschichte des Buchwesens* 16 (1976): 291–318.

Stegmann, Dirk. "Zum Verhältnis von Großindustrie und Nationalsozialismus 1930–1933. Ein Beitrag zur Geschichte der sog. Machtergreifung." *Archiv für Sozialgeschichte* 13 (1973): 399–482.

———. "Zwischen Repression und Manipulation: Konservative Machteliten und Arbeiter- und Angestelltenbewegung 1910–1918. Ein Beitrag zur Vorgeschichte der DAP/NSDAP." *Archiv für Sozialgeschichte* 12 (1972): 351–432.

Stöckel, Sigrid, ed. *Die "rechte Nation" und ihr Verleger. Politik und Popularisierung im J. F. Lehmanns Verlag 1890–1979.* Berlin: J. F. Lemann, 2002.

Strenge, Irene. *Kurt von Schleicher. Politik im Reichswehrministerium am Ende der Weimarer Republik.* Berlin: Duncker & Humblot, 2006.

———. *Machtübernahme 1933 — Alles auf legalem Weg.* Berlin: Duncker & Humblot, 2002.

Streubel, Christiane. "Frauen der politischen Rechten in Kaiserreich und Republik. Ein Überblick und Forschungsbericht." *Historical Social Research/Historische Sozialforschung* 28 (2003): 103–66.

———. *Radikale Nationalistinnen. Agitation und Programmatik rechter Frauen in der Weimarer Republik.* Frankfurt and New York: Campus Verlag, 2006.

Striesow, Jan. *Die Deutschnationale Volkspartei und die Völkisch-Radikalen 1918–1922.* 2 vols. Frankfurt: Haag und Herschen, 1981

Struve, Walter. *Elites against Democracy: Leadership Ideals in Bourgeois Political Thought in Germany, 1890–1933.* Princeton, NJ: Princeton University Press, 1973.

Stupperich, Amrei. *Volksgemeinschaft oder Arbeitersolidarität. Studien zur Arbeitnehmerpolitik in der Deutschnationalen Volkspartei (1918–1933).* Göttingen and Zurich: Musterschmidt-Verlag, 1982.

Süchting-Hänger, Andrea. *"Gewissen der Nation." Nationales Engagement und politisches Handeln konservativer Frauenorganisationen 1900 bis 1937.* Düsseldorf: Droste, 2002.

Szejnmann, Claus-Christian W. *Nazism in Central Germany: The Brownshirts in Red Saxony.* New York and Oxford: Berghahn Books, 1999.

Tautz, Joachim. *Militärische Jugendpolitik in der Weimarer Republik. Die Jugendorganisation des Stahlhelm, Bund der Frontsoldaten: Jungstahlhelm und Scharnhorst, Bund deutscher Jungmannen.* Regensburg: Roderer, 1998.

Terhalle, Maximilian. *Deutschnational in Weimar. Die politische Biographie des Reichstagsabgeordneten Otto Schmidt(-Hannover) 1888–1971.* Cologne, Weimar, and Vienna: Böhlau Verlag, 2009.

Trippe, Christiane F. *Konservative Verfassungspolitik 1918–1923. Die DNVP als Opposition in Reich und Ländern.* Düsseldorf: Droste, 1995.

Turner, Henry Ashby, Jr. "'Alliance of Elites' as a Cause of Weimar's Collapse and Hitler's Triumph." In *Die deutsche Staatskrise 1930–1933. Handlungsspielräume und Alternativen,* ed. Heinrich August Winkler, 205–14. Munich: R. Oldenbourg, 1992.

———. "Emil Kirdorf and the Nazi Party." *Central European History* 1 (1968): 324–44.

———. *German Big Business and the Rise of Hitler.* Oxford: Oxford University Press, 1985.

———. "Hitlers Einstellung zu Wirtschaft und Gesellschaft vor 1933." *Geschichte und Gesellschaft* 2 (1976): 89–117.

———. "Großunternehmertum und Nationalsozialismus 1930–1933. Kritisches und Ergänzendes zu zwei neuen Forschungsbeiträgen." *Historische Zeitschrift* 221 (1975): 18–68.

Tyrell, Albrecht. "Der Wegbereiter—Hermann Göring als politischer Beauftragter Hitlers in Berlin 1930–1932/33." In *Demokratie und Diktatur. Geist und Gestalt politischer Herrschaft in Deutschland und Europa. Festschrift für Karl Dietrich Bracher,* ed. Manfred Funke et al., 178–97. Düsseldof: Droste, 1987.

Ulbricht, Justus H. "Völkische Publizistik in München. Verleger, Verlage und Zeitschriften im Vorfeld des Nationalsozialismus." In *München—Hauptstadt der Bewegung." Bayerns Metropole und der Nationalsozialismus,* 131–36. Munich: Klinkhardt und Biermann, 1993.

Ulmer, Martin. *Antisemitismus in Stuttgart 1871–1933. Studien zum öffentlichen Diskurs und Alltag.* Berlin: Metropol Verlag, 2011.

Vogel, Wieland. *Katholische Kirche und Nationale Kampfverbände in der Weimarer Republik.* Paderborn: Schöningh, 1989.

Vogelsang, Thilo. *Reichswehr, Staat und NSDAP. Beiträge zur Deutschen Geschichte 1930–1932.* Stuttgart: Deutsche Verlags-Anstalt, 1962.

Volkov, Sulamit. *Germans, Jews, and Antisemites.* Cambridge: Cambridge University Press, 2006.

Vollnhals, Clemens. "Oswald Spengler und der Nationalsozialismus. Das Dilemma eines konservativen Revolutionärs." *Telaviver Jahrbuch für Deutsche Geschichte* 13 (1984): 263–303.

Volkmann, Peer Oliver. *Heinrich Brüning (1885–1970). Nationalist ohne Heimat. Eine Teilbiographie.* Düsseldorf: Droste, 2007.

von der Goltz, Anna. *Hindenburg: Power, Myth, and the Rise of Nazism.* Oxford and New York: Oxford University Press, 2009.

von Klemperer, Klemens. *Germany's New Conservatism: Its History and Dilemma in the Twentieth Century*. Princeton, NJ: Princeton University Press, 1972.

Walkenhorst, Peter. *Nation—Volk—Rasse. Radikaler Nationalismus im Deutschen Kaiserreich 1890–1914*. Göttingen: Vandenhoeck & Ruprecht, 2006.

Walker, David P. "The German Nationalist People's Party: The Conservative Dilemma in the Weimar Republic." *Journal of Contemporary History* 14 (1979): 627–47.

Weber, Reinhold. *Bürgerpartei und Bauernbund in Württemberg. Konservative Parteien im Kaiserreich und in Weimar (1895–1933)*. Düsseldorf: Droste, 2004.

———. "Das 'Geheime Deutschland' und das 'Geistige Bad Harzburg'. Friedrich Glum und das Dilemma des demokratischen Konservatismus am Ende der Weimarer Republik." In *Von der Aufgabe der Freiheit. Politische Verantwortung und bürgerliche Gesellschaft im 19. und 20. Jahrhundert. Festschrift für Hans Mommsen zum 5. November 1995*, ed. Christian Jansen, Lutz Niethammer, and Bernd Weisbrod, 285–308. Berlin: Akademie Verlag, 1995.

Weisbrod, Bernd. "Die Befreiung von den 'Tariffesseln'. Deflationspolitik als Krisenstrategie der Unternehmer in der Ära Brüning." *Geschichte und Gesellschaft* 11 (1985): 295–325.

———. "Economic power and political stability reconsidered: heavy industry in Weimar Germany." *Social History* 4 (1979): 241–63.

———. "Gewalt in der Politik. Zur politischen Kultur in Deutschland zwischen den beiden Weltkriegen." *Geschichte in Wissenschaft und Unterricht* 43 (1992): 391–404.

———. "Industrial Crisis Strategy in the Great Depression." In *Economic Crisis and Political Crisis: The Weimar Republic, 1924–1933*, ed. Jürgen von Kruedener, 45–62. New York, Oxford, and Munich: Berg Publishers, 1990.

———. "Kriegerische Gewalt und männlicher Fundamentalismus. Ernst Jüngers Beitrag zur konservativen Revolution." *Geschichte in Wissenschaft und Unterricht* 49 (1998): 542–58.

———. *Schwerindustrie in der Weimarer Republik. Interessenpolitik zwischen Stabilisierung und Krise*. Wuppertal: Peter Hammer, 1978.

Weiß, Dieter J. "Katholischer Konservatismus am Scheideweg—Die 'Historisch-politische Blätter' und die 'Gelben Hefte'." In *Konservative Zeitschriften zwischen Kaiserreich und Diktatur*, ed. Hans-Christof Kraus, 97–114. Berlin: Duncker & Humblot, 2003.

Weiß, Hermann, and Hoser, Paul, eds. *Die Deutschnationalen und die Zerstörung der Weimarer Republik. Aus dem Tagebuch von Reinhold Quaatz 1928–1933*. Munich, R. Oldenbourg, 1989.

Wengst, Udo. "Heinrich Brüning und die 'konservative Alternative'. Kritische Anmerkungen zu neuen Thesen über die Endphase der Weimarer Republik." *Aus Politik und Zeitgeschichte. Beilage zum Parlament*, 1980/50B (13 December 1980): 19–26.

———. "Der Reichsverband der Deutschen Industrie in den ersten Monaten des Dritten Reiches. Ein Beitrag zum Verhältnis von Großindustrie und Nationalsozialismus." *Vierteljahrshefte für Zeitgeschichte* 28 (1980): 94–110.

———. "Schlange-Schöningen, Ostsiedlung und die Demission der Regierung Brüning." *Geschichte in Wissenschaft und Unterricht* 30 (1979): 538–51.

————. "Unternehmerverbände und Gewerkschaften in Deutschland im Jahre 1930." *Vierteljahrshefte für Zeitgeschichte* 25 (1977): 99–119.

Wilhelm, Hermann. *Dichter, Denker, Fememörder. Rechtsradikalismus und Antisemitismus in München von der Jahrhundertwende bis 1921.* Berlin: Transit, 1989.

Williamson, John G. *Karl Helfferich, 1872–1924: Economist, Financier, Politician.* Princeton, NJ: Princeton University Press, 1971.

Wirsching, Andreas, ed. *Das Jahr 1933. Die nationalsozialistische Machteroberung und die deutsche Gesellschaft.* Göttingen: Wallstein Verlag, 2009.

Winkler, Heinrich August. "Die deutsche Gesellschaft der Weimarer Republik und der Antisemitismus—Juden als Blitzableiter." In *Vorurteil und Völkermord. Entwicklungslinien des Antisemitismus*, ed. Wolfgang Benz and Werner Bergmann, 341–62. Freiburg, Basel, and Vienna: Herder, 1997.

————. *Weimar 1918–1933. Die Geschichte der ersten deutschen Demokratie.* Munich: C. H. Beck, 1998.

————, ed. *Die deutsche Staatskrise 1930–1933. Handlungsspielräume und Alternativen.* Munich: R. Oldenbourg, 1992.

Witt, Peter-Christian. "Konservatismus als 'Überparteilichkeit.' Die Beamten der Reichskanzlei zwischen Kaiserreich und Weimarer Republik 1900–1933." In *Deutscher Konservatismus im 19. und 20. Jahrhundert. Festschrift für Fritz Fischer*, ed. Dirk Stegmann, Bernd-Jürgen Wendt, and Peter-Christian Witt, 231–80. Bonn: Verlag Neue Gesellschaft, 1983.

Wolff-Rohé, Stephanie. *Der Reichsverband der Deutschen Industrie 1919–1924/25.* Frankfurt: Peter Lang, 2001.

Woods, Roger. *The Conservative Revolution in the Weimar Republic.* New York: St. Martin's Press, 1996.

Wulf, Peter. "Antisemitismus in bürgerlichen und bäuerlichen Parteien und Verbände in Schleswig-Holstein (1918–1924)." *Jahrbuch für Antisemitismusforschung* 11 (2002): 52–75.

————. "Ernst Oberfohren und die DNVP am Ende der Weimarer Republik." In *"Wir bauen das Reich." Aufstieg und erste Herrschaftsjahre des Nationalsozialismus in Schleswig-Holstein*, ed. Erich Hoffman and Peter Wulf, 165–87. Neumünster: Karl Wachholtz Verlag, 1983.

Zollitsch, Wolfgang. "Adel und adlige Machteliten in der Endphase der Weimarer Republik. Standespolitik und agrarische Interessen." In *Die deutsche Staatskrise 1930–1933. Handlungsspielräume und Alternativen*, ed. Heinrich August Winkler, 239–56. Munich: R. Oldenbourg, 1992.

————. "Die Erosion des traditionellen Konservatismus. Ländlicher Adel in Preußen zwischen Kaiserreich und Weimarer Republik." In *Parteien im Wandel. Vom Kaiserreich zur Weimarer Republik. Rekrutierung—Qualifizierung—Karrieren*, ed. Dieter Dowe, Jürgen Kocka, and Heinrich August Winkler, 161–82. Munich: R. Oldenbourg, 1999.

————. "Orientierungskrise und Zerfall des authoritären Konsenses: Adel und Bürgertum zwischen autoritärem Parlamentarismus, konservative Revolution und nationalsozialistischem Führeradel 1928–1933." In *Adel und Bürgertum in Deutschland II. Entwicklungslinien und Wendepunkte im 20. Jahrhundert*, ed. Hans Reif, 213–33. Berlin: Akademie Verlag, 2001.

———. "Das Scheitern des 'governementalen' Rechte. Tilo von Wilmowsky und die organisierten Interessen in der Staatskrise von Weimar." In *Demokratie in Deutschland. Chancen und Gefährdungen im 19. Und 20. Jahrhundert,* ed. Wolther von Kieseritzky and Klaus-Peter Sick, 254–73. Munich: C. H. Beck, 1999.

Index

Lohmann, Karl, 148
Lossow, Otto Hermann, 174
Lucius, Eduard, 140, 148
Ludendorff, Erich, 31, 87, 150, 209
Lüninck, Baron Ferdinand von, 223,
    232–33
    and DNVP, 233
    Law for the Restoration of the Civil
        Service, 233
    letter to Catholic espicopate,
        232–33
Lüninck, Baron Hermann von, 223
Luther, Hans, 228
Lutheran Academic Society (Lübeck),
    251

Mackensen, August von, 8
Mahraun, 14, 150, 196, 205–14
    acceptance of the Weimar
        Republic, 210
    arrest (1933), 213
    revised stance on antisemitism,
        210–11
    See also Young German Order
Main Assembly of the German
    Associations of Travelers'
    Welfare (Hauptversammlung
    der Deutschen
    Wandererfürsorgeverbände), 252
Malinowski, Stefan, 7, 230
Maltzahn von, 70
Mannheim, Karl, 277
Marcks, Erich, 280, 283
Maria Laach, 223, 235
Marx, Karl, 81
Marx, Wilhelm, 38
Marxism, 54
Maschinenwerke Augsburg-
    Nürnberg (MAN), 171
Mecklenburg, 85
Meesmann, Otto, 155
Meinecke, Friedrich, 167
Meissner, Otto, 280
mental illness, 245, 248
    as punishment for sin, 253
Michels, Robert, 277
milieu, Protestant-National Liberal,
    116

Moehler, Armin, 284
Moeller van den Bruck, Arthur, 223
Mohr, Herbert, 196
Mommsen, Hans, 4
monarchism, 29–30, 32, 35, 37,
    48–49, 52–53, 60–63. 67, 69, 71,
    125, 225
Mosse, George L., 9, 167,
Müffling, Wilhelm von, 61
Müller, Arthur, 149
Müller, Hermann, 40
Müller-Otfried, Paula, 90
Mussolini, Benito, 146, 275

Nagel, Hans, 95
National Association of Jewish Front
    Soldiers (Reichsbund jüdischer
    Frontsoldaten/RjF), 203
National Club of 1919 (Berliner
    Nationalklub von 1919), 61,
    172
National Rural League (Reichs-
    Landbund or RLB), 5, 82, 141,
    151
National Socialist German Workers'
    Party (National Socialist
    German Workers' Party/
    NSDAP), 2–3, 5, 10, 13, 42, 70–
    71, 85, 95, 135, 140–42, 144–45,
    152–54, 170, 178, 180, 182–83,
    195, 198, 203, 237, 272, 275, 279,
    282–83
    attacks on Stahlhelm, 212
    attacks on Young German Order,
        211–12
    bourgeois associational life, 144
    civil service, 152
    conflict with the non-Nazi Right,
        178
    elections: Reichstag 1930, 152;
        Reichstag July 1932, 153
    farmers, 152
    independent middle classes, 152
    Nazi-conservative symbiosis, 10
    negotiations with the Center in
        Prussia, 183
    party leadership crisis (1921),
        171–72